P9-ECZ-737

READINGS ON RELIGION:
FROM INSIDE AND OUTSIDE

READINGS ON RELIGION
FROM INSIDE
AND OUTSIDE

Edited by
Robert S. Ellwood, Jr.

University of Southern California

Prentice-Hall, Inc., Englewood Cliffs, New Jersey 07632

Library of Congress Cataloging in Publication Data

Main entry under title:
Readings on religion.

   1. Religion—Addresses, essays, lectures.
I. Ellwood, Robert S., (date)
BL25.R23   208   77–17973
ISBN 0–13–760942–6

CAMROSE LUTHERAN COLLEGE
LIBRARY

For Christine

© 1978 by Prentice-Hall, Inc.
Englewood Cliffs, New Jersey 07632

All rights reserved. No part of this book may
be reproduced in any form or by any means
without permission in writing from the publisher.

Printed in the United States of America

10   9   8   7   6   5   4   3   2   1

BL
25
.R23 21,285

PRENTICE-HALL INTERNATIONAL, INC., *London*
PRENTICE-HALL OF AUSTRALIA PTY. LIMITED, *Sydney*
PRENTICE-HALL OF CANADA, LTD., *Toronto*
PRENTICE-HALL OF INDIA PRIVATE LIMITED, *New Delhi*
PRENTICE-HALL OF JAPAN, INC., *Tokyo*
PRENTICE-HALL OF SOUTHEAST ASIA PTE. LTD., *Singapore*
WHITEHALL BOOKS LIMITED, *Wellington, New Zealand*

CONTENTS

CHAPTER TWO

TRIBE AND TOWN: THE HISTORY OF RELIGION

CHAPTER THREE
SPIRALS OF CONSCIOUSNESS: THE PSYCHOLOGY OF RELIGION   85

CHAPTER FOUR
DANCING BEFORE GOD: RELIGIOUS SYMBOL AND RITE   131

CHAPTER FIVE

TRANSCENDENT ASSEMBLIES: SOCIOLOGY OF RELIGION   175

CHAPTER SIX

UNEARTHLY PATTERNS IN THE MIND: THE CONCEPTUAL LIFE OF RELIGION   235

CHAPTER SEVEN
FUTURES BAZAAR: OPTIONS AND ISSUES IN RELIGION TODAY AND TOMORROW

TWO KINDS OF REVERENCE: AN INTRODUCTORY COMMENT

Religion is the relation of humankind to invisible realities that transcend the ordinary and suggest the ultimate *and* that are expressed in distinctive concepts, practices, and sociological configurations. Religion can be perceived in two ways: from inside—from the perspective of one for whom the religion under consideration represents a direct, intentional commitment and an accepted view of reality; and from outside —from the perspective of one not so committed or accepting but who is attempting to understand it. The outside approach to religion or a religion can, of course, be critical or disparaging. Nevertheless, it is important to realize that it can also be a genuine attempt at empathic appreciation of the faith of others.

Indeed, both modes of perception can be of spiritual value and full of reverence. Nothing can quite compare, even as nothing can compare with a priceless pearl, with the inner warmth and peace of one who has a single and secure faith. Yet there are spiritual treasures along the wayside of another path as well. The one who seeks to understand and value the faiths of others will find himself or herself growing in awareness, in sensitivity to what it would mean to be another, and so in love for humankind. He or she will also grow in self-knowledge, for submerged aspects of the explorer's own being will be quickened to life by contact with other folk for whom that aspect is important.

In this book we shall endeavor to increase our understanding of the religious life of mankind through reading selections on religion old and new, near and far. About half are written by "insiders" to the religion under discussion; about half by "ousiders," mostly empathic, a few critical. The inside-outside pattern is made more complicated by the fact that many readers are outsiders to what is being written about by an insider and may often identify more with the perspective of outsiders on many religions, even if they have a religion of their own. Coming to terms with all of this is, however, part of coming to understand religion in human life.

It could be argued that religion cannot really be understood from books and, especially, from short passages. It is true that no words can fully communicate the inwardness of a personal spiritual experience or of another spiritual culture. Yet a countervailing truth, one that reinforces the value of the second form of reverence mentioned above, needs to be recognized too. Events and experiences have their real, human meaning not only in themselves but also as they are remembered, portrayed in art, and written about. It is only through this process that experiences receive interpretations that explain their meaning, fit them into a world view, and determine how they will affect future events. Selections like those in this anthology, then, are not just secondhand pieces *about* religion. Whether from inside or outside, they *are* religion in the sense that they are parts of the process by which religious experience is interpreted so that it interacts with the rest of human life. Accounts of religion from outside can play this role as much as those from inside. People have become Buddhists because of accounts of Buddhism by writers not themselves Buddhist.

In compiling this anthology, I have endeavored to strike a balance not only between inside and outside accounts but also between different levels and styles of religious writing. There is material that is ancient and modern, popular and scholarly, simple and profound. This is to illustrate that religion can be written about from different perspectives and in different ways. Selections in this book represent most of the major religions of the world but not in a systematic or balanced manner, since that is the subject of my textbook in world religions, *Many Peoples, Many Faiths*, and its accompanying anthology, *Words of the World's Religions*. Enough of non-Western religion appears in the present book to keep focused in the reader's mind the idea that religion is not just a matter of the sort of churches, temples, and synagogues in America. The bulk of the material, however, is European and American, since most students are more familiar with that tradition and so perhaps find various points about religion more understandable if illustrated from out of it.

The order of chapters in this book follows that in *Introducing Religion: From Inside and Outside*, a textbook in religious studies. Both books are basically built around the three forms of religious expression articulated by the sociologist of religion Joachim Wach: the theoretical (the conceptual—myths and ideas), the practical (practices—such as rites, services, forms of prayer and meditation, pilgrimage), and the sociological (the types of groups, forms of leadership, relation of religion to society). In my books, however, I have put them in a different order and added material on the meaning, history, psychology, and future of religion. The textbook and this anthology could be used together by students and teachers; but there are no internal cross-references, and the two could also be used separately.

It is my hope that these readings will encourage many readers to explore further the fascinating world of religious studies and will help induce, in the way best for each, a sense of both kinds of religious reverence.

CHAPTER ONE

DRAMAS FROM INFINITY: RELIGION AND ITS MEANING

What is religion? It can be considered the relation of humankind to invisible realities that transcend the ordinary, suggest the ultimate, and are expressed in distinctive concepts, practices, and sociological configurations. That is, religion is like a drama in which a person—or a society —acts out and thinks out who he or she really is in relation to all being, visible and invisible, and to infinity itself, the unlimited and unconditioned—God—that is the backdrop and the source of meaning for our being. Religion accepts this perspective on our being and strives to find ways in which the *real self* (the self in relation to totality) can be acted out or subjectively realized. Religion finds many ways to do this. Some of the main ones are illustrated in this chapter and can be thought of as pairs of opposites; this fact in itself suggests the complex task of religion as it mediates between this world and infinity and the human needs for both social and individualistic expression.

Religion appears as rite, suggesting that in formally structured group action a person can leave behind the limitations of ordinary existence. For this there is the biblical account of Solomon's dedication of the temple in Jerusalem. Religion also appears as inward, subjective transformation. For this we have an account of the departure for religious life of a very famous Buddhist monk in ancient China.

Religion is clearly a way in which a society itself establishes the symbols and structures that give meaning to the people within it; on this

1

are some words from a distinguished sociologist. Yet even in the modern world, people experience in religion a sense of transcendence, of something above and beyond their own society and even this universe; another sociologist of distinction speaks on this. The complexity of the matter is suggested by the role of *symbols*, entities or ideas that appear in this world yet in a special way seem to participate in something beyond it and serve as links to the beyond. Religious symbols are tangible expressions of the *sacred*, that which is above the human level but gives it meaning and power. Passages on symbols and on the sacred by noted writers interpret these ideas. Two inside accounts do the same in personal terms: an account of the experience of the sacred in the form of the goddess Isis by a classical writer and an account of finding identity through religion's reconciliation of important symbols by a famous modern convert to Christianity.

Finally, religion as establisher of rules or constraints in a society through the guilt or shame, as well as the social opprobrium, it can impose and religion as giver of ecstasy are another polarity. These two sides go together, for each psychologically prepares a person for the experience of the other and both suggest another reality than this. This polarity also suggests religion's complexity.

For those within religion, however, its complexity is easily understood. It makes an individual feel like a real self, as though he or she had become who he or she really is.

RELIGION AS RITE

The following passage from the Old Testament epitomizes not only rite but also the spirit of what might be called *official religion,* the sunny religion of a community feeling successful and blessed, unified with its sovereign and its God, and able to praise and thank that God expansively. These feelings are typically expressed in solemn but joyful ceremonies; the spirit of participation and of the confidence it induces is appropriate to the mood, as is the lofty language of King Solomon's prayer. Israel had defeated her enemies, the state was unified, the temple was built, and the promises of old seemed fulfilled and the future assured under God's favor. This mighty rite clearly bespeaks all these convictions. None were to prove quite what they seemed on that bright day, but the splendor and meaning of religious rite is recalled with every remembrance of it.

I Kings 8: 1–30

8 Then Solomon assembled the elders of Israel and all the heads of the tribes, the leaders of the fathers' houses of the people of Israel, before King Solomon in Jerusalem, to bring up the ark of the covenant of the Lord out of the city of David, which is Zion. ²And all the men of Israel assembled to King Solomon at the feast in the month Eth'anim, which is the seventh month. ³ And all the elders of Israel came, and the priests took up the ark. ⁴And they brought up the ark of the Lord, the tent of meeting, and all the holy vessels that were in the tent; the priests and the Levites brought them up. ⁵And King Solomon and all the congregation of Israel, who had assembled before him, were with him before the ark, sacrificing so many sheep and oxen that they could not be counted or numbered. ⁶Then the priests brought the ark of the covenant of the Lord to its place, in the inner sanctuary of the house, in the most holy place, underneath the wings of the cherubim. ⁷For the cherubim spread out their wings over the place of the ark, so that the cherubim made a covering above the ark and its poles. ⁸And the poles were so long that the ends of the poles were seen from the holy place before the inner sanctuary; but they could not be seen from outside; and they are there to this day. ⁹There was nothing in the ark except the two tables of stone which Moses put there at Horeb, where the Lord made a covenant with the people of Israel, when they came out of the land of Egypt. ¹⁰And when the priests came out of the holy place, a cloud filled the house of the Lord, ¹¹so that the priests could not stand to minister because of the cloud; for the glory of the Lord filled the house of the Lord.

¹²Then Solomon said, "The Lord has set the sun in the heavens, but has said that he would dwell in thick darkness. ¹³I have built thee an exalted house, a place for thee to dwell in forever." ¹⁴Then the king faced about, and blessed all the assembly of Israel, while all

I Kings 8: 1–30, from the Revised Standard Version of the Bible, copyrighted 1946, 1952, © 1971, 1973, by the National Council of the Churches of Christ in the U.S.A. Reprinted by permission.

the assembly of Israel stood. ¹⁵And he said, "Blessed be the LORD, the God of Israel, who with his hand has fulfilled what he promised with his mouth to David my father, saying, ¹⁶'Since the day that I brought my people Israel out of Egypt, I chose no city in all the tribes of Israel in which to build a house, that my name might be there; but I chose David to be over my people Israel.' ¹⁷Now it was in the heart of David my father to build a house for the name of the LORD, the God of Israel. ¹⁸But the LORD said to David my father, 'Whereas it was in your heart to build a house for my name, you did well that it was in your heart; ¹⁹nevertheless you shall not build the house, but your son who shall be born to you shall build the house for my name.' ²⁰Now the LORD has fulfilled his promise which he made; for I have risen in the place of David my father, and sit on the throne of Israel, as the LORD promised, and I have built the house for the name of the LORD, the God of Israel. ²¹And there I have provided a place for the ark, in which is the covenant of the LORD which he made with our fathers, when he brought them out of the land of Egypt."

²²Then Solomon stood before the altar of the LORD in the presence of all the assembly of Israel, and spread forth his hands toward heaven; ²³and said, "O LORD, God of Israel, there is no God like thee, in heaven above or on earth beneath, keeping covenant and showing steadfast love to thy servants who walk before thee with all their heart; ²⁴who hast kept with thy servant David my father what thou didst declare to him; yea, thou didst speak with thy mouth, and with thy hand hast fulfilled it this day. ²⁵Now therefore, O LORD, God of Israel, keep with thy servant David my father what thou hast promised him, saying, 'There shall never fail you a man before me to sit upon the throne of Israel, if only your sons take heed to their way, to walk before me as you have walked before me.' ²⁶Now therefore, O God of Israel, let thy word be confirmed, which thou hast spoken to thy servant David my father.

²⁷"But will God indeed dwell on the earth? Behold, heaven and the highest heaven cannot contain thee; how much less this house which I have built! ²⁸Yet have regard to the prayer of thy servant and to his supplication, O LORD my God, hearkening to the cry and to the prayer which thy servant prays before thee this day; ²⁹that thy eyes may be open night and day toward this house, the place of which thou hast said, 'My name shall be there,' that thou mayest hearken to the prayer which thy servant offers toward this place. ³⁰And hearken thou to the supplication of thy servant and of thy people Israel, when they pray toward this place; yea, hear thou in heaven thy dwelling place; and when thou hearest, forgive."

RELIGION AS SUBJECTIVE
TRANSFORMATION

Religion can also be a process of inner change through which one becomes a real self and attains unification with infinite reality through psychological unfolding. The following selection is an account, allegedly autobiographical although perhaps actually transcribed by disciples, of the life of a great Chinese patriarch of Ch'an, or Dhyana, Buddhism (better known in the West by its Japanese name, Zen). He was Hui-neng (A.D. 638–713). We can follow the story of how this young man, who was of modest background and illiterate, was awakened by accidentally hearing scripture and attained preeminence as he showed the depth of his wisdom. He grasped that the "Essence of Mind," consciousness itself, was always pure, free, and unbounded. The fact that he lived in a monastery with its rites and often difficult interpersonal relationships indicates that subjective transformation was not apart from other aspects of religion; yet certainly here it, rather than the role of religion in society as a whole, is the most important thing.

The Diamond Sutra
and the Sutra of Hui-Neng

Once, when the Patriarch had arrived at Pao Lin Monastery, Prefect Wei of Shao Chou and other officials went there to ask him to deliver public lectures on Buddhism in the hall of Ta Fan Temple in the City (of Canton).

In due course, there were assembled (in the lecture hall) Prefect Wei, government officials and Confucian scholars, about thirty each, and bhikkhus, bhikkhunis, Taoists and laymen to the number of about one thousand. After the Patriarch had taken his seat, the congregation in a body paid him homage and asked him to preach on the fundamental laws of Buddhism. Whereupon, His Holiness delivered the following address:

Reprinted by special arrangement with Shambhala Publications, Inc., 1123 Spruce St., Boulder, Colorado. From *The Diamond Sutra and the Sutra of Hui-Neng*, translated by A. F. Price and Wong Mou-Lam. Copyright 1969. Some notes omitted.

Learned Audience, our Essence of Mind (literally, self-nature) which is the seed or kernel of enlightenment (Bodhi) is pure by nature, and by making use of this mind alone we can reach Buddhahood directly. Now let me tell you something about my own life and how I came into possession of the esoteric teaching of the Dhyana (or the Zen) School.

My father, a native of Fan Yang, was dismissed from his official post and banished to be a commoner in Hsin Chou in Kwangtung. I was unlucky in that my father died when I was very young, leaving my mother poor and miserable. We moved to Kwang Chou (Canton) and were then in very bad circumstances.

I was selling firewood in the market one day, when one of my customers ordered some to be brought to his shop. Upon delivery being made and payment received, I left the shop, outside of which I found a man reciting a sutra. As soon as I heard the text of this sutra my mind at once became enlightened. Thereupon I asked the man the name of the book he was reciting and was told that it was the Diamond Sutra (Vajracchedika or Diamond Cutter). I further enquired whence he came and why he recited this particular sutra. He replied that he came from Tung Ch'an Monastery in the Huang Mei District of Ch'i Chou; that the Abbot in charge of this temple was Hung Yen, the Fifth Patriarch; that there were about one thousand disciples under him; and that when he went there to pay homage to the Patriarch, he attended lectures on this sutra. He further told me that His Holiness used to encourage the laity as well as the monks to recite this scripture, as by doing so they might realise their own Essence of Mind, and thereby reach Buddhahood directly.

It must be due to my good karma in past lives that I heard about this, and that I was given ten taels for the maintenance of my mother by a man who advised me to go to Huang Mei to interview the Fifth Patriarch. After arrangements had been made for her, I left for Huang Mei, which took me less than thirty days to reach.

I then went to pay homage to the Patriarch, and was asked where I came from and what I expected to get from him. I replied, "I am a commoner from Hsin Chou of Kwangtung. I have travelled far to pay you respect and I ask for nothing but Buddhahood." "You are a native of Kwangtung, a barbarian? How can you expect to be a Buddha?" asked the Patriarch. I replied, "Although there are northern men and southern men, north and south make no difference to their Buddha-nature. A barbarian is different from Your Holiness physically, but there is no difference in our Buddha-nature." He was going to speak further to me, but the presence of other disciples made him stop short. He then ordered me to join the crowd to work.

"May I tell Your Holiness," said I, "that Prajna (transcendental Wisdom) often rises in my mind. When one does not go astray from one's own Essence of Mind, one may be called the 'field of merits.'[1] I do not know what work Your Holiness would ask me to do."

"This barbarian is too bright," he remarked. "Go to the stable and speak no more." I then withdrew myself to the backyard and was told by a lay brother to split firewood and to pound rice.

More than eight months after, the Patriarch saw me one day and said, "I know your knowledge of Buddhism is very sound, but I have to refrain from speaking to you lest evil doers should do you harm. Do you understand?" "Yes, Sir, I do," I replied. "To avoid people taking notice of me, I dare not go near your hall."

The Patriarch one day assembled all his disciples and said to them, "The question of incessant rebirth is a momentous one. Day after day, instead of trying to free yourselves from this bitter sea of life and death, you seem to go after tainted merits only (i.e., merits which will cause rebirth). Yet merits will be of no help, if your Essence of Mind is obscured. Go and seek for Prajna (wisdom) in your own mind and then write me a stanza (gatha) about it. He who understands what the Essence of Mind is will be given the robe (the insignia of the Patriarchate) and the Dharma (i.e., the esoteric teaching of the Dhyana School), and I shall make him the Sixth Patriarch. Go away quickly. Delay not in writing the stanza, as deliberation is quite unnecessary and of no use. The man who has realised the Essence of Mind can speak of it at once, as soon as he is spoken to about it; and he cannot lose sight of it, even when engaged in battle."

Having received this instruction, the disciples withdrew and said to one another, "It is of no use for us to concentrate our mind to write the stanza and submit it to His Holiness, since the Patriarchate is bound to be won by Shen Hsiu, our instructor. And if we write perfunctorily, it will only be a waste of energy." Upon hearing this, all of them made up their minds not to write and said, "Why should we take the trouble? Hereafter, we will simply follow our instructor, Shen Hsiu, wherever he goes, and look to him for guidance."

---

[1]A title of honour given to monks, as they afford the best opportunities to others to sow the 'seed' of merits.

Meanwhile, Shen Hsiu reasoned thus with himself. "Considering that I am their teacher, none of them will take part in the competition. I wonder whether I should write a stanza and submit it to His Holiness. If I do not, how can the Patriarch know how deep or superficial my knowledge is? If my object is to get the Dharma, my motive is a pure one. If I were after the Patriarchate, then it would be bad. In that case, my mind would be that of a worldling and my action would amount to robbing the Patriarch's holy seat. But if I do not submit the stanza, I shall never have a chance of getting the Dharma. A very difficult point to decide, indeed!"

In front of the Patriarch's hall there were three corridors, the walls of which were to be painted by a court artist, named Lu Chen, with pictures from the Lankavatara (Sutra) depicting the transfiguration of the assembly, and with scenes showing the genealogy of the five Patriarchs for the information and veneration of the public.

When Shen Hsiu had composed his stanza he made several attempts to submit it to the Patriarch, but as soon as he went near the hall his mind was so perturbed that he sweated all over. He could not screw up courage to submit it, although in the course of four days he made altogether thirteen attempts to do so.

Then he suggested to himself, "It would be better for me to write it on the wall of the corridor and let the Patriarch see it for himself. If he approves it, I shall come out to pay homage, and tell him that it is done by me; but if he disapproves it, then I shall have wasted several years in this mountain in receiving homage from others which I by no means deserve! In that case, what progress have I made in learning Buddhism?"

At 12 o'clock that night he went secretly with a lamp to write the stanza on the wall of the south corridor, so that the Patriarch might know what spiritual insight he had attained. The stanza read:

> *Our body is the Bodhi-tree,*
> *And our mind a mirror bright.*
> *Carefully we wipe them hour by hour,*
> *And let no dust alight.*

As soon as he had written it he left at once for his room; so nobody knew what he had done. In his room he again pondered: "When the Patriarch sees my stanza tomorrow and is pleased with it, I shall be ready for the Dharma; but if he says that it is badly done, it will mean that I am unfit for the Dharma, owing to the misdeeds in previous lives which thickly becloud my mind. It is difficult to know what the Patriarch will say about it!" In this vein he kept on thinking until dawn, as he could neither sleep nor sit at ease.

But the Patriarch knew already that Shen Hsiu had not entered the door of enlightenment, and that he had not known the Essence of Mind.

In the morning, he sent for Mr. Lu, the court artist, and went with him to the south corridor to have the walls there painted with pictures. By chance, he saw the stanza. "I am sorry to have troubled you to come so far," he said to the artist. "The walls need not be painted now, as the Sutra says, 'All forms or phenomena are transient and illusive.' It will be better to leave the stanza here, so that people may study it and recite it. If they put its teaching into actual practice, they will be saved from the misery of being born in these evil realms of existence (gatis). The merit gained by one who practises it will be great indeed!"

He then ordered incense to be burnt, and all his disciples to pay homage to it and to recite it, so that they might realise the Essence of Mind. After they had recited it, all of them exclaimed, "Well done!"

At midnight, the Patriarch sent for Shen Hsiu to come to the hall, and asked him whether the stanza was written by him or not. "It was, Sir," replied Shen Hsiu. "I dare not be so vain as to expect to get the Patriarchate, but I wish Your Holiness would kindly tell me whether my stanza shows the least grain of wisdom."

"Your stanza," replied the Patriarch, "shows that you have not yet realised the Essence of Mind. So far you have reached the 'door of enlightenment,' but you have not yet entered it. To seek for supreme enlightenment with such an understanding as yours can hardly be successful.

"To attain supreme enlightenment, one must be able to know spontaneously one's own nature or Essence of Mind, which is neither created nor can it be annihilated. From ksana to ksana (thought-moment to thought-moment), one should be able to realise the Essence of Mind all the time. All things will then be free from restraint (i.e., emancipated). Once the Tathata (Suchness, another name for the Essence of Mind) is known, one will be free from delusion for ever; and in all circumstances one's mind will be in a state of 'Thusness.' Such a state of mind is absolute Truth. If you can see things in such a frame of mind you will have known the Essence of Mind, which is supreme enlightenment.

"You had better go back to think it over again for a couple of days, and then submit me another stanza. If your stanza shows that you have entered the 'door of enlightenment,' I will transmit you the robe and the Dharma."

Shen Hsiu made obeisance to the Patriarch and left. For several days, he tried in vain to write another stanza. This upset his mind so much that he was as ill at ease as if he were in a nightmare, and he could find comfort neither in sitting nor in walking.

Two days after, it happened that a young boy who was passing by the room where I was pounding rice recited loudly the stanza written by Shen Hsiu. As soon as I heard it, I knew at once that the composer of it had not yet realised the Essence of Mind. For although I had not been taught about it at that time, I already had a general idea of it.

"What stanza is this?" I asked the boy. "You barbarian," he replied, "don't you know about it? The Patriarch told his disciples that the question of incessant rebirth was a momentous one, that those who wished to inherit his robe and Dharma should write him a stanza, and that the one who had an understanding of the Essence of Mind would get them and be made the Sixth Patriarch. Elder Shen Hsiu wrote this 'Formless' Stanza on the wall of the south corridor and the Patriarch told us to recite it. He also said that those who put its teaching into actual practice would attain great merit, and be saved from the misery of being born in the evil realms of existence."

I told the boy that I wished to recite the stanza too, so that I might have an affinity with its teaching in future life. I also told him that although I had been pounding rice there for eight months I had never been to the hall, and that he would have to show me where the stanza was to enable me to make obeisance to it.

The boy took me there and I asked him to read it to me, as I am illiterate. A petty officer of the Chiang Chou District named Chang Tih-Yung, who happened to be there, read it out to me. When he had finished reading I told him that I also had composed a stanza, and asked him to write it for me. "Extraordinary indeed," he exclaimed, "that you also can compose a stanza!"

"Don't despise a beginner," said I, "if you are a seeker of supreme enlightenment. You should know that the lowest class may have the sharpest wit, while the highest may be in want of intelligence. If you slight others, you commit a very great sin."

"Dictate your stanza," said he. "I will take it down for you. But do not forget to deliver me, should you succeed in getting the Dharma!"

My stanza read:

There is no Bodhi-tree,
Nor stand of a mirror bright.
Since all is void,
Where can the dust alight?

When he had written this, all disciples and others who were present were greatly surprised. Filled with admiration, they said to one another, "How wonderful! No doubt we should not judge people by appearance. How can it be that for so long we have made a Bodhisattva incarnate work for us?"

Seeing that the crowd was overwhelmed with amazement, the Patriarch rubbed off the stanza with his shoe, lest jealous ones should do me injury. He expressed the opinion, which they took for granted, that the author of this stanza had also not yet realised the Essence of Mind.

Next day the Patriarch came secretly to the room where the rice was pounded. Seeing that I was working there with a stone pestle, he said to me, "A seeker of the Path risks his life for the Dharma. Should he not do so?" Then he asked, "Is the rice ready?" "Ready long ago," I replied, "only waiting for the sieve." He knocked the mortar thrice with his stick and left.

Knowing what his message meant, in the third watch of the night I went to his room. Using the robe as a screen so that none could see us, he expounded the Diamond Sutra to me. When he came to the sentence, "One should use one's mind in such a way that it will be free from any attachment," I at once became thoroughly enlightened, and realised that all things in the universe are the Essence of Mind itself.

"Who would have thought," I said to the Patriarch, "that the Essence of Mind is intrinsically pure! Who would have thought that the Essence of Mind is intrinsically free from becoming or annihilation! Who would have thought that the Essence of Mind is intrinsically self-sufficient! Who would have thought that the Essence of Mind is intrinsically free from change! Who would have thought that all things are the manifestation of the Essence of Mind!"

Knowing that I had realised the Essence of Mind, the Patriarch said, "For him who does not know his own mind there is no use learning Buddhism. On the other hand, if he knows his own mind and sees intuitively his own nature, he is a Hero, a 'Teacher of gods and men,' 'Buddha'."

RELIGION AS SOCIAL CONSTRUCTION OF MEANING

The following passage is by sociologist of religion Peter L. Berger (who has also written very positively on transcendence in religion) and is on religion as an endeavor by a human society to make itself a part of the cosmos. Here *nomos* (Greek for "law") means the human social order with its structures of authority, morality, ritual, and so on, and *cosmos* means the universe itself, including gods and infinity. Note especially the last sentence, "religion is the audacious attempt to conceive of the entire universe as being humanly significant." Religion means that the stars, the powers of universal creation and destruction, have a special relation to human beings and the human social order, and what is behind the stars is also concerned with our morals, rites, and internal transformations. Religious "dramas from infinity" spell this out.

The Sacred Canopy

Peter L. Berger

Whenever the socially established nomos attains the quality of being taken for granted, there occurs a merging of its meanings with what are considered to be the fundamental meanings inherent in the universe. Nomos and cosmos appear to be co-extensive. In archaic societies, nomos appears as a microcosmic reflection, the world of men as expressing meanings inherent in the universe as such. In contemporary society, this archaic cosmization of the social world is likely to take the form of "scientific" propositions about the nature of men rather than the nature of the universe. Whatever the historical variations, the tendency is for the meanings of the humanly constructed order to be projected into the universe as such. It may readily be seen how this projection tends to stabilize the tenuous nomic constructions, though the mode of this stabilization will have to be investigated further. In any case, when the nomos is taken for granted as appertaining to the "nature of things," understood

Excerpts from *The Sacred Canopy* by Peter L. Berger, pp. 24–28. Copyright © 1967 by Peter L. Berger. Used by permission of Doubleday & Company, Inc. Notes omitted.

cosmologically *or* anthropologically, it is endowed with a stability deriving from more powerful sources than the historical efforts of human beings. It is at this point that religion enters significantly into our argument.

Religion is the human enterprise by which a sacred cosmos is established. Put differently, religion is cosmization in a sacred mode. By sacred is meant here a quality of mysterious and awesome power, other than man and yet related to him, which is believed to reside in certain objects of experience. This quality may be attributed to natural or artificial objects, to animals, or to men, or to the objectivations of human culture. There are sacred rocks, sacred tools, sacred cows. The chieftain may be sacred, as may be a particular custom or institution. Space and time may be assigned the same quality, as in sacred localities and sacred seasons. The quality may finally be embodied in sacred beings, from highly localized spirits to the great cosmic divinities. The latter, in turn, may be transformed into ultimate forces or principles ruling the cosmos, no longer conceived of in personal terms but still endowed with the status of sacredness. The historical manifestations of the sacred vary widely, though there are certain uniformities to be observed cross-culturally (no matter here whether these are to be interpreted as resulting from cultural diffusion or from an inner logic of man's religious imagination). The sacred is apprehended as "sticking out" from the normal routines of everyday life, as something extraordinary and potentially dangerous, though its dangers can be domesticated and its potency harnessed to the needs of everyday life. Although the sacred is apprehended as other than man, yet it refers to man, relating to him in a way in which other non-human phenomena (specifically, the phenomena of non-sacred nature) do not. The cosmos posited by religion thus both transcends and includes man. The sacred cosmos is confronted by man as an immensely powerful reality other than himself. Yet this reality addresses itself to him and locates his life in an ultimately meaningful order.

On one level, the antonym to the sacred is the profane, to be defined simply as the absence of sacred status. All phenomena are profane that do not "stick out" as sacred. The routines of everyday life are profane unless, so to speak, proven otherwise, in which latter case they are conceived of as being infused in one way or another with sacred power (as in sacred work, for instance). Even in such cases, however, the sacred quality attributed to the ordinary events of life *itself* retains its extraordinary character, a character that is typically reaffirmed through a variety of rituals and the loss of which is tantamount to secularization, that is, to a conception of the events

in question as *nothing but* profane. The dichotomization of reality
into sacred and profane spheres, however related, is intrinsic to the
religious enterprise. As such, it is obviously important for any
analysis of the religious phenomenon.

On a deeper level, however, the sacred has another opposed
category, that of chaos. The sacred cosmos emerges out of chaos and
continues to confront the latter as its terrible contrary. This
opposition of cosmos and chaos is frequently expressed in a variety
of cosmogonic myths. The sacred cosmos, which transcends and
includes man in its ordering of reality, thus provides man's ultimate
shield against the terror of anomy. To be in a "right" relationship
with the sacred cosmos is to be protected against the nightmare
threats of chaos. To fall out of such a "right" relationship is to be
abandoned on the edge of the abyss of meaninglessness. It is not
irrelevant to observe here that the English "chaos" derives from a
Greek word meaning "yawning" and "religion" from a Latin one
meaning "to be careful." To be sure, what the religious man is
"careful" about is above all the dangerous power inherent in the
manifestations of the sacred themselves. But behind this danger is
the other, much more horrible one, namely that one may lose all
connection with the sacred and be swallowed up by chaos. All the
nomic constructions, as we have seen, are designed to keep this
terror at bay. In the sacred cosmos, however, these constructions
achieve their ultimate culmination—literally, their apotheosis.

Human existence is essentially and inevitably externalizing
activity. In the course of externalization men pour out meaning into
reality. Every human society is an edifice of externalized and
objectivated meanings, always intending a meaningful totality. Every
society is engaged in the never completed enterprise of building a
humanly meaningful world. Cosmization implies the identification of
this humanly meaningful world with the world as such, the former
now being grounded in the latter, reflecting it or being derived from
it in its fundamental structures. Such a cosmos, as the ultimate
ground and validation of human nomoi, need not necessarily be
sacred. Particularly in modern times there have been thoroughly
secular attempts at cosmization, among which modern science is by
far the most important. It is safe to say, however, that originally *all*
cosmization had a sacred character. This remained true through most
of human history, and not only through the millennia of human
existence on earth preceding what we now call civilization. Viewed
historically, most of man's worlds have been sacred worlds. Indeed,
it appears likely that only by way of the sacred was it possible for
man to conceive of a cosmos in the first place.

It can thus be said that religion has played a strategic part in the human enterprise of world-building. Religion implies the farthest reach of man's self-externalization, of his infusion of reality with his own meanings. Religion implies that human order is projected into the totality of being. Put differently, religion is the audacious attempt to conceive of the entire universe as being humanly significant.

TRANSCENDENCE

The following passage is part of an essay by the sociologist Robert N. Bellah entitled "Transcendence in Contemporary Piety." The essay often refers to the poetry of Wallace Stevens. It is of interest to us because it raises, in a very modern context, the meaning of transcendence, or the experience of that which is greater than the ordinary and the ground of religion. Bellah points out that humans have a deep-seated need for transcendence and that inner experience (see the selection from Maslow), society, and history can sometimes answer that need. Finally, however, we turn to words such as God, Being, and so on that are just symbols but, insofar as they have meaning at all, point to something beyond individual, society, and history. Nevertheless, the issue remains open as to whether these word-symbols point to one transcendent reality, or none, or many.

Beyond Belief:
Essays on Religion
in a Post-Traditional World

Robert N. Bellah

Reality may be encountered in the self as well as in the "external" world. Augustine said, "Men go to gape at mountain peaks, at the boundless tides of the sea, the broad sweep of rivers, the encircling ocean and the motions of the stars: and yet they leave themselves unnoticed; they do not marvel at themselves." He further argued that it is precisely "within" that we should begin our search for God. But

From pp. 198–99, 200–201, 202–203 in *Beyond Belief: Essays on Religion in a Post-Traditional World* by Robert N. Bellah. Copyright © 1970 by Robert N. Bellah. Reprinted by permission of Harper & Row, Publishers, Inc. Notes omitted.

in those vast inner regions that we can never know completely
Augustine recognized that there are other realities besides the
divine: "For no one is known to another so intimately as he is
known to himself, and yet no one is so well known even to himself
that he can be sure as to his conduct on the morrow." The heights
and depths of the inner life have been among the central realities of
religious men in many times and cultures. The overwhelming reality
of the inner life precludes any simple use of the word "subjective,"
as though the inner life were less "real" that external things. Above
all the inner life is not a matter of personal whim or simple control of
the ego. It is precisely its "constraining" nature, its "objectivity,"
which makes it a vehicle for transcendence.

It is with respect to unsatisfied desires and longings that
overwhelm all men at certain times and largely dominate the
existence of many that the "externality" of the inner life is most
pronounced. These "deficiency needs," to use Abraham Maslow's
terms, have by and large been viewed negatively by the great
religious traditions, though they exist in partly disguised form in the
central myths and theologies of many religions. We have learned
today not simply to flee from these desires, like St. Anthony in the
desert, but to take them seriously, indeed to view them as revelatory.
An existence that is so deeply unsatisfying that one's very biological
organism cries out against it is revealed by that fact alone as needing
change. This is not to say that deficiency needs are the only reality or
that satisfying them willy-nilly is the only morally legitimate course
of action. Deficiency needs must be considered in terms of a whole
that must include many other structures and processes. But
deficiency needs cannot just be dismissed or denied; they must be
taken as one indication of the structure of reality.

The inner experience not of need but of fulfillment has always
been the chief "inner" dimension of transcendent reality. Herbert
Richardson has recently argued that the chief aspects of such a
religious experience are the feelings of wholeness, rightness, and
well-being. Unlike the experience of deficiency, the experience of
fulfillment tends to overcome all opposition, to be as much immanent
as transcendent. Yet it is viewed subsequently as a revelation about
reality, not simply as an aesthetic or emotional experience of a purely
"subjective" sort. Such experiences are as basic in Western
spirituality as in Asian religions. In Christianity one needs to think
only, for example, of Paul on the road to Damascus, of Augustine in
the garden in Milan, or of Martin Luther, Blaise Pascal, Jonathan
Edwards, or Paul Tillich to see that in different periods and with
different theologies the experience itself has remained central. This is

not to say that the categories of interpretation do not differ significantly between various religions.

.   .   .

Without some such experience of transcendence consideration of it must probably remain abstract, verbal, and theoretical. Yet individual experience alone is an inadequate basis for knowledge of reality. Science proceeds on the assumption that experiments must be replicable, and indeed, scientific evidence is treated skeptically if it rests on the work of only one investigator and has not been duplicated by others. Traditionally religious men have acted on a parallel assumption. Individual religious experience must be checked against the experience of others. A religious tradition is in fact a community of religious experience. This is not to say that the religious experience of a community always takes precedence over that of an individual when there is a conflict between them. But if an innovator fails to arouse any response from others and if others cannot participate in his new modes of experience, then his religious innovation dies with himself and has no meaning for human religious history.

Religious experience is almost impossible without some form of group support. Maslow has indicated the necessity of adequate social arrangements for dealing with deficiency needs as a prerequisite for personal growth toward self-realization. Religious institutions are social settings for the encouragement of the spiritual life. When they seem no longer capable of fulfilling their function for significant numbers of people then revolutionary or reformist action to improve the situation also takes group form. Every great innovator has required his band of disciples and his lay sympathizers.

In a word, society, too, is a locus for the confrontation with reality. In the work of Emile Durkheim, society becomes almost the representative of a reality principle much like Freud's. It is society, according to Durkheim, that disciplines the individual, raises him above his petty desires and interests, and supports his rational capacity to deal objectively with the structures of reality. Durkheim sees society not only as a hard taskmaster but as the source of the best in man, for it is only in and through society that he can be fully human. In this perhaps Durkheim betrays his rabbinic heritage in that he holds not only that we should obey the law, but that it is worthy of our love.

It is also through society that man encounters history. There is a historical dimension at the level of personality. But it is in society that one's individual life history and history as collective experience intersect. History is the proving ground for both personal and social values. Given structures, personal and social, may prove inadequate in the face of the contingencies and catastrophes of history. In history reality is encountered as judgment, and no finite structure is ever entirely adequate to that encounter. Since history reveals the inadequacy of every empirical society, it becomes clear that society no more than the individual is a final repository of transcendence. Rather every society is itself forced to appeal to some higher jurisdiction, to justify itself not entirely on its actual performance but through its commitment to unrealized goals or values. The kind of symbolism that societies develop to indicate their commitment to higher values and define their legitimacy itself varies in historical perspective. But there is no society that can avoid such symbolism. Even in the most complex modern societies it is necessary.

.   .   .

Our analysis, then, forces us to consider the symbols that transcend individual and society, symbols that attempt to grasp reality as a whole, symbols like God, Being, Nothingness, and Life, which individuals and societies have used to make sense of themselves and give direction to their actions. These symbols may emerge out of individual, social, and historical experiences but they are not identical with them. They are not symbols for empirical realities in any scientifically verifiable sense. In some respects they are systems of pure terminology, displaying what Kenneth Burke has called the principle of perfection that he finds inherent in language itself. But these great summary symbols that refer to the totality of being, to the transcendent dimension of reality, and to the differentiated terminologies which have grown up around them, cannot be dismissed as "subjective" just because they are not in a simple sense "objective" in their reference. They are neither objective nor subjective, neither cosmological nor psychological. Rather, they are relational symbols that are intended to overcome precisely such dichotomies of ordinary conceptualization and bring together the coherence of the whole of experience.

It seems clear that we cannot distinguish reality as such from our symbolizations of it. Being human we can only think in symbols, only make sense of any experience in symbols. But these considerations reopen the issue of our confrontation with reality conceived of as standing over-against us. For that formulation seems to imply somehow that we stand outside of reality, that there is a split between ourselves and reality. But that is not the case. We participate in reality and not passively but actively. Thus in another mood Stevens can emphasize not the otherness of reality but its openness: "Reality is not what it is. It consists of the many realities which it can be made into."

SYMBOLISM

Symbols of transcendence are not simply passive objects, like works of art; they are also actions done, rituals performed, or thoughts thought. In the following passage a well-known philosopher of symbolism discusses the role and background of ritualized symbols, showing their roots in, among other things, the play of children. Notice the importance of imitation, but schematized, abbreviated imitation; this sort of ritualization can be seen in, for example, eating in the Christian Holy Communion.

Philosophy in a New Key

Susanne Langer

With the formalization of overt behavior in the presence of the sacred objects, we come into the field of *ritual.* This is, so to speak, a complement to the life-symbols; for as the latter present the basic facts of human existence, the forces of generation and achievement and death, so the rites enacted at their contemplation formulate and record man's response to those supreme realities. Ritual "expresses feelings" in the logical rather than the physiological sense. It may have what Aristotle called "cathartic" value, but that is not its characteristic; it is primarily an *articulation* of feelings. The ultimate product of such articulation is not a simple emotion, but a complex, permanent *attitude.* This attitude, which is the worshipers' response to the insight given by the sacred symbols, is an emotional pattern, which governs all individual lives. It cannot be recognized through any clearer medium than that of formalized gesture; yet in this cryptic form it *is* recognized, and yields a strong sense of tribal or congregational unity, of rightness and security. A rite regularly performed is the constant reiteration of sentiments toward "first and last things"; it is not a free expression of emotions, but a disciplined rehearsal of "right attitudes."

But emotional attitudes are always closely linked with the exigencies of current life, colored by immediate cares and desires, by

Reprinted by permission of the publishers from *Philosophy in a New Key* by Susanne Langer. Cambridge, Mass.: Harvard University Press. Copyright © 1942, 1951, 1957 by the President and Fellows of Harvard College; renewed 1970 by Susanne Knauth Langer. Notes omitted.

specific memories and hopes. Since the sacra are consciously regarded not as symbols of Life and Death, but as life-givers and death-dealers, they are not only revered, but also besought, trusted, feared, placated with service and sacrifice. Their power is invoked for the salvation of worshipers in times of danger. They can break the drought, end famine, stay a pestilence, or turn the tide of battle. The sacred ark going up before the Children of Israel gives them their victory. Held by the Philistines, it visits disease on its captors. Its efficacy is seen in every triumph of the community, every attainment and conquest. Specific events as well as definite feelings become associated with a Holy of Holies, and seek expression round the altar.

This is the source of *mimetic* ritual. The memory of celebrated events is strong in the celebration that renders thanks to the saving Power; it enters, perhaps quite unconsciously at first, into the gestures and shouts traditionally conveying such thanks. The story is retold, because it reveals the character of the Holy One, and as the telling soon becomes a formula, the gesticulations that accompany it become traditional gestures, new bodily expressions that can be woven into ritual patterns. The flourish of swords that accompanies the recall of a great exploit is presently carried out at definite points in the narrative, so that the congregation may join in it, as it joins in shouts like "Hallelujah," "Iacchos," or "Amen" at recognized periods. The gesture acquires a swing and rhythm of its own so it can be performed in genuine unison. At the end of the story it may be elaborated into a long demonstration, a "sword-dance."

Another and even more obvious origin of mimetic rites lies not in sacred story, but in supplication. Here conception is even more vivid, more urgent than in memory; an act is to be suggested and recommended to the only Being that can perform it, the Holy One; the suppliants, in their eagerness to express their desire, naturally break into pantomime. Representations of the act mingle with gestures of entreaty. And just as the expressive virtue of sacra is conceived as physical virtue, so the symbolic power of mimetic rites is presently regarded as causal efficacy; hence the world-wide and world-old belief in sympathetic magic. It really sinks to the inane conception of "magic" only when one assumes a *direct* relation between the mimicked event and the expected real one; in so far as the pantomime is enacted before a fetish, a spirit, or God, it is intended to move this divine power to act, and is simply a primitive prayer. We are often told that savage religion begins in magic; but the chances are, I think, that magic begins in religion. Its typical form—the confident, practical *use* of a formula, a brew, and a rite to achieve a physical effect—is the empty shell of a religious act.

Confused, inferior minds may retain it, even in a society that no longer thinks in terms of hidden agency, but sees causally connected phenomena; and so we come to the absurd practice of a "magic" that is supposed to *defy* natural law.

Religion is a gradual envisagement of the essential pattern of human life, and to this insight almost any object, act, or event may contribute. There is no ingredient in ritual that may not also be found outside it. Sacred objects are not intrinsically precious, but derive their value from their religious use. Formalized expressive gesture occurs in the most casual social intercourse, in greetings, marks of deference, or mock defiance (like the grimaces school-children make behind the back of an unpopular teacher, mainly for each other's benefit). As for mimetic gestures, they are the current and often unconscious accompaniment of all dramatic imagination. It need not be of serious or important acts. Mimicry is the natural symbolism by which we represent activities to our minds. It is so obvious a semantic that even where no act is carried out, but every idea merely suggested, pantomime is universally understood. Victor the Wild Boy of Aveyron, and even Wild Peter who was less intelligent, could understand mimetic expression at once, without any training, though neither ever learned language.

Before a symbolic form is put to public religious use—before it serves the difficult art of presenting really profound ideas—it has probably had a long career in a much homelier capacity. Long before men perform *rites* which enact the phases of life, they have learned such acting in play. And the play of children is very instructive if we would observe the peculiarly intellectual (non-practical) nature of gesture. If its purpose were, as is commonly supposed, to *learn by imitation,* an oft-repeated enactment should come closer and closer to reality, and a familiar act be represented better than a novel one; instead of that we are apt to find no attempt at *carrying out* the suggested actions of the shared day-dreams that constitute young children's play.

"Now I go away"—three steps away from the center of the game constitute this process. "And you must be crying"—the deserted one puts her hands before her face and makes a little pathetic sound. "Now I sew your fairy dress"—a hand with all five fingertips pressed together describes little circles. But the most convincingly symbolic gesture is that of eating. Children are interested in eating, and this much-desired occasion arises often in their games. Yet their imitation of that process is perhaps their least realistic act. There is no attempt to simulate the use of a spoon or other implement; the hand that carries the imaginary food to the mouth moves with the speed of a short clock-pendulum, the lips whisper "B-b-b-b-b." This sort of imitation would never serve the purpose of learning an activity. It is an abbreviated, schematized form of an action. Whether or no the child could perform the act is irrelevant; eating is an act learned long ago, sewing is probably a total mystery. Yet the imitation of sewing, though clumsy, is not as poor as that of the banquet.

The better an act is understood and the more habitually it is associated with a symbolic gesture, the more formal and cursory may be the movement that represents it. Just as the white settlers of this country first called an Indian feast a "Pow! Wow! Wow!" and later referred to it quite offhandedly as "a pow-wow," so a child's representation of sewing, fighting, or other process will be really imitative at first, but dwindle to almost nothing if the game is played often. It becomes an act of *reference* rather than of representation.

.   .   .

The universality of the concepts which religion tries to formulate draws all nature into the domain of ritual. The apparently misguided efforts of savages to induce rain by dancing and drumming are not practical mistakes at all; they are rites in which the rain has a part. White observers of Indian rain-dances have often commented on the fact that in an extraordinary number of instances the downpour really "results." Others, of a more cynical turn, remark that the leaders of the dance know the weather so well that they time their dance to meet its approaching changes and simulate "rain-making." This may well be the case; yet it is not a pure imposture. A "magic" effect is one which *completes a rite.* No savage tries to induce a snowstorm in midsummer, nor prays for the ripening of fruits entirely out of season, as he certainly would if he considered his dance and prayer the physical causes of such events. He dances *with* the rain, he invites the elements to do their part, as they are thought to be somewhere about and merely irresponsive. This accounts for the fact that no evidence of past failures discourages his practices; for if heaven and earth do not answer him, the rite is simply *unconsummated;* it was not therefore a "mistake." Its failure can be redeemed by finding some extenuating circumstance, some "counter-charm" that explains the miscarriage of the usual climax. There is no evil intent in the devices of medicine men to insure, or even to simulate, answers to magical invocations; for the most important virtue of the rite is not so much its practical as its religious success. Rain-making may well have begun in the celebration of an imminent shower after long drought; that the first harbinger clouds would be greeted with entreaty, excitement, and mimetic suggestion is obvious. The ritual evolves while a capricious heaven is making up its mind. Its successive acts mark the stages that bring the storm nearer. Its real import—its power to articulate a relation between man and nature, vivid at the moment—can be recognized only in the metaphorical guise of a physical power to induce the rain.

Sympathetic magic, springing from mimetic ritual, belongs mainly to tribal, primitive religion. There is, however, a type of ceremonial that runs the whole gamut from the most savage to the most civilized piety, from blind compulsive behavior, through magical conjuring, to the heights of conscious expression: that is the Sacrament.

COSMOS AND CHAOS

In endeavoring to make the social order a significant part of the cosmos (that is, the universe itself, seen as ordered and meaningful) through symbol, rite, and inner transformation and to bring individuals into this process, religion must distinguish between that which is *in* and that which is *out of* the order of meaning. This is a sorting-out that happens on every level, including for the scrupulous the subtlest of thoughts and moral gestures. It is, however, expressed symbolically in very large gestures as well. In the following passage, a prominent historian of religion shows ways in which traditional societies have distinguished between "cosmos and chaos" in territory. One can often see parallel attitudes today in groups of people with religious self-identities. Comparable spatial symbols of a sacred place as opposed to that which is outside can also be observed on smaller scale in the architecture of churches and temples; in the gates, doors, anterooms, and successive barriers between the holiest sanctuaries within them and the world outside; and in the approaches to sacred pilgrimage cities like Mecca.

The Sacred and the Profane
Mircea Eliade

One of the outstanding characteristics of traditional societies is the opposition that they assume between their inhabited territory and the unknown and indeterminate space that surrounds it. The former is the world (more precisely, our world), the cosmos; everything

From *The Sacred and the Profane* by Mircea Eliade, copyright © 1957 by Rowohlt Taschenbuch Verlag GmbH; copyright © 1959 by Harcourt Brace Jovanovich, Inc., and reprinted with their permission.

outside it is no longer a cosmos but a sort of "other world," a foreign, chaotic space, peopled by ghosts, demons, "foreigners" (who are assimilated to demons and the souls of the dead). At first sight this cleavage in space appears to be due to the opposition between an inhabited and organized—hence cosmicized—territory and the unknown space that extends beyond its frontiers; on one side there is a cosmos, on the other a chaos. But we shall see that if every inhabited territory is a cosmos, this is precisely because it was first consecrated, because, in one way or another, it is the work of the gods or is in communication with the world of the gods. The world (that is, our world) is a universe within which the sacred has already manifested itself, in which, consequently, the break-through from plane to plane has become possible and repeatable. It is not difficult to see why the religious moment implies the cosmogonic moment. The sacred reveals absolute reality and at the same time makes orientation possible; hence it *founds the world* in the sense that it fixes the limits and establishes the order of the world.

All this appears very clearly from the Vedic ritual for taking possession of a territory; possession becomes legally valid through the erection of a fire altar consecrated to Agni. "One says that one is installed when one has built a fire altar [*gārhapatya*] and all those who build the fire altar are legally established" (*Shatapatha Brāhmana*, VII, 1, 1, 1–4). By the erection of a fire altar Agni is made present, and communication with the world of the gods is ensured; the space of the altar becomes a sacred space. But the meaning of the ritual is far more complex, and if we consider all of its ramifications we shall understand why consecrating a territory is equivalent to making it a cosmos, to *cosmicizing* it. For, in fact, the erection of an altar to Agni is nothing but the reproduction—on the microcosmic scale—of the Creation. The water in which the clay is mixed is assimilated to the primordial water; the clay that forms the base of the altar symbolizes the earth; the lateral walls represent the atmosphere, and so on. And the building of the altar is accompanied by songs that proclaim which cosmic region has just been created (*Shatapatha Brāhmana* I, 9, 2, 29, etc.). Hence the erection of a fire altar—which alone validates taking possession of a new territory—is equivalent to a cosmogony.

An unknown, foreign, and unoccupied territory (which often means, "unoccupied by our people") still shares in the fluid and larval modality of chaos. By occupying it and, above all, by settling in it, man symbolically transforms it into a cosmos through a ritual repetition of the cosmogony. What is to become "our world" must first be "created," and every creation has a paradigmatic model—the creation of the universe by the gods. When the Scandinavian colonists took possession of Iceland (*land-náma*) and cleared it, they regarded the enterprise neither as an original undertaking nor as human and profane work. For them, their labor was only repetition of a primordial act, the transformation of chaos into cosmos by the divine act of creation. When they tilled the desert soil, they were in fact repeating the act of the gods who had organized chaos by giving it a structure, forms, and norms.[1]

Whether it is a case of clearing uncultivated ground or of conquering and occupying a territory already inhabited by "other" human beings, ritual taking possession must always repeat the cosmogony. For in the view of archaic societies everything that is not "our world" is not yet a world. A territory can be made ours only by creating it anew, that is, by consecrating it. This religious behavior in respect to unknown lands continued, even in the West, down to the dawn of modern times. The Spanish and Portuguese conquistadores, discovering and conquering territories, took possession of them in the name of Jesus Christ. The raising of the Cross was equivalent to consecrating the country, hence in some sort to a "new birth." For through Christ "old things are passed away; behold, all things are become new" (II Corinthians, 5, 17). The newly discovered country was "renewed," "recreated" by the Cross.

EXPERIENCE OF THE SACRED

When the sacred, the transcendent, the holy, and the referent of all religious symbols and rites, is actually experienced, it can be a powerful and overwhelming thing that is not a mere problem in philosophy. The following is a description by the Roman writer Apuleius of a vision of Isis, the Egyptian goddess identified with the moon who in the Roman world had an elaborate initiatory cult of her own and was regarded by her followers, of whom the author was one, as the highest deity. Under many names she was the supreme and merciful one eager to receive the worship of her children. This passage is in a novel; the hero had through magic been given the body of a donkey but following this vision was told that because of his faith he would be relieved of

---

[1] Cf. Mircea Eliade, *The Myth of the Eternal Return*, New York, Pantheon Books, Bollingen Series XLVI, 1954, pp. 11 ff.

that burden. Yet this passage is generally held to come out of deep Isaic faith and to reflect in fictionalized form its experience of the sacred. Note that the vision is not divorced from the cultic life of the faith but rather leads naturally to participation in Isaic ceremonies and initiation, seeming to merge into the more human joy of a procession of Isaic devotees and to find a response in the beauty of nature itself.

The Golden Ass

Apuleius

About the first watch of the night I was aroused by sudden panic. Looking up I saw the full orb of the Moon shining with peculiar lustre and that very moment emerging from the waves of the sea. Then the thought came to me that this was the hour of silence and loneliness when my prayers might avail. For I knew that the Moon was the primal Goddess of supreme sway; that all human beings are the creatures of her providence; that not only cattle and wild beasts but even inorganic objects are vitalized by the divine influence of her light; that all the bodies which are on earth, or in the heavens, or in the sea, increase when she waxes, and decline when she wanes. Considering this, therefore, and feeling that Fate was now satiated with my endless miseries and at last licensed a hope of salvation, I determined to implore the august image of the risen Goddess.

So, shaking off my tiredness, I scrambled to my feet and walked straight into the sea in order to purify myself. I immersed my head seven times because (according to the divine Pythagoras) that number is specially suited for all ritual acts; and then, speaking with lively joy, I lifted my tear-wet face in supplication to the irresistible Goddess:

'Queen of Heaven, whether you are fostering Ceres the motherly nurse of all growth, who (gladdened at the discovery of your lost daughter) abolished the brutish nutriment of the primitive acorn and pointed the way to gentler food (as is yet shown in the tilling of the fields of Eleusis); or whether you are celestial Venus who in the first moment of Creation mingled the opposing sexes in the generation of mutual desires, and who (after sowing in humanity

From Jack Lindsay, translator, *The Golden Ass by Apuleius*. Bloomington and London: Indiana University Press, 1932, 1967, pp. 235–39. Reprinted by permission of the publisher.

the seeds of indestructible continuing life) are now worshipped in the wave-washed shrine of Paphos; or whether you are the sister of Phoebus, who be relieving the pangs of childbirth travail with soothing remedies have brought safe into the world lives innumerable, and who are now venerated in the thronged sanctuary of Ephesus; or whether you are Proserpine, terrible with the howls of midnight, whose triple face has power to ward off all the assaults of ghosts and to close the cracks in the earth, and who wander through many a grove, propitiated in divers manners, illuminating the walls of all cities with beams of female light, nurturing the glad seeds in the earth with your damp heat, and dispensing abroad your dim radiance when the sun has abandoned us—O by whatever name, and by whatever rites, and in whatever form, it is permitted to invoke you, come now and succour me in the hour of my calamity. Support my broken life, and give me rest and peace after the tribulations of my lot. Let there be an end to the toils that weary me, and an end to the snares that beset me. Remove from me the hateful shape of a beast, and restore me to the sight of those that love me. Restore me to Lucius, my lost self. But if an offended god pursues me implacably, then grant me death at least since life is denied me.'

Having thus poured forth my prayer and given an account of my bitter sufferings, I drowsed and fell asleep on the same sand-couch as before. But scarcely had I closed my eyes before a god-like face emerged from the midst of the sea with lineaments that gods themselves would revere. Then gradually I saw the whole body (resplendent image that it was) rise out of the scattered deep and stand beside me.

I shall not be so brave as to attempt a description of this marvellous form, if the poverty of human language will not altogether distort what I have to say, or if the divinity herself will deign to lend me a rich enough stock of eloquent phrase. First, then, she had an abundance of hair that fell gently in dispersed ringlets upon the divine neck. A crown of interlaced wreaths and varying flowers rested upon her head; and in its midst, just over the brow, there hung a plain circlet resembling a mirror or rather a miniature moon—for it emitted a soft clear light. This ornament was supported on either side by vipers that rose from the furrows of the earth; and above it blades of corn were disposed. Her garment, dyed many colours, was woven of fine flax. One part was gleaming white; another was yellow as the crocus; another was flamboyant with the red of roses. But what obsessed my gazing eyes by far the most was her pitch-black cloak that shone with a dark glow. It was wrapped round her, passing from under the right arm over the left shoulder and fastened with a knot like the boss of a shield. Part of it fell down in pleated folds and swayed gracefully with a knotted fringe along the hem. Upon the embroidered edges and over the whole surface sprinkled stars were burning; and in the centre a mid-month moon breathed forth her floating beams. Lastly, a garland wholly composed of every kind of fruit and flower clung of its own accord to the fluttering border of that splendid robe.

Many strange things were among her accoutrements. In her right hand she held a brazen sistrum, a flat piece of metal curved like a girdle, through which there passed some little rods—and when with her arm she vibrated these triple chords they produced a shrill sharp cry. In her left hand she bore an oblong golden vessel shaped like a boat, on the handle of which (set at the most conspicuous angle) there coiled an asp raising its head and puffing out its throat. The shoes that covered her ambrosial feet were plaited from the palm, emblem of victory.

Such was the goddess as breathing forth the spices of pleasant Arabia she condescended with her divine voice to address me.

'Behold, Lucius,' she said, 'moved by your prayer I come to you —I, the natural mother of all life, the mistress of the elements, the first child of time, the supreme divinity, the queen of those in hell, the first among those in heaven, the uniform manifestation of all the gods and goddesses—I, who govern by my nod the crests of light in the sky, the purifying wafts of the ocean, and the lamentable silences of hell—I, whose single godhead is venerated all over the earth under manifold forms, varying rites, and changing names. Thus, the Phrygians that are the oldest human stock call me Pessinuntia, Mother of the Gods. The aboriginal races of Attica call me Cecropian Minerva. The Cyprians in their island-home call me Paphian Venus. The archer Cretans call me Diana Dictynna. The three-tongued Sicilians[1] call me Stygian Proserpine. The Eleusinians call me the ancient goddess Ceres. Some call me Juno. Some call me Bellona. Some call me Hecate. Some call me Rhamnusia. But those who are enlightened by the earliest rays of that divinity the sun, the Ethiopians, the Arii, and the Egyptians who excel in antique lore, all worship me with their ancestral ceremonies and call me by my true name, Queen Isis.

'Behold, I am come to you in your calamity. I am come with solace and aid. Away then with tears. Cease to moan. Send sorrow

---

[1]'Three-tongued Sicilians': The islanders changed from Sicilian to Greek to Latin. The Arii are of Parthian Aria.

packing. Soon through my providence shall the sun of your salvation arise. Hearken therefore with care unto what I bid. Eternal religion has dedicated to me the day which will be born from the womb of this present darkness. Tomorrow my priests will offer to me the first fruits of the year's navigation. They will consecrate in my name a new-built ship. For now, the tempests of the winter are lulled; the roaring waves of the sea are quieted; and the waters are again navigable. You must await this ceremony, without anxiety and without wandering thoughts. For the priest at my suggestion will carry in the procession a crown of roses attached to the sistrum in his right hand; and you must unhesitatingly push your way through the crowd, join the procession, and trust in my good will. Approach close to the priest as if you meant to kiss his hand, and gently crop the roses. Instantly you will slough the hide of this beast on which I have long looked with abhorrence.

'Fear for no detail of the work to which I once put my hand. Even at this moment of time in which I appear before you, I am also in another place instructing my priest in a vision what is to be brought to pass. By my command the crush of people will open to give you way; and despite all the gay rites and ferial revelries not one of my worshippers will feel disgust because of the unseemly shape in which you are incarcerated. Neither will any one of them misinterpret your sudden metamorphosis or rancorously use it against you.

'Only remember, and keep the remembrance fast in your heart's deep core, that all the remaining days of your life must be dedicated to me, and that nothing can release you from this service but death. Neither is it aught but just that you should devote your life to her who redeems you back into humanity. You shall live blessed. You shall live glorious under my guidance; and when you have travelled your full length of time and you go down into death, there also (on that hidden side of earth) you shall dwell in the Elysian Fields and frequently adore me for my favours. For you will see me shining on amid the darkness of Acheron and reigning in the Stygian depths.

'More, if you are found to merit my love by your dedicated obedience, religious devotion, and constant chastity, you will discover that it is within my power to prolong your life beyond the limits set to it by Fate.'

At last the end of this venerable oracle was reached, and the invincible Goddess ebbed back into her own essence. No time was lost. Immediately snapping the threads of sleep, and wrung with a sweat of joy and terror, I wakened. Wondering deeply at so direct a manifestation of the Goddess's power, I sprinkled myself with salt water; and eager to obey her in every particular, I repeated over to myself the exact words in which she had framed her instructions. Soon the sun of gold arose and sent the clouds of thick night flying; and lo, a crowd of people replenished the streets, filing in triumphal religious procession. It seemed to me that the whole world, independent of my own high spirits, was happy. Cattle of every kind, the houses, the very day, all seemed to lift serene faces brimful with jollity. For sunny and placid weather had suddenly come upon us after a frosty yesterday; and the tuneful birdlets, coaxed out by the warmths of the Spring, were softly singing sweet hymns of blandishment to the Mother of the Stars, the Producer of the Seasons, the Mistress of the Universe. The trees also, both those that blossomed into fruit and those that were content to yield only sterile shade, were loosed by the southerly breezes; and glistening gaily with their budded leaves, they swished their branches gently in sibilant sighs. The crash of storm was over; and the waves, no longer mountainous with swirling foam, lapped quietly upon the shore. The dusky clouds were routed; and the heavens shone with clear sheer splendour of their native light.

FINDING IDENTITY
THROUGH RELIGION

The author of the following passage, C. S. Lewis, has subsequent to the experience recounted here written a number of extremely popular Christian-oriented books. Notice, apart from his reluctance, the way in which this process of finding religious faith was a process of harmonizing the symbols in his life and of finding in the midst of them his real self. In the realm of symbols, his main problem was making the symbolic word *God* truly transcendent rather than just a creature of his thought. He wanted to keep part of his life independent but realized that the price of this would be disunion within himself. That independence was important to him because he had been brought up by a father and strict schoolmasters who had interfered with him all too much. Nevertheless, the thirst for transcendent unity beyond all private thoughts and feelings prevailed.

Surprised by Joy

C. S. Lewis

Really, a young Atheist cannot guard his faith too carefully. Dangers lie in wait for him on every side. You must not do, you must not even try to do, the will of the Father unless you are prepared to "know of the doctrine." All my acts, desires, and thoughts were to be brought into harmony with universal Spirit. For the first time I examined myself with a seriously practical purpose. And there I found what appalled me; a zoo of lusts, a bedlam of ambitions, a nursery of fears, a harem of fondled hatreds. My name was legion.

Of course I could do nothing—I could not last out one hour—without continual conscious recourse to what I called Spirit. But the fine, philosophical distinction between this and what ordinary people call "prayer to God" breaks down as soon as you start doing it in earnest. Idealism can be talked, and even felt; it cannot be lived. It became patently absurd to go on thinking of "Spirit" as either ignorant of, or passive to, my approaches. Even if my own philosophy were true, how could the initiative lie on my side? My own analogy, as I now first perceived, suggested the opposite: if Shakespeare and Hamlet could ever meet, it must be Shakespeare's doing.[1] Hamlet could initiate nothing. Perhaps, even now, my Absolute Spirit still differed in some way from the God of religion. The real issue was not, or not yet, there. The real terror was that if you seriously believed in even such a "God" or "Spirit" as I admitted, a wholly new situation developed. As the dry bones shook and came together in that dreadful valley of Ezekiel's, so now a philosophical theorem, cerebrally entertained, began to stir and heave and throw off its gravecloths, and stood upright and became a living presence. I was to be allowed to play at philosophy no longer. It might, as I say, still be true that my "Spirit" differed in some way from "the God of popular religion." My Adversary waived the point. It sank into utter unimportance. He would not argue about it. He only said, "I am the Lord"; "I am that I am"; "I am."

From C. S. Lewis, *Surprised by Joy*. London: Collins Fontana Books, 1959, pp. 180–83. Reprinted by permission.

[1] i.e. Shakespeare could, in principle, make himself appear as Author within the play, and write a dialogue between Hamlet and himself. The "Shakespeare" within the play would of course be at once Shakespeare and one of Shakespeare's creatures. It would bear some analogy to Incarnation.

People who are naturally religious find difficulty in understanding the horror of such a revelation. Amiable agnostics will talk cheerfully about "man's search for God." To me, as I then was, they might as well have talked about the mouse's search for the cat. The best image of my predicament is the meeting of Mime and Wotan in the first act of *Seigfried; hier brauch' ich nicht Spärer noch Späher, Einsam will ich* . . . (I've no use for spies and snoopers. I would be private. . . .)

Remember, I had always wanted, above all things, not to be "interfered with." I had wanted (mad wish) "to call my soul my own." I had been far more anxious to avoid suffering than to achieve delight. I had always aimed at limited liabilities. The supernatural itself had been to me, first, an illicit dram, and then, as by a drunkard's reaction, nauseous. Even my recent attempt to live my philosophy had secretly (I now knew) been hedged round by all sorts of reservations. I had pretty well known that my ideal of virtue would never be allowed to lead me into anything intolerably painful; I would be "reasonable." But now what had been an ideal became a command; and what might not be expected of one? Doubtless, by definition, God was Reason itself. But would He also be "reasonable" in that other, more comfortable, sense? Not the slightest assurance on that score was offered me. Total surrender, the absolute leap in the dark, were demanded. The reality with which no treaty can be made was upon me. The demand was not even "All or nothing." I think that stage had been passed, on the bus-top when I unbuckled my armour and the snow-man started to melt. Now, the demand was simply "All."

You must picture me alone in that room at Magdalen, night after night, feeling, whenever my mind lifted even for a second from my work, the steady, unrelenting approach of Him whom I so earnestly desired not to meet. That which I greatly feared had at last come upon me. In the Trinity Term of 1929 I gave in, and admitted that God was God, and knelt and prayed; perhaps, that night, the most dejected and reluctant convert in all England. I did not then see what is now the most shining and obvious thing; the Divine humility which will accept a convert even on such terms. The Prodigal Son at least walked home on his own feet. But who can duly adore that Love which will open the high gates to a prodigal who is brought in kicking, struggling, resentful, and darting his eyes in every direction for a chance of escape? The words *compelle intrare*, compel them to come in, have been so abused by wicked men that we shudder at them; but, properly understood, they plumb the depth of the Divine mercy. The hardness of God is kinder than the softness of men, and His compulsion is our liberation.

RELIGION
AS ESTABLISHER
OF CONSTRAINTS

One function of religion in society is its role as enforcer of norms of attitude and behavior. Behind this function is an assumption that, if the human society is indeed part of the cosmos, human transgressions affect this relationship negatively and that the transgressions of one person affect everyone. It also means that just as the transcendent can be expressed through symbol and rite so can transgressions be dealt with in this way. The following passage, by a distinguished anthropologist, alludes to these matters among the Nuer people of the Sudan. Note the ways in which transgression, ritual, sin, disease, and individual and communal guilt are interrelated. Through all these processes, the effect is finally for the religion to reinforce by spiritual sanctions the behavior norms of the community. This constraints-establishing function of religion is, however, tied with the next, the giving of ecstasy; typically the ecstatic joy of religion is most accessible to those who have observed its constraints.

Nuer Religion

E. E. Evans-Pritchard

Woc is used in a number of contexts in which the sense is getting rid of something, especially by wiping it out. It is the ritual ones which more particularly concern us. The first cut across the forehead at initiation is called the *woc dhol*, the wiping out of boyhood. The final rites of marriage are said to wipe out maidenhood. As we have noted, the mortuary ceremony is called *col woc*, the wiping out of death and mourning with their association of debt. The word is also used in reference to sacrifices made on account of a transgression. Sacrifice is said to *woc*, wipe out, *nueer, rual, kor,* and *thiang,* and indeed any *duer,* fault. The transgressor is healed by the blotting out of his transgression. God turns away, as the Nuer put it. He does not

From E. E. Evans-Pritchard, *Nuer Religion*. Oxford: The Clarendon Press, 1956, pp. 190–93. Reprinted by permission of Oxford University Press. Notes omitted.

regard it any more, so it ceases to be. When used in reference to sacrifices made on account of sins the word has thus the sense of expiation, and it is interesting that the same word which Nuer use for wiping out a transgression means in Dinka 'to err', 'to sin', and 'offence'. We have in the words *dop* and *woc* two ideas which throw much light on the way Nuer regard sins and sacrifices made in consequence of them. Sin, as has been noted, is something which destroys and which tracks down. Two other characteristics of it are now revealed. It can spread and it can be wiped out by sacrifice. But though sin is regarded as bringing about a condition of the person which is contagious, the uncleanness is not simply a physical impurity which can be washed or purged away. It is also a spiritual state which can only be changed by sacrifice; and not even sacrifice is sufficient by itself to change it, only sacrifice which carries with it the will and desire of the sinner. What gives emphasis to the physical quality of the condition is the fact that the consequences of sin, which in a sense form part of it, are physical. This brings us to a very important matter, the identification of disease with sin.

Nuer may speak, as we have seen, of the consequences of a sin by the same word (in which the interdiction is also implied) as they use when they speak of the sin itself. *Rual* is incest, and it is also syphilis and yaws. *Nueer* is a breach of certain interdictions, and it is also the violent sickness which follows the breach. *Thiang* is a breach of the weaning interdiction, and it is also the dysentery the breach causes. Different diseases have different names, it is true, but if the sin which brought the sickness about is known it is spoken of by the name of the sin. The particular form of the sickness, the particular consequences which have resulted from the sin, are of secondary interest. Had the man suffered from a different ailment it would have been from the same cause. Therefore one may say that where there is a state of sin such sickness as it appears in is a symptom of the sin, or even in a sense is the sin. Even where there has been no breach of a specific interdiction, and there is consequently not the same verbal identification, any sickness tends to be regarded as the operation of Spirit on account of some fault on the part of the sick person or of someone closely related to him, and it may simply be said to be *kwoth*, meaning that it is the action of Spirit. A sickness may always be a sign of some fault. No attempt may be made to discover whether there has been a fault or not or what the fault, if any, was, but Nuer think that a man would not be sick if there had been no error, though the thought is not always expressed.

Since sickness is the action of Spirit therapeutic treatment is sacramental. The sickness is only a symptom of the spiritual condition of the person, which is the underlying cause of the crisis; and it can only be cured by expiation—sacrifice—for the sin which has brought it about. This, then, is a further characteristic of sin. It causes physical misfortune, usually sickness, which is identified with it, so that the healing of the sickness is felt to be also the wiping out of the sin. When Nuer say that sacrifice wipes out the *giak*, the badness or evil, they do not just mean that the sickness will depart but also that what may have caused it will be no more. When a serious sin has been committed sacrifice is made before there are any signs of sickness.

So far we have been discussing certain definite ideas and conventions. Certain violations of specific interdictions are held to be divinely punished and these have special names, *nueer*, *rual*, and so forth. But they are covered by the general term *dueri*, faults. That term covers also breaches of any social convention. There is, therefore, no convenient terminological distinction in Nuer which we can follow in translation to mark off faults of the kind we have been considering and have called sins from faults of some other kind. Moreover, God is regarded as the guardian of the social order and his intervention as a possible sanction for any rule of conduct. We cannot, therefore, make an absolute distinction between what we have called sins and other faults. We can only say that the religious sanction is more severe, and more definite, and tends also to be more exclusive, in the case of the faults we have been discussing than in cases of other faults.

A *duer*, fault, of any kind may, as we have earlier noted, bring about divine punishment. It may do so through the action of a curse or of ghostly vengeance, and as in such cases God is thought to be the arbiter the fault involves to some extent the idea of divine intervention and consequently the need for sacrifice; and a misfortune may be attributed to a curse of the living or to anger of the ghosts and hence to injuries done to them. It may do so through fetishes, though, as we have noted, there is some ambiguity and confusion about their morality. Particular calamities are not otherwise attributed to specific breaches of custom, and I have never seen or heard of sacrifices performed on account of such breaches. Serious sickness, the commonest occasion of sacrifice, in all cases I have examined, was attributed, when attributed to anything, to an infraction of one of the interdictions we have been discussing, to seizure or possession by a spirit, generally seizure on account of neglect of obligations to it, to ghostly vengeance, or to a fetish, and not simply to failure to observe the social code. But we have to bear in mind that when there is sickness not attributed to some specific cause sacrifice is, nevertheless, performed to cover any or all unknown causes and that among such causes may be moral faults which have caught up with the sick man in his sickness, and this is so because God has taken notice of them.

Consequently, such moral faults as meanness, disloyalty, dishonesty, slander, lack of deference to seniors, and so forth, cannot be entirely dissociated from sin, for God may punish them even if those who have suffered from them take no action of their own account. Nuer seem to regard moral faults as accumulating and creating a condition of the person predisposing him to disaster, which may then fall upon him on account of some act or omission which might not otherwise and by itself have brought it about. This is further suggested by the custom of confession at certain sacrifices, when it is necessary to reveal all resentments and grievances a man may have in his heart towards others. This may be rather a peculiar kind of confession, that of other people's shortcomings, but the point is that the faults together with the feelings they have engendered are placed on the victim and flow away into the earth with its blood.

RELIGION AS GIVER OF ECSTASY

The release of inward joy through religion is suggested by the following account from the life of Sri Ramakrishna (1836–86), a great modern Hindu saint, referred to here simply as the Master. He reflects on various ways toward knowing God: the way of jnana or knowledge and the way of bhakti or devotion to God (Brahman, spoken of as existence-knowledge-bliss) in one of his incarnate human forms such as Rama or Krishna or even as Durga, the Great Mother goddess. Above all, though, the very thought of these symbols of transcendence can produce ecstasy or deep samadhi or meditation in the Master. Ecstasy may be the fruit of a holy life, following the constraints of religion, but goes far beyond that; in it all the constraints and symbols may be thought of as internalized and then themselves harmonized on a transcendent level.

The Gospel
of Sri Ramakrishna

The Master went with the devotees to the northeast verandah of his
room. Among them was a householder from the village of
Dakshineswar, who studied Vedānta philosophy at home. He had
been discussing Om with Kedar before the Master. He said, "This
Eternal Word, the Anāhata Śabda, is ever present both within and
without."

Master: "But the Word is not enough. There must be
something indicated by the Word. Can your name alone make me
happy? Complete happiness is not possible for me unless I see you."

Devotee: "That Eternal Word itself is Brahman."

Master (to Kedar): "Oh, don't you understand? He upholds the
doctrine of the rishis of olden times. They once said to Rāma: 'O
Rāma, we know You only as the son of Daśaratha. Let sages like
Bharadvāja worship You as God Incarnate. We want to realize
Brahman, the Indivisible Existence-Knowledge-Bliss Absolute.' At
these words Rāma smiled and went away."

Kedar: "Those rishis could not recognize Rāma as an
Incarnation of God. They must have been fools."

Master (seriously): "Please don't say such a thing. People
worship God according to their tastes and temperaments. The mother
cooks the same fish differently for her children, that each one may
have what suits his stomach. For some she cooks the rich dish of
pilau. But not all the children can digest it. For those with weak
stomachs she prepares soup. Some, again, like fried fish or pickled
fish. It depends on one's taste.

"The rishis followed the path of jnāna. Therefore they sought to
realize Brahman, the Indivisible Existence-Knowledge-Bliss Absolute.
But those who follow the path of devotion seek an Incarnation of
God, to enjoy the sweetness of bhakti. The darkness of the mind
disappears when God is realized. In the Purāna it is said that it was
as if a hundred suns were shining when Rāma entered the court.
Why, then, weren't the courtiers burnt up? It was because the
brilliance of Rāma was not like that of a material object. As the lotus

From Swami Nikhilananda, translator, *The Gospel of Sri Ramakrishna*. New York:
Ramakrishna-Vivekananda Center, 1942, pp. 188–90, 567–68. Reprinted by permission
of the Ramakrishna-Vivekananda Center. Notes omitted.

blooms when the sun rises, so the lotus of the heart of the people assembled in the court burst into blossom."

As the Master uttered these words, standing before the devotees, he suddenly fell into an ecstatic mood. His mind was withdrawn from external objects. No sooner did he say, "the lotus of the heart burst into blossom", than he went into deep samādhi. He stood motionless, his countenance beaming and his lips parted in a smile.

After a long time he returned to the normal consciousness of the world. He drew a long breath and repeatedly chanted the name of Rāma, every word showering nectar into the hearts of the devotees. The Master sat down, the others seating themselves around him.

Master (to the devotees): "Ordinary people do not recognize the advent of an Incarnation of God. He comes in secret. Only a few of His intimate disciples can recognize Him. That Rāma was both Brahman Absolute and a perfect Incarnation of God in human form was known only to twelve rishis. The other sages said to Him, 'Rāma, we know You only as Daśaratha's son.'

"Can everyone comprehend Brahman, the Indivisible Existence-Knowledge-Bliss Absolute? He alone has attained perfect love of God who, having reached the Absolute, keeps himself in the realm of the Relative in order to enjoy the divine līlā. A man can describe the ways and activities of the Queen if he has previously visited her in England. Only then will his description of the Queen be correct. Sages like Bharadvāja adored Rāma and said: 'O Rāma, You are nothing but the Indivisible Satchidānanda. You have appeared before us as a human being, but You look like a man because You have shrouded Yourself with Your own māyā.' These rishis were great devotees of Rāma and had supreme love for God."

Presently some devotees from Konnagar arrived, singing kirtan to the accompaniment of drums and cymbals. As they reached the northeast verandah of Sri Ramakrishna's room, the Master joined in the music, dancing with them intoxicated with divine joy. Now and then he went into samādhi, standing still as a statue. While he was in one of these states of divine unconsciousness, the devotees put thick garlands of jasmine around his neck. The enchanting form of the Master reminded the devotees of Chaitanya, another Incarnation of God. The Master passed alternately through three moods of divine consciousness: the inmost, when he completely lost all knowledge of the outer world; the semi-conscious, when he danced with the devotees in an ecstasy of love; and the conscious, when he joined them in loud singing. It was indeed a sight for the gods, to see the Master standing motionless in samādhi, with fragrant garlands hanging from his neck, his countenance beaming with love, and the devotees singing and dancing around him.

When it was time for his noon meal, Sri Ramakrishna put on a new yellow cloth and sat on the small couch. His golden complexion, blending with his yellow cloth, enchanted the eyes of the devotees.

.   .   .

It was the third day of the Durgā Pujā. The Master had been awake in his room as Dakshineswar since early morning. The morning worship in the Kāli temple was over and the orchestra had played the morning melodies in the nahabat. Brāhmins and gardeners, basket in hand, were plucking flowers for the worship of the Divine Mother. Bhavanath, Baburam, Niranjan, and M. had spent the night at Dakshineswar, sleeping on the porch of the Master's room. As soon as they awoke they saw Sri Ramakrishna dancing in an ecstatic mood. He was chanting: "Victory to Mother Durgā! Hallowed be the name of Durgā!" He was naked and looked like a child as he chanted the name of the Blissful Mother. After a few moments he said: "Oh, the bliss of divine ecstasy! Oh, the bliss of divine drunkenness!" Then he repeatedly chanted the name of Govinda: "O Govinda! My life! My soul!"

The devotees sat on their beds and with unwinking eyes watched Sri Ramakrishna's spiritual mood. Hazra was living at the temple garden. Latu was also living there to render the Master personal service. Rakhal was still at Vrindāvan. Narendra visited Sri Ramakrishna now and then. He was expected that day.

The devotees washed their faces. The Master took his seat on a mat on the north verandah. Bhavanath and M. sat beside him. Other devotees were coming in and out of the room.

Master (to Bhavanath):   "The truth is that ordinary men cannot easily have faith. But an Iśvarakoti's faith is spontaneous. Prahlāda burst into tears while writing the letter 'ka'. It reminded him of Krishna. It is the nature of jīvas to doubt. They say yes, no doubt, but—

"Hazra can never be persuaded to believe that Brahman and Śakti, that Śakti and the Being endowed with Śakti, are one and the same. When the Reality appears as Creator, Preserver, and Destroyer, we call It Śakti; when It is inactive, we call It Brahman. But really It is one and the same thing—indivisible. Fire naturally brings to mind its power to burn; and the idea of burning naturally brings to mind the idea of fire. It is impossible to think of the one without the other.

"So I prayed to the Divine Mother: 'O Mother! Hazra is trying to upset the views of this place. Either give him right understanding or take him from here.' The next day he came to me and said, 'Yes, I agree with you.' He said that God exists everywhere as All-pervading Consciousness."

Bhavanath (smiling):   "Did what Hazra said really make you suffer so much?"

Master: "You see, I am now in a different mood. I can't shout and carry on heated discussions with people. I am not in a mood now to argue and quarrel with Hazra. Hriday said to me at Jadu Mallick's garden house, 'Uncle, don't you want to keep me with you?' 'No,' I said, 'I am no longer in a mood to get into heated arguments with you.'

"What is knowledge and what is ignorance? A man is ignorant so long as he feels that God is far away. He has knowledge when he knows that God is here and everywhere.

"When a man has true knowledge he feels that everything is filled with Consciousness. At Kāmārpukur I used to talk to Shibu, who was then a lad four or five years old. When the clouds rumbled and lightning flashed, Shibu would say to me: 'There, uncle! They're striking matches again!' (*All laugh.*) One day I noticed him chasing grasshoppers by himself. The leaves rustled in the near-by trees. 'Hush! Hush!' he said to the leaves. 'I want to catch the grasshoppers.' He was a child and saw everything throbbing with consciousness. One cannot realize God without the faith that knows no guile, the simple faith of a child.

CHAPTER TWO

TRIBE AND TOWN: THE HISTORY OF RELIGION

The story of religion is a vast and varied one, but some awareness of it is essential to the full understanding of any religion. The story begins far back in the animal world with patterns of ritualization and norms for behavior in a group that somewhat parallel human religion. It culminates (thus far) with the response of traditional religions to modernization and with the interpretation of religion by modern philosophers and social thinkers.

In between, religion appears as symbol systems clustering around what in every period of development is the source of life and the basic image of self. Nothing is more characteristic of the religion of hunting cultures than a sense of the sacred potency of the animal and the power of the shaman who, as a human able to go into trance or work magic, knows the secrets of spirits. He can master animal souls and find lost or strayed human spirits to divine or heal. In archaic agricultural societies, the sacred model is instead, at least for farmers, the plant with its cycles of seasonal death and rebirth and its need to receive sacrificed life in order to give life.

The next stage is the ancient agrarian empire, such as that of Egypt, Babylon, or China, with its emphasis on the sacred king and the ritually expressed order believed to emanate from him. Pursuing the stability beloved by the farmer with his need for regular seasons and his orientation toward a single village and tract of land, its whole symbology is typically directed toward placing human society and geography into a divine and secure cosmos in which chaos is predictably defeated.

Yet new things were stirring in the world of the ancient empires. As society became stable, complex, and relatively secure economically, new images of self appeared alongside those sacred symbols related to food, tribe, and shamanistic rapture. Individuals, increasingly able to make decisions and control their own lives and deaths, came to feel and articulate depth and infinity. Thus, religions centered on personal initiation and salvation occurred more and more, and finally there appeared the great religious founders—Zoroaster, the Buddha, Jesus the Christ, Muhammad. From their work came religious movements that, for the first time on a large scale, swept across national and cultural boundaries to become international. They presented an image of human subjectivity as able to attain horizonless consciousness, or immortal salvation, or citizenship in a new heaven and earth and as liable to absolute judgment for its decisions.

In a real sense, the ancient form of discovery of the self found its culmination in the devotion to personal saviors, gods, saints, and holy men characteristic of the next stage, medievalism. In both East and West, the Middle Ages meant fervent devotion to sacred personalities who were luminous images of the ideal archetypal hero, mother, and child. They bespoke a sense of one's own personality as adequate to make heartfelt commitments or express profound love.

The modern religious experience, shaped by forces such as the Protestant Reformation in Europe and comparable movements in other cultures, has had to contend with still more new discoveries about the nature of human destiny. Modernization has forced a new encounter with historical time through rapid social change; things change in far-reaching ways through industrialization, urbanization, and the birth of new nations and do not change back. It has had to deal with a new sense of pluralism—the discovery that each person must live with and decide among a great number of options in faith and life style and that the spiritual security of the narrow village with only one church or temple is gone forever. Finally and perhaps most significant of all, the modern intellectual climate has produced a spirit of what might be called *self-reflexiveness*, that is, the capacity to analyze everything human, including religion, from outside points of view—historical, sociological, psychological, or philosophical. While not wholly unknown to the ancients, this newly pervasive atmosphere of self-reflexiveness has meant that religion does not operate in a vacuum, even within a person, but is always in dialogue with other values, other intellectual ways of interpreting things, and other possible worlds of meaning.

ANIMAL PRECURSORS
OF RELIGION

There are many patterns of behavior in the animal world that suggest human religion. While it is certainly not suggested that animals have religion in the same sense as humans, since expression of meaning through language and the concepts that go with it are inseparable from religion as we know it, it is possible that some behavior often interpreted religiously by humans is shared by animals. One of these patterns would certainly be ritualization, the repetition (often, as Susanne Langer points out, in a truncated form that is itself symbolic) of a deeply important event fraught with fear and meaning. Religious rites, or personal religious practices and memories, can have this character, with the repetition itself meaningful and reassuring although different in emotional quality from the original event. The following passage, by a very distinguished student of animal behavior, describes ritualization in a greylag goose. The second selection, by a well-known naturalist, relates a striking event in the wild. While in this powerful account there is a great deal of reading in of human feeling, in a deeper sense it is to the point. Nature's main concern is that in the aggregate life outstay death, and if religion universally says anything with one voice, it is this same message on the human plane.

On Aggression

Konrad Lorenz

One indispensable element which simple animal traditions have in common with the highest cultural traditions of man is habit. Indubitably it is habit which, in its tenacious hold on the already acquired, plays a similar part in culture as heredity does in the phylogenetic origin of rites. Once an unforgettable experience brought home to me how similar the basic function of habit can be in such dissimilar processes as the simple formation of path habits in a goose and the cultural development of sacred rites in Man. At the

From *On Aggression* by Konrad Lorenz, copyright © 1963 by Dr. G. Borotha-Schoeler Verlag, Wien; English translation copyright © 1966 by Konrad Lorenz. Reprinted by permission of Harcourt Brace Jovanovich, Inc., and of Methuen and Co., Ltd.

time, I was making observations on a young greylag goose which I had reared from the egg and which had transferred to me, by that remarkable process called imprinting, all the behavior patterns that she would normally have shown to her parents. In her earliest childhood, Martina had acquired a fixed habit: when she was about a week old I decided to let her walk upstairs to my bedroom instead of carrying her up, as until then had been my custom. Greylag geese resent being touched, and it frightens them, so it is better to spare them this indignity if possible. In our house in Altenberg the bottom part of the staircase, viewed from the front door, stands out into the middle of the right-hand side of the hall. It ascends by a right-angled turn to the left, leading up to the gallery on the first floor. Opposite the front door is a very large window. As Martina, following obediently at my heels, walked into the hall, the unaccustomed situation suddenly filled her with terror and she strove, as frightened birds always do, toward the light. She ran from the door straight toward the window, passing me where I now stood on the bottom stair. At the window, she waited a few moments to calm down, then, obedient once more, she came to me on the step and followed me up to my bedroom. This procedure was repeated in the same way the next evening, except that this time her detour to the window was a little shorter and she did not remain there so long. In the following days there were further developments: her pause at the window was discontinued and she no longer gave the impression of being frightened. The detour acquired more and more the character of a habit, and it was funny to see how she ran resolutely to the window and, having arrived there, turned without pausing and ran just as resolutely back to the stairs, which she then mounted. The habitual detour to the window became shorter and shorter, the 180° turn became an acute angle, and after a year there remained of the whole path habit only a right-angled turn where the goose, instead of mounting the bottom stair at its right-hand end, nearest the door, ran along the stair to its left and mounted it at right angles.

One evening I forgot to let Martina in at the right time, and when I finally remembered her it was already dusk. I ran to the front door, and as I opened it she thrust herself hurriedly and anxiously through, ran between my legs into the hall and, contrary to her usual custom, in front of me to the stairs. Then she did something even more unusual: she deviated from her habitual path and chose the shortest way, skipping her usual right-angle turn and mounting the stairs on the right-hand side, "cutting" the turn of the stairs and starting to climb up. Upon this, something shattering happened:

arrived at the fifth step, she suddenly stopped, made a long neck, in geese a sign of fear, and spread her wings as for flight. Then she uttered a warning cry and very nearly took off. Now she hesitated a moment, turned around, ran hurriedly down the five steps and set forth resolutely, like someone on a very important mission, on her original path to the window and back. This time she mounted the steps according to her former custom from the left side. On the fifth step she stopped again, looked around, shook herself and greeted, behavior mechanisms regularly seen in greylags when anxious tension has given place to relief. I hardly believed my eyes. To me there is no doubt about the interpretation of this occurrence: the habit had become a custom which the goose could not break without being stricken by fear.

This interpretation will seem odd to some people but I can testify that similar behavior is well known to people familiar with the higher animals. Margaret Altmann, who studied wapiti and moose in their natural surroundings and followed their tracks for months in the company of her old horse and older mule, made very significant observations on her two hoofed collaborators. If she had camped several times in a certain place, she could never afterward move her animals past that place without at least "symbolically" stopping and making a show of unpacking and repacking.

The Immense Journey
Loren Eiseley

I have said that I saw a judgment upon life, and that it was not passed by men. Those who stare at birds in cages or who test minds by their closeness to our own may not care for it. It comes from far away out of my past, in a place of pouring waters and green leaves. I shall never see an episode like it again if I live to be a hundred, nor do I think that one man in a million has ever seen it, because man is an intruder into such silences. The light must be right, and the observer must remain unseen. No man sets up such an experiment. What he sees, he sees by chance.

Copyright © 1956 by Loren Eiseley. Reprinted from *The Immense Journey*, by Loren Eiseley, pp. 173–75, by permission of Random House, Inc.

You may put it that I had come over a mountain, that I had slogged through fern and pine needles for half a long day, and that on the edge of a little glade with one long, crooked branch extending across it, I had sat down to rest with my back against a stump. Through accident I was concealed from the glade, although I could see into it perfectly.

The sun was warm there, and the murmurs of forest life blurred softly away into my sleep. When I awoke, dimly aware of some commotion and outcry in the clearing, the light was slanting down through the pines in such a way that the glade was lit like some vast cathedral. I could see the dust motes of wood pollen in the long shaft of light, and there on the extended branch sat an enormous raven with a red and squirming nestling in his beak.

The sound that awoke me was the outraged cries of the nestling's parents, who flew helplessly in circles about the clearing. The sleek black monster was indifferent to them. He gulped, whetted his beak on the dead branch a moment and sat still. Up to that point the little tragedy had followed the usual pattern. But suddenly, out of all that area of woodland, a soft sound of complaint began to rise. Into the glade fluttered small birds of half a dozen varieties drawn by the anguished outcries of the tiny parents.

No one dared to attack the raven. But they cried there in some instinctive common misery, the bereaved and the unbereaved. The glade filled with their soft rustling and their cries. They fluttered as though to point their wings at the murderer. There was a dim intangible ethic he had violated, that they knew. He was a bird of death.

And he, the murderer, the black bird at the heart of life, sat on there, glistening in the common light, formidable, unmoving, unperturbed, untouchable.

The sighing died. It was then I saw the judgment. It was the judgment of life against death. I will never see it again so forcefully presented. I will never hear it again in notes so tragically prolonged. For in the midst of protest, they forgot the violence. There, in that clearing, the crystal note of a song sparrow lifted hesitantly in the hush. And finally, after painful fluttering, another took the song, and then another, the song passing from one bird to another, doubtfully at first, as though some evil thing were being slowly forgotten. Till suddenly they took heart and sang from many throats joyously together as birds are known to sing. They sang because life is sweet and sunlight beautiful. They sang under the brooding shadow of the raven. In simple truth they had forgotten the raven, for they were the singers of life, and not of death.

RELIGION
IN HUNTING CULTURES

The following passage on the religion of the Chukchee, a hunting and herding people of Siberia who are located on the coasts opposite Alaska, gives a vivid example of the world of the primitive hunter. Notice the emphasis on cosmic orientation, the role of the shaman, and the spiritual relation to the economic animals—especially in the deities who are protectors of the reindeer and the walrus. Sacrifice and the shaman's trances are the main means of communicating with the rich invisible world of gods, souls, and spirits that surrounds the Chukchee. It is not a chaotic world, though; it has a definite structure, with ways for shamans and spirits to pass from one realm of reality to another.

Aboriginal Siberia

M. A. Czaplicka

Benevolent supernatural beings are called by the Chukchee *vairgit*, i.e.'beings'. The most important are the 'benevolent beings sacrificed to' (*taaronyo vairgit*), those to whom the people bring sacrifices. They live in twenty-two different 'directions' of the Chukchee compass. The chief of these beings is the one residing in the zenith, which is called 'being-a-crown' (*kanoirgin*), or 'middle-crown' (*ginon-kanon*). Mid-day, the Sun, and the Polar Star are often identified with the 'middle-crown'. The Dawn and the Twilight are 'wife-companions', several of the tales describing them as being married to one wife. The 'directions' of the evening are together called 'Darkness'. Sacrifices are made to them only on special occasions, and are often mingled with those offered to the *kelet* ('evil spirits') of the earth.

The sun, moon, stars, and constellations are also known as *vairgit*; but the sun is a special *vairgin*, represented as a man clad in a bright garment, driving dogs or reindeer. He descends every evening to his wife, the 'Walking-around-Woman'. The moon is also represented as a man. He is not a *vairgin*, however, but the son of a *kele* of the lower worlds. He has a lasso, with which he catches

From M. A. Czaplicka, *Aboriginal Siberia*. Oxford: The Clarendon Press, 1914, 1969, pp. 256–61. Reprinted by permission of Oxford University Press. Notes omitted.

people who look too fixedly at him. Shamans invoke the moon in incantations and spells.

Among the stars, the pole-star is the principal *vairgin*, and is most often referred to as *unpener*, 'the pole-stuck star', a name which, Mr. Bogoras asserts, is universal throughout Asia.

There are several other *vairgit* beneficent to man, which Bogoras supposes to be merely vague and impersonal names of qualities. 'They represent a very loose and indefinite personification of the creative principle of the world, and are similar to Vakanda or Great Manitou of the Indians,' he says. Their names are Tenan-tomgin ('Creator', lit. 'One who induces things to be created'); Girgol-vairgin ('Upper-Being'); Marginen ('World', literally 'The Outer-One'); Yaivac-vairgin ('Merciful-Being'); Yagtac-vairgin ('Life-giving Being'); Kinta-vairgin ('Luck-giving Being'). These do not receive special sacrifices, but are all, except 'Creator', mentioned at the sacrifices to the Dawn, Zenith, and Midday. The 'Luck-giving Being' is sometimes represented as a raven, but the Creator is never so represented by the Chukchee (as he is among the Koryak), although he is sometimes known as 'the outer garment of the Creator'. The Chukchee, however, have many tales about Big-Raven, whom they call Tenan-tomgin.

Besides these 'Beings', the Reindeer Chukchee have also a 'Reindeer-Being' (*Qoren-vairgin*), who watches over the herds; and the Maritime people have their 'Beings of the Sea' (*Anga-vairgit*), of whom the most important are Keretkun and his wife, sometimes called Cinei-new. They live on the sea-bottom or in the open sea, where they have a large floating house. They are larger than men, have black faces, and head-bands of peculiar form, and are clad in long white garments made of walrus-gut adorned with many small tassels. Another sea-spirit is the 'Mother of the Walrus', living at the bottom of the sea, and armed with two tusks like a walrus. Besides her, there is still another sea-spirit like a walrus, which is believed to work harm to people, crawling into their houses at night. These walrus-beings do not receive regular sacrifices, and sometimes assist the shaman in the capacity of *kelet*. Keretkun, however, is the recipient of sacrifices at the autumn ceremonials. The Asiatic Eskimo have sea-deities similar to those of the Maritime Chukchee.

The Chukchee classify the winds also as 'Beings', whose names are mentioned in incantations, the local prevailing wind being always regarded in a given locality as the chief of these 'Beings'.

Spirits of tents and houses are called 'House-Beings' (*Yara-vairgit*). They are attached to houses, not to people, and if a house is destroyed they cease to exist with it. If the inhabitants of a house abandon it, the house-spirits turn into very dangerous earth-spirits. A small share of every important sacrifice is placed for them on the ground in the corners of the sleeping-room.

Other spirits, which are neither *kelet* nor *vairgit*, also exist; e.g. the spirits of intoxicating mushrooms, which form a 'Separate Tribe' (*Yanra-varat*).

Some 'Beings' have so called 'assistants' (*viyolet*) which receive a share of the sacrifices. The 'assistant' is very often represented as a raven or as half a raven. Even the *kelet* have 'assistants'.

All the forests, rivers, lakes, and the classes of animals are animated by 'masters' (*aunralit*) or 'owners' (*etinvit*). Sometimes the Chukchee call these *kelet*—a word which, though it usually means 'evil spirits', sometimes is used in the simple sense of 'spirits'. Wild animals are said to have the same sort of households as the Chukchee themselves and to imitate men in their actions. For instance, 'one family of eagles has a slave, Rirultet, whom they stole from the earth a long time ago. He prepares food for all of them, and his face has become blackened with soot.' Animals, like spirits, can take the form of men. The ermine and the owl become warriors on certain occasions; the mice become hunters. 'In most cases, animals, while impersonating human beings, retain some of their former qualities, which identify them as beings of a special class, acting in a human way, but different from mankind.' So the fox-woman retains her strong smell, and the goose-woman does not take animal food.

Lifeless objects, especially if they have originally been parts of living organisms, may become endowed with life; e.g. skins ready for sale may turn at night into reindeer, and walk about.

These various 'owners' are very often of the *kelet* class; but, according to Bogoras, no Chukchee will confess to having made sacrifices to evil spirits, except under extraordinary circumstances.

Bogoras divides the *kelet* of the Chukchee into three classes: (*a*) invisible spirits, bringing disease and death; (*b*) bloodthirsty cannibal spirits, the enemies of Chukchee warriors especially; (*c*) spirits which assist the shaman during shamanistic performances.

Kelet of the class (*a*) are said to live underground, and to have also an abode above the earth; but they never come from the sea, for, according to a Chukchee proverb 'nothing evil can come from the sea'.

The *kelet* do not remain in their homes, but wander abroad and seek for victims. They are too numerous to be distinguished by special names. Some of them are one-eyed; they have all sorts of strange faces and forms, most of them being very small. They are organized in communities resembling those of men. On the Pacific shores they are often known as *rekkenit* (sing. *rekken*). These have various monstrous forms, and animals which are born with any deformity are sacrificed to them. The *kelet* have an especial fondness for the human liver. This belief is the origin of the Chukchee custom of opening a corpse to discover from the liver which spirit has killed the deceased. The class (*b*), which is especially inimical to warriors, is spoken of chiefly in the tales. While incantations and charms are employed against spirits of the first class, against the giant cannibal *kelet* of the second category ordinary weapons of war are used. These spirits once formed a tribe of giants living on the Arctic shore, but being much harassed by the Chukchee, they changed themselves into invisible spirits.

The third class (*c*) is that of shamanistic spirits, sometimes called 'separate spirits' or 'separate voices'. They take the forms of animals, plants, icebergs, &c., and can change their form very quickly—and also their temper; on account of this last peculiarity the shaman must be very punctilious in keeping his compact with them. The shaman says of them, 'These are my people, my own little spirits.' We do not find in Bogoras any reference to benevolent shamanistic spirits or assistants of the shamen.

Besides these typical evil spirits, there is also a class of 'monsters'. Among these the chief is the killer-whale, which is surrounded by a taboo among all Arctic peoples: any one who kills a killer-whale is sure to die very soon. These monsters in winter are transformed into wolves and prey upon the reindeer of the Chukchee. An exaggerated representation of a polar bear also appears as one of the 'monsters'. The mammoth plays an important part in Chukchee beliefs. It is said to be the reindeer of the *kelet*. If the tusks are seen above ground, this is a bad omen, and unless an incantation is uttered something untoward will happen.

'According to one story, some Chukchee men found two mammoth-tusks protruding from the earth. They began to beat the drum and performed several incantations. Then the whole carcass of the mammoth came to sight. The people ate the meat. It was very nutritious and they lived on it all winter. When the bones were stripped of all the meat, they put them together again, and in the morning they were again covered with meat. Perhaps this story has for its foundation the finding of a mammoth-carcass good for eating, as happened on the Obi in the eighteenth century, and also more recently in the Kolyma country.

'Because of these beliefs, the search for ivory of the mammoth was tabooed in former times. Even now, a man who finds a mammoth-tusk has to pay for it to the "spirit" of the place by various sacrifices. The search for such tusks is considered a poor pursuit for a man, notwithstanding the high price which the ivory brings.'

In the pictorial representations of these 'monsters', or, rather, exaggerated animals, all which have a reindeer as the foremost figure are intended to represent benevolent spirits; while others in which a dog, horse, or mammoth stands in front, represent *kelet*.

Monstrous worms, blackbeetles, birds, and fish are the other exaggerated animal forms which Bogoras calls 'monsters'.

The soul is called *uvirit* or *uvekkirgin* ('belonging to the body'). Another term is *tetkeyun*, meaning 'vital force of living being'. The soul resides in the heart or the liver, and animals and plants as well as men possess it. One hears, however, more about other 'souls'— those which belong to various parts of the body: e.g. there is a limb-soul, nose-soul, &c. And so a man whose nose is easily frost-bitten is said to be 'short of souls'. Very often the soul assumes the form of a beetle, and hums like a bee in its flight. When a man loses one of his souls, he may obtain its return through a shaman, who, if he cannot discover the whereabouts of the missing soul, can send a portion of his own into the person who has suffered this loss. If a *kele* steals a soul, he carries it into his own dark abode, and there binds its limbs to prevent its escaping. In one of the tales 'a *kele* forces a stolen soul to watch his lamp and trim it'. Bogoras knew of a case of a man who struck his wife with a firebrand, and when the woman died after two days, and her relatives had examined her body and found no injury to any organ, they said that the husband's blow had injured her soul.

'*Kelet* also have souls of their own, which may be lost or spirited away by shamans.'

According to the Chukchee belief there are several worlds, one above another. Some reckon five such worlds, others seven or nine. A hole, under the pole-star, forms a passage from one world to the other, and through this hole shamans and spirits pass from one to another of the worlds. Another way to reach the other world is to take a step downwards in the direction of the dawn. There are also other 'worlds' in the 'directions' of the compass, one under the sea, another small dark 'world' vaguely described as being above, which is the abode of the female *kele*-birds. Some of the stars also are distinct 'worlds' with their own inhabitants. The sky, they say, is a 'world' too, and touches our earth at the horizon, where at four points there are gates. When the wind blows these gates are believed to be opening.

RELIGION
AND ARCHAIC AGRICULTURE

The basic point of agricultural religion is to establish a relationship with the earth and the giving of fertility to the earth. For this reason a deity of the earth, usually a goddess, is important. Gods representing the sky powers of sun and rain that cause the earth to bring forth a harvest and myths of the marriage of heaven and earth are also important. Images, rites, and magic seek to enhance fertility, sometimes through the example of human sexuality and often with sacrifice on the principle of life for life. Frequently the sacred king is regarded as a quasi-divine giver of fertility, in his role of mediator between the human and cosmic orders, and is responsible for weather and crops as well as political affairs. His rituals, perhaps his sacred marriage, have a direct bearing on the fields. Finally, human life may be assimilated with the agricultural pattern; just as its festival cycle revolves around seedtime with its fertility-giving rites and the celebrative harvest festival, so life, death, and immortality can be seen on the model of the plant that dies but is born again from the interred seed. Deities in agricultural societies, especially those of grain and life, may show a similar cycle in their myths and cults. The following passage alludes to most of these themes in the religion of the pre-Christian Nordic peoples of Scandinavia.

Scandinavian Mythology

H. R. Ellis Davidson

The Deities of the Earth

While Odin and Thor were counted among the family of the Aesir, the gods and goddesses who brought peace and plenty to men were known as the Vanir, deities who bore many different names. The god who stands out most prominently in the literature is called Freyr, a name meaning

Reproduced by permission of The Hamlyn Publishing Group Limited from *Scandinavian Mythology* by H. R. Ellis Davidson, pp. 74–83, 85–86. Copyright © 1969 by H. R. Ellis Davidson.

'Lord'. His twin sister was Freyja, 'Lady', and their father was the god Njord. Freyr was said to have been worshipped by the Swedes at Uppsala in the late Viking Age, along with Thor and Odin, and to have been represented in the temple there by a phallic image. He was described as the god who dispensed peace and plenty to men, and who was invoked at marriages. We possess one tiny but powerfully modelled little phallic figure, found at Rällinge in Sweden, which is believed to be a representation of this god. There are indications that the ritual of the divine marriage formed part of the cult of Freyr, and Saxo refers to some kind of dramatic miming which took place at Uppsala in his honour. He himself, or perhaps the devotees of Odin, about whom Saxo seems to know a good deal, considered such practices degrading and unmanly.

The Wooing of Gerd.   The myth of Freyr's wooing of the maiden Gerd is preserved in one of the Edda poems, and also told by Snorri. Freyr one day climbed into the seat of Odin, from which he could see into all the worlds. Northwards, in the underworld, he caught sight of a beautiful maiden coming out of her father's hall. Her arms were so white that their radiance lit up air and sea, and Freyr was overcome by desire for her, and could neither eat nor sleep. He sent his servant Skirnir on a long and perilous journey to woo the maiden for him, giving him his own sword and a horse which could carry him to the underworld. Skirnir at length reached the hall of the giant Gymir who was the father of Gerd. She refused the golden apples of the gods and the precious ring Draupnir which he offered her, and he had to threaten her with the magic sword and with the wrath of the gods, before she finally consented to meet Freyr in a grove in nine nights' time, to become his bride. The poem ends with a cry of impatience from the god because the time of waiting seems so long.

The usual interpretation given to this myth is that it represents the wooing of the earth by the sky, resulting in a rich harvest. But it is certainly not a simple presentation of this idea, for the confrontation of Skirnir with Gerd is complicated with esoteric dialogue about magic and the land of the dead, and he threatens her with a second death with all its attendant horrors.

The radiance of Gerd which lights up air and sea, and the introduction of Skirnir, whose name means Bright One, and who is otherwise unknown, suggest that there is some connection with the journey of the sun over the sky and down into the underworld. It is possible that the ritual of the divine marriage was linked with the reappearance of the sun after the winter darkness, or with the spring solstice. Certainly, of all the gods it is Freyr who appears to be most closely linked with the sun, although he cannot be viewed as a sun god, as was once supposed. The nine nights of waiting imposed on him are referred to again as preceding the supposed marriage of Freyja to the giant Thrym, and may have been a regular part of the pattern of a marriage ceremony.

The Dead King.   There is a close link between Freyr and the dead kings of Sweden who continued to benefit their people after their deaths. Snorri tells us in the history of the Ynglings, the early Swedish kings at Uppsala, that it was Freyr who set up the holy place there where the temple stood, and where we know that the royal burial mounds of the fifth and sixth centuries formed a centre of power and sanctity. Because of the prosperity which Freyr had brought to the Swedes when he ruled them, it is said that they worshipped him and took his name, calling themselves Ynglings after Yngvi-Freyr. His death was concealed from the people until a great howe, or burial mound, was ready to receive him, with a door and three holes in it, into which treasures were placed in the form of gold, silver and copper. These were the people's offerings for plenty, and for three years they brought them, thinking that Freyr still lived. When they learned that he was dead, they realised that he must be still helping them, as the seasons continued to be good, and they called him the god of the earth.

There was a similar tradition in Denmark of a king whose name, Frodi, could mean 'wise' or 'fruitful', or rather a series of kings bearing this name, according to Saxo. One of them, like Freyr, was associated with a time of great prosperity, and was carried round the land in a wagon after death. The people believed he still lived, until he was finally buried in a howe. Offerings were also made to a dead king in Norway, an ancestor of Olaf the Holy called Olaf 'Elf of Geirstad'. Before he died Olaf commanded that every man should take half a mark of silver into his burial mound, and he prophesied that if a famine came to the land men would sacrifice to him.

The door made in the burial mound of Freyr implies that it was possible to enter the mound of the dead king and perform rites there, as in the great megalithic tombs of the past, although the royal graves of the Migration period were not collective ones like those of neolithic times. We find a reference in Snorri's history of the kings to wooden men, presumably images of Freyr, taken from one of his mounds and sent from Sweden to Norway. A number of wooden figures, some of them male phallic ones, from a period before the Viking Age, were preserved in the peat bogs. One from Jutland, a rough but powerful phallic symbol with a strangely dignified face, may represent a less sophisticated image of Freyr, the god of fecundity, than the little bronze man of the Viking Age.

The King from the Sea.   The god as worshipped in Sweden appears to represent a divine king of the past, a ruler in a distant golden age and the founder of the nation. Another figure of this type was known to the Anglo-Saxons as Scyld. He was said to have come to Denmark across the sea as a little child in a boat laden with treasures, and to have become their king, bringing them much prosperity. At his death, they laid his body in a ship, filled with weapons and the treasures of the nation, and sent it out to sea, so that it might carry their king back to the place from whence he came: such is the story told at the beginning of the epic poem *Beowulf.*

The story of a child coming over the sea to rule men and bringing them wealth and plenty was long remembered both by Anglo-Saxons and Scandinavians, and sometimes it was said that a sheaf of corn lay in the boat which brought the child to their land. Other similar gods of whom we know little include Ing, whose name was linked with Freyr when he was called Yngvi-Freyr and who was said to have travelled in a wagon over the sea, and Ull, who was said to have used a shield as a boat. They may have been divine ancestor-kings, after whom places and sometimes tribes were believed to have been named.

Wagon and Ships.   The idea of a fertility deity who travels in a wagon through the land after death, or over the sea in a boat, is a familiar image in the literature. He brings blessing to men, visiting them periodically, apparently as part of the seasonal ceremonies. This may be seen as a development of the myth of the wagon of the sun, of much importance in the Bronze Age, when both wagon and ship were potent symbols apparently used to represent the sun's journey across the sky and down into the underworld. As in Ancient Egypt, it seems as if the dead king in early times was associated with this journey and with the blessing of his people, judging from the fragments of belief about the gods of the Vanir which have survived in myths.

We have also some archaeological evidence for the practice of carrying the god round the land. Beautiful and elaborate little wagons have been reconstructed from fragments found in the earth. Two were found at Dejbjerg in Denmark, broken in pieces and left, apparently as an offering, in a peat bog. They are thought to date from about the second century A.D. From a much later period we have a superbly carved wagon, whose carvings seem to have mythological significance, recovered from the Oseberg ship burial in Norway which took place at the close of the ninth century. This wagon formed part of the furnishing of an elaborate ship burial. Ships were used for funerals of both men and women and were buried in graves in seventh century East Anglia, and in Sweden and Norway up to the end of the Viking period.

It seems likely that such graves were prepared for worshippers of the Vanir. Freyr himself, according to Snorri, counted among his greatest treasures the ship *Skidbladnir,* said to be large enough to contain all the gods, and yet able to be folded up and kept in a pouch when not in use. The evidence suggests that ships were used both as offerings and also in processions in the Bronze Age. Examples of processional ships can be found well into the Middle Ages. The use of ships in carnivals, and the hanging of model ships in churches, sometimes taken out and carried in procession to bless the fields, has continued in Denmark and other northern countires into modern times.

The Goddess Nerthus.   At the beginning of the Christian era, the Roman historian Tacitus wrote a detailed account of the journey of the goddess Nerthus, known also as Mother Earth, when she travelled in a wagon round certain parts of Denmark. Her wagon was drawn by oxen and presumably held some symbol of the goddess, but only her priests were permitted to see inside. After her journey the wagon and its contents were cleansed in a sacred lake. The slaves who performed the rite were afterwards put to death, to preserve the sanctity of the deity. The wagon of Nerthus was welcomed with great rejoicing, and all fighting ceased throughout the land at the time of its appearance.

Freyr's Progress.   We hear also of an image of Freyr carried in a wagon in Sweden at the end of the Viking Age, although this is a late story and seems to have been told in order to poke fun at the credulous Swedes, who continued with such superstitions after Norway had been converted. According to the story, a young Norwegian who had fled to Sweden because of a disagreement with King Olaf Tryggvason, was invited by a priestess, called the 'wife' of the god Freyr, to accompany the wagon of the god on its autumn progress round the Swedish farms. She was an attractive young woman, and Gunnar was very willing to go, but when the wagon was stuck in an early snowstorm on a mountain road, Freyr himself came out in anger and attacked Gunnar. The hero appealed to the Christian god of King Olaf, and overthrew the heathen deity. He then put on the robes of the god and took his place when they visited the autumn feasts. The Swedes were most impressed to find that Freyr could eat and drink and even, as subsequently became apparent, get his wife with child. They held this to be a splendid omen, and so increased their offerings to the god. At this point King

Olaf, hearing what was going on, summoned Gunnar home, and he escaped taking with him his wife and child and carrying off a large amount of treasure.

.   .   .

Sacrifice to Freyr.   Sacrifices to Freyr are mentioned in the literature, although no details are given about them. There is mention of a horse about to be sacrificed to him at his temple in Thrandheim. Sometimes an ox was said to be sacrificed, as in the saga of the hero Glum. Glum's enemy, a devout worshipper of Freyr, made such a sacrifice in order to gain the god's help, and got the desired result. Glum on the other hand aroused the hostility of Freyr when he shed blood on a field sacred to the god, which stood by the temple of Freyr and bore a name which has been interpreted as 'Certain Giver'. It was suggested by Frazer and others following him that early kings of Scandinavia were regularly sacrificed for the good of the land and the prosperity of the people. Stories in the histories of the kings sometimes suggest something of the kind, for a number of them meet with strange and violent ends, and sometimes their wives are said to be responsible for bringing these upon them.

There is some evidence, as has been shown, that kings and members of the royal family were offered to Odin by hanging. But the possibility must be borne in mind that in Freyr's cult, as in Ancient Egypt, it was the natural death of the king, a time of crisis and danger, which was marked by elaborate rites connected with the god. Yet another possibility, for which there is evidence from Mesopotamia, is that the sacrifice of a substitute, and not the real king, took place at times of famine and peril.

RELIGION
IN THE ANCIENT EMPIRES

The official religion of the ancient empires, whether in China or Babylon, Egypt or India, was essentially that of all archaic agricultural societies, with a special emphasis on the role of the sacred emperor and his court. The following passage from the ancient Chinese Book of Rites gives an excellent picture of the role of the emperor, particularly in relation to agriculture and the cosmic order in which he was regarded as a pivotal part. These are the rites for the first month of spring. For this month, as for every season, there was an elaborate system of correspondences—stars, colors, smells, and elements— as well as rites to harmonize and enhance the forces of nature operative in that month. The court and especially the emperor, whose harmony with what nature was doing was so critically important, wore clothes and ate food corresponding to this total pattern. Then the sovereign performed appropriate rituals, culminating in this case with his plowing the first furrows to inaugurate the planting season ritually and to endow it with his sacred power. Notice that the passage ends with a set of prohibitions for the season of new life—there is a time for everything, and a time when a thing is not appropriate—and a statement of the dire results of performing the wrong rituals for the season, which would create disastrous disharmony between nature and the rites of the human order.

The Yueh Ling

1.   In the first month of spring the sun is in Shih, the star culminating at dusk being Shen [Orion], and that culminating at dawn Wei [Scorpio].

2.   Its days are chia and yi.

3.   Its divine ruler is T'ai Hao, and the (attending) spirit is Kou-mang.

4.   Its creatures are the scaly.

5.   Its musical note is chüeh and its pitch-tube is the t'ai-ts'ou.

6.   Its number is eight; its taste is sour; its smell is rank.

7.   Its sacrifice is that at the door, and of the parts of the victim the spleen has the foremost place.

8.   The east winds resolve the cold. Creatures that have been torpid during the winter begin to move. The fishes rise up to the ice. Otters sacrifice fish. The wild geese make their appearance.

9.   The son of Heaven occupies the apartment on the left of the Ching Yang (Fane); rides in the carriage with the phoenix (bells),

From the Yueh Ling section of the *Li Ki, I–X,* pp. 249–57, in the *Sacred Books of the East.* Oxford: The Clarendon Press, 1885. Reprinted by permission of the Oxford University Press. Notes omitted. Romanizations modernized.

CAMROSE LUTHERAN COLLEGE
LIBRARY

drawn by the azure-dragon (horses), and carrying the green flag; wears the green robes, and the (pieces of) green jade (on his cap and at his girdle pendant). He eats wheat and mutton. The vessels which he uses are slightly carved, (to resemble) the shooting forth (of plants).

10.   In this month there takes place the inauguration of spring. Three days before this ceremony, the Grand recorder informs the son of Heaven, saying, 'On such and such a day is the inauguration of the spring. The energies of the season are fully seen in wood.' On this the son of Heaven devotes himself to self-purification, and on the day he leads in person the three ducal ministers, his nine high ministers, the feudal princes (who are at court), and his Great officers, to meet the spring in the eastern suburb; and on their return, he rewards them all in the court.

11.   He charges his assistants to disseminate (lessons of) virtue, and harmonise the governmental orders, to give effect to the expressions of his satisfaction and bestow his favours; down to the millions of the people. Those expressions and gifts thereupon proceed, every one in proper (degree and direction).

12.   He also orders the Grand recorder to guard the statutes and maintain the laws, and (especially) to observe the motions in the heavens of the sun and moon, and of the zodiacal stars in which the conjunctions of these bodies take place, so that there should be no error as to where they rest and what they pass over; that there should be no failure in the record of all these things, according to the regular practice of early times.

13.   In this month the son of Heaven on the first (hsin) day prays to God for a good year; and afterwards, the day of the first conjunction of the sun and moon having been chosen, with the handle and share of the plough in the carriage, placed between the man-at-arms who is its third occupant and the driver, he conducts his three ducal ministers, his nine high ministers, the feudal princes and his Great officers, all with their own hands to plough the field of God. The son of Heaven turns up three furrows, each of the ducal ministers five, and the other ministers and feudal princes nine. When they return, he takes in his hand a cup in the great chamber, all the others being in attendance on him and the Great officers, and says, 'Drink this cup of comfort after your toil.'

14.   In this month the vapours of heaven descend and those of the earth ascend. Heaven and earth are in harmonious co-operation. All plants bud and grow.

15.   The king gives orders to set forward the business of husbandry. The inspectors of the fields are ordered to reside in the lands having an eastward exposure, and (see that) all repair the marches and divisions (of the ground), and mark out clearly the paths and ditches. They must skilfully survey the mounds and rising grounds, the slopes and defiles, the plains and marshes, determining what the different lands are suitable for, and where the different grains will grow best. They must thus instruct and lead on the people, themselves also engaging in the tasks. The business of the fields being thus ordered, the guiding line is first put in requisition, and the husbandry is carried on without error.

16.   In this month orders are given to the chief director of Music to enter the college, and practise the dances (with his pupils).

17.   The canons of sacrifice are examined and set forth, and orders are given to sacrifice to the hills and forests, the streams and meres, care being taken not to use any female victims.

18.   Prohibitions are issued against cutting down trees.

19.   Nests should not be thrown down; unformed insects should not be killed, nor creatures in the womb, nor very young creatures, nor birds just taking to the wing, nor fawns, nor should eggs be destroyed.

20.   No congregating of multitudes should be allowed, and no setting about the rearing of fortifications and walls.

21.   Skeletons should be covered up, and bones with the flesh attached to them buried.

22.   In this month no warlike operations should be undertaken; the undertaking of such is sure to be followed by calamities from Heaven. The not undertaking warlike operations means that they should not commence on our side.

23.   No change in the ways of heaven is allowed; nor any extinction of the principles of earth; nor any confoundng of the bonds of men.

24.   If in the first month of spring the governmental proceedings proper to summer were carried out, the rain would fall unseasonably, plants and trees would decay prematurely, and the states would be kept in continual fear. If the proceedings proper to autumn were carried out, there would be great pestilence among the people; boisterous winds would work their violence; rain would descend in torrents; orach, fescue, darnel, and southernwood would grow up together. If the proceedings proper to winter were carried out, pools of water would produce their destructive effects, snow and frost would prove very injurious, and the first sown seeds would not enter the ground.

RELIGIOUS FOUNDERS

It was within the general context of the ancient empires and their religious style that the first fruits of the next great stage in religion emerged: the great national and international religions that are traced back to a single founder, such as Zoroaster, Confucius, Lao-tzu, the Buddha, Jesus the Christ, and Muhammad. These founders are very special persons indeed. Not only do they contain within themselves, in the eyes of their followers, the fullness of harmony with the cosmic and divine order aimed at by the old rituals of the sacred king, but they also represent a new revelation and a new *way* of understanding the divine, through the lens of a personality transparent to God or his word. The following is a fictionalized description of an encounter with the Buddha that is from a very popular modern novel of the spiritual life. In its simple and elegant way, the passage gives an unforgettable impression of the power and grace of this new kind of personality, the religious founder.

Siddhartha

Hermann Hesse

Gotama

In the town of Savathi every child knew the name of the Illustrious Buddha and every house was ready to fill the almsbowls of Gotama's silently begging disciples. Near the town was Gotama's favorite abode, the Jetavana grove, which the rich merchant Anathapindika, a great devotee of the Illustrious One, had presented to him and his followers.

The two young ascetics, in their search of Gotama's abode, had been referred to this district by tales and answers to their questions, and on their arrival in Savathi, food was offered to them immediately at the first house in front of which door they stood silently begging. They partook of food and Siddhartha asked the lady who handed him the food:

"Good lady, we should very much like to know where the Buddha, the Illustrious One, dwells, for we are two Samanas from

From Hermann Hesse, *Siddhartha*, translated by Hilda Rosner, pp. 27–31. Copyright 1951 by New Directions Publishing Corporation. Reprinted by permission of New Directions Publishing Corporation.

the forest and have come to see the Perfect One and hear his teachings from his own lips."

The woman said: "You have come to the right place, O Samanas from the forest. The Illustrious One sojourns in Jetavana, in the garden of Anathapindika. You may spend the night there, pilgrims, for there is enough room for the numerous people who flock here to hear the teachings from his lips."

Then Govinda rejoiced and happily said: "Ah, then we have reached our goal and our journey is at an end. But tell us, mother of pilgrims, do you know the Buddha? Have you seen him with your own eyes?"

The woman said: "I have seen the Illustrious One many times. On many a day I have seen him walk through the streets, silently, in a yellow cloak, and silently hold out his almsbowl at the house doors and return with his filled bowl."

Govinda listened enchanted and wanted to ask many more questions and hear much more, but Siddhartha reminded him that it was time to go. They expressed their thanks and departed. It was hardly necessary to enquire the way, for quite a number of pilgrims and monks from Gotama's followers were on the way to Jetavana. When they arrived there at night, there were continual new arrivals. There was a stir of voices from them, requesting and obtaining shelter. The two Samanas who were used to life in the forest, quickly and quietly found shelter and stayed there till morning.

At sunrise they were astounded to see the large number of believers and curious people who had spent the night there. Monks in yellow robes wandered along all the paths of the magnificent grove. Here and there they sat under the trees, lost in meditation or engaged in spirited talk. The shady gardens were like a town, swarming with bees. Most of the monks departed with their almsbowls, in order to obtain food for their midday meal, the only one of the day. Even the Buddha himself went begging in the morning.

Siddhartha saw him and recognized him immediately, as if pointed out to him by a god. He saw him, bearing an almsbowl, quietly leaving the place, an unassuming man in a yellow cowl.

"Look," said Siddhartha softly to Govinda, "there is the Buddha."

Govinda looked attentively at the monk in the yellow cowl, who could not be distinguished in any way from the hundreds of other monks, and yet Govinda soon recognized him. Yes, it was he, and they followed him and watched him.

The Buddha went quietly on his way, lost in thought. His peaceful countenance was neither happy nor sad. He seemed to be smiling gently inwardly. With a secret smile, not unlike that of a healthy child, he walked along, peacefully, quietly. He wore his gown and walked along exactly like the other monks, but his face and his step, his peaceful downward glance, his peaceful downward-hanging hand, and every finger of his hand spoke of peace, spoke of completeness, sought nothing, imitated nothing, reflected a continual quiet, an unfading light, an invulnerable peace.

And so Gotama wandered into the town to obtain alms, and the two Samanas recognized him only by his complete peacefulness of demeanor, by the stillness of his form, in which there was no seeking, no will, no counterfeit, no effort—only light and peace.

"Today we will hear the teachings from his own lips," said Govinda.

Siddhartha did not reply. He was not very curious about the teachings. He did not think they would teach him anything new. He, as well as Govinda, had heard the substance of the Buddha's teachings, if only from second and third-hand reports. But he looked attentively at Gotama's head, at his shoulders, at his feet, at his still, downward-hanging hand, and it seemed to him that in every joint of every finger of his hand there was knowledge; they spoke, breathed, radiated truth. This man, this Buddha, was truly a holy man to his fingertips. Never had Siddhartha esteemed a man so much, never had he loved a man so much.

They both followed the Buddha into the town and returned in silence. They themselves intended to abstain from food that day. They saw Gotama return, saw him take his meal within the circle of his disciples—what he ate would not have satisfied a bird—and saw him withdraw to the shades of the mango tree.

In the evening, however, when the heat abated and everyone in the camp was alert and gathered together, they heard the Buddha preach. They heard his voice, and this also was perfect, quiet and full of peace. Gotama talked about suffering, the origin of suffering, the way to release from suffering. Life was pain, the world was full of suffering, but the path to the release of suffering had been found. There was salvation for those who went the way of the Buddha.

The Illustrious One spoke in a soft but firm voice, taught the four main points, taught the Eightfold Path; patiently he covered the usual method of teaching with examples and repetition. Clearly and quietly his voice was carried to his listeners—like a light, like a star in the heavens.

When the Buddha had finished—it was already night—many pilgrims came forward and asked to be accepted into the community, and the Buddha accepted them and said: "You have listened well to the teachings. Join us then and walk in bliss; put an end to suffering."

MEDIEVAL RELIGION

The Middle Ages, in both East and West, were times of carefully logical philosophical systems based on religion—survivors within the mind of the ancient order unifying cosmos, society, and ritual—and also of passionate devotional systems that half-deliberately broke through order and philosophy to assert that the simple faith and fervent devotion of a full and real person toward an ideal saintly or divine image of personhood could bring one closer than rite or reason to divinity. This was the message of bhakti or devotionalism in Hinduism, Pure Land Buddhism in East Asia, Sufism in Islam, and the devotion toward Jesus, the Virgin Mary, and the saints that so proliferated in medieval Christianity. The following passage from a very famous book on the medieval spirit gives an excellent discussion of this matter, with special emphasis on devotion to the Blessed Virgin Mary and the hymns that it inspired. There is also allusion to certain other medieval themes, scholastic doctrine and the inevitability of death.

Mont-St.-Michel and Chartres

Henry Adams

The schools had already proved one or two points which need never have been discussed again. In essence, religion was love; in no case was it logic. Reason can reach nothing except through the senses; God, by essence, cannot be reached through the senses; if He is to

From Henry Adams, *Mont-St.-Michel and Chartres*. Garden City, N.Y.: Doubleday Anchor Books, 1959, pp. 361–64, 368–69. Copyright 1905 by Henry Adams. Copyright 1933 by Charles Francis Adams. Reprinted by permission of Houghton Mifflin Company.

be known at all, He must be known by contact of spirit with spirit, essence with essence; directly; by emotion; by ecstasy; by absorption of our existence in His; by substitution of his spirit for ours. The world had no need to wait five hundred years longer in order to hear this same result reaffirmed by Pascal. Saint Francis of Assisi had affirmed it loudly enough, even if the voice of Saint Bernard had been less powerful than it was. The Virgin had asserted it in tones more gentle, but any one may still see how convincing, who stops a moment to feel the emotion that lifted her wonderful Chartres spire up to God.

The Virgin, indeed, made all easy, for it was little enough she cared for reason or logic. She cared for her baby, a simple matter, which any woman could do and understand. That, and the grace of God, had made her Queen of Heaven. The Trinity had its source in her—totius Trinitatis nobile Triclinium—and she was maternity. She was also poetry and art. In the bankruptcy of reason, she alone was real.

So Guillaume de Champeaux, half a century dead, came to life again in another of his creations. His own Abbey of Saint-Victor, where Abélard had carried on imaginary disputes with him, became the dominant school. As far as concerns its logic, we had best pass it by. The Victorians needed logic only to drive away logicians, which was hardly necessary after Bernard had shut up the schools. As for its mysticism, all training is much alike in idea, whether one follows the six degrees of contemplation taught by Richard of Saint-Victor, or the eightfold noble way taught by Gautama Buddha. The theology of the school was still less important, for the Victorians contented themselves with orthodoxy only in the sense of caring as little for dogma as for dialectics; their thoughts were fixed on higher emotions. Not Richard the teacher, but Adam the poet, represents the school to us, and when Adam dealt with dogma he frankly admitted his ignorance and hinted his indifference; he was, as always, conscientious; but he was not always, or often, as cold. His statement of the Trinity is a marvel; but two verses of it are enough:

Digne loqui de personis	Of the Trinity to reason
Vim transcendit rationis,	Leads to licence or to treason
Excedit ingenia.	Punishment deserving
Quid sit gigni, quid processus,	What is birth and what procession
Me nescire sum professus,	Is not mine to make profession,

Sed fide non dubia.	Save with faith unswerving.
Qui sic credit, non festinet,	Thus professing, thus believing,
Et a via non declinet	Never insolently leaving
Insolenter regia.	The highway of our faith,
Servet fidem, formet mores,	Duty weighing, law obeying,
Nec attendat ad errores	Never shall we wander straying
Quos damnat Ecclesia.	Where heresy is death.

Such a school took natural refuge in the Holy Ghost and the Virgin—Grace and Love—but the Holy Ghost, as usual, profited by it much less than the Virgin. Comparatively little of Adam's poetry is expressly given to the Saint Esprit, and too large a part of this has a certain flavour of dogma:

Qui procedis ab utroque Genitore Genitoque Pariter, Paraclite!	The Holy Ghost is of the Father and of the Son; neither made nor created nor begotten, but proceeding.
Amor Patris, Filiique Par amborum et utrique Compar et consimilis!	The whole three Persons are coeternal together; and coequal.

This sounds like a mere versification of the Creed, yet when Adam ceased to be dogmatic and broke into true prayer, his verse added a lofty beauty even to the Holy Ghost; a beauty too serious for modern rhyme:

Oh, juvamen oppressorum,	Oh, helper of the heavy-laden,
Oh, solamen miserorum,	Oh, solace of the miserable,
Pauperum refugium,	Of the poor, the refuge,
Da contemptum terrenorum!	Give contempt of earthly pleasures!
Ad amorem supernorum	To the love of heavenly treasures
Trahe desiderium!	Lift our hearts' desire!
Consolator et fundator,	Consolation and foundation,
Habitator et amator,	Dearest friend and habitation
Cordium humilium,	Of the lowly-hearted,
Pelle mala, terge sordes,	Dispel our evil, cleanse our foulness,

Et discordes fac concordes,	And our discords turn to concord,
Et affer praesidium!	And bring us succour!

Adam's scholasticism was the most sympathetic form of mediaeval philosophy. Even in prose, the greatest writers have not often succeeded in stating simply and clearly the fact that infinity can make itself finite, or that space can make itself bounds, or that eternity can generate time. In verse, Adam did it as easily as though he were writing any other miracle—as Gaultier de Coincy told the Virgin's—and any one who thinks that the task was as easy as it seems, has only to try it and see whether he can render into a modern tongue any single word which shall retain the whole value of the word which Adam has chosen:

Ne periret homo reus	To death condemned by awful sentence,
Redemptorem misit Deus,	God recalled us to repentance,
Pater unigenitum;	Sending His only Son;
Visitavit quos amavit	Whom He loved He came to cherish;
Nosque vitae revocavit	Whom His justice doomed to perish,
Gratia non meritum.	By grace to life He won.
Infinitus et Immensus,	Infinity, Immensity,
Quem non capit ullus sensus	Whom no human eye can see
Nec locorum spatia,	Or human thought contain,
Ex eterno temporalis,	Made of Infinity a space
Ex immenso fit localis,	Made of Immensity a place,
Ut restauret omnia.	To win us Life again.

The English verses, compared with the Latin, are poor enough, with the canting jingle of a cheap religion and a thin philosophy, but by contrast and comparison they give higher value to the Latin. One feels the dignity and religious quality of Adam's chants the better for trying to give them an equivalent. One would not care to hazard such experiments on poetry of the highest class like that of Dante and Petrarch, but Adam was conventional both in verse and thought, and aimed at obtaining his effects from the skilful use of the Latin sonorities for the purposes of the chant. With dogma and metaphysics he dealt boldly and even baldly as he was required to do, and successfully as far as concerned the ear or the voice; but poetry was hardly made for dogma; even the Trinity was better expressed mathematically than by rhythm. With the stronger emotions, such as terror, Adam was still conventional, and showed that he thought of the chant more than of the feeling and exaggerated the sound beyond the value of the sense.

Adam loved. His verses express the Virgin; they are graceful, tender, fervent, and they hold the same dignity which cannot be translated:

In hac valle lacrimarum	In this valley full of tears,
Nihil dulce, nihil carum,	Nothing softens, nothing cheers,
Suspecta sunt omnia;	All is suspected lure;
Quid hic nobis erit tutum,	What safety can we hope for, here,
Cum nec ipsa vel virtutum	When even virtue faints for fear
Tuta sit victoria!	Her victory be not sure!
Caro nobis adversatur,	Within, the flesh a traitor is,
Mundus carni suffragatur	Without, the world encompasses,
In nostram perniciem;	A deadly wound to bring.
Hostis instat, nos infestans,	The foe is greedy for our spoils,
Nunc se palam manifestans,	Now clasping us within his coils,
Nunc occultans rabiem.	Or hiding now his sting.
Et peccamus et punimur,	We sin, and penalty must pay,
Et diversis irretimur	And we are caught, like beasts of prey,
Laqueis venantium.	Within the hunter's snares.
O Maria, mater Dei,	Nearest to God! oh, Mary Mother!
Tu, post Deum, summa spei,	Hope can reach us from none other,
Tu dulce refugium;	Sweet refuge from our cares;
Tot et tantis irretiti,	We have no strength to struggle longer,

Non valemus his reniti	For our bonds are more and stronger
Ne vi nec industria;	Than our hearts can bear!
Consolatrix miserorum,	You who rest the heavy-laden,
Suscitatrix mortuorum,	You who lead lost souls to Heaven,
Mortis rompe retia!	Burst the hunter's snare!

The art of this poetry of love and hope, which marked the mystics, lay of course in the background of shadows which marked the cloister. 'Inter vania nihil vanius est homine.' Man is an imperceptible atom always trying to become one with God. If ever modern science achieves a definition of energy, possibly it may borrow the figure: Energy is the inherent effort of every multiplicity to become unity. Adam's poetry was an expression of the effort to reach absorption through love, not through fear; but to do this thoroughly he had to make real to himself his own nothingness; most of all, to annihilate pride, for the loftiest soul can comprehend that an atom—say, of hydrogen—which is proud of its personality, will never merge in a molecule of water. The familiar verse: 'Oh, why should the spirit of mortal be proud?' echoes Adam's epitaph to this day:

Haeres peccati, natura filius irae,	Heir of sin, by nature son of wrath,
Exiliique reus nascitur omnis homo.	Condemned to exile, every man is born.
Unde superbit homo, cujus conceptio culpa,	Whence is man's pride, whose conception fault,
Nasci poena, labor vita, necesse mori?	Birth pain, life labour, and whose death is sure?

RELIGION AND MODERNIZATION

Religion has always been in a process of adjustment to its age and its environment. In this respect the modern age is no different from any other, but it has been a time of more rapid change than most previous ages and of unprecedented changes—such as industry, technology, rapid communication, new political systems, and widespread education—of a sort that profoundly affect the daily lives of ordinary people. It is with changes like these that traditional religions, grounded in earlier ages, have had to contend. They have sometimes contended very well, sometimes less well, but never without grievous wrenching and struggle. The following passage gives an impression of the nature of this struggle in the case of one religion, Islam.

The Concept of Progress and Islamic Law

Noel J. Coulson

"All innovation is the work of the devil." These alleged words of the founder Prophet of Islam, Muhammad, do not merely reflect the innate conservatism and the deep-seated attachment to tradition that were so strong among the Arab peoples who formed the first adherents of the faith. They also express a principle that became a fundamental axiom of religious belief in Islamic communities everywhere—namely, that the code of conduct represented by the religious law, or Shari`a, was fixed and final in its terms and that any modification would necessarily be a deviation from the one legitimate and valid standard.

Among Muslim peoples, therefore, it is what we may call the traditional or classical Islamic concept of law and its role in society that constitutes a most formidable obstacle to progress. Western jurisprudence has provided a number of different answers to questions about the nature of law, finding its source variously in the orders of a political superior, in the breasts of the judiciary, in the "silent, anonymous forces" of evolving society, or in the very nature of the universe itself. For Islam, however, this same question admits of only one answer, which the religious faith itself supplies. Law is the command of Allah, and the acknowledged function of Muslim jurisprudence from the beginning was simply to discover the terms of that command.

The religious code of conduct thus established was an all-embracing one, in which every aspect of human relationships was

Reprinted with permission of Macmillan Publishing Co., Inc., from "The Concept of Progress in Islamic Law" by Noel J. Coulson, pp. 74–76, 90–92, in *Religion and Progress in Modern Asia*, ed. Robert N. Bellah. Copyright © by The Free Press, 1965.

regulated in meticulous detail. Furthermore, the law, having once achieved perfection of expression, was in principle static and immutable, for Muhammad was the last of the Prophets, and after his death in A.D. 632 there could be no further direct communication of the divine will to man. Thenceforth the religious law was to float above Muslim society as a disembodied soul, representing the eternally valid ideal toward which society must aspire.

In classical Islamic theory therefore, law does not grow out of or develop along with an evolving society, as is the case with Western systems, but is imposed from above. In the Islamic concept, human thought unaided cannot discern the true values and standards of conduct; such knowledge can be attained only through divine revelation, and acts are good or evil exclusively because Allah has attributed this quality to them. Law therefore precedes and is not preceded by society; it controls and is not controlled by society. Although in Western systems the law is molded by society, in Islam exactly the converse is true. The religious law provides the comprehensive, divinely ordained, and eternally valid master plan to which the structure of state and society must ideally conform.

Obviously the clash between the dictates of the rigid and static religious law and any impetus for change or progress that a society may experience poses for Islam a fundamental problem of principle. The Muslim countries of the Near and Middle East have sought the solution in a process that may be generally termed "legal modernism." It is the purpose of this paper to appreciate in broad outline the nature and efficacy of that solution. I propose that we focus our attention upon one particular legal reform introduced in Tunisia in 1957: the outright prohibition of polygamy, which represented a complete break with the legal tradition of some thirteen centuries. I have chosen this particular case not because polygamy is one of the most pressing social problems in Islam today —it is generally not so—but because, first, it involves the status of the family, where the influence of the traditional religious law has always been strongest; second, it highlights various issues in legal reform that are common to Muslim communities the world over; and, finally, it is one of the most extreme and significant examples of the process of legal modernism, which not only may radically alter the shape of Islamic society but also may affect the very nature of the Islamic religion itself. Our approach to the subject must be essentially historical, for it is only in the light of past tradition that the significance of legal modernism and its potential role in the future development of Islamic peoples may be properly assessed.

Traditional Muslim jurisprudence is an example of a legal science almost totally divorced from historical considerations. Islamic orthodoxy views the elaboration of the law as a process of scholastic endeavor completely independent of and in isolation from considerations of time and place, and the work of individual jurists during the formative period is measured by the single standard of its intrinsic worth in the process of discovery of the divine command. Master architects were followed by builders who implemented the plans; successive generations of craftsmen made their own particular contributions to the fixtures, fittings, and interior decor until, the task completed, future jurists were simply to serve as passive caretakers of the eternal edifice. This elaboration of the system of Allah's commands lacks any true dimension of historical depth. Recent researches by scholars, however, have shown that the genesis of Islamic religious law lay in a complex process of historical growth intimately connected with current social conditions and extending over the first three centuries of Islam.

In its efforts to solve the problem of the clash between the dictates of traditional law and the demands of modern society, legal modernism, as it appears in its most extreme stage, the Tunisian reform, rests upon the premise that the will of Allah was never expressed in terms so rigid or comprehensive as the classical doctrine maintained but that it enunciated broad general principles that admit of varying interpretations and varying applications according to the circumstances of the time. Modernism, therefore, is a movement toward a historical exegesis of the divine revelation and, as such, can find its most solid foundation in the early historical growth of Shari`a law that we have described. For recent scholarship and research have demonstrated that Shari`a law originated as the implementation of the precepts of divine revelation within the framework of current social conditions, and in so doing they have provided a basis of historical fact to support the ideology underlying legal modernism. Once the classical theory is viewed in its true historical perspective, as only one stage in the evolution of the Shari`a, modernist activities no longer appear as a total departure from the one legitimate position but preserve the continuity of Islamic legal tradition by taking up again the attitude of the earliest jurists of Islam and reviving a corpus whose growth had been artificially arrested, that had lain dormant for a period of ten centuries.

It cannot be said, however, that legal modernism has yet reached the stage in which it provides a completely satisfactory answer to the problems of law and society in present-day Islam. Traditionalist elements condemn some modernist activities like the unwarranted manipulation of the texts of divine revelation to force from them meanings in accord with the preconceived purposes of the reformers. This manipulation, argue the traditionalists, is, in substance if not in form, nothing less than the secularization of the law. Modernist jurisprudence does in fact often wear an air of opportunism, adopting *ad hoc* solutions out of expediency, and does not yet rest upon systematic foundations or principles consistently applied. "Social engineers" the modernists certainly are, inasmuch as their activities are shaping the law to conform with the needs of society. Yet if Islamic jurisprudence is to remain faithful to its fundamental ideals, it cannot regard the needs and aspirations of society as the *exclusive* determinants of the law. These elements can legitimately operate to mold the law only within the bounds of such norms and principles as have been irrevocably established by divine command.

Looking to the future, therefore, it appears to be the primary task of Muslim jurisprudence to ascertain the precise limits and implications of the original core of divine revelation. And this task will perhaps come to involve a reorientation of the traditional attitude toward the reported precedents of the Prophet, not only in terms of their authenticity, but also in terms of the nature of their authority once authenticity is duly established. And it seems axiomatic that, when the precepts of divine revelation have been so established, they must form the fundamental and invariable basis of any system of law that purports to be a manifestation of the will of Allah.

THREE NINETEENTH-CENTURY VIEWS OF RELIGION

One result of the modernization process in Europe in the nineteenth century was a new and intense look at religion, especially its role in society. Many thinkers were concerned not only with understanding religion from the point of view of metaphysics but also seeing what effect it had on individuals and on human society within the stream of history. The rapid pace of change was bringing forth a new appreciation of our human existence in historical time and of the fact that the profoundest depths of our thoughts and the smallest details of our lives were shaped by where we were in history and the forces that moved history. The following selections are writings from three nineteenth-century thinkers whose perception of religion must be dealt with by anyone attempting an informed twentieth-century understanding of it. Other major figures of comparable importance from the nineteenth and early twentieth centuries appear in other sections of this book.

The theologian Friedrich Schleiermacher (1768–1834), responding in part to the exalted feelings of the romantic movement and the new sense of expansiveness in the universe and of human potential wrought by science and revolution, taught that religion is at base a feeling but a special kind of feeling, a feeling for the infinite. In the following passage, from his *On Religion: Speeches to its Cultured Despisers* (1799), he argues that religion or piety is this contemplative feeling for the infinite and not simply a species of knowledge, science, or ethics. A life is empty unless it gives place to the side of human nature that can submit to openness toward the infinite, called God.

For the philosopher Georg W. F. Hegel (1770–1831), history is a process by which spirit—consciousness—comes to know itself and realize that it is its only perfect object of knowing. Religion through the ages is a manifestation of this process; the idea of God in a period corresponds to mankind's developing self-knowledge, and each stage in religion can be expressed in an overarching abstract idea. The subsequent passage, "Lectures on the Philosophy of Religion," expresses this. While some details of the Hegelian system may be outdated, the problem of spiritual and developmental meaning in history remains the crux of the whole crisis of modernity.

Economic and political philosopher Karl Marx (1818–1883) turned Hegel on his head by accepting a dialectical process of historical development but arguing that it was spurred by the interplay of economic rather than spiritual forces. It is the economic structure of a society and the kind of relations between people it engenders—whether of exploitation and alienation or of harmony—that control the nature of human life and even of subjective thought. Religion is simply an expression of this process, a misleading means by which we try to rationalize or alleviate what is really going on for economic reasons—doubtless because one class is exploiting another. For this reason religion, with its dreams, only gets in the way of significant change. Key lines from *Capital*, "The German Ideology," and "Toward the Critique of Hegel's Philosophy of Right" for understanding the Marxist approach to religion are the following: "The religious world is but a reflex of the real world," "Consciousness is therefore from the very beginning a social product" (that is, the way we think and feel is a result of the kind of society we live in), and *"Man makes religion, religion does not make man."*

On Religion:
Speeches to its Cultured Despisers

Friedrich Schleiermacher

It is true that religion is essentially contemplative. You would never
call anyone pious who went about in impervious stupidity, whose
sense is not open for the life of the world. But this contemplation is
not turned, as your knowledge of nature is, to the existence of a
finite thing, combined with and opposed to another finite thing. It
has not even, like your knowledge of God—if for once I might use an
old expression—to do with the nature of the first cause, in itself and
in its relation to every other cause and operation. The contemplation
of the pious is the immediate consciousness of the universal
existence of all finite things, in and through the Infinite, and of all
temporal things in and through the Eternal. Religion is to seek this
and find it in all that lives and moves, in all growth and change, in
all doing and suffering. It is to have life and to know life in
immediate feeling, only as such an existence in the Infinite and
Eternal. Where this is found religion is satisfied, where it hides itself
there is for her unrest and anguish, extremity and death. Wherefore
it is a life in the infinite nature of the Whole, in the One and in the
All, in God, having and possessing all things in God, and God in all.
Yet religion is not knowledge and science, either of the world or of
God. Without being knowledge, it recognizes knowledge and
science. In itself it is an affection, a revelation of the Infinite in the
finite, God being seen in it and it in God.

Similarly, what is the object of your ethics, of your science of
action? Does it not seek to distinguish precisely each part of human
doing and producing, and at the same time to combine them into a
whole, according to actual relations? But the pious man confesses
that, as pious, he knows nothing about it. He does, indeed,
contemplate human action, but it is not the kind of contemplation
from which an ethical system takes its rise. Only one thing he seeks
out and detects, action from God, God's activity among men. If your
ethics are right, and his piety as well, he will not, it is true,
acknowledge any action as excellent which is not embraced in your
system. But to know and to construct this system is your business,
ye learned, not his. If you will not believe, regard the case of

From Friedrich Schleiermacher, *On Religion: Speeches to its Cultured Despisers,*
translated by John Oman. (New York: Harper & Row, Publishers, Inc., 1958), pp.
36–38. Reprinted by permission of Harper & Row, Publishers, Inc., and Routledge &
Kegan Paul, London.

women. You ascribe to them religion, not only as an adornment, but you demand of them the finest feeling for distinguishing the things that excel: do you equally expect them to know your ethics as a science?

It is the same, let me say at once, with action itself. The artist fashions what is given him to fashion, by virtue of his special talent. These talents are so different that the one he possesses another lacks; unless someone, against heaven's will, would possess all. But when anyone is praised to you as pious, you are not accustomed to ask which of these gifts dwell in him by virtue of his piety. The citizen—taking the word in the sense of the ancients, not in its present meagre significance—regulates, leads, and influences in virtue of his morality. But this is something different from piety. Piety has also a passive side. While morality always shows itself as manipulating, as self-controlling, piety appears as a surrender, a submission to be moved by the Whole that stands over against man. Morality depends, therefore, entirely on the consciousness of freedom, within the sphere of which all that it produces falls. Piety, on the contrary, is not at all bound to this side of life. In the opposite sphere of necessity, where there is no properly individual action, it is quite as active. Wherefore the two are different. Piety does, indeed, linger with satisfaction on every action that is from God, and every activity that reveals the Infinite in the finite, and yet it is not itself this activity. Only by keeping quite outside the range both of science and of practice can it maintain its proper sphere and character. Only when piety takes its place alongside of science and practice, as a necessary, an indispensable third, as their natural counterpart, not less in worth and splendour than either, will the common field be altogether occupied and human nature on this side complete.

Lectures on the Philosophy of Religion

G. W. F. Hegel

Now in development as such, insofar as it has not as yet reached its goal, the moments of the notion are still in a state of separation or mutual exclusion, so that the reality has not as yet come to be equal to the notion or conception. The finite religions are the appearance in

From G. W. F. Hegel, *On Art, Religion, Philosophy*, ed. J. Glenn Gray (New York: Harper & Row, 1970), pp. 200–206. Reprinted by permission of the publisher.

history of these moments. In order to grasp these in their truth, it is necessary to consider them under two aspects; on the one hand, we have to consider how God is known, how he is characterised; and on the other, how the subject at the same time knows itself. For the two aspects the objective and subjective have but one foundation for their further determination, and but one specific character pervades them both. The idea which a man has of God corresponds with that which he has of himself, of his freedom. Knowing himself in God, he at the same time knows his imperishable life in God; he knows of the truth of his being, and therefore the idea of the *immortality of the soul* here enters as an essential moment into the history of religion. The ideas of God and of immortality have a necessary relation to each other; when a man knows truly about God, he knows truly about himself, too: the two sides correspond to each other. At first God is something quite undetermined; but in the course of the development of the human mind, the consciousness of that which God is gradually forms and matures itself, losing more and more of its initial indefiniteness, and with this the development of true *self-consciousness* advances also. The proofs of the existence of God are included also within the sphere of this progressive development, it being their aim to set forth the necessary elevation of the spirit to God. For the diversity of the characteristics which in this process of elevation are attributed to God is fixed by the diversity of the points of departure, and this diversity again has its foundation in the nature of the historical stage of actual self-consciousness which has been reached. The different forms which this elevation of the spirit takes will always indicate the metaphysical spirit of the period in question, for this corresponds to the prevalent idea of God and the sphere of worship.

If we now attempt to indicate in a more precise way the divisions of this stage of definite religion, we find that what is of primary importance here is the manner of the divine manifestation. God is manifestation, not in a general sense merely, but as being spirit he determines himself as appearing to himself; that is to say, he is not object in the general sense, but is object to himself.

1. As for manifestation generally, or abstract manifestation, it is What is Natural in general. Manifestation is being for other, an externalisation of things mutually distinct, and one, in fact, which is immediate and not yet reflected into itself. This logical determination is taken here in its concrete sense as the natural world. What is for an "Other" exists for this very reason in a sensuous form. The thought, which is for another thought, which, as having being, is to be posited as distinct, that is to say, as something which exists as an independent subject in reference to the other, is only capable of

being communicated by the one to the other through the sensuous medium of sign or speech, in fact by bodily means.

But since God exists essentially only as appearing to himself, that abstract attitude of man to nature does not belong to religion; on the contrary, in religion nature is only a moment of the divine, and therefore must, as it exists for the religious consciousness, have also the characteristic note of the spiritual mode of existence in it. It thus does not remain in its pure, natural element, but receives the characteristic quality of the divine which dwells in it. It cannot be said of any religion that in it men have worshipped the sun, the sea, or nature; when they worship these objects, the latter no longer have for the worshippers the prosaic character which they have for ourselves. Even while these objects are for them divine, they still, it is true, remain natural; but when they become objects of religion, they at once assume a spiritual aspect. The contemplation of the sun, the stars, etc., as individual natural phenomena, is outside the sphere of religion. The so-called prosaic manner of looking at nature, as the latter exists for consciousness when regarding it through the understanding, betokens a separation which comes later; its presence is consequent on much deeper and more thoroughgoing reflection. Not till the spirit or mind has posited itself independently for itself, and as free from nature, does the latter appear to it as an Other, as something external.

The first mode of manifestation then, in the form of nature namely, has the subjectivity, the spiritual nature of God as its centre in a general sense only, and consequently these two determinations have not as yet come into relation through reflection. When this takes place, it constitutes the second mode of manifestation.

2.   In himself or potentially God is Spirit; this is our notion or conception of him. But for this very reason He must be posited too as spirit, and this means that the manner of his manifestation must be itself a *spiritual* one, and consequently the negation of the natural. And for this it is necessary that his determinateness, the Idea on the side of reality, be equal to the conception; and the relation of reality to the divine conception is complete when spirit exists as spirit; that is to say, when both the conception and reality exist as this spirit. To begin with, however, we see that the form of nature constitutes that determinateness of the conception of God, or the aspect of reality belonging to the Idea. The emergence of the spiritual element of subjectivity out of nature accordingly appears at first merely as a conflict between the two sides, which are still entangled with one another in that conflict. Therefore this stage of definite religion, too,

remains in the sphere of what is natural, and in fact constitutes, in common with the preceding one, the stage of the religion of nature.

3. It is actually within the definite religions as they succeed each other that spirit in its movement attempts to make the determinateness correspond with the notion or conception, but this determinateness appears here as still abstract, or, to put it otherwise, the notion appears as still the finite notion. These attempts, in which the principle of the preceding stages, namely, essence, or essential being, strives to comprehend itself as infinite inwardness are: (1) the Jewish religion; (2) the Greek; (3) the Roman. The God of the Jews is oneness or soleness, which as such continues to be abstract unity, and is not as yet concrete in itself. This God is indeed God in the spirit, but does not exist as yet *as* spirit. He is something not presented to sense, an abstraction of thought, which has not as yet that fulness in itself which constitutes it spirit. The freedom which the notion seeks to reach through self-development in the Greek religion, still lives under the sway of the sceptre of necessity of essence; and the notion as it appears in and seeks to win its independence in the Roman religion is still limited, since it is related to an external world which stands opposite to it, in which it is only to be objective, and is, therefore, external adaptation to an end, or external purposiveness.

These are the principal specific forms which here present themselves as the modes of the reality of spirit. As *determinate* they are inadequate to the notion or conception of spirit, and are finite in character, and this infinitude, namely, that there is one God, this abstract affirmation, is finite also. This determination of the manifestation of God in consciousness as pure ideality of the one, as abolition of the manifold character of external manifestation, might perhaps be contrasted with the religion of nature as being that which is true, but it is really only *one* form of determinateness as against the totality of the notion of spirit. It corresponds with this totality just as little as its opposite does. These definite religions are not in fact as yet the true religion; and in them God is not as yet known in his true nature, since there is wanting to them the absolute content of spirit.

Revealed Religion

Manifestation, development, and determination or specification do not go on *ad infinitum* and do not cease *accidentally*. True progress consists rather in this: that this reflexion of the notion into itself stops short, inasmuch as it really returns into itself. Thus manifestation is itself infinite in nature; the content is in accordance with the conception of spirit, and the manifestation is, like spirit, in and for itself. The notion or conception of religion has in religion become objective to itself. Spirit, which is in and for itself, has now no longer individual forms, determinations of itself, before it, as it unfolds itself. It knows itself no longer as spirit in any definite form or limitation but has now overcome those limitations, this finiteness, and is actually what it is potentially. This knowledge of spirit for itself or actually, as it is in itself or potentially, is the being in-and-for-itself of spirit as exercising knowledge, the perfected, absolute religion, in which it is revealed what spirit, what God is; this is the Christian religion.

That spirit, as it does in all else, must in religion also run through its natural course, is necessarily bound up with the conception of spirit. Spirit is only spirit when it exists for itself as the negation of all finite forms, as this absolute ideality.

I form ideas, I have perceptions, and here there is a certain definite content, as, for instance, this house, and so on. They are my perceptions, they present themselves to me; I could not, however, present them to myself if I did not grasp this particular content in myself, and if I had not posited it in a simple, ideal manner in myself. Ideality means that this definite external existence, these conditions of space, of time, and matter, this separateness of parts, is done away with in something higher, in that I know this external existence, these forms of it are not ideas which are mutually exclusive, but are comprehended, grasped together in me in a simple manner.

Spirit is knowledge; but in order that knowledge should exist, it is necessary that the content of that which it knows should have attained to this ideal form, and should in this way have been negated. What spirit is must in that way have become its own, it must have described this circle; and these forms, differences, determinations, finite qualities, must have existed in order that it should make them its own.

This represents both the way and the goal—that spirit should have attained to its own notion or conception, to that which it implicitly is, and in this way only, the way which has been indicated in its abstract moments, does it attain it. Revealed religion is manifested religion, because in it God has become wholly manifest. Here all is proportionate to the notion; there is no longer anything secret in God. Here, then, is the consciousness of the developed conception of spirit, of reconciliation, not in beauty, in joyousness, but *in the spirit*. Revealed religion, which was hitherto still veiled, and did not exist in its truth, came at its own time. This was not a chance time, dependent on someone's liking or caprice, but determined on in the essential, eternal counsel of God; that is, in the eternal reason, wisdom of God; it is the notion of the reality or fact itself, the divine notion, the notion of God Himself, which determines itself to enter on this development, and has set its goal before it.

This course thus followed by religion is the true theodicy; it exhibits all products of spirit, every form of its self-knowledge, as necessary, because spirit is something living, working, and its impulse is to press on through the series of its manifestations towards the consciousness of itself as embracing all truth.

Capital

Karl Marx

The religious world is but the reflex of the real world. And for a society based upon the production of commodities, in which the producers in general enter into social relations with one another by treating their products as commodities and values, whereby they reduce their individual private labour to the standard of homogeneous human labour—for such a society, Christianity with its *cultus* of abstract man, more especially in its bourgeois developments, Protestantism, Deism, &c., is the most fitting form of religion. In the ancient Asiatic and other ancient modes of production, we find that the conversion of products into commodities, and therefore the conversion of men into producers of commodities, holds a subordinate place, which, however, increases in importance as the primitive communities approach nearer and nearer to their dissolution. Trading nations, properly so called, exist in the ancient world only in its interstices, like the gods of Epicurus in the Intermundia, or like Jews in the pores of Polish society. Those ancient social organisms of production are, as compared with bourgeois society, extremely simple and transparent. But they are founded either on the immature development of man individually, who has not yet severed the umbilical cord that unites him with his fellow men in a primitive tribal community, or upon direct relations of subjection. They can arise and exist only when the development of the productive power of labour has not risen beyond a low stage,

From Karl Marx, *Capital*, translated by Samuel Moore and Edward Aveling. New York: Modern Library, pp. 91–92. Copyright © 1906 Charles H. Kerr and Co.

and when, therefore, the social relations within the sphere of material life, between man and man, and between man and Nature, are correspondingly narrow. This narrowness is reflected in the ancient worship of Nature, and in the other elements of the popular religions. The religious reflex of the real world can, in any case, only then finally vanish, when the practical relations of everyday life offer to man none but perfectly intelligible and reasonable relations with regard to his fellowmen and to nature.

The life-process of society, which is based on the process of material production, does not strip off its mystical veil until it is treated as production by freely associated men, and is consciously regulated by them in accordance with a settled plan. This, however, demands for society a certain material groundwork or set of conditions of existence which in their turn are the spontaneous product of a long and painful process of development.

The German Ideology

Karl Marx
and Friedrich Engels

Thus it is quite obvious from the start that there exists a materialistic connection of men with one another, which is determined by their needs and their mode of production and which is as old as men themselves. This connection is ever taking on new forms and thus presents a "history" independently of the existence of any political or religious nonsense which would hold men together on its own.

Only now, after having considered four moments, four aspects of the fundamental historical relationships, do we find that man also possesses "consciousness"; but, even so, not inherent, not "pure" consciousness. From the start the "spirit" is afflicted with the curse of being "burdened" with matter, which here makes its appearance in the form of agitated layers of air, sounds—in short, of language. Language is as old as consciousness; language is practical consciousness, as it exists for other men, and for that reason is really beginning to exist for me personally as well; for language, like consciousness, arises only from the need, the necessity, of

From Karl Marx and Friedrich Engels, ed. R. Pascal, "The German Ideology," in Lewis S. Feuer, ed., *Basic Writings on Politics and Philosophy: Karl Marx and Friedrich Engels*. (Garden City, N. Y.: Doubleday Anchor Books, 1959), pp. 251–52. Reprinted by permission of Lawrence & Wishart, Ltd., London, and of Lewis S. Feuer.

intercourse with other men. Where there exists a relationship, it exists for me: the animal has no "relations" with anything, cannot have any. For the animal, its relation to others does not exist as a relation. Consciousness is therefore from the very beginning a social product and remains so as long as men exist at all. Consciousness is at first, of course, merely consciousness concerning the immediate sensuous environment and consciousness of the limited connection with other persons and things outside the individual who is growing self-conscious. At the same time it is consciousness of nature, which first appears to men as a completely alien, all-powerful, and unassailable force, with which men's relations are purely animal and by which they are overawed like beasts; it is thus a purely animal consciousness of nature (natural religion).

We see here immediately: this natural religion or animal behavior toward nature is determined by the form of society and vice versa. Here, as everywhere, the identity of nature and man appears in such a way that the restricted relation of men to nature determines their restricted relation to one another, and their restricted relation to one another determines men's restricted relation to nature, just because nature is as yet hardly modified historically; and, on the other hand, man's consciousness of the necessity of associating with the individuals around him is the beginning of the consciousness that he is living in society at all.

Toward the Critique of Hegel's Philosophy of Right

Karl Marx

For Germany the *criticism of religion* is in the main complete, and criticism of religion is the premise of all criticism.

The *profane* existence of error is discredited after its *heavenly oratio pro aris et focis*[1] has been rejected. Man, who looked for a superman in the fantastic reality of heaven and found nothing there

---

From Karl Marx, "Toward the Critique of Hegel's Philosophy of Right," in Lewis S. Feuer, ed., *Basic Writings on Politics and Philosophy: Karl Marx and Friedrich Engels*. (Garden City, N. Y.: Doubleday Anchor Books, 1959), pp. 262–63. Reprinted by permission of Lewis S. Feuer.

[1][Speech for the altars and hearths.]

but the *reflection* of himself, will no longer be disposed to find but the *semblance* of himself, the non-human [*Unmensch*], where he seeks and must seek his true reality.

The basis of irreligious criticism is: *Man makes religion,* religion does not make man. In other words, religion is the self-consciousness and self-feeling of man, who either has not yet found himself or has already lost himself again. But *man* is no abstract being, squatting outside the world. Man is *the world of man,* the state, society. This state, this society produce religion, *a perverted world consciousness,* because they are *a perverted world.* Religion is the general theory of that world, its encyclopedic compendium, its logic in a popular form, its spiritualistic *point d'honneur,* its enthusiasm, its moral sanction, its solemn completion, its universal ground for consolation and justification. It is *the fantastic realization* of the human essence because the *human essence* has no true reality. The struggle against religion is therefore mediately the fight against *the other world,* of which religion is the spiritual *aroma.*

Religious distress is at the same time the *expression* of real distress and the *protest* against real distress. Religion is the sigh of the oppressed creature, the heart of a heartless world, just as it is the spirit of an unspiritual situation. It is the *opium* of the people.

The abolition of religion as the *illusory* happiness of the people is required for their *real* happiness. The demand to give up the illusions about its condition is the *demand to give up a condition which needs illusions.* The criticism of religion is therefore *in embryo the criticism of the vale of woe,* the *halo* of which is religion.

Criticism has plucked the imaginary flowers from the chain not so that man will wear the chain without any fantasy or consolation, but so that he will shake off the chain and cull the living flower. The criticism of religion disillusions man, to make him think and act and shape his reality like a man who has been disillusioned and has come to reason, so that he will revolve round himself and therefore round his true sun. Religion is only the illusory sun, which revolves round man as long as he does not revolve round himself.

The task of history, therefore, once the *world beyond the truth* has disappeared, is to establish the *truth of this world.* The immediate *task of philosophy,* which is at the service of history, once the *saintly form* of human self-alienation has been unmasked, is to unmask self-alienation in its *unholy forms.* Thus the criticism of heaven turns into the criticism of the earth, the *criticism of religion* into the *criticism of right,* and the *criticism of theology* into the *criticism of politics.* . . .

CHAPTER THREE

SPIRALS
OF CONSCIOUSNESS:
THE PSYCHOLOGY
OF RELIGION

The high branches of religion reach toward infinity and draw light from it, but religion has roots that twist deeply into the winding caverns of the mind. Religion as we know it is intertwined with how we remember things, how we have dealt with fears and shocks and even incipient madness, and how we have traversed the forests of childhood and the jungles of adolescence.

These are roots of religion discussed by psychology, but that discipline is equally concerned with the exploration of states of consciousness, from lethargy and depression to ecstasy. This exploration is highly relevant to understanding religion because religion characteristically values certain states of consciousness—mystical rapture, repentant introspection—above others.

None of these investigations necessarily explains away religion by reducing it to something else. Description of psychological states and processes does not in itself answer the ultimate questions of why anything is, or is thought, at all; those answers depend in large part on the cognitive value, or value as sources of real knowledge, we assign to various states and processes of consciousness. That value is not self-evident in the state or process itself and finally comes from a combination of psychology with other perspectives on meaning.

We could, for example, agree with psychoanalysis that thinking of

God as "Father" is a perpetuation into adulthood of a pattern of thought based in early childhood. Whether we feel a child's perception of fundamental relationships is likely to be more acute than an adult's, or very inadequate compared to that of a mature person, is another question.

In exploring the roots of religion in the mind, we begin with the famous passage about the search for God in memory in the autobiography of the Christian saint and theologian Augustine. He becomes aware that within memory he finds the tracks that have led him to God; yet he does not find that God himself dwells there. Next the works of some modern psychological theorists, Freud, Jung, and Piaget, whose works seem relevant to understanding the psychological sources of religion, are explored. Then, as a sort of interlude, writings pertinent to understanding religion in childhood and adolescence are looked at. Writings relevant to understanding the interpretation of religion suggested by two new and important contemporary interpretative schools of psychology, the humanistic and behavioristic, are then presented. Finally there are two passages representative of areas of special interest in contemporary psychology that are especially pertinent to religious studies. One is on the creation of private worlds of meaning in schizophrenia, and the other on psychic research and its suggestion, at least, of data that parallel traditional religious affirmation of miracles.

All in all, psychology appears to be the modern discipline that most tramples the same courts as did religion in the past, divining the hidden wellsprings of human motivation and meaning. Nevertheless, religion past and present cannot be understood without reference to philosophy and sociology as well.

AUGUSTINE ON MEMORY

Few religious writers of any age have explored the depths of the mind and the fountainheads of motivation as did the Christian bishop and theologian Augustine (354–430) in his autobiographical Confessions. The following is a famous passage from that work in which he searches for God in memory, finding that through memory he learns how near God has ever been to him. Yet it is not precisely in memory that God is found, for he is also new and dwells not only in him but also everywhere else.

Confessions of St. Augustine

See now how great a space I have covered in my memory, in search of Thee, O Lord; and I have not found Thee outside it. For I find nothing concerning Thee but what I have remembered from the time I first learned of Thee. From that time, I have never forgotten Thee. For where I found truth, there I found my God, who is Truth Itself, and this I have not forgotten from the time I first learned it. Thus from the time I learned of Thee, Thou hast remained in my memory, and there do I find Thee, when I turn my mind to Thee and find delight in Thee. These are my holy delights, which in Thy mercy Thou hast given me, looking upon my poverty.

But where in my memory do You abide, Lord, where in my memory do You abide? What resting-place have You claimed as Your own, what sanctuary built for Yourself? You have paid this honour to my memory, that You deign to abide in it; but I now come to consider in what part of it You abide. In recalling You to mind I have mounted beyond those parts of memory which I have in common with the beasts, in that I did not find You among the images of corporeal things; and I came to those parts in which are kept the affections of my mind, and I could not find You there. And I came in to the innermost seat of my mind—which the mind has in my memory, since the mind remembers itself—and You were not there: because, just as You are not a corporeal image, or any affection of any living man such as we have when we are glad or sad, when we desire, fear, remember, forget and all such things: so You are not the mind itself, because You are the Lord God of the mind, and all these things suffer change, but You remain unchangeable over all: and yet You deign to dwell in my memory, ever since the time I first learned of You. And indeed why do I seek in what place of my memory You dwell as though there were places in my memory? Certain I am that You dwell in it, because I remember You since the time I first learned of You, and because I find You in it when I remember You.

In what place then did I find You to learn of You? For You were not in my memory, before I learned of You. Where then did I find You to learn of You, save in Yourself, above myself? Place there is

From *Confessions of St. Augustine* in the translation of F. J. Sheed. Copyright, 1943, Sheed and Ward, Inc., New York. Reprinted by permission.

none, we go this way and that, and place there is none. You, who are Truth, reside everywhere to answer all who ask counsel of You, and in one act reply to all though all seek counsel upon different matters. And You answer clearly, but all do not hear clearly. All ask what they wish, but do not always hear the answer that they wish. That man is Your best servant who is not so much concerned to hear from You what he wills as to will what he hears from You.

Late have I loved Thee, O Beauty so ancient and so new; late have I loved Thee! For behold Thou wert within me, and I outside; and I sought Thee outside and in my unloveliness fell upon those lovely things that Thou hast made. Thou wert with me and I was not with Thee. I was kept from Thee by those things, yet had they not been in Thee, they would not have been at all. Thou didst call and cry to me and break open my deafness: and Thou didst send forth Thy beams and shine upon me and chase away my blindness: Thou didst breathe fragrance upon me, and I drew in my breath and do now pant for Thee: I tasted Thee, and now hunger and thirst for Thee: Thou didst touch me, and I have burned for Thy peace.

SIGMUND FREUD

Sigmund Freud (1856–1939), the great father of modern psychoanalysis, views religion as perpetuation into adult life of childhood ways of perceiving reality. While it may sometimes help a person to make a working adjustment, in itself religion is *neurotic*—that is, a source of destructive inner conflicts—because (like all civilization) it does not correspond with reality as it really is and requires repression of certain drives. Freud recognizes, of course, that civilization requires some neuroses and repression but to justify them on the grounds of the further neurotic and repressive, and false, systems called religion only makes matters worse for individuals and societies. This is discussed in the following passage. There is also reference to Freud's theory, presented in *Totem and Taboo*, that religion began far back in prehistoric times when a band of brothers killed their father and, feeling simultaneous liberation and guilt, made the father an invisible God. This is a mythologizing of Freud's basic theory of the Oedipus Complex—that unconsciously boys resent the father and wish to replace him but have desire toward the mother and wish her love—which, as this passage indicates, he believes to be the basis of religion and much else as well.

The Future of an Illusion

Sigmund Freud

Even in present-day man purely reasonable motives can effect little against passionate impulsions. How much weaker then must they have been in the human animal of primaeval times! Perhaps his descendants would even now kill one another without inhibition, if it were not that among those murderous acts there was one—the killing of the primitive father—which evoked an irresistible emotional reaction with momentous consequences. From it arose the commandment: Thou shalt not kill. Under totemism this commandment was restricted to the father-substitute; but it was later extended to other people, though even to-day it is not universally obeyed.

But, as was shown by arguments which I need not repeat here, the primal father was the original image of God, the model on which later generations have shaped the figure of God. Hence the religious explanation is right. God actually played a part in the genesis of that prohibition; it was His influence, not any insight into social necessity, which created it. And the displacement of man's will on to God is fully justified. For men knew that they had disposed of their father by violence, and in their reaction to that impious deed, they determined to respect his will thenceforward. Thus religious doctrine tells us the historical truth—though subject, it is true, to some modification and disguise—whereas our rational account disavows it.

We now observe that the store of religious ideas includes not only wish-fulfilments but important historical recollections. This concurrent influence of past and present must give religion a truly incomparable wealth of power. But perhaps with the help of an analogy yet another discovery may begin to dawn on us. Though it is not a good plan to transplant ideas far from the soil in which they grew up, yet here is a conformity which we cannot avoid pointing out. We know that a human child cannot successfully complete its development to the civilized stage without passing through a phase of neurosis sometimes of greater and sometimes of less distinctness. This is because so many instinctual demands which will later be unserviceable cannot be suppressed by the

Reprinted from *The Future of an Illusion* by Sigmund Freud, translated from the German and edited by James Strachey. By permission of W. W. Norton & Company, Inc. Copyright © 1961 by James Strachey. Also printed in *The Standard Edition of the Complete Psychological Works of Sigmund Freud*, vol. 21, revised and edited by James Strachey. By permission of Sigmund Freud Copyrights Ltd., The Institute of Psychoanalysis, and The Hogarth Press Ltd. Notes omitted.

rational operation of the child's intellect but have to be tamed by acts of repression, behind which, as a rule, lies the motive of anxiety. Most of these infantile neuroses are overcome spontaneously in the course of growing up, and this is especially true of the obsessional neuroses of childhood. The remainder can be cleared up later still by psycho-analytic treatment. In just the same way, one might assume, humanity as a whole, in its development through the ages, fell into states analogous to the neuroses, and for the same reasons—namely because in the times of its ignorance and intellectual weakness the instinctual renunciations indispensable for man's communal existence had only been achieved by it by means of purely affective forces. The precipitates of these processes resembling repression which took place in prehistoric times still remained attached to civilization for long periods. Religion would thus be the universal obsessional neurosis of humanity; like the obsessional neurosis of children, it arose out of the Oedipus complex, out of the relation to the father. If this view is right, it is to be supposed that a turning-away from religion is bound to occur with the fatal inevitability of a process of growth, and that we find ourselves at this very juncture in the middle of that phase of development. Our behaviour should therefore be modelled on that of a sensible teacher who does not oppose an impending new development but seeks to ease its path and mitigate the violence of its irruption. Our analogy does not, to be sure, exhaust the essential nature of religion. If, on the one hand, religion brings with it obsessional restrictions, exactly as an individual obsessional neurosis does, on the other hand it comprises a system of wishful illusions together with a disavowal of reality, such as we find in an isolated form nowhere else but in amentia, in a state of blissful hallucinatory confusion. But these are only analogies, by the help of which we endeavour to understand a social phenomenon; the pathology of the individual does not supply us with a fully valid counterpart.

It has been repeatedly pointed out (by myself and in particular by Theodor Reik) in how great detail the analogy between religion and obsessional neurosis can be followed out, and how many of the peculiarities and vicissitudes in the formation of religion can be understood in that light. And it tallies well with this that devout believers are safeguarded in a high degree against the risk of certain neurotic illnesses; their acceptance of the universal neurosis spares them the task of constructing a personal one.

Our knowledge of the historical worth of certain religious doctrines increases our respect for them, but does not invalidate our proposal that they should cease to be put forward as the reasons for the precepts of civilization. On the contrary! Those historical residues have helped us to view religious teachings, as it were, as neurotic relics, and we may now argue that the time has probably come, as it does in an analytic treatment, for replacing the effects of repression by the results of the rational operation of the intellect. We may foresee, but hardly regret, that such a process of remoulding will not stop at renouncing the solemn transfiguration of cultural precepts, but that a general revision of them will result in many of them being done away with. In this way our appointed task of reconciling men to civilization will to a great extent be achieved. We need not deplore the renunciation of historical truth when we put forward rational grounds for the precepts of civilization. The truths contained in religious doctrines are after all so distorted and systematically disguised that the mass of humanity cannot recognize them as truth. The case is similar to what happens when we tell a child that new-born babies are brought by the stork. Here, too, we are telling the truth in symbolic clothing, for we know what the large bird signifies. But the child does not know it. He hears only the distorted part of what we say, and feels that he has been deceived; and we know how often his distrust of the grown-ups and his refractoriness actually take their start from this impression. We have become convinced that it is better to avoid such symbolic disguisings of the truth in what we tell children and not to withhold from them a knowledge of the true state of affairs commensurate with their intellectual level.

CARL G. JUNG

Carl G. Jung (1875–1961) was a student and disciple of Freud who broke with him, partly on the issue of religion. For Jung, the goal of psychological development is *individuation*, the emergence of the true individual or self. In this process it is necessary to arrange the various parts of consciousness into a harmonious pattern. The parts are drives and styles of behavior that can be identified—and are so identified in dreams and myths—with *archetypes*, or godlike forms—the wise father, the great mother, the youth, the shadow. If a person is carried away by any one of them, the result is destructive. Their polarities should be balanced off to make a pattern—a mandala like those of the East—in which the individuated self, often represented by the archetype of the true God or Christ, can appear. While all of this is within the psyche itself, Jung recognizes the great value of religion in helping one to identify and organize the archetypes and to transit through spiritual growth. The following passages from his autobiography discuss these matters; the second passage deals with an esoteric text and with a dream Jung himself had—both are important Jungian sources of wisdom about the archetypes and the individuation process. A person's dreams are perhaps the best clues to where he or she is in the process and to what the individual should do next.

Memories, Dreams, Reflections

Carl G. Jung

Just as all energy proceeds from opposition, so the psyche too possesses its inner polarity, this being the indispensable prerequisite for its aliveness, as Heraclitus realized long ago. Both theoretically and practically, polarity is inherent in all living things. Set against this overpowering force is the fragile unity of the ego, which has come into being in the course of millennia only with the aid of countless protective measures. That an ego was possible at all appears to spring from the fact that all opposites seek to achieve a state of balance. This happens in the exchange of energy which results from the collision of hot and cold, high and low, and so on. The energy underlying conscious psychic life is pre-existent to it and therefore at first unconscious. As it approaches consciousness it first appears projected in figures like mana, gods, daimons, etc., whose numen seems to be the vital source of energy, and in point of fact is so as long as these supernatural figures are accepted. But as these fade and lose their force, the ego—that is the empirical man—seems to come into possession of this source of energy, and does so in the fullest meaning of this ambiguous statement: on the one hand he seeks to seize this energy, to possess it, and even imagines that he does possess it; and on the other hand he is possessed by it.

   This grotesque situation can, to be sure, occur only when the contents of consciousness are regarded as the sole form of psychic existence. Where this is the case, there is no preventing inflation by projections coming home to roost. But where the existence of an unconscious psyche is admitted, the contents of projection can be received into the inborn instinctive forms which predate

From *Memories, Dreams, Reflections*, by C. G. Jung, edited by Aneila Jaffe, translated by Richard and Clara Winston, pp. 346–49, 196–99. Copyright© 1962, 1963 by Random House, Inc. Reprinted by permission of Pantheon Books, a division of Random House, Inc. Notes omitted.

consciousness. Their objectivity and autonomy are thereby preserved, and inflation is avoided. The archetypes, which are pre-existent to consciousness and condition it, appear in the part they actually play in reality: as a priori structural forms of the stuff of consciousness. They do not in any sense represent things as they are in themselves, but rather the forms in which things can be perceived and conceived. Naturally, it is not merely the archetypes that govern the particular nature of perceptions. They account only for the collective component of a perception. As an attribute of instinct they partake of its dynamic nature, and consequently possess a specific energy which causes or compels definite modes of behavior or impulses; that is, they may under certain circumstances have a possessive or obsessive force (numinosity!). The conception of them as *daimonia* is therefore quite in accord with their nature.

If anyone is inclined to believe that any aspect of the *nature* of things is changed by such formulations, he is being extremely credulous about words. The real facts do not change, whatever names we give them. Only we ourselves are affected. If one were to conceive of "God" as "pure Nothingness," that has nothing whatsoever to do with the fact of a superordinate principle. We are just as much possessed as before; the change of name has removed nothing at all from reality. At most we have taken a false attitude toward reality if the new name implies a denial. On the other hand, a positive name for the unknowable has the merit of putting us into a correspondingly positive attitude. If, therefore, we speak of "God" as an "archetype," we are saying nothing about His real nature but are letting it be known that "God" already has a place in that part of our psyche which is pre-existent to consciousness and that He therefore cannot be considered an invention of consciousness. We neither make Him more remote nor eliminate Him, but bring Him closer to the possibility of being experienced. This latter circumstance is by no means unimportant, for a thing which cannot be experienced may easily be suspected of non-existence. This suspicion is so inviting that so-called believers in God see nothing but atheism in my attempt to reconstruct the primitive unconscious psyche. Or if not atheism, then Gnosticism—anything, heaven forbid, but a psychic reality like the unconscious. If the unconscious is anything at all, it must consist of earlier evolutionary stages of our conscious psyche. The assumption that man in his whole glory was created on the sixth day of Creation, without any preliminary stages, is after all somewhat too simple and archaic to satisfy us nowadays. There is pretty general agreement on that score. In regard to the psyche, however, the archaic conception holds on tenaciously: the psyche has no antecedents, is a *tabula rasa*, arises anew at birth, and is only what it imagines itself to be.

Consciousness is phylogenetically and ontogenetically a secondary phenomenon. It is time this obvious fact were grasped at last. Just as the body has an anatomical prehistory of millions of years, so also does the psychic system. And just as the human body today represents in each of its parts the result of this evolution, and everywhere still shows traces of its earlier stages—so the same may be said of the psyche. Consciousness began its evolution from an animal-like state which seems to us unconscious, and the same process of differentiation is repeated in every child. The psyche of the child in its preconscious state is anything but a *tabula rasa*; it is already preformed in a recognizably individual way, and is moreover equipped with all specifically human instincts, as well as with the a priori foundations of the higher functions.

On this complicated base, the ego arises. Throughout life the ego is sustained by this base. When the base does not function, stasis ensues and then death. Its life and its reality are of vital importance. Compared to it, even the external world is secondary, for what does the world matter if the endogenous impulse to grasp it and manipulate it is lacking? In the long run no conscious will can ever replace the life instinct. This instinct comes to us from within, as a compulsion or will or command, and if—as has more or less been done from time immemorial—we give it the name of a personal daimon we are at least aptly expressing the psychological situation. And if, by employing the concept of the archetype, we attempt to define a little more closely the point at which the daimon grips us, we have not abolished anything, only approached closer to the source of life.

. . .

During those years, between 1918 and 1920, I began to understand that the goal of psychic development is the self. There is no linear evolution; there is only a circumambulation of the self. Uniform development exists, at most, only at the beginning; later, everything points toward the center. This insight gave me stability, and gradually my inner peace returned. I knew that in finding the mandala as an expression of the self I had attained what was for me the ultimate. Perhaps someone else knows more, but not I.

Some years later (in 1927) I obtained confirmation of my ideas about the center and the self by way of a dream. I represented its essence in a mandala which I called "Window on Eternity." The picture is reproduced in *The Secret of the Golden Flower*. A year later I painted a second picture, like wise a mandala, with a golden castle in the center. When it was finished, I asked myself, "Why is this so Chinese?" I was impressed by the form and choice of colors, which seemed to me Chinese, although there was nothing outwardly Chinese about it. Yet that was how it affected me. It was a strange coincidence that shortly afterward I received a letter from Richard Wilhelm enclosing the manuscript of a Taoist-alchemical treatise entitled *The Secret of the Golden Flower,* with a request that I write a commentary on it. I devoured the manuscript at once, for the text gave me undreamed-of confirmation of my ideas about the mandala and the circumambulation of the center. That was the first event which broke through my isolation. I became aware of an affinity; I could establish ties with something and someone.

In remembrance of this coincidence, this "synchronicity," I wrote underneath the picture which had made so Chinese an impression upon me: "In 1928, when I was painting this picture, showing the golden, well-fortified castle, Richard Wilhelm in Frankfurt sent me the thousand-year-old Chinese text on the yellow castle, the germ of the immortal body."

This is the dream I mentioned earlier: I found myself in a dirty, sooty city. It was night, and winter, and dark, and raining. I was in Liverpool. With a number of Swiss—say, half a dozen—I walked through the dark streets. I had the feeling that there we were coming from the harbor, and that the real city was actually up above, on the cliffs. We climbed up there. It reminded me of Basel, where the market is down below and then you go up through the Totengässchen ("Alley of the Dead"), which leads to a plateau above and so to the Petersplatz and the Peterskirche. When we reached the plateau, we found a broad square dimly illuminated by street lights, into which many streets converged. The various quarters of the city were arranged radially around the square. In the center was a round pool, and in the middle of it a small island. While everything round about was obscured by rain, fog, smoke, and dimly lit darkness, the little island blazed with sunlight. On it stood a single tree, a magnolia, in a shower of reddish blossoms. It was as though the tree stood in the sunlight and were at the same time the source of light. My companions commented on the abominable weather, and obviously did not see the tree. They spoke of another Swiss who was living in Liverpool, and expressed surprise that he should have settled here. I was carried away by the beauty of the flowering tree and the sunlit island, and thought, "I know very well why he has settled here." Then I awoke.

On one detail of the dream I must add a supplementary comment: the individual quarters of the city were themselves arranged radially around a central point. This point formed a small open square illuminated by a larger street lamp, and constituted a small replica of the island. I knew that the "other Swiss" lived in the vicinity of one of these secondary centers.

This dream represented my situation at the time. I can still see the grayish-yellow raincoats, glistening with the wetness of the rain. Everything was extremely unpleasant, black and opaque—just as I felt then. But I had had a vision of unearthly beauty, and that was why I was able to live at all. Liverpool is the "pool of life." The "liver," according to an old view, is the seat of life—that which "makes to live."

This dream brought with it a sense of finality. I saw that here the goal had been revealed. One could not go beyond the center. The center is the goal, and everything is directed toward that center. Through this dream I understood that the self is the principle and archetype of orientation and meaning. Therein lies its healing function. For me, this insight signified an approach to the center and therefore to the goal. Out of it emerged a first inkling of my personal myth.

After this dream I gave up drawing or painting mandalas. The dream depicted the climax of the whole process of development of consciousness. It satisfied me completely, for it gave a total picture of my situation. I had known, to be sure, that I was occupied with something important, but I still lacked understanding, and there had been no one among my associates who could have understood. The clarification brought about by the dream made it possible for me to take an objective view of the things that filled my being.

JEAN PIAGET

The Swiss psychologist Jean Piaget (b.1896) has written little that is specifically about the psychology of religion, but his celebrated work on how children learn and how they perceive and construct their world in the mind has very important implications for the psychology of religion. He emphasizes that the world as we know it is rooted in several stages of sensory and perceptive development. The infant at first relates to things only through a combination of sensory perception and motor activity. Reality is learned through a flexible, trial-and-error process that includes the use of imagination. An understanding of this process is helpful to understanding both the religious outlook of children and all world views, including those of religion, insofar as they are results of this process. The following passage provides a simple introduction to some of Piaget's ideas.

Piaget

David Elkind

What then is it about Piaget's work and theory that has made him so influential despite his controversial ideas and his somewhat unacceptable (at least to a goodly portion of the academic community) research methodology? The fact is that, theory and method aside, his descriptions of how children come to know and think about the world ring true to everyone's ear. When Piaget says that children believe that the moon follows them when they go for a walk at night, that the name of the sun is in the sun and that dreams come in through the window at night, it sounds strange and is yet somehow in accord with our intuitions. In fact, it was in trying to account for these strange ideas (which are neither innate, because they are given up as children grow older, nor acquired, because they are not taught by adults) that Piaget arrived at his revolutionary theory of knowing.

In the past, two kinds of theories have been proposed to account for the acquisition of knowledge. One theory, which might be called *camera* theory, suggests that the mind operates in much the same way as a camera does when it takes a picture. This theory assumes that there is a reality that exists outside of our heads and that is completely independent of our knowing processes. As does a camera, the child's mind takes pictures of this external reality, which it then stores up in memory. Differences between the world of adults and the world of children can thus be explained by the fact that adults have more pictures stored up than do the children. Individual differences in intelligence can also be explained in terms of the quality of the camera, speed of the film and so on. On this analogy,

From David Elkind, "Piaget," *Human Behavior*, vol. 4, no. 8 (August 1975), 25–31. Copyright © 1975 *Human Behavior* Magazine. Reprinted by permission.

dull children would have less precise cameras and less sensitive film than brighter children.

A second, less popular theory of knowing asserts that the mind operates not as a camera but rather as a projector. According to this view, infants come into the world with a built-in film library that is part of some natural endowment. Learning about the world amounts to running these films through a projector (the mind), which displays the film on a blank screen—the world. This theory asserts then that we never learn anything new, that nothing really exists outside of our heads and that the whole world is a product of our own mental processes. Differences between the world of adults and the world of children can be explained by arguing that adults have projected a great many more films than have children. And individual differences can be explained in terms of the quality of the projection equipment or the nature and content of the films.

The projector theory of knowing has never been very popular because it seems to defy common sense. Bishop Berkeley, an advocate of this position, was once told that he would be convinced that the world was not all in his head if, when walking about the streets of London, the contents of a slop bucket chanced to hit him on the head. The value of the projector, sometimes called the *idealistic* or *platonic* theory of knowing, has been to challenge the copy theorists and to force them to take account of the part that the human imagination plays in constructing the reality that seems to exist so independently of the operations of the human mind.

In contrast to these ideas, Piaget has offered a nonmechanical, creative or *constructionist* conception of the process of human knowing. According to Piaget, children construct reality out of their experiences with the environment in much the same way that artists paint a picture from their immediate impressions. A painting is never a simple copy of the artist's impressions, and even a portrait is "larger" than life. The artist's construction involves his or her experience but only as it has been transformed by the imagination. Paintings are always unique combinations of what the artists have taken from their experience and what they have added to it from their own scheme of the world.

In the child's construction of reality, the same holds true. What children understand reality to be is never a copy of what was received by their *sense* impressions; it is always transformed by their own ways of knowing. For example, once I happened to observe a friend's child playing at what seemed to be "ice-cream wagon." He dutifully asked customers what flavor ice cream they desired and then scooped it into make-believe cones. When I suggested that he was the ice-cream man, however, he disagreed. And when I asked what he was doing, he replied, "I am going to college." It turned out his father had told him that he had worked his way through college by selling Good Humor ice cream from a wagon. The child has recreated his own reality from material offered by the environment. From Piaget's standpoint, we can never really know the environment but only our reconstructions of it. Reality, he believes, is always a reconstruction of the environment and never a copy of it.

Looked at from this standpoint, the discrepancies between child and adult thought appear in a much different light than they do for the camera and projector theories. Those theories assume that there are only quantitative differences between the child and adult views of the world, that children are "miniature adults" in mind as well as in appearance. In fact, of course, children are not even miniature adults physically. And intellectually, the child's reality is qualitatively different from the adult's because the child's means for constructing reality out of environmental experiences are less adequate than those of the adult. For Piaget, the child progressively constructs and reconstructs reality until it approximates that of adults.

To be sure, Piaget recognizes the pragmatic value of the copy theory of knowing and does not insist that we go about asserting the role of our knowing processes in the construction of reality. He does contend that the constructionist theory of knowing has to be taken into account in education. Traditional education is based on a copy theory of knowing that assumes that if given the words, children will acquire the ideas they represent. A constructionist theory of knowing asserts just the reverse—that children must attain the concepts before the words have meaning. Thus Piaget stresses that children must be active in learning, that they have concrete experiences from which to construct reality and that only in consequence of their mental operations on the environment will they have the concepts that will give meaning to the words they hear and read. This approach to education is not new and has been advocated by such workers as Pestalozzi, Froebel, Montessori and Dewey. Piaget has, however, provided an extensive empirical and theoretical basis for an educational program in which children are allowed to construct reality through active engagements with the environment.

In order to illustrate perceptions of religion and patterns of religious development characteristic of the child, the following true account of childhood religion as remembered by a young woman who grew up in America in the 1950s and 1960s was written especially for this book. The author, who prefers to be anonymous, gives a vivid impression of the integration of religious concepts in the child's view of the world. Specifics, of course, vary greatly depending on the individual, the culture, and the particular church or religion to which the child is exposed. Nevertheless, such matters as the very concrete imagination—note the picturing of the soul—and the close interaction between relation to parents and relation to God (or gods) is made apparent.

Remembrances
of Childhood Faith

Anonymous

Because my parents belonged to two separate Protestant denominations, I had only two short spurts of formal religious training till I was finally baptized at age ten. But my parents believed in God and there was talk of God in my home; also my best friend next door was a Roman Catholic, and she often tried to initiate me into the mysteries of "Catechism."

I was first introduced to the image of the soul when I was almost five. My mother was driving my siblings and me somewhere and I believe our Catholic neighbor kids and their mother were with us. At any rate the subject was brought up and we were told we had this thing called a "soul" in our brains. Only God could see it, and when we died if it was white we could go to Heaven but if we'd been bad and it was black, we'd be sent to the Other Place. I got a clear image in my head that haunted me till I was in my early teens, of a roundish thing about the size of a saucer that shone like a pearl. Whenever I did something bad (especially if I got away with it) or lied in school, I could see little black flecks appear on the saucer and I would worriedly promise myself I would do something good soon, to clear it up. Conversely when I did something I was praised for I felt good inside, and my mental image of my soul would regain some of its whiteness.

From my first experience at Sunday School (lasting about three months) when I was five I formed an image of God as a white-bearded old man in white robes, sitting on a gold throne atop a cloud. I knew he could see everything I did although I can remember a couple of different occasions when, having stolen some sweets from the kitchen when my parents weren't around, I hid the contraband under my blouse so God wouldn't see it. I believed implicitly that God punished bad children just as surely as my father did, only his ways were more insidious: either he caused my father to find out and give me a spanking or else he caused something bad to happen to me. In fact, my image of God's personality and sense of justice was directly bound up with my father's same. My upbringing was strict: Severe spankngs were our lot if we broke rules, and it was my father who administered them. But after one of those spankings, he usually came into our rooms and hugged us, and let us come out again. This meant we had "paid up" for our breach, and were now even with the world again. I was sure that God's forgiveness worked the same way: If I did something bad God would make something bad happen to me, then I would be forgiven. On the other hand, it was my father who suggested sudden treats if he was pleased with us ("into the car, kids, those report cards deserve a trip to Disneyland!"), and it was he that kissed us at night, and if we were sick he always murmured "You're God's perfect child" before he tucked us in.

This strong sense of a balance of justice was central to my concept of religion. My whole life as a child seemed to prove that if you were good, you got paid, and if you were bad you just as surely paid for it. My father was judge, jury, prosecutor, and executioner in our home. I looked to God for the same sort of treatment, only in a larger sense. God knew, and could do, everything: My father could not. If my father punished me for something my brother had done, it was God making me get it for something awful I'd done (and gotten away with) before. God was the center of all power. Jesus was a beautiful but nebulous figure who liked lambs and children and in whose name we prayed, but he didn't mean much else to me till I was nine and started attending Sunday School regularly. I learned his story but it was powerless for me till the second time I wrestled with death fears and a cracking sense of that balance of justice, when I was fifteen. I repeated over and over in my mind "Jesus died for our sins, he died so we can go to Heaven"; it calmed me down so I could step back from the abyss till the next time. From then on Jesus and his mercy was the saving grace in an ugly world that made no sense. God receded into an invisible power way off in the distance who never directly lifted a hand once men made their choices to do evil or good.

Prayer to me as a child was a magical formula that created a "hotline" to God. If I knelt at my bedside and said "Dear God in Heaven," it was like lifting the phone and dialing Paradise. I asked God to bless friends and whichever members of my family I wasn't mad at that night, I asked for what I wanted, then I had to close with "In Jesus' name I pray, Amen," or it was like leaving the phone off the hook. If I'd done something awful I said I was sorry and told God why I'd done it. There were two kinds of prayer: little ones when you went about daily business and needed something on the spur of the moment, and big ones, where you knelt and made a temple of your hands at bedtime. It worked, too: When I was seven I prayed every night for weeks that a certain girl in another class would make friends with me. She was a celebrity to the second graders—she had waist-length black hair that I coveted, and she was taking ballet lessons so she got to be in all the school pageants, but our brothers had a fight once so she never failed to stick her tongue out at me whenever she saw me. One day she finally relented when our classes were sharing the tetherball area, and she let me play with her hair. After that she tolerated my adulation along with the rest of the girls', and I was jubilant. I remember I could hardly wait to thank God that night, and after school, feeling a good deed was called for, I offered to do the dishes (ugh!) all by myself.

Other areas of Christian mythology were much less important to me. If I understood them, they existed (like all the lands in fantasy stories existed—I believed fervently in those). If they made no sense, like the Bible and all its boring "begats," "spakes," and weird names, they were relegated to the level of "Catholic business," which my parents assured me wasn't necessary to get to Heaven. Angels did God's legwork on earth: I was in agreement with my neighbor over that. But Jesus' mother Mary was only important at Christmas, along with Santa, and praying to her was "Catholic." When the neighbor girl and I started the first grade, she started preaching to me. It was a sort of one-upmanship game, and I believed everything she said. One day she came back from her Catechism class and told me triumphantly there were two kinds of people in the world, Catholic and Public, and the Catholics were going to Heaven and the Publics (like me) were going to the Other Place (to say that word—though we all knew it—not only would earn an instant terrible spanking, but would result in millions of black flecks on the soul). I ran home crying and my father assured me that it wasn't true, God loved everybody. "That's just Catholic talk," he said, and armed with that, I was afterwards able to stand up to my friend's frequent promises of doom for us Publics.

I first learned the concept of Hell when I was in kindergarten, from my babysitter. She was pretty, had a long ponytail, let us jump on the beds and dress up, and everything she said I believed without question. She told us one night that bad kids grow up into bad people, and bad people go to Hell after they die. Though she described it enthusiastically (we were a great audience for things gory), I wasn't too worried about the place: I associated it with criminals and old people, and until I was ten I didn't think I had to grow up. I was more interested in the power of the word itself. Spanking words were always interesting to us—we used to have contests to see who would say them the loudest—but since Hell was also a bad word for God, and he heard us even if our parents didn't, I preferred to stick to relatively safe ones like fink and poopoo.

The night of my tenth birthday I realized that I was going to grow up: In three more birthdays I'd be a teenager, and even worse, in ten more I'd be a grown-up. And grown-ups were old and they got wrinkles, never had any fun, and they died (like my grandmother had recently done). Dying meant no more birthdays, which made me cry. Then I realized God couldn't see us and we him till we died. It was then Hell became a reality, but I still wasn't too afraid of it. The balance of justice was still central for me—even my Catholic neighbor agreed that God could take away sins—and if my mental image of my soul could be kept white, I didn't have to worry.

By the time I hit puberty my world view was expanding, and I began to look at adults (my parents especially) with a critical eye. Not only did I see them make mistakes, I realized they preached one thing and did another, quite deliberately in some instances. But at the same time I was acutely aware of the ephemeral quality of time, especially of life, and I couldn't hate my parents for their mistakes; I would not have them forever. They were people, had to die some day, and so had a right to any happiness they could get. Perhaps I should mention that our homelife during my teen years was miserable, second only to the cruelties of school life. One disaster after another kept life in a constant turmoil, and I began to yearn for peace and happiness—the two things one seemed to lose when one lost childhood. Often I hated those around me, but occasionally I would see them striving (vainly) for peace as time slipped by and I would feel sympathy for them, but I was not comforted and I felt close to no one.

My sense of loneliness peaked when I was sixteen; as my life hit its nadir shortly after my birthday, I started a three-month wrestle with apostasy. My childhood sense of balance had been cracked to bits and with it my simplistic view of religion. The question of God's existence loomed before me like a black abyss. I stood on the edge and looked down and felt soul-sickened for night after night; I read what I could during the day to find answers. I was a constant churchgoer at the time—I sang in the choir and I helped teach the first and second grades in Sunday School. It never occured to me to discuss this directly with my pastor or fellow teachers because I was ashamed of my lack of faith, but I did ask oblique and leading questions of them and of people outside the church whom I particularly admired.

Religious writings were unsatisfactory because they were full of confusing phrases interlarded with coy euphemisms, cliches, and false humility. English literature was crowded with people who asked the same questions, but their answers were often desolate and senselessly narrow; for me it was better children's literature and fantasy that rang true. I could not believe the universe had no meaning or was accidental, and I turned away from "adult" literature. I reimmersed myself in the world of childhood, through literature, since the reality was forever denied me. For me the decision was the right one. Works like Madeline L'Engle's *A Wrinkle in Time* and C. S. Lewis' Narnia stories presented world views that I could believe in. My emotions were twofold when I finished reading these tales: *Sehnsucht,* when I was crashed back into the screaming real world by the last pages, and hope because I'd seen underneath the storylines glimmerings of peace, meaning, and joy.

ADOLESCENT RELIGION

The religion of adolescence has a very special quality of its own. This is the period in life of exciting but often painful transition from childhood to adulthood. It is marked by rapid changes, by emotional ups and downs, by an urge to explore many different ideas and lifestyles, by sometimes stormy relations with family, and by immense emotional feelings that may lead to passionate relations with the opposite sex and also, when combined with a characteristic adolescent idealism and surety, to intense conversion experiences and religious commitments.

The two following passages, one from a seventeenth century relative of the editor and one from a well-known twentieth-century psychologist, illustrate some aspects of adolescent religion. The first is from the autobiography of Thomas Ellwood, a prominent early Quaker who was later secretary to the poet John Milton and editor of the journals of George Fox, founder of the Society of Friends or Quakers. The autobiography was written when Ellwood was middle-aged, but these paragraphs describe events in 1659, when he was about twenty. The Quakers, with their emphasis on inward light and sincerity, were then very unpopular with both the authorities and the other churches, but they were growing. Notice here the power and completeness of Ellwood's conversion, the sense of new identity and dedication to a cause it gave him, and the rift it created with his father.

The second passage is from an often-cited article that deals with the modern, and especially adolescent, tendency to see life as a series of experiences or even a series of commitments. Even if the cases given are somewhat extreme, in America as in the Orient the adolescent relation to religion is not always the beginning of a lifelong commitment such as that of Thomas Ellwood but may be a rapid series of experiments, experiences, and temporary involvements.

The History of Thomas Ellwood

Thomas Ellwood

I had a desire to go to another meeting of the Quakers, and bade my father's man inquire if there was any in the country thereabouts. He thereupon told me he had heard at Isaac Penington's that there was to be a meeting at High Wycombe on Thursday next.

Thither therefore I went, though it was seven miles from me; and that I might be rather thought to go out a-coursing than to a meeting, I let my greyhound run by my horse's side.

When I came there, and had set up my horse at an inn, I was at a loss how to find the house where the meeting was to be. I knew it not, and was ashamed to ask after it; wherefore, having ordered the ostler to take care of my dog, I went into the street and stood at the inn gate, musing with myself what course to take. But I had not

From Thomas Ellwood, *The History of Thomas Ellwood* (London: George Routledge and Sons, 1885), pp. 28–31, 39–41, 44–46.

stood long ere I saw a horseman riding along the street, whom I remembered I had seen before at Isaac Penington's, and he put up his horse at the same inn. Him therefore I resolved to follow, supposing he was going to the meeting, as indeed he was.

Being come to the house, which proved to be John Raunce's, I saw the people sitting together in an outer room; wherefore I stepped in and sat down on the first void seat, the end of a bench just within the door, having my sword by my side and black clothes on, which drew some eyes upon me. It was not long ere one stood up and spoke, whom I was afterwards well acquainted with; his name was Samuel Thornton, and what he said was very suitable and of good service to me, for it reached home as if it had been directed to me.

As soon as ever the meeting was ended and the people began to rise, I, being next the door, stepped out quickly, and hastening to my inn, took horse immediately homewards, and (so far as I remember) my having been gone was not taken notice of by my father.

This latter meeting was like the clinching of a nail, confirming and fastening in my mind those good principles which had sunk into me at the former. My understanding began to open, and I felt some stirrings in my breast, tending to the work of a new creation in me. The general trouble and confusion of mind, which had for some days lain heavy upon me and pressed me down, without a distinct discovery of the particular cause for which it came, began now to wear off, and some glimmerings of light began to break forth in me, which let me see my inward state and condition towards God. The light, which before had shone in my darkness, and the darkness could not comprehend it, began now to shine out of darkness, and in some measure discovered to me what it was that had before clouded me and brought that sadness and trouble upon me. And now I saw that although I had been in a great degree preserved from the common immoralities and gross pollutions of the world, yet the spirit of the world had hitherto ruled in me, and led me into pride, flattery, vanity, and superfluity, all which was naught. I found there were many plants growing in me which were not of the heavenly Father's planting, and that all these, of whatever sort or kind they were, or how specious soever they might appear, must be plucked up.

Now was all my former life ripped up, and my sins by degrees were set in order before me. And though they looked not with so black a hue and so deep a dye as those of the lewdest sort of people did, yet I found that all sin (even that which had the fairest or finest show, as well as that which was more coarse and foul) brought guilt, and with and for guilt, condemnation on the soul that sinned. This I felt, and was greatly bowed down under the sense thereof.

Now also did I receive a new law—an inward law superadded to the outward—the law of the spirit of life in Christ Jesus, which wrought in me against all evil, not only in deed and in word, but even in thought also; so that everything was brought to judgment, and judgment passed upon all. So that I could not any longer go on in my former ways and course of life, for when I did, judgment took hold upon me for it.

.   .   .

Early next morning I got up, and found my spirit pretty calm and quiet, yet not without a fear upon me lest I should slip and let fall the testimony which I had to bear. And as I rode a frequent cry ran through me to the Lord, in this wise: "Oh, my God, preserve me faithful, whatever befalls me: suffer me not to be drawn into evil, how much scorn and contempt soever may be cast upon me."

Thus was my spirit exercised on the way almost continually; and when I was come within a mile or two of the city, whom should I meet upon the way coming from thence but Edward Burrough. I rode in a montero-cap (a dress more used then than now), and so did he; and because the weather was exceedingly sharp, we both had drawn our caps down, to shelter our faces from the cold, and by that means neither of us knew the other, but passed by without taking notice one of the other; till a few days after, meeting again, and observing each other's dress, we recollected where we had so lately met. Then thought I with myself, oh, how glad should I have been of a word of encouragement and counsel from him when I was under that weighty exercise of mind! But the Lord saw it was not good for me, that my reliance might be wholly upon Him, and not on man.

When I had set up my horse I went directly to the hall where the sessions were held, where I had been but a very little while before a knot of my old acquaintances, espying me, came to me. One of these was a scholar in his gown, another a surgeon of that city (both my school-fellows and fellow-boarders at Thame school), and the third a country gentleman with whom I had long been very familiar.

When they were come up to me they all saluted me after the usual manner, pulling off their hats and bowing, and saying, "Your humble servant, sir," expecting no doubt the like from me. But when they saw me stand still, not moving my cap, nor bowing my knee in way of congee to them, they were amazed, and looked first one upon another, then upon me, and then one upon another again, for a while, without speaking a word.

At length the surgeon, a brisk young man, who stood nearest to me, clapping his hand in a familiar way upon my shoulder, and smiling on me, said, "What, Tom! a Quaker?" To which I readily and cheerfully answered, "Yes, a Quaker." And as the words passed out of my mouth I felt joy spring in my heart; for I rejoiced that I had not been drawn out by them into a compliance with them, and that I had strength and boldness given me to confess myself to be one of that despised people.

They stayed not long with me nor said any more, that I remember to me; but looking somewhat confusedly one upon another, after a while took their leave of me, going off in the same ceremonious manner as they came on.

.   .   .

On this nag I designed to ride next day to Isaac Penington's, and in order thereunto arose betimes and got myself ready for the journey; but because I would pay all due respect to my father, and not go without his consent, or knowledge at the least, I sent one up to him (for he was not yet stirring) to acquaint him that I had a purpose to go to Isaac Penington's, and desired to know if he pleased to command me any service to them. He sent me word he would speak with me before I went, and would have me come up to him, which I did, and stood by his bedside.

Then, in a mild and gentle tone, he said: "I understand you have a mind to go to Mr. Penington's." I answered, "I have so."—"Why," said he, "I wonder why you should. You were there, you know, but a few days ago, and unless you had business with them, don't you think it will look oddly?"—I said, "I thought not."—"I doubt," said he, "you'll tire them with your company, and make them think they shall be troubled with you."—"If," replied I, "I find anything of that, I'll make the shorter stay."—"But," said he, "can you propose any sort of business with them, more than a mere visit?"—"Yes," said I, "I propose to myself not only to see them, but to have some discourse with them."—"Why," said he, in a tone a little harsher, "I hope you don't incline to be of their way."—"Truly," answered I, "I like them and their way very well, so far as I yet understand it; and I am willing to go to them that I may understand it better."

Thereupon he began to reckon up a beadroll of faults against the Quakers, telling me they were a rude, unmannerly people, that would not give civil respect or honour to their superiors, no not to magistrates; that they held many dangerous principles; that they were an immodest shameless people; and that one of them stripped himself stark naked, and went in that unseemly manner about the streets, at fairs and on market days, in great towns.

To all the other charges I answered only, "That perhaps they might be either misreported or misunderstood, as the best of people had sometimes been." But to the last charge of going naked, a particular answer, by way of instance, was just then brought into my mind and put into my mouth, which I had not thought of before, and that was the example of Isaiah, who went naked among the people for a long time (Isaiah xx. 4). "Ay," said my father, "but you must consider that he was a prophet of the Lord, and had an express command from God to go so."—"Yes, sir," replied I, "I do consider that; but I consider also, that the Jews, among whom he lived, did not own him for a prophet, nor believe that he had such a command from God. And," added I, "how know we but that this Quaker may be a prophet too, and might be commanded to do as he did, for some reason which we understand not?"

This put my father to a stand; so that, letting fall his charges against the Quakers, he only said, "I would wish you not to go so soon, but take a little time to consider of it; you may visit Mr. Penington hereafter."—"Nay, sir," replied I, "pray don't hinder my going now, for I have so strong a desire to go that I do not well know how to forbear." And as I spoke those words, I withdrew gently to the chamber door, and then hastening down stairs, went immediately to the stable, where finding my horse ready bridled, I forthwith mounted, and went off, lest I should receive a countermand.

Protean Man

Robert J. Lifton

My work with the Chinese was done in Hong Kong, in connection with a study of the process of "thought reform" (or "brainwashing") as conducted on the mainland. I found that Chinese intellectuals of varying ages, whatever their experience with thought reform itself, had gone through an extraordinary set of what I at that time called identity fragments—combinations of belief and emotional involvement—each of which they could readily abandon in favor of another. I remember particularly the profound impression made upon me by the extraordinary history of one young man in particular: beginning as a "filial son" or "young master," that elite status of an only son in an upper-class Chinese family; then feeling himself an abandoned and betrayed victim, as

From "Protean Man," in *Boundaries* by Robert J. Lifton. Copyright 1967, 1968, 1969 by Robert J. Lifton. This article first appeared in *Partisan Review*, XXXV, 1 (Winter 1968). Reprinted by permission of Simon & Schuster, Inc.

traditional forms collapsed during civil war and general chaos, and his father, for whom he was to long all his life, was separated from him by political and military duties; then a "student activist" in rebellion against the traditional culture in which he had been so recently immersed (as well as against a Nationalist Regime whose abuses he had personally experienced); leading him to Marxism and to strong emotional involvement in the Communist movement; then, because of remaining "imperfections," becoming a participant in a thought reform program for a more complete ideological conversion; but which, in his case, had the opposite effect, alienating him, so he came into conflict with the reformers and fled the country; then, in Hong Kong, struggling to establish himself as an "anti-Communist writer"; after a variety of difficulties, finding solace and meaning in becoming a Protestant convert; and following that, still just thirty, apparently poised for some new internal (and perhaps external) move.

Even more dramatic were the shifts in self-process of a young Japanese whom I interviewed in Tokyo and Kyoto from 1960 to 1962. I shall mention one in particular as an extreme example of this protean pattern, though there were many others who in various ways resembled him. Before the age of twenty-five he had been all of the following: a proper middle-class Japanese boy, brought up in a professional family within a well-established framework of dependency and obligation; then, due to extensive contact with farmers' and fishermen's sons brought about by wartime evacuation, a "country boy" who was to retain what he described as a life-long attraction to the tastes of the common man; then, a fiery young patriot who "hated the Americans" and whose older brother, a kamikaze pilot, was saved from death only by the war's end; then a youngster confused in his beliefs after Japan's surrender, but curious about rather than hostile toward American soldiers; soon an eager young exponent of democracy, caught up in the "democracy boom" which swept Japan; at the same time a young devotee of traditional Japanese arts—old novels, Chinese poems, kabuki and flower arrangement; during junior high and high school, an all-round leader, outstanding in studies, student self-government and general social and athletic activities; almost simultaneously, an outspoken critic of society at large and of fellow students in particular for their narrow careeerism, on the basis of Marxist ideas current in Japanese intellectual circles; yet also an English-speaking student, which meant, in effect, being in still another vanguard and having a strong interest in things American; then, midway through high school, experiencing what he called a "kind of neurosis" in which he lost interest in everything he was doing and, in quest of a "change in mood," took advantage of an opportunity to become an exchange student for one year at an American high school; became a convert to many aspects of American life, including actually being baptized as a Christian under the influence of a minister he admired who was also his American "father," and returned to Japan only reluctantly; as a "returnee," found himself in many ways at odds with his friends and was accused by one of "smelling like butter" (a traditional Japanese phrase for Westerners); therefore re-immersed himself in "Japanese" experience—sitting on *tatami,* indulging in quiet, melancholy moods, drinking tea and so on; then became a *ronin*—in feudal days, a samurai without a master, now a student without a university—because of failing his examinations for Tokyo University (a sort of Harvard, Yale, Columbia and Berkeley rolled into one), and as is the custom, spending the following year preparing for the next round rather than attend a lesser institution; once admitted, found little to interest him until becoming an enthusiastic *Zengakuren* activist, with full embrace of its ideal of "pure Communism" and a profound sense of fulfillment in taking part in the planning and carrying out of student demonstrations; but when offered a high position in the organization during his junior year, abruptly became an *ex-Zengakuren* activist by resigning, because he felt he was not suited for "the life of a revolutionary"; then an aimless dissipator, as he drifted into a pattern of heavy drinking, marathon mah-jongg games and affairs with bar-girls; but when the time came, had no difficulty gaining employment with one of Japan's mammoth industrial organizations (and one of the *bêtes noires* of his Marxist days) and embarking upon the life of a young executive or *sarariman* (salaried man)—in fact doing so with eagerness, careful preparation and relief, but at the same time having fantasies and dreams of kicking over the traces, sometimes violently, and embarking upon a world tour (largely Hollywood-inspired) of exotic and sophisticated pleasure-seeking.

RELIGION
IN HUMANISTIC PSYCHOLOGY

One of the most significant movements in recent psychology, especially for the student of religion, is humanistic psychology. Its father, Abraham Maslow (1908–70), argues that the true nature of the human person and the psyche should be ascertained not from studying mentally sick or neurotic patients but by examining those who are supremely happy and creative, especially persons in moments of a *being-state*—during which all needs are felt to be met, there is no sense of deprivation, and the psyche is functioning bountifully. Those moments are often those of greatest creativity, as well as moments of supreme achievement in sports, interpersonal relations, or performance. Maslow calls them *peak experiences* and points to their similarity to many religious accounts of mystical experiences. He is sympathetic toward religion because he believes that religion, at least at its best, aims at this same kind of fulfillment of one's being. In the following passage Maslow discusses basic characteristics of the peak experience; the parallels to many religious experiences are evident.

Religions, Values, and Peak Experiences

Abraham Maslow

Religious Aspects of Peak Experiences

Practically everything that happens in the peak-experiences, naturalistic though they are, could be listed under the headings of religious happenings, or indeed have been in the past considered to be only religious experiences.

1.   For instance, it is quite characteristic in peak-experiences that the whole universe is perceived as an integrated and unified whole. This is not as simple a happening as one might imagine from the bare words themselves. To have a clear perception (rather than a purely abstract and verbal philosophical acceptance) that the universe is all of a piece and that one has his place in it—one is a part of it, one belongs in it—can be so profound and shaking an experience that it can change the person's character and his Weltanschauung forever after. In my own experience I have two subjects who, because of such an experience, were totally, immediately, and permanently cured of (in one case) chronic anxiety neurosis and, in the other case, of strong obsessional thoughts of suicide.

This, of course, is a basic meaning of religious faith for many people. People who might otherwise lose their "faith" will hang onto it because it gives a meaningfulness to the universe, a unity, a single philosophical explanation which makes it all hang together. Many orthodoxly religious people would be so frightened by giving up the notion that the universe has integration, unity, and, therefore,

From *Religions, Values, and Peak Experiences*, by Abraham Maslow, the Kappa Delta Pi Lecture Series. Copyright © 1964 by Kappa Delta Pi. Reprinted by permission of Kappa Delta Pi, an Honor Society in Education, P.O. Box A, West Lafayette, Indiana 47906.

meaningfulness (which is given to it by the fact that it was all created by God or ruled by God or *is* God) that the only alternative for them would be to see the universe as a totally unintegrated chaos.

2.   In the cognition that comes in peak-experiences, characteristically the percept is exclusively and fully attended to. That is, there is tremendous concentration of a kind which does not normally occur. There is the truest and most total kind of visual perceiving or listening or feeling. Part of what this involves is a peculiar change which can best be described as non-evaluating, non-comparing, or non-judging cognition. That is to say, figure and ground are less sharply differentiated. Important and unimportant are also less sharply differentiated, i.e., there is a tendency for things to become equally important rather than to be ranged in a hierarchy from very important to quite unimportant. For instance, the mother examining in loving ecstasy her new-born infant may be enthralled by every single part of him, one part as much as another one, one little toenail as much as another little toenail, and be struck into a kind of religious awe in this way. This same kind of total, non-comparing acceptance of everything, as if everything were equally important, holds also for the perception of people. Thus it comes about that in peak-experience cognition a person is most easily seen per se, in himself, by himself, uniquely and idiosyncratically as if he were the sole member of his class. Of course, this is a very common aspect not only of religious experience but of most theologies as well, i.e., the person is unique, the person is sacred, one person in principle is worth as much as any other person, everyone is a child of God, etc.

3.   The cognition of being (B-cognition) that occurs in peak-experiences tends to perceive external objects, the world, and individual people as more detached from human concerns. Normally we perceive everything as relevant to human concerns and more particularly to our own private selfish concerns. In the peak-experiences, we become more detached, more objective, and are more able to perceive the world as if it were independent not only of the perceiver but even of human beings in general. The perceiver can more readily look upon nature as if it were there in itself and for itself, not simply as if it were a human playground put there for human purposes. He can more easily refrain from projecting human purposes upon it. In a word, he can see it in its own Being (as an end in itself) rather than as something to be used or something to be afraid of or something to wish for or to be reacted to in some other personal, human, self-centered way. That is to say, B-cognition, because it makes human irrelevance more possible, enables us thereby to see more truly the nature of the object in itself. This is a little like talking about god-like perception, superhuman perception.

The peak-experience seems to lift us to greater than normal heights so that we can see and perceive in a higher than usual way. We become larger, greater, stronger, bigger, taller people and tend to perceive accordingly.

4.   To say this in a different way, perception in the peak-experiences can be relatively ego-transcending, self-forgetful, egoless, unselfish. It can come closer to being unmotivated, impersonal, desireless, detached, not needing or wishing. Which is to say, that it becomes more object-centered than ego-centered. The perceptual experience can be more organized around the object itself as a centering point rather than being based upon the selfish ego. This means in turn that objects and people are more readily perceived as having independent reality of their own.

5.   The peak-experience is felt as a self-validating, self-justifying moment which carries its own intrinsic value with it. It is felt to be a highly valuable—even uniquely valuable—experience, so great an experience sometimes that even to attempt to justify it takes away from its dignity and worth. As a matter of fact, so many people find this so great and high an experience that it justifies not only itself but even living itself. Peak-experiences can make life worthwhile by their occasional occurrence. They give meaning to life itself. They prove it to be worthwhile. To say this in a negative way, I would guess that peak-experiences help to prevent suicide.

6.   Recognizing these experiences as end-experiences rather than as means-experiences makes another point. For one thing, it proves to the experiencer that there are ends in the world, that there are things or objects or experiences to yearn for which are worthwhile in themselves. This in itself is a refutation of the proposition that life and living is meaningless. In other words, peak-experiences are one part of the operational definition of the statement that "life is worthwhile" or "life is meaningful."

7.   In the peak-experience there is a very characteristic disorientation in time and space, or even the lack of consciousness of time and space. Phrased positively, this is like experiencing universality and eternity. Certainly we have here, in a very operational sense, a real and scientific meaning of "under the aspect of eternity." This kind of timelessness and spacelessness contrasts very sharply with normal experience. The person in the peak-experiences may feel a day passing as if it were minutes or also a minute so intensely lived that it might feel like a day or a year or an eternity even. He may also lose his consciousness of being located in a particular place.

8.   The world seen in the peak-experiences is seen only as beautiful, good, desirable, worthwhile, etc. and is never experienced as

evil or undesirable. The world is accepted. People will say that then they understand it. Most important of all for comparison with religious thinking is that somehow they become reconciled to evil. Evil itself is accepted and understood and seen in its proper place in the whole, as belonging there, as unavoidable, as necessary, and, therefore, as proper. Of course, the way in which I (and Laski also) gathered peak-experiences was by asking for reports of ecstasies and raptures, of the most blissful and perfect moments of life. Then, of course, life *would* look beautiful. And then all the foregoing might seem like discovering something that had been put in a priori. But observe that what I am talking about is the perception of evil, of pain, of disease, of death. In the peak-experiences, not only is the world seen as acceptable and beautiful, but, and this is what I am stressing, the bad things about life are accepted more totally than they are at other times. It is as if the peak-experience reconciled people to the presence of evil in the world.

9. Of course, this is another way of becoming "god-like." The gods who can contemplate and encompass the whole of being and who, therefore, understand it must see it as good, just, inevitable, and must see "evil" as a product of limited or selfish vision and understanding. If we could be god-like in this sense, then we, too, out of universal understanding would never blame or condemn or be disappointed or shocked. Our only possible emotions would be pity, charity, kindliness, perhaps sadness or amusement. But this is precisely the way in which self-actualizing people do at times react to the world, and in which all of us react in our peak-experiences.

10. Perhaps my most important finding was the discovery of what I am calling B-values or the intrinsic values of Being. (See Appendix G.) When I asked the question, "How does the world look different in peak-experiences?", the hundreds of answers that I got could be boiled down to a quintessential list of characteristics which, though they overlap very much with one another can still be considered as separate for the sake of research. What is important for us in this context is that this list of the described characteristics of the world as it is perceived in our most perspicuous moments is about the same as what people through the ages have called eternal verities, or the spiritual values, or the highest values, or the religious values. What this says is that facts and values are not totally different from each other; under certain circumstances, they fuse. Most religions have either explicitly or by implication affirmed some relationship or even an overlapping or fusion between facts and values. For instance, people not only existed but they were also sacred. The world was not only merely existent but it was also sacred.

11.   B-cognition in the peak-experience is much more passive and receptive, much more humble, than normal perception is. It is much more ready to listen and much more able to hear.

12.   In the peak-experience, such emotions as wonder, awe, reverence, humility, surrender, and even worship before the greatness of the experience are often reported. This may go so far as to involve thoughts of death in a peculiar way. Peak-experiences can be so wonderful that they can parallel the experience of dying, that is of an eager and happy dying. It is a kind of reconciliation and acceptance of death. Scientists have never considered as a scientific problem the question of the "good death"; but here in these experiences, we discover a parallel to what has been considered to be the religious attitude toward death, i.e., humility or dignity before it, willingness to accept it, possibly even a happiness with it.

13.   In peak-experiences, the dichotomies, polarities, and conflicts of life tend to be transcended or resolved. That is to say, there tends to be a moving toward the perception of unity and integration in the world. The person himself tends to move toward fusion, integration, and unity and away from splitting, conflicts, and oppositions.

14.   In the peak-experiences, there tends to be a loss, even though transient, of fear, anxiety, inhibition, of defense and control, of perplexity, confusion, conflict, of delay and restraint. The profound fear of disintegration, of insanity, of death, all tend to disappear for the moment. Perhaps this amounts to saying that fear disappears.

15.   Peak-experiences sometimes have immediate effects or aftereffects upon the person. Sometimes their aftereffects are so profound and so great as to remind us of the profound religious conversions which forever after changed the person. Lesser effects could be called therapeutic. These can range from very great to minimal or even to no effects at all. This is an easy concept for religious people to accept, accustomed as they are to thinking in terms of conversions, of great illuminations, of great moments of insight, etc.

16.   I have likened the peak-experience in a metaphor to a visit to a personally defined heaven from which the person then returns to earth. This is like giving a naturalistic meaning to the concept of heaven. Of course, it is quite different from the conception of heaven as a place somewhere into which one physically steps after life on this earth is over. The conception of heaven that emerges from the peak-experiences is one which exists all the time all around us, always available to step into for a little while at least.

17.   In peak-experiences, there is a tendency to move more closely to a perfect identity, or uniqueness, or to the idiosyncracy of the person or to his real self, to have become more a real person.

18.   The person feels himself more than at other times to be responsible, active, the creative center of his own activities and of his own perceptions, more self-determined, more a free agent, with more "free will" than at other times.

19.   But it has also been discovered that precisely those persons who have the clearest and strongest identity are exactly the ones who are most able to transcend the ego or the self and to become selfless, who are at least relatively selfless and relatively egoless.

20.   The peak-experiencer becomes more loving and more accepting, and so he becomes more spontaneous and honest and innocent.

21.   He becomes less an object, less a thing, less a thing of the world living under the laws of the physical world, and he becomes more a psyche, more
a person, more subject to the psychological laws, especially the laws of what people have called the "higher life."

22.   Because he becomes more unmotivated, that is to say, closer to non-striving, non-needing, non-wishing, he asks less for himself in such moments. He is less selfish. (We must remember that the gods have been considered generally to have no needs or wants, no deficiencies, no lacks, and to be gratified in all things. In this sense, the unmotivated human being becomes more god-like.)

23.   People during and after peak-experiences characteristically feel lucky, fortunate, graced. A common reaction is "I don't deserve this." A common consequence is a feeling of gratitude, in religious persons, to their God, in others, to fate or to nature or to just good fortune. It is interesting in the present context that this can go over into worship, giving thanks, adoring, giving praise, oblation, and other reactions which fit very easily into orthodox religious frameworks. In that context we are accustomed to this sort of thing— that is, to the feeling of gratitude or all-embracing love for everybody and for everything, leading to an impulse to do something good for the world, an eagerness to repay, even a sense of obligation and dedication.

24.   The dichotomy or polarity between humility and pride tends to be resolved in the peak-experiences and also in self-actualizing persons. Such people resolve the dichotomy between pride and humility by fusing them into a single complex superordinate unity, that is by being proud (in a certain sense) and also humble (in a certain sense). Pride (fused with humility) is not

hubris nor is it paranoia; humility (fused with pride) is not masochism.

25.   What has been called the "unitive consciousness" is often given in peak-experiences, i.e., a sense of the sacred glimpsed *in* and *through* the particular instance of the momentary, the secular, the worldly.

RELIGION IN BEHAVIORISTIC PSYCHOLOGY

Another important modern school of psychological theory is behaviorism. Endeavoring to understand human beings in a scientific way, behavioristic psychologists are concerned with studying human feelings and behavior as adaptations to environments, responses to outer stimuli, and results of inner biological processes. With this study has grown a conviction that these conditions are manageable and can and should be managed (as they have always been through such means as wearing clothes and building houses) to make for maximum human happiness. Modern behaviorists have correspondingly felt that such inner subjective processes of thought as have been dealt with by psychoanalysts and humanistic psychologists are not the proper study of psychology—nor are philosophy or religion or trying to base one's life on such abstractions as freedom, dignity, duty, virtue, and the like. All these and the theoretical idea of a self upon which they are founded are just subjective merry-go-rounds that fascinate us but keep us from the scientific study of ways to make people happier through better control of our environment and biology. The first thing to do is to recognize that our behavior is in fact controlled by an environment that demands specific responses, and not by a subjective, autonomous will; thus, the way to change human behavior is to change the environment first, not to moralize.

Needless to say, religionists and behaviorists have generally had no high opinion of each other's causes, but the dialogue between them is thought-provoking and increasingly important. One of the best-known and most vehement of behaviorist thinkers is B. F. Skinner; the following passage from his writing deals with issues highly relevant to religion. Note his fundamental disagreement with C. S. Lewis, whom he quotes and who was introduced earlier in this book. Note also Skinner's far-reaching optimism about the potential of human destiny. If we take full responsibility for scientifically planning our future in the billions of years ahead of us in this universe, there is hardly any limit to what we might become.

Beyond Freedom and Dignity

B. F. Skinner

Philosophies are also spoken of as things possessed. A man is said to speak or act in certain ways because he has a particular philosophy— such as idealism, dialectical materialism, or Calvinism. Terms of this kind summarize the effect of environmental conditions which it would now be hard to trace, but the conditions must have existed and should not be ignored. A person who possesses a "philosophy of freedom" is one who has been changed in certain ways by the literature of freedom.

The issue has had a curious place in theology. Does man sin because he is sinful, or is he sinful because he sins? Neither question points to anything very useful. To say that a man is sinful because he sins is to give an operational definition of sin. To say that he sins because he is sinful is to trace his behavior to a supposed inner trait. But whether or not a person engages in the kind of behavior called sinful depends upon circumstances which are not mentioned in either question. The sin assigned as an inner possession (the sin a person "knows") is to be found in a history of reinforcement. (The expression "God-fearing" suggests such a history, but piety, virtue, the immanence of God, a moral sense, or morality does not. As we have seen, man is not a moral animal in the sense of possessing a special trait or virtue; he has built a kind of social environment which induces him to behave in moral ways.)

These distinctions have practical implications. A recent survey of white Americans is said to have shown that "more than half blamed the inferior educational and economic status of blacks on 'something about Negroes themselves.' " The "something" was further identified as "lack of motivation," which was to be distinguished from *both* genetic and environmental factors. Significantly, motivation was said to be associated with "free will." To neglect the role of the environment in this way is to discourage any inquiry into the defective contingencies responsible for a "lack of motivation."

From *Beyond Freedom and Dignity*, by B. F. Skinner. Copyright © 1971 by B. F. Skinner. Reprinted by permission of Alfred A. Knopf, Inc.

It is in the nature of an experimental analysis of human behavior that it should strip away the functions previously assigned to autonomous man and transfer them one by one to the controlling environment. The analysis leaves less and less for autonomous man to do. But what about man himself? Is there not something about a person which is more than a living body? Unless something called a self survives, how can we speak of self-knowledge or self-control? To whom is the injunction "Know thyself" addressed?

. . .

The picture which emerges from a scientific analysis is not of a body with a person inside, but of a body which *is* a person in the sense that it displays a complex repertoire of behavior. The picture is, of course, unfamiliar. The man thus portrayed is a stranger, and from the traditional point of view he may not seem to be a man at all. "For at least one hundred years," said Joseph Wood Krutch, "we have been prejudiced in every theory, including economic determinism, mechanistic behaviorism, and relativism, that reduces the stature of man until he ceases to be man at all in any sense that the humanists of an earlier generation would recognize." Matson has argued that "the empirical behavioral scientist . . . denies, if only by implication, that a unique being, called Man, exists." "What is now under attack," said Maslow, "is the 'being' of man." C. S. Lewis put it quite bluntly: Man is being abolished.

There is clearly some difficulty in identifying the man to whom these expressions refer. Lewis cannot have meant the human species, for not only is it not being abolished, it is filling the earth. (As a result it may eventually abolish itself through disease, famine, pollution, or a nuclear holocaust, but that is not what Lewis meant.) Nor are individual men growing less effective or productive. We are told that what is threatened is "man *qua* man," or "man in his humanity," or "man as Thou not It," or "man as a person not a thing." These are not very helpful expressions, but they supply a clue. What is being abolished is autonomous man—the inner man, the homunculus, the possessing demon, the man defended by the literatures of freedom and dignity.

His abolition has long been overdue. Autonomous man is a device used to explain what we cannot explain in any other way. He has been constructed from our ignorance, and as our understanding increases, the very stuff of which he is composed vanishes. Science does not dehumanize man, it de-homunculizes him, and it must do so if it is to prevent the abolition of the human species. To man *qua* man we readily say good riddance. Only by dispossessing him can we turn to the real causes of human behavior. Only then can we turn from the inferred to the observed, from the miraculous to the natural, from the inaccessible to the manipulable.

. . .

It is only autonomous man who has reached a dead end. Man himself may be controlled by his environment, but it is an environment which is almost wholly of his own making. The physical environment of most people is largely man-made. The surfaces a person walks on, the walls which shelter him, the clothing he wears, many of the foods he eats, the tools he uses, the vehicles he moves about in, most of the things he listens to and looks at are human products. The social environment is obviously man-made—it generates the language a person speaks, the customs he follows, and the behavior he exhibits with respect to the ethical, religious, governmental, economic, educational, and psychotherapeutic institutions which control him. The evolution of a culture is in fact a kind of gigantic exercise in self-control. As the individual controls himself by manipulating the world in which he lives, so the human species has constructed an environment in which its members behave in a highly effective way. Mistakes have been made, and we have no assurance that the environment man has constructed will continue to provide gains which outstrip the losses, but man as we know him, for better or for worse, is what man has made of man.

This will not satisfy those who cry "Victim!" C. S. Lewis protested: ". . . the power of man to make himself what he pleases . . . means . . . the power of some men to make other men what they please." This is inevitable in the nature of cultural evolution. The controlling *self* must be distinguished from the controlled self, even when they are both inside the same skin, and when control is exercised through the design of an external environment, the selves are, with minor exceptions, distinct. The person who unintentionally or intentionally introduces a new cultural practice is only one among possibly billions who will be affected by it. If this does not seem like an act of self-control, it is only because we have misunderstood the nature of self-control in the individual.

When a person changes his physical or social environment "intentionally"—that is, in order to change human behavior, possibly including his own—he plays two roles: one as a controller, as the designer of a controlling culture, and another as the controlled, as the product of a culture. There is nothing inconsistent about this; it follows from the nature of the evolution of a culture, with or without intentional design.

The human species has probably not undergone much genetic change in recorded time. We have only to go back a thousand generations to reach the artists of the caves of Lascaux. Features which bear directly on survival (such as resistance to disease) change substantially in a thousand generations, but the child of one of the Lascaux artists transplanted to the world of today might be almost indistinguishable from a modern child. It is possible that he would learn more slowly than his modern counterpart, that he could maintain only a smaller repertoire without confusion, or that he would forget more quickly; we cannot be sure. But we can be sure that a twentieth-century child transplanted to the civilization of Lascaux would not be very different from the children he met there, for we have seen what happens when a modern child is raised in an impoverished environment.

Man has greatly changed himself as a person in the same period of time by changing the world in which he lives. Something of the order of a hundred generations will cover the development of modern religious practices, and something of the same order of magnitude modern government and law. Perhaps no more than twenty generations will account for modern industrial practices, and possibly no more than four or five for education and psychotherapy. The physical and biological technologies which have increased man's sensitivity to the world around him and his power to change that world have taken no more than four or five generations.

Man has "controlled his own destiny," if that expression means anything at all. The man that man has made is the product of the culture man has devised. He has emerged from two quite different processes of evolution: the biological evolution responsible for the human species and the cultural evolution carried out by that species. Both of these processes of evolution may now accelerate because they are both subject to intentional design. Men have already changed their genetic endowment by breeding selectively and by changing contingencies of survival, and they may now begin to introduce mutations directly related to survival. For a long time men have introduced new practices which serve as cultural mutations, and they have changed the conditions under which practices are selected. They may now begin to do both with a clearer eye to the consequences.

Man will presumably continue to change, but we cannot say in what direction. No one could have predicted the evolution of the human species at any point in its early history, and the direction of intentional genetic design will depend upon the evolution of a culture which is itself unpredictable for similar reasons. "The limits of perfection of the human species," said Étienne Cabet in *Voyage en Icarie*, "are as yet unknown." But, of course, there are no limits. The human species will never reach a final state of perfection before it is exterminated—"some say in fire, some in ice," and some in radiation.

RELIGION AND MADNESS

Just as it is well known that some people become religious fanatics and build a highly unstable personality structure around religious notions, so it is also well known that the world of the insane often seems to parallel that of religion—it has its myths and visions, its saviors and demons. This raises some far-reaching and perhaps disturbing questions. Are the insane really the most religious of people? Are they perhaps not insane but closer to true but invisible realities? Or is religion itself just a socially accepted way of being a little crazy?

The following passage by a psychiatrist presents fascinating material relevant to thinking about this issue. Note that the author shows that the fantasy of the disturbed young man not only parallels motifs of religious myth and initiation but also has a meaning that religion helps us to understand. He also indicates that the value of such myths and rituals is different when they are purely private, and so *separate* individuals from society, and when they are public, and so provide an ideational basis for *uniting* people into a society.

The Far Side of Madness

John Weir Perry

This inner world of the psychotic does not look like the one we know outwardly, but it is recognizable as a view of the cosmos familiar in myth and ritual forms since ancient times. For it is a world in which there is a center, a cosmic axis running through and connecting the human world with the Sky World and the Underworld. In this center

From John Weir Perry, *The Far Side of Madness*, © 1974, pp. 9–11. Reprinted by permission of Prentice-Hall, Inc., Englewood Cliffs, New Jersey. Notes omitted.

powerful events take place. There, the psychotic individual has died and has found himself in an afterlife state. There, occurs a clash of opposite powers, of light and dark halves of the world, either threatening disintegration or maintaining integration of the whole of the cosmic order. There, he is thrown back in time to the Creation and the first beginnings, and he repeats the evolution of the world step by step. There, he is raised up into a position of supremacy, of world rulership or spiritual leadership. There, a new birth or rebirth takes place in association with an extraordinary marriage to some divine personage. And, finally, around this center come resolutions of cosmic proportions in the form of a redeemed society and a quadrated world structure in harmonious equipoise of four continents, powers, races, creeds, or elements.

An example is the experience of a young man of thirty-three (case number 3) who was markedly withdrawn and disturbed, delusional and hallucinating. He gave me an account of his experiences as they were occurring to him. They may be reassembled and summarized as follows:

He spoke of himself as beneath everyone and lonely, and called himself "skunk." On the other hand, when he was admitted, he felt he was "brought here by God" and was especially chosen to serve Our Lady. He had ideas of play-acting going on, and said that the people helping him were Hollywood actors. In his first interview, he drew a diagram on the wall tile which described a square, a circle, and a cross, all concentric; at the center he stressed a point and identified it with himself; from then on he spoke of himself or the Holy Ghost as being at the center. At this center there was a "going up and down," for he was to go to Hell and Purgatory and back, these being the "Three Ways of Initiation"; a little earlier he felt that he was "making the way of the cross" and imagined he felt the nails in him. At other times he thought he was being poisoned and sometimes shouted, "Go ahead, kill me, kill me." He thought of time as going backward, and he drew a diagram of the sun at the center of the cosmos and the four directions as time in reverse, called "back-o'clock." He saw the world divided in a mortal struggle between Catholicism and the forces of the Devil, in the form of the Sodality of Our Lady leading the war against communism; it was Bishop Sheen against the Movie Set (the Reds). Sometimes he heard the Devil talking to him. The world was about to be ruled by Our Lady of Fatima, of whom he was a special apostle and chief defender. He felt an urgent need to marry and gave indications of great aggravation when there was any hint of a homosexual advance toward him on the ward and was put into a tremendous rage on these occasions. He saw himself as having the characteristics and powers of Christ, and as being the Second Coming; thus he drew diagrams of himself as the Holy Ghost in a quaternity of Father, Mary, Jesus, and himself as Holy Ghost (called

"Dope" on one occasion). Also, he was the successor to the fifteenth President. One day he gazed upward and said he was seeing the Immaculate Conception; all redheads were recognized as Mary, whom he was to marry; one was Cora, which meant the Sacred Heart; one Rose, or the Rose of Sharon; and one Claire, the moon, or "claire de lune." Along with these ideas of wedding Mary were many comments about birth, and a wish for twelve babies. Claire's image seemed indistinguishable from his sister's, and he associated this with conception, with birth; this was like an egg, which he drew. He also thought of the "fourth degree of initiation" as a rebirth. He envisioned a splendid new order to be brought into the world by the World Mission of Our Lady of Fatima; there was a ceremony in which candle lights were carried from the altar as a center, to all parts of the world; this would be Victory in Heaven; in this order there would be tolerance for all colors and creeds without discrimination. He drew this as a world in four segments in the form of a rosary in four colors—the "World Mission Rosary"—representing the four races and creeds and continents.

Are we to write off this ideation as just gibberish or just the distortions of the mundane world by a diseased mind? Is it merely an archaic mode of thinking, a so-called primary process gone berserk and of no use in the modern mind? It might seem so, at first glance, if it were not a close replica of the highest myth and ritual forms of the central religious practices of archaic times. These were the ceremonial death and renewal of the year and of the sacral king and his kingdom, out of which other religious forms have differentiated and evolved in the centuries since. A modern psychiatrist would give, in an unhesitating pronouncement, a diagnosis of paranoid schizophrenia to the sacral kings of Mesopotamia of the third millennium B.C. who called themselves "King of the Universe" and "Son of the God," suckled by the Goddess. But it is a madness in which our most revered traditions of government and of religion are solidly rooted.

Far from dismissing this ideation as crazy nonsense, we would do well to seek out in every possible way the meanings of this language of the unconscious, emotional psyche. For there is every indication that this process emerges as the psyche's own way of dissolving old states of being, and of creatively bringing to birth its new starts—its own way of forming visions of a renewed self and of a new design of life with revivified meanings in one's world.

In my opinion the real pathology in psychosis does not reside in the "mental content," the images and the symbolic sequences. All of that appears to be natural psychic process, present and working in all of us. This is normal madness, so to speak. The schizophrenic "disorder" lies rather in the ego, which suffers from a constricted consciousness that has been educated out of its needed contact with the natural elements of the psychic life, both emotion and image. The madness is perhaps required but comes in overwhelming strength. The need of the schizoid personality is to learn to perceive symbolic meanings as they pertain to the living of one's psychic life, and thus to keep connected with the ever-enriching wellsprings of the emotions which nourish that life. The problem of the prepsychotic state is how to discover the impassioned life, and nature has its own answer in the form of a turbulent ordeal, a trial by immersion in the source of the passions—that is, a psychosis.

For this reason it is absolutely vital to the psychotic person's welfare that the response from his surroundings be in accord with the nature of the experience he is undergoing. A damaging and disqualifying view in terms of psychopathology gives him instant dismay and a sense of isolation. Many of the signs of "insanity" are manifestations of the individual's withdrawal from a hostile emotional setting, including the psychiatric one. If, on the other hand, the person's journey into the unconscious psyche is given the empathy and understanding it deserves, his experience feels like the "altered state of consciousness" that it is, and not like craziness. Then, too, the psyche can get on with its work without having to combat an uncomprehending environment. If psychiatry could learn to cooperate with rather than combat nature, we might be of more benefit to persons meeting their developmental crises.

RELIGION AND PARANORMAL EXPERIENCE

The range of psychological experiences to which, if claims made for them are true, the labels psychic or paranormal can be applied is a wide one: telepathy, precognition, retrocognition, psychokinesis (the moving of objects by mental power alone), and astral projection (travel out of the body). What all these and comparable phenomena have in common is a suggestion of the existence or transmission of mental awareness and influence independent of the physical body and, often, of time. While these phenomena are not in themselves religion, they are obviously of interest to religious studies because they appear to parallel the miracles and prophecies of religious traditions and may shed some light on the nonphysical modes of existence claimed for the souls, angels, and gods of religion. Nowhere is this interest greater than in investigations of evidence of the survival of the human personality after physical death.

The following passage is from a book summarizing the experiences claimed by persons who were clinically dead but then resuscitated. While by no means certain, the hypothesis is possible that what they experienced was a foretaste of what most or all people experience at death and after. The recollections of a large number of persons showed a striking similarity. All the individuals remembered one or more of such elements as noise, passing through a dark tunnel, being out of the body and seeing the body from above, meeting with others believed dead, a review of their life, coming to a border or limit from which (if they were to return to this life as would be the case with those who now tell the tale) they were turned back. Perhaps the experience with greatest religious significance is the commonly reported meeting with a "being of light" who is like a transcendent guardian of the other side.

Life After Life

Raymond A. Moody, Jr.

The Being of Light

What is perhaps the most incredible common element in the accounts I have studied, and is certainly the element which has the most profound effect upon the individual, is the encounter with a very bright light. Typically, at its first appearance this light is dim, but it rapidly gets brighter until it reaches an unearthly brilliance. Yet, even though this light (usually said to be white or "clear") is of an indescribable brilliance, many make the specific point that it does not in any way hurt their eyes, or dazzle them, or keep them from seeing other things around them (perhaps because at this point they don't have physical "eyes" to be dazzled).

Despite the light's unusual manifestation, however, not one person has expressed any doubt whatsoever that it was a being, a being of light. Not only that, it is a personal being. It has a very definite personality. The love and the warmth which emanate from this being to the dying person are utterly beyond words, and he feels completely surrounded by it and taken up in it, completely at ease and accepted in the presence of this being. He senses an irresistible magnetic attraction to this light. He is ineluctably drawn to it.

From Raymond A. Moody, Jr., *Life After Life* (Atlanta, Ga.: Mockingbird Books, Inc., 1975), pp. 45–49. Reprinted by permission of Mockingbird Books, Inc.

Interestingly, while the above description of the being of light is utterly invariable, the identification of the being varies from individual to individual and seems to be largely a function of the religious background, training, or beliefs of the person involved. Thus, most of those who are Christians in training or belief identify the light as Christ and sometimes draw Biblical parallels in support of their interpretation. A Jewish man and woman identified the light as an "angel." It was clear, though, in both cases, that the subjects did not mean to imply that the being had wings, played a harp, or even had a human shape or appearance. There was only the light. What each was trying to get across was that they took the being to be an emissary, or a guide. A man who had had no religious beliefs or training at all prior to his experience simply identified what he saw as "a being of light." The same label was used by one lady of the Christian faith, who apparently did not feel any compulsion at all to call the light "Christ."

Shortly after its appearance, the being begins to communicate with the person who is passing over. Notably, this communication is of the same direct kind which we encountered earlier in the description of how a person in the spiritual body may "pick up the thoughts" of those around him. For, here again, people claim that they did not hear any physical voice or sounds coming from the being, nor did they respond to the being through audible sounds. Rather, it is reported that direct, unimpeded transfer of thoughts takes place, and in such a clear way that there is no possibility whatsoever either of misunderstanding or of lying to the light.

Furthermore, this unimpeded exchange does not even take place in the native language of the person. Yet, he understands perfectly and is instantaneously aware. He cannot even translate the thoughts and exchanges which took place while he was near death into the human language which he must speak now, after his resuscitation.

The next step of the experience clearly illustrates the difficulty of translating from this unspoken language. The being almost immediately directs a certain thought to the person into whose presence it has come so dramatically. Usually the persons with whom I have talked try to formulate the thought into a question. Among the translations I have heard are: "Are you prepared to die?", "Are you ready to die?", "What have you done with your life to show me?", and "What have you done with your life that is sufficient?" The first two formulations, which stress "preparation" might at first seem to have a different sense from the second pair, which emphasize "accomplishment." However, some support for my own feeling that everyone is trying to express the same thought comes from the narrative of one woman who put it this way:

> The first thing he said to me was, that he kind of asked me if I was ready to die, or what I had done with my life that I wanted to show him.

Furthermore, even in the case of more unusual ways of phrasing the "question," it turns out, upon elucidation, to have much the same force. For example, one man told me that during his "death,"

> The voice asked me a question: "Is it worth it?" And what it meant was, did the kind of life I had been leading up to that point seem worthwhile to me then, knowing what I then knew.

Incidentally, all insist that this question, ultimate and profound as it may be in its emotional impact, is not at all asked in condemnation. The being, all seem to agree, does not direct the question to them to accuse or to threaten them, for they still feel the total love and acceptance coming from the light, no matter what their answer may be. Rather, the point of the question seems to be to make them think about their lives, to draw them out. It is, if you will, a Socratic question, one asked not to acquire information but to help the person who is being asked to proceed along the path to the truth by himself. Let us look at some firsthand accounts of this fantastic being.

> 1. I heard the doctors say that I was dead, and that's when I began to feel as though I were tumbling, actually kind of floating, through this blackness, which was some kind of enclosure. There are not really words to describe this. Everything was very black, except that, way off from me, I could see this light. It was a very, very brilliant light, but not too large at first. It grew larger as I came nearer and nearer to it.
>
> I was trying to get to that light at the end, because I felt that it was Christ, and I was trying to reach that point. It was not a frightening experience. It was more or less a pleasant thing. For immediately, being a Christian, I had connected the light with Christ, who said, "I am the light of the world." I said to myself, "If this is it, if I am to die, then I know who waits for me at the end, there in that light."
>
> 2. I got up and walked into the hall to go get a drink, and it was at that point, as they found out later, that my appendix ruptured. I became very weak, and I fell down. I began to feel a sort of drifting, a movement of my real being in and out of my body, and to hear beautiful music. I floated on

down the hall and out the door onto the screened-in porch. There, it almost seemed that clouds, a pink mist really, began to gather around me, and then I floated right straight on through the screen, just as though it weren't there, and up into this pure crystal clear light, an illuminating white light. It was beautiful and so bright, so radiant, but it didn't hurt my eyes. It's not any kind of light you can describe on earth. I didn't actually see a person in this light, and yet it has a special identity, it definitely does. It is a light of perfect understanding and perfect love.

The thought came to my mind, "Lovest thou me?" This was not exactly in the form of a question, but I guess the connotation of what the light said was, "If you do love me, go back and complete what you began in your life." And all during this time, I felt as though I were surrounded by an overwhelming love and compassion.

3.   I knew I was dying and that there was nothing I could do about it, because no one could hear me. . . . I was out of my body, there's no doubt about it, because I could see my own body there on the operating room table. My soul was out! All this made me feel very bad at first, but then, this really bright light came. It did seem that it was a little dim at first, but then it was this huge beam. It was just a tremendous amount of light, nothing like a big bright flashlight, it was just too much light. And it gave off heat to me; I felt a warm sensation.

It was a bright yellowish white—more white. It was tremendously bright; I just can't describe it. It seemed that it covered everything, yet it didn't prevent me from seeing everything around me—the operating room, the doctors and nurses, everything. I could see clearly, and it wasn't blinding.

At first, when the light came, I wasn't sure what was happening, but then, it asked, it kind of asked me if I was ready to die. It was like talking to a person, but a person wasn't there. The light's what was talking to me, but in a voice.

Now, I think that the voice that was talking to me actually realized that I wasn't ready to die. You know, it was just kind of testing me more than anything else. Yet, from the moment the light spoke to me, I felt really good —secure and loved. The love which came from it is just unimaginable, indescribable. It was a fun person to be with! And it had a sense of humor, too—definitely!

CHAPTER FOUR

DANCING BEFORE GOD: RELIGIOUS SYMBOL AND RITE

Dancing is among the oldest of religious practices, from the festive dances of primitive peoples and the shaman's scenario to David's dancing before the Ark of the Covenant in Jerusalem. Sacred dance epitomizes the essence of the religious symbol and typifies the second of the three forms of religious expression—which is closely linked to the idea of symbol—that is, religious practices.

Philosophical definitions of symbol vary, though generally they first distinguish between symbol and sign. A sign, like a stop sign, gives a message but has nothing intrinsic to do with the message itself. The cross on a Christian church, however, not only tells where the house of worship is located but also is a continual reminder of its background and meaning. It is a symbol. The word *symbol* comes from Greek for "fall with" and suggests that a symbol is inseparable from something else of weight. In the words of Paul Tillich, a symbol "participates in" what it symbolizes. It establishes a connection between the present object of the senses and the mind's reserve associations of memory and feeling that give it special meaning. Symbols are of many kinds: actions, social groups, visual representations in picture or image, sounds, words, ideas. If the symbol is religious, the association is with the transcendent and the real self.

Religious rites may be thought of as *orchestrations of symbols*. They use words, music, gestures, art, architecture, and intentional groups to evoke a special or sacred time and space—the service and the temple, where those for whom the symbols have communicative meaning discover the transcendent and one's true nature close at hand. Sacred dance, the most multi-media of all religious expression, suggests all of this. Dancing may use the same amount of energy as a corresponding amount of work, but it feels different; this indicates that there are qualitative as well as quantitative differences in ways of acting that may have to do with differences in reference, goal, subjective meaning, and implied relation to the universe of the acts. Dancing may make you feel more like yourself and also more like a harmonizing part of society and the whole cosmos. If it is sacred dance, its gestures may act out patterns that set a meaning-code against the cosmos. They may weave out the life of a god, the order of creation, or the rhythm of events such as planting and harvest that bear transcendent meaning as indicators of the cycles of cosmic life. Dance is a symbol; the rhythm and harmony and the suspension of ordinary thought make participating in it participation in something more, the community and the gods with their divine pattern.

All symbols and rites are like dance in these respects, though they use different media. They are all openings into vast realms of transcendent meaning for those who hold their keys, as those drab gates or rabbit-holes in stories that offer access to secret gardens or fabulous kingdoms. (Perhaps it is no accident that even social dances are often associated with brilliant dress and a fantasy atmosphere.)

In this chapter we explore first some important theoretical understandings of symbol in religion. Then we look at several examples and aspects of symbol in action in rite and initiation. Finally, we consider the important distinction between public and private symbols.

PAUL TILLICH
ON SYMBOLS

The following is an important statement on symbols by the modern Protestant theologian Paul Tillich (1886–1965). It is in the context of discussing God and language about God. Tillich first affirms that the statement that God is being itself is nonsymbolic, but all other statements we can make about God are symbolic, since they take some finite part of human experience and apply it to God. To do that, however, is what symbols are for. As Tillich indicates in his distinction between signs and symbols, the latter participate in what they symbolize, but they are not *wholly* what they symbolize in the way that God is being itself. Rather they cut both ways, toward the unbounded and also toward the world of finite forms where, nonetheless, hints of something more are sometimes glimpsed. Thus, while the language of symbol may sometimes be untrue in a literal-minded sense, it is far from unreal.

Systematic Theology
Paul Tillich

The statement that God is being-itself is a nonsymbolic statement. It does not point beyond itself. It means what it says directly and properly; if we speak of the actuality of God, we first assert that he is not God if he is not being-itself. Other assertions about God can be made theologically only on this basis. Of course, religious assertions do not require such a foundation for what they say about God; the foundation is implicit in every religious thought concerning God. Theologians must make explicit what is implicit in religious thought and expression; and, in order to do this, they must begin with the most abstract and completely unsymbolic statement which is possible, namely, that God is being-itself or the absolute.

However, after this has been said, nothing else can be said about God as God which is not symbolic. As we already have seen, God as being-itself is the ground of the ontological structure of being without being subject to this structure himself. He *is* the structure; that is, he has the power of determining the structure of everything that has being. Therefore, if anything beyond this bare assertion is said about God, it no longer is a direct and proper statement, no longer a concept. It is indirect, and it points to something beyond itself. In a word, it is symbolic.

The general character of the symbol has been described. Special emphasis must be laid on the insight that symbol and sign are different; that, while the sign bears no necessary relation to that to which it points, the symbol participates in the reality of that for which it stands. The sign can be changed arbitrarily according to the demands of expediency, but the symbol grows and dies according to the correlation between that which is symbolized and the persons who receive it as a symbol. Therefore, the religious symbol, the symbol which points to the divine, can be a true symbol only if it participates in the power of the divine to which it points.

From *Systematic Theology*, vol. 1, by Paul Tillich, pp. 238–41. Copyright © 1951 by The University of Chicago Press. Reprinted by permission.

There can be no doubt that any concrete assertion about God must be symbolic, for a concrete assertion is one which uses a segment of finite experience in order to say something about him. It transcends the content of this segment, although it also includes it. The segment of finite reality which becomes the vehicle of a concrete assertion about God is affirmed and negated at the same time. It becomes a symbol, for a symbolic expression is one whose proper meaning is negated by that to which it points. And yet it also is affirmed by it, and this affirmation gives the symbolic expression an adequate basis for pointing beyond itself.

The crucial question must now be faced. Can a segment of finite reality become the basis for an assertion about that which is infinite? The answer is that it can, because that which is infinite is being-itself and because everything participates in being-itself. The *analogia entis* is not the property of a questionable natural theology which attempts to gain knowledge of God by drawing conclusions about the infinite from the finite. The *analogia entis* gives us our only justification of speaking at all about God. It is based on the fact that God must be understood as being-itself.

The truth of a religious symbol has nothing to do with the truth of the empirical assertions involved in it, be they physical, psychological, or historical. A religious symbol possesses some truth if it adequately expresses the correlation of revelation in which some person stands. A religious symbol *is* true if it adequately expresses the correlation of some person with final revelation. A religious symbol can die only if the correlation of which it is an adequate expression dies. This occurs whenever the revelatory situation changes and former symbols become obsolete. The history of religion, right up to our own time, is full of dead symbols which have been killed not by a scientific criticism of assumed superstitions but by a religious criticism of religion. The judgment that a religious symbol *is* true is identical with the judgment that the revelation of which it is the adequate expression is true. This double meaning of the truth of a symbol must be kept in mind. A symbol *has* truth: it is adequate to the revelation it expresses. A symbol *is* true: it is the expression of a true revelation.

Theology as such has neither the duty nor the power to confirm or to negate religious symbols. Its task is to interpret them according to theological principles and methods. In the process of interpretation, however, two things may happen: theology may discover contradictions between symbols within the theological circle and theology may speak not only as theology but also as religion. In the first case, theology can point out the religious dangers and the theological errors which follow from the use of certain symbols; in the second case, theology can become prophecy, and in this role it may contribute to a change in the revelatory situation.

Religious symbols are double-edged. They are directed toward the infinite which they symbolize *and* toward the finite through which they symbolize it. They force the infinite down to finitude and the finite up to infinity. They open the divine for the human and the human for the divine. For instance, if God is symbolized as "Father," he is brought down to the human relationship of father and child. But at the same time this human relationship is consecrated into a pattern of the divine-human relationship. If "Father" is employed as a symbol for God, fatherhood is seen in its theonomous, sacramental depth. One cannot arbitrarily "make" a religious symbol out of a segment of secular reality. Not even the collective unconscious, the great symbol-creating source, can do this. If a segment of reality is used as a symbol for God, the realm of reality from which it is taken is, so to speak, elevated into the realm of the holy. It no longer is secular. It is theonomous. If God is called the "king," something is said not only about God but also about the holy character of kinghood. If God's work is called "making whole" or "healing," this not only says something about God but also emphasizes the theonomous character of all healing. If God's self-manifestation is called "the word," this not only symbolizes God's relation to man but also emphasizes the holiness of all words as an expression of the spirit. The list could be continued. Therefore, it is not surprising that in a secular culture both the symbols for God and the theonomous character of the material from which the symbols are taken disappear.

A final word of warning must be added in view of the fact that for many people the very term "symbolic" carries the connotation of nonreal. This is partially the result of confusion between sign and symbol and partially due to the identification of reality with empirical reality, with the entire realm of objective things and events. Both reasons have been undercut explicitly and implicitly in the foregoing chapters. But one reason remains, namely, the fact that some theological movements, such as Protestant Hegelianism and Catholic modernism, have interpreted religious language symbolically in order to dissolve its realistic meaning and to weaken its seriousness, its power, and its spiritual impact. This was not the purpose of the classical essays on the "divine names," in which the symbolic character of all affirmations about God was strongly emphasized and explained in religious terms, nor was it a consequence of these essays. Their intention and their result was to give to God and to all his relations to man more reality and power than a nonsymbolic and therefore easily superstitious interpretation could give them. In this sense symbolic interpretation is proper and necessary; it enhances rather than diminishes the reality and power of religious language, and in so doing it performs an important function.

MIRCEA ELIADE
ON SYMBOLS

The following passage summarizes the religious characteristics of symbols from the point of view of a famous historian of religion. The basic point is that through symbol the *world* itself— in the sense of cosmos, the divinely established order—speaks, for symbol indicates its structure. Symbol bespeaks many things at once, however, and so articulates both system and paradox. Nevertheless, challenging mystery of that order is always inherent in what engages humans deeply enough to give birth to profound discovery and creativity.

Methodological Remarks on the Study of Religious Symbolism

Mircea Eliade

The symbol is not a mere reflection of objective reality. It reveals something more profound and more basic. Let us try to enumerate the different aspects of depths of this revelation.

1. Religious symbols are capable of revealing a modality of the real or a structure of the World that is not evident on the level of immediate experience. In order to illustrate in what sense the symbol

From Mircea Eliade, "Methodological Remarks on the Study of Religious Symbolism," in *The History of Religions: Esssays in Methodology,* ed. Mircea Eliade and Joseph M. Kitagawa. Copyright © 1959 by The University of Chicago Press. Reprinted by permission.

aims at a modality of the real which is inaccessible to human experience, let us recall a single example, the symbolism of water, which is capable of expressing the pre-formal, the virtual, and the chaotic. This is clearly not a matter of rational knowledge; rather does the living consciousness grasp reality through the symbol, anterior to reflection. It is by such graspings that the World is constituted. Later, as these meanings expand, they will lead to the first reflections on the ultimate foundation of the World, i.e., to all cosmologies and ontologies, from the time of the Vedas to the pre-Socratics.

As to the capacity of symbols to reveal a profound structure of the World, we may recall what has been said above pertaining to the principal meanings of the Cosmic Tree. This symbol *reveals the World as a living totality,* periodically regenerating itself and, because of this regeneration, continually fruitful, rich, and inexhaustible. In this case also, it is not a question of a reflective knowledge, but of an immediate intuition of a "cipher" of the World. The World "speaks" through the symbol of the Cosmic Tree, and this "word" is understood directly. The *World* is apprehended as *life,* and in primitive thought, *life is an aspect of being.*

The religious symbols which point to the structures of life reveal a more profound, more mysterious life than that which is known through everyday experience. They unveil the miraculous, inexplicable side of life, and at the same time the sacramental dimensions of human existence. "Deciphered" in the light of religious symbols, human life itself reveals a hidden side; it comes from "another part," from far off; it is "divine" in the sense that it is the work of the gods or of supernatural beings.

2.   This leads us to a second general remark: for the primitive, *symbols are always religious* because they point to something *real* or to a *structure of the world.* For on the archaic levels of culture, the *real*— that is, the powerful, the meaningful, the living—is equivalent to the *sacred.* On the other hand, the World is a creation of gods or supernatural beings; to unfold a structure of the World is equivalent to revealing a secret or a "ciphered" signification of divine workmanship. For this reason archaic religious symbols imply an ontology. It is, of course, a question of a presystematic ontology, the expression of a judgment about the world and simultaneously about human existence, a judgment that is not formulated in concepts and which rarely lends itself to conceptualization.

3.   An essential characteristic of religious symbolism is its *multivalence,* its capacity to express simultaneously a number of meanings whose continuity is not evident on the plane of immediate

experience. The symbolism of the moon, for example, reveals a connatural solidarity between the lunar rhythms, temporal becoming, water, the growth of plants, the female principle, death and resurrection, human destiny, weaving, and so forth.[1] In the final analysis, the symbolism of the moon reveals a correspondence of mystical order between the various levels of cosmic reality and certain modalities of human existence. Let us note that this correspondence becomes evident neither spontaneously in immediate experience nor through critical reflection. It is the result of a certain mode of "being present" in the world.

Even admitting that certain functions of the moon have been discovered through attentive observation of the lunar phases (for example, the relationship with rain and menstruation), it is hard to conceive that lunar symbolism in its totality has been constituted by a rational process. It is quite another order of knowledge that discloses, for example, the "lunar destiny" of human existence, the fact that man is "measured" by the temporal rhythms illustrated by the phases of the moon, that he is fated to die but, quite like the moon which reappears after three days of darkness, man too can begin his existence anew, that in any case he nourishes the hope in a life after death, assured or ameliorated through an initiation ritual.

4.   This capacity of religious symbolism to reveal a multitude of structurally coherent meanings has an important consequence. The symbol is thus able to reveal a perspective in which heterogeneous realities are susceptible of articulation into a whole, or even of integration into a "system." In other words, the religious symbol allows man to discover a certain unity of the World and, at the same time, to disclose to himself his proper destiny as an integrating part of the World. Let us keep in mind this example of lunar symbolism. We then understand the sense in which the different meanings of lunar symbols form a sort of "system." On different levels (cosmological, anthropological, "spiritual"), the lunar rhythm reveals structures that can be homologized, that is to say, modalities of existence subject to the laws of time and of cyclic becoming, existences destined to a "life" which carries in its very structure death and rebirth. Owing to the symbolism of the moon, the World no longer appears as an arbitrary assemblage of heterogeneous and divergent realities. The diverse cosmic levels communicate with each other; they are "bound together" by the same lunar rhythm, just as human life also is "woven together" by the moon and is predestined by the "spinning" goddesses.

[1]Cf. Eliade, *Patterns in Comparative Religion*, pp. 154 ff.

Another example will illustrate even better this capacity of symbols to open up a perspective through which things can be grasped and articulated into a system. The symbolism of night and darkness—which can be discerned in the cosmogonic myths, in initiation rites, in iconographies portraying nocturnal or subterranean animals—reveals the structural solidarity between precosmic and prenatal darkness on the one hand, and death, rebirth, and initiation on the other.[2] This makes possible not only the intuition of a certain mode of being, but also the understanding of the "place" of this mode of being in the constitution of the World and of the human condition. The symbolism of the Cosmic Night allows man to imagine what preceded him and preceded the World, to understand how things came into existence, and where things "existed" before they came to be. It is not an act of speculation, but a direct grasp of this mystery—that things had a beginning, and that all that preceded and concerns this beginning has a considerable weight for human existence. One has only to recall the great importance attached to the initiation rites implying a *regressus ad uterum*, through which man believes he can begin a new existence, or the numerous ceremonials designed to reactualize periodically the primordial "chaos" in order to regenerate the world and human society.

5.   Perhaps the most important function of religious symbolism —important above all because of the role which it will play in later philosophical speculations—is its capacity for expressing paradoxical situations, or certain structures of ultimate reality, otherwise quite inexpressible. One example will suffice: the symbolism of the Symplegades,[3] as it may be deciphered in numerous myths, legends, and images presenting the paradoxical passage from one mode of being to another, such as transfer from this world to another world, from the Earth to Heaven or Hell, or passage from a profane mode of existence to a spiritual existence. The most frequent images are: passing between two rocks or two icebergs that bump together continuously, between two mountains in continual motion, between the jaws of a monster, or penetrating and withdrawing unhurt from a *vagina dentata*, or entering a mountain that has no opening. We understand what all these images point to; if there exists the possibility of a "passage," this cannot be realized except "in spirit,"

[2]It is equally necessary to add that darkness symbolizes precosmic "chaos" as well as orgy (social confusion) and "folly" (dissolution of the personality).

[3]Cf. Ananda K. Coomaraswamy, "Symplegades," in *Homage to George Sarton*, ed. M. F. Ashley Montagu (New York, 1947), pp. 463–88; cf. also Carl Hentze, *Tod, Auferstehung, Weltordung* (Zurich, 1955), esp. pp. 45 ff.

giving this term all the meanings that it has in archaic societies, i.e., referring to a disincarnated mode of being as well as the imaginary world and the world of ideas. One can pass through a Symplegade insofar as one is able to act "spiritually," insofar as one proves that one possesses imagination and intelligence and, consequently, is capable of detaching oneself from immediate reality.[4] No other symbol of the "difficult passage"—not even the celebrated motif of the thin bridge like the blade of a sword or the edge of the razor to which allusion is made in the *Katha Upanishad* (iii, 14)—reveals better than the Symplegades that there is a mode of being inaccessible to immediate experience, and that one cannot attain to this mode of being except through renouncing the naïve belief in the inexpungeability of matter.

One could make similar remarks about the capacity of symbols to express the contradictory aspects of ultimate reality. Cusanus considered the *coincidentia oppositorum* as the most appropriate definition of the nature of God. But for many centuries this symbol had already been used to signify that which we call the "totality" or the "absolute" as well as the paradoxical coexistence in the divinity of polar and antagonistic principles. The conjunction of the Serpent (or of another symbol of the chthonian darkness and of the non-manifest) and of the Eagle (symbol of solar light and of the manifest) express, in iconography or in myths, the mystery of the totality or of cosmic unity.[5] Although the concepts of polarity and of the *coincidentia oppositorum* have been used in a systematic fashion since the beginnings of philosophical speculation, the symbols that dimly revealed them were not the result of critical reflection, but of an existential tension. In accepting his presence in the world, precisely as man found himself before the "cipher" or "word" of the world, he came to encounter the mystery of the contradictory aspects of a reality or of a "sacrality" that he was led to consider compact and homogeneous. One of the most important discoveries of the human spirit was naïvely anticipated when, through certain religious symbols, man guessed that the polarities and the antimonies could be articulated as a unity. Since then, the negative and sinister aspects of the cosmos and of the gods have not only found a justification, but have revealed themselves as an integral part of all reality or sacrality.

6. Finally, it is necessary to underline the *existential value* of

---

[4]Eliade, *Birth and Rebirth*, chap. iv.
[5]Eliade, *Patterns in Comparative Religion*, pp. 419 ff.

religious symbolism, that is, the fact that a symbol always aims at a *reality or a situation in which human existence is engaged.* It is above all this existential dimension that marks off and distinguishes symbols from concepts. Symbols still keep their contact with the profound sources of life; they express, one might say, the "spiritual as lived" *(le spirituel vécu).* This is why symbols have, as it were, a "numinous aura"; they reveal that the modalities of the spirit are at the same time manifestations of life, and, consequently, they directly engage human existence. The religious symbol not only unveils a structure of reality or a dimension of existence; by the same stroke it brings a *meaning* into human existence. This is why even symbols aiming at the ultimate reality conjointly constitute existential revelations for the man who deciphers their message.

The religious symbol translates a human situation into cosmological terms and vice versa; more precisely, it reveals the continuity between the structures of human existence and cosmic structures. This means that man does not feel himself "isolated" in the cosmos, but that he "opens out" to a world which, thanks to a symbol, proves "familiar." On the other hand, the cosmological values of symbols enable him to leave behind the subjectivity of a situation and to recognize the objectivity of his personal experiences.

It follows that he who understands a symbol not only "opens out" to the objective world, but at the same time succeeds in emerging from his particular situation and in attaining a comprehension of the universal. This is explained by the fact that symbols have a way of causing immediate reality, as well as particular situations, to "burst." Whenever a tree incarnates the World Tree or when a spade is associated with the phallus and agricultural work with the act of generation, for example, one could say that the immediate reality of these objects or actions "bursts" or "explodes" under the irruptive force of a more profound reality. The same might be said of an individual situation, let us say, that of the neophyte locked up in the initiation hut. The symbolism "bursts" the bonds of this particular situation, making it exemplary, that is to say, indefinitely repeatable in many and varied contexts (because the initiation hut is likened to the maternal womb and at the same time to the belly of a monster and to Hell, and the darkness symbolizes the Cosmic Night, the preformal, the fetal state of the world, etc.). Consequently, because of the symbol, the individual experience is "awakened" and transmuted in a spiritual act. To "live" a symbol and to decipher its message correctly implies an opening toward the Spirit and, finally, access to the universal.

CLAUDE LÉVI- STRAUSS
ON SYMBOL

The following passage is from the difficult but important writings of the French anthropologist Claude Lévi-Strauss. He speaks here just of myth, although his comments could cover the whole gamut of symbolic expression. Elsewhere, for example, he speaks of kinship systems as being of the same order as language and, thus, as symbolic in a manner comparable to that here argued for myth; the same argument is made in his book *The Raw and the Cooked* for the order of items on the "menu" characteristic of a culture. The point is that a culture by definition is a network of symbols on all levels; a culture affects every area of the life of those within it, and everything shaped by a culture is a symbol of that culture. Symbols are really units of a language, comparable to words. The meaning lies not in the individual words so much as in the sentences they make and finally in the grand sentence that is the whole culture, whose basic message *is* culture reflecting the human intellect with its characteristic ways of thinking.

In this passage from "The Structural Study of Myth," Lévi-Strauss states that myth is to be understood by comparison to language—which he does through the use of some technical terminology from linguistics—even though mythical language may have special properties. Each part of it can only be understood in relation to the whole. To understand the story of Little Red Riding Hood, we need to understand not only her meaning and that of the wolf but also the dynamics and dialectic of their relationship. Moreover, Lévi-Strauss tells us, we need to take into account all the variants. To understand Little Red Riding Hood and what the popularity of this story in our culture has to say about the culture, we have to look at all the different ways it has been told, from the medieval fairy tale to modern kindergarten retellings and racy burlesque versions.

All these ideas are of immense importance for understanding religion. Just as no part of a myth can be rightly understood apart from its relationships and variants, so no part of a religious rite, belief system, or sociological structure can be understood apart from its pattern of relationship to the rest of the religious system or its historical and contemporary variants within the religion. A vast number of both popular and scholarly misconceptions about all sorts of things religious have resulted from taking them out of context and failing to grasp that their meaning could not be gotten without understanding their relationships and their variants.

The Structural Study of Myth

Claude Lévi-Strauss

A remark can be introduced at this point which will help to show the originality of myth in relation to other linguistic phenomena. Myth is the part of language where the formula *traduttore, traditore* reaches its lowest truth value. From that point of view it should be placed in the gamut of linguistic expressions at the end opposite to that of poetry, in spite of all the claims which have been made to prove the contrary. Poetry is a kind of speech which cannot be translated except at the cost of serious distortions; whereas the mythical value of the myth is preserved even through the worst translation. Whatever our ignorance of the language and the culture of the people where it originated, a myth is still felt as a myth by any reader anywhere in the world. Its substance does not lie in its style, its original music, or its syntax, but in the *story* which it tells. Myth is language, functioning on an especially high level where meaning succeeds practically at "taking off" from the linguistic ground on which it keeps on rolling.

To sum up the discussion at this point, we have so far made the following claims: (1) If there is a meaning to be found in mythology, it cannot reside in the isolated elements which enter into the composition of a myth, but only in the way those elements are combined. (2) Although myth belongs to the same category as language, being, as a matter of fact, only part of it, language in myth exhibits specific properties. (3) Those properties are only to be found *above* the ordinary linguistic level, that is, they exhibit more complex features than those which are to be found in any other kind of linguistic expression.

If the above three points are granted, at least as a working hypothesis, two consequences will follow: (1) Myth, like the rest of language, is made up of constituent units. (2) These constituent units presuppose the constituent units present in language when analyzed on other levels—namely, phonemes, morphemes, and sememes—but they, nevertheless, differ from the latter in the same way as the latter

From Claude Lévi-Strauss, "The Structural Study of Myth." Reproduced by permission of the American Folklore Society, from the *Journal of American Folklore* 68 (270), 1955, and of the author.

differ among themselves; they belong to a higher and more complex order. For this reason, we shall call them *gross constituent units.*

How shall we proceed in order to identify and isolate these gross constituent units or mythemes? We know that they cannot be found among phonemes, morphemes, or sememes, but only on a higher level; otherwise myth would become confused with any other kind of speech. Therefore, we should look for them on the sentence level. The only method we can suggest at this stage is to proceed tentatively, by trial and error, using as a check the principles which serve as a basis for any kind of structural analysis: economy of explanation; unity of solution; and ability to reconstruct the whole from a fragment, as well as later stages from previous ones.

The technique which has been applied so far by this writer consists in analyzing each myth individually, breaking down its story into the shortest possible sentences, and writing each sentence on an index card bearing a number corresponding to the unfolding of the story.

Practically each card will thus show that a certain function is, at a given time, linked to a given subject. Or, to put it otherwise, each gross constituent unit will consist of a *relation.*

However, the above definition remains highly unsatisfactory for two different reasons. First, it is well known to structural linguists that constituent units on all levels are made up of relations, and the true difference between our *gross* units and the others remains unexplained; second, we still find ourselves in the realm of a non-reversible time, since the numbers of the cards correspond to the unfolding of the narrative. Thus the specific character of mythological time, which as we have seen is both reversible and non-reversible, synchronic and diachronic, remains unaccounted for. From this springs a new hypothesis, which constitutes the very core of our argument: The true constituent units of a myth are not the isolated relations but *bundles of such relations,* and it is only as bundles that these relations can be put to use and combined so as to produce a meaning. Relations pertaining to the same bundle may appear diachronically at remote intervals, but when we have succeeded in grouping them together we have reorganized our myth according to a time referent of a new nature, corresponding to the prerequisite of the initial hypothesis, namely a two-dimensional time referent which is simultaneously diachronic and synchronic, and which accordingly integrates the characteristics of *langue* on the one hand, and those of *parole* on the other. To put it in even more linguistic terms, it is as though a phoneme were always made up of all its variants.

RITE

The following description of an important Shinto rite from Japan, the *Kanname-sai,* or Harvest Festival at the Grand Shrine of Ise, is an introduction to the orchestration of symbols that is religious rite. Ise is the shrine of two principle Shinto deities of national importance: Amaterasu, the solar goddess and ancestress of the imperial line in the Inner Shrine; and Toyouke, a goddess of food at the Outer Shrine. Ise holds a number of auxiliary shrines of other deities as well. The whole complex could be called a Shinto national cathedral. The rites at Ise are very ancient and stylized and are less occasions of popular devotion than of very solemn and quiet enactments of timeless ritual. For this very reason, they give a classic example of pure rite. A pattern common to many traditional rites throughout the world comes through in this description: preparation through abstinence and meditation, presentation of offerings, prayer, and finally a means for general participation (the sacred time of the ritual). The main point to note is that rite has a definite structure that presents its own message about the relation of society and deity and of time and eternity.

Harvest and Renewal at the Grand Shrine of Ise

Robert S. Ellwood, Jr.

We shall now proceed to a description of the Kanname-sai or Harvest Festival of the Grand Shrine. This is the culminating event of the Ise liturgical cycle, for the Shinto calendar revolves around Harvest as the Christian calendar centers upon Easter. The Harvest first-fruits offerings are presented in the two major shrines on successive nights; in the Outer Shrine on October 15th, in the Inner on the 16th. In each case the nocturnal offering is enacted twice; at 10 p.m. and again beginning at 2 a.m. Each ceremony lasts approximately two hours. At noon of the following the imperial offerings are

From Robert S. Ellwood, Jr., "Harvest and Renewal at the Grand Shrine of Ise," *Numen,* vol. XV, no. 3 (November 1968), 172–77, 180–82. Most notes omitted. Reprinted by permission of N. V. Boekhandel & Drukkerij voorheen E. J. Brill, Leiden, Netherlands.

presented in the same shrine as the ceremony of the night before, and then the rite for that shrine is completed at 5 p.m. with sacred dance (kagura). The writer observed these rites as far as possible (for no non-participant, even if a Shinto priest, is allowed within the inner fence) in October of 1966.

The clergy practice abstinence by residing in the Purification House (Saikan) of the shrine in which they will officiate before the ceremony. During this period they will wear only pure white clothes, eat only food prepared in the Purification House over a "pure fire" (made by wood friction with an archaic string-and-axle device) and are allowed no outside communication except with the Shrine Office and the Imperial Messengers. Nothing impure—that is, primarily, nothing pertaining to blood, sickness, decay, or death—is to reach their five senses. Apart from these rather negative precautions, however, no particular practices are followed save for purifying the body by bathing. One understands that while more serious priests may endeavor to study, there is also a deal of joviality and chatter.

The Harvest Festival ceremonies proper begin at 5 p.m. on the 15th. The first observance is the very interesting Okitama or Distant-Sea-Spirit (or perhaps Starting-Spirit) Rite. At the northeast corner of the Outer Fence of the Inner Shrine is a small fane, acutally just two or three small Stones, of the Deity Okitama. Nearby is a similar shrine to Miyabi no Kami (from *Miya*, "Palace" or "Shrine" and *bi*, "fire" or, from the character, "around the site"), who has sometimes been identified with Ōmiyanome, the great patroness of palace activities often mentioned in the *Engishiki* prayers. At Ise both of these deities are held to be protective kami of the shrine area whose blessing should be invoked before any major activity takes place within their domain. The name Okitama suggests that the rite may be a remnant of an ancient cultus of marine deities who came in from the sea to bless the crops. However, the two also remind one of the kind of deities found in the lists of protective deities of the Imperial Palace in the *Engishiki* and *Kogoshūi*. A prayer and offering are presented.

Next, another rite with interesting primordial overtones is held in the Nakanoe, or space between the two middle fences, of the Inner Shrine. This is the Miura or divination to determine if any of the clergy are impure and hence unable to participate in the rite. The clergy arrange themselves in two files before the inner gate. Until the Meiji reforms of the early 1870's a *kannagi* was seated in the gate. She said a norito or prayer, then plucked the strings of a *koto* (Japanese zither) three times, then sang for the descent of the kami. The song, at least as ancient as the *Kenkyū Nenjūgyōji* (12th century), consisted of some syllables difficult of interpretation, and then these lines: "Kami of heaven, kami of the lands, come down! Of thunderbolts also, come down! From over the Great Bay, from under the Great Bay, come in!"

Then she read the names of each of the clergy and, with each name, plucked the strings of the *koto*. If the sound was true, that priest was allowed to participate, but if untrue, he was disqualified, and presumed to have kept the purification period inadequately.

However the Miura is now simplified somewhat. The priestess does not participate, but rather an assistant priest hits the strings of the instrument with his ritual wand (*shaku*) as he reads the lines. Each priest bows and whistles by sucking in his breath as his name is read. The song is not now used. It is said that it is very unlikely that a priest would actually be disqualified. When I observed the rite, the Miura was held in the Yojoden rather than the court-yard because of rain. After the ceremony the clergy left the enclosure in procession, wearing white robes, the tall black *eboshi* caps, and held above them yellow paper umbrellas. As usual, at a place on the path marked by a stone, they offered *kihai* (worship) toward the "Rough Spirit" Shrine with claps and bowing.

At 10 p.m. the major ceremony of making the offerings in the Outer Shrine begins. The pattern is approximately the same on the two nights, but following the usual practice of Japanese scholars I will present here the usage as it is observed in the Inner Shrine, and then mention the one or two differences of relative significance.

On the hour, at the sound of a drum three times, the clergy emerge, perhaps twenty-five or thirty, from the Purification House. They first proceed to the Pure Fire House (Imibi Yaden) to get the offerings, which have been prepared and arranged in three large palanquin boxes of white unfinished wood. The offerings are purified by waving sakaki branches over them. Then the boxes are lifted, each by two priests. Others carry torches, and lanterns are lit along the path to the Shrine. Total silence is kept, but the heavy wooden shoes resound like snare drums on the white gravel trail. Usually the procession will be led by the Saishu with a staff, but when I observed the rite she was absent owing to illness.

First they proceed to the Minie Chosa, a floorless lodge located opposite the outer gate of the Inner Shrine. Here one of the offerings, the abalone, is symbolically cooked by mixing it with salt, and all are significantly offered here first. At the back of this lodge, just behind a fire, are three black primitive-looking stones. These represent Toyouke, the Food Goddess of the Outer Shrine. Just as on ordinary days all offerings to both deities are made in the Outer Shrine Food House (Mikeden), they are now first presented here.

For this rite, three tables have been set up inside this small lodge. The clergy align themselves on either side at right angles to the tables. Here the food is arranged. Three priests advance to remove it from the boxes and set it up. The center table is for the food for the Inner Shrine main deity, Amaterasu, the others for the two Aidono or companion altars (deities) who share the Inner Shrine with her, Ame no Tachikara and Yorotsu Hata Toyo Akitsu Hime. Next three other priests advance, one to each table, and enact cutting and cooking, using a ritual sword and ritual chopsticks. Then a higher priest (Negi) advances and using the chopsticks arranges the salt on the abalone as a purifier. Others next restore the offerings to the chests.

The Chosa lodge ceremony is done only in the Inner Shrine rite. The Outer Shrine has no Chosa building, and the offerings are prepared as usual in its ancient Mikeden. Before the Meiji reforms, the Chosa ceremony was not done in that building, but the offerings were taken to the River over a bridge used only at that time and symbolically prepared there. Here we see the idea of associating purification with the River, so deeply ingrained in the traditions of Ise. The spiritual preparation of the clergy was also formerly accomplished across the River rather than in the present Purification House.

Next the procession bears the offerings up the steps to the Inner Court. They are taken past the four fences, and the clergy line up with them before the Shōden, the inner house which is the dwelling place of the great deity. This area inside the fourth fence is entered only three times a year, at the Harvest Festival and the two Tsukinami Feasts of June and December which resemble it structurally.

As the clergy advance with the offerings into the Inner Court (Naiin), Shinto music, shrill, unmelodious, uncanny, is played on reed flutes. This music is played in Shinto rites on three occasions: the presentation of offerings, the withdrawal of offerings, and for kagura or sacred dance. They make offerings only while it is sounding, as though without its support no man would dare approach the deity. With all inside, the gates of the Inner Court are closed, and the priests are no longer visible to the observer. Only two participants remain visible; two priests seat themselves on either side of the middle court outside these gates, and each lights a bonfire before him. The music continues to flow from within. The fires and strange tones in the autumn darkness evoke a strong feeling of the mysterious activity of deity within the sacred enclosure.

Inside, three low tables are set up. The food dishes are arranged in a most orderly manner on the tables, together with the sake cups on tiny clay pillars. The vessels are all of the *doki* type made especially for the Grand Shrine, of unglazed pottery identical with that of Neolithic Japan and used only once. At the top of the tables is a set of chopsticks and in the center three cups each for four kinds of sake. Surrounding them are various bowls of rice and of several kinds of fish, seaweed, vegetables, salt, and water. No flesh meat is offered.

First the sake is solemnly poured into the cups for the deities. Next as the music stops the Chief Priest recites *sotto voce*, in a nasal tone, the text of the prayer, which begins, in elegant language, "From the High Plain of Heaven, depending on the Great Imperial Goddess, we are blessed in a year of awesome wonders through the labors of the officials and people of the land under heaven with eightfold and luxuriant sheaves."

All worship by clapping and bowing eight times. Second and third offerings of sake are poured, each followed by eightfold clapping, and music is played. Now is the time of the divine banquet, the most sacred moment.

Next a custom is observed in which two priests go outside the Inner fence and proceed to its four corners, offering at each sake, dried abalone, fish, and so forth, clapping and bowing at each four times.

The clappings have been audible from where the observers are standing. Then with music the offerings are taken up, replaced in the boxes, and the party withdraws carrying them. It is now about midnight, and the evening offering is completed in the Main Shrine. The clergy now process to the "Rough Spirit" Shrine, after having obtained another box of offerings for it from the Pure Fire House. A few priests have been standing watch there all evening. A somewhat briefer ceremony of prayer and offering is enacted before the *aramitama*. Here, however, the observer can better see the full procedure.

Then, beginning at 2 a.m., the entire service in the Main Shrine and the "Rough Spirit" Shrine is repeated. Shinto always loves duplication, whether of shrines or ceremonies, particularly at Ise, and doubtless this represents something fundamental to its experience of the divine. We may recall that the same twofold (or perhaps one should say fourfold) rite is performed on consecutive nights at the two shrines.

.   .   .

The third and final major division of the Harvest Festival is then held at 5 p.m.

This is the kagura or sacred dancing held in the Yojoden. At this hour a selected number of clergy enter that pavilion. Within, they align themselves along the sides while other clergy who will serve as musicians form a silent single file outside the building toward its entry. A ranking priest (Negi) goes to the inner gate where the *tamagushi* branches had been placed in the previous ceremony, bows, takes one of them, and returns with it to the Yojoden. He then solemnly presents it to the priest who is to be dancer. Holding the *tamagushi* he begins the kagura, which is always a long and ancient Court dance called Ninjo-mai. The use of the *tamagushi* provides another example of the passing of it to indicate the person who is the spiritual center of the activity. During the dance, torches for illumination are burning within the Yojoden, and music is played. The dances are not visible to the observer. It is said to re-create the divine age, evoked by the solemn offerings which called down the deities of that other time. Thus the Harvest Festival ends.

The threefold pattern—nocturnal offering, imperial offerings at noon, kagura—then is enacted twice on successive nights and days at the two major shrines. The main difference is that the Minie Chosa rite is not equivalated in the Outer Shrine. Possibly this recalls, especially in the former practice of preparing the Inner Shrine offerings on the island, ways in which the Inner Shrine cultus was conducted before the association between the two became so intimate.

There is a certain amount of "follow up" over succeeding days. At the present a folk dance festival is held on the grounds of the Inner Shrine beginning on the last day of the Kanname-sai. Amateur groups in traditional costume from all over Japan display their traditional dances. A carnival is held on the streets of Ise city. Thus the austere ritual of the Grand Shrine is somewhat mitigated through certain of those popular festivities which are, in principle, extensions of the same final phase of Shinto worship represented by kagura.

Offerings are made to the lesser shrines of the system over the next few days, the work being completed by the priests (not the Envoys, who return immediately) by the 25th.[1]

The four basic elements of Shinto worship may be remembered as purification, presentation, petition, and participation. It is obvious that these elements are well represented at the Kanname-sai. There is purification of the clergy in the Purification House before the ceremony and of the elements in the Pure Fire House—not to mention the special conditions of purity under which they have been produced. The presentation of the offerings and its corollary, petition in the form of prayer or norito, is in fact accomplished three times at each of the Main Shrines. The reasons for the nocturnal duplication are, like other secrets of Ise, lost in antiquity, but the separation of the shrine offerings from the imperial offerings clearly crystallizes historical movement.

The element of participation is, in the average Shinto *matsuri* or festival, the most conspicuous feature. During the work of prayer and offering, confined to the few priests and lay dignitaries ensconced in the prayer hall, rows of carnival stalls are being set up in the courtyard, and groups of wrestlers, dancers, musicians, and young men who will carry the divine presence in the *mikoshi* or palanquin will be impatiently waiting to begin activity. But at the Grand Shrine, given its dignified pace and spacious grounds, the distance between offering and participation seems not inconsiderable. The popular elements are obviously modern and contrived; and in any

---

[1]When the offerings are taken to the group of four shrines dedicated respectively to the primal parents, Izanami and Izanagi, and the "rough" and "smooth" spirits of Tsukiyomi, the moon god, two groups of priests are dispatched at the same time, one to handle ceremonies at the primal parents' shrine, the other the Tsukiyomi shrines. It is traditional that at each pair of shrines the two groups move through the ritual rapidly to see which can finish first. This does not suggest irreverence so much as the rivalry between two men's groups typical of New Year's in Japanese popular religion. For example, at the "Winter Peak" of the Yamabushi on Mt. Haguro, New Year's is essentially a rivalry between two lodges into which the members of the Yamabushi order divide themselves. It is expressed in mock debate, duplication of rituals, and finally a sledge race. (See H. Byron Earhart, "Four Ritual Periods of Haguro Shugendō in Northeastern Japan," *History of Religions*, Vol. 5, No. 1 (Summer, 1965), pp. 101–04.) One is also reminded of the ancient theme of interspersing sacred time with levity and burlesque, as in the case of the "ritual clowns" of the American Indians or the Boy Bishops and "Lords of Misrule" of the Middle Ages.

case have no close intimacy with the shrine rite in either time or space; the Grand Shrine rite which does hold this function, the sacred dance, is the least visible of all to any save participating clergy. One realizes that Ise, as an institution of the Great Tradition of the Court and a sacred center for the entire nation, cannot operate on the immediate popular level. It must either turn inward to its divine life, or else remain equally mysterious and accessible to all whether local or remote, in dependence not on level of visibility but on degree of spiritual rapport. Created at the dawn of historical time in Japan to preserve the power and ethos of archaism when that world seemed already slipping away, and having become stylized but virtually immobile ever since, its inner and ritual life creates a time of almost stellar distance, which only tangentially brushes the world outside its gates.

FESTIVAL

The following passage by a distinguished contemporary novelist is on Sukos, perhaps the most delightful and colorful of Jewish festivals. It is descended from the ancient Israelite harvest festival, but notice that it has also been given a meaning that makes history sacred—the huts remind us of those the people of Israel lived in while crossing the desert with Moses. Notice also that the festival is the sort of occasion that delights children—and those others who have not lost the gift of childlike delight—and makes the tradition a thing of joy for them. Finally, though, we move from this agrarian festival to the Sh'mini Atzeres, the festival of the law, which balances it by showing that ritual and religious festivity as symbols of identity are rooted not only in the seasonal cycle and sacred history but also—and this has been especially manifested in Judaism—in the structures of religious life now. There is something particularly Jewish about celebrating an object as emblematic of hard study and disciplined life as the Torah (the first five books of the Bible containing the Law of Moses) and in showing merriment over the way this very discipline brings one close to God. Yet all religious festivals in various ways show how the people of that tradition relate to nature, where they come from, and how they live now; all festivals are, like Sukos and Sh'mini Atzeres, miniaturizations of the tradition's whole spiritual life.

This Is My God

Herman Wouk

We are back in the light of the full moon, the moon of the autumnal equinox, the fifteenth of Tishri. Everything that the earth will yield this year lies heaped in the storehouses: the fruit, the grain, the wine, the oil: piles of yellow and green and red, vats brimming purple and gold. The farmers of ancient Israel, like farmers in all lands and times, gather for the autumn thanksgiving.

The full moon sheds its light on every man, woman, and child in Palestine. Nobody is indoors. The law of Moses requires that for seven days and nights all Jews live in huts partially roofed by green boughs, palm branches, or piles of reeds. In these frail structures the families feast, and sing, and visit, and sleep. At the mercy of the weather, they live as their ancestors did in the desert, in the first forty years of independence, before they conquered Canaan.

Sukos is so pre-eminently a gay and rollicking time that its Talmudic name is simply *The Festival*. For a folk settled in a rich farm country, contemplating their heaping harvests, the suko custom may have helped to limit the smugness of prosperity. In the suko under the night sky, wind and rain could at any moment make life dismal. The moon shone through the loose ceiling of boughs, the old warning of the way fortune changes. The stars—the law suggests that the stars be visible through the roof—may have been reminders that life at its richest is a brief spark in a black mystery. Or so you can interpret the ordinance, if you will. Moses wrote that by dwelling in huts once a year Israel would remember that they had once lived in sukos in the desert, and he went no further.

With the dispersion of the Jews to colder climates, the customs surrounding the sukos have changed. There are pious Jews who still sleep in the hut when the weather permits it, but most of them today confine their observance to eating meals and praying there.

In American Jewish life, especially with the rise of suburban communities, Sukos is recovering much of its old charm and excitement. For the harvest-time hut (the archaic word is "tabernacle") is a perfect instrument for delighting and instructing

Excerpts from *This Is My God* by Herman Wouk. Copyright © 1959, 1970 by The Abe Wouk Foundation, Inc. Used by permission of Doubleday & Company, Inc.

the children. Those who mourn the absence of something like a Christmas tree in our customs have never given the suko a thought, or more likely have not heard of it.

You can construct the hut in your own yard. There are portable ready-made sukos which take most of the work out of the job. What is wanted is nothing more than three or four walls, some slats of wood at the top, and the covering for the roof—branches, boughs, grass, reeds. There has to be room in the suko for a table and chairs. Decorating the suko becomes a pleasant game of improvising patterns with fruits, vegetables, flowers, and anything else that adds color and gaiety. The small children dart in and out of the booth, playing some version of cops-and-robbers, as the children doubtless did in the hills of Judah thirty centuries ago when the suko was going up. Older children help in decorating the suko or they take over the job entirely, and find enormous fun in doing it. The heaps of fruit, flowers, corn, squash dwindle on the table. The bare walls of the suko disappear under living patterns of yellow, scarlet, and green.

Night falls. The family dines by candlelight and moonlight in the open air, in the curious hut filled with harvest fragrance. The old holiday melodies and chants sound strangely new outdoors. Maybe it is so cool that they dine in coats. Maybe the weather holds, and they have an idyllic dinner alfresco, in the scented gloom of the suko. Sometimes it rains, and a half-annoyed half-hilarious scramble indoors ensues. The charm of broken routine, of a new colorful way of doing familiar things, makes Sukos a seven-day picnic—one that is dedicated and charged with symbol, as well as delightful.

In the city, these pleasures of Sukos are hard to come by. Community meals in a hut on the roof or in the yard of a synagogue are the best that many people can manage. Even that much is a vivid reminder of what Sukos can be.

The Palm Branch

The law of Sukos reads, "And you shall take the fruit of a pleasant tree, and palm branches, and thick leafy boughs, and willows of the brook, and rejoice before your Lord God."

This is not a suggestion of improvised decoration, but the basis of one of Judaism's spectacular symbols, the rite of the palm branch.

The *esrog* is a fragrant yellow fruit native to Palestine, much like a lemon but larger, with a curious brownish button at the tip, the withered blossom which never wholly drops off. The worshipper takes in one hand a green palm branch wreathed at the base with fresh willow and myrtle, and the yellow esrog in the other; and he marches with these tokens of the ancient Palestinian harvest in formal synagogue processions, and waves them in the Hallelujah chants. It is not hard to get willow twigs and myrtle in almost any country. But palm branches do not grow in Copenhagen, nor do esrogs in Quebec. International shipment of these articles begins long before Sukos. By the time the holiday comes, any Jew who wants to perform the rite of the palm branch is usually able to do so.

Distant in time and place as we are from the Palestine of David and Solomon, the sight of palm branches waving to a Hebrew chant in an American synagogue stirs echoes of a great past. So does the Hosannah procession, a parade led by the cantor carrying the Scroll of the Law, followed by all who have the branch and fruit. In the old country it was often only the rich man of the town who could own a *lulav* (palm branch) and esrog. The congregation bought a set out of its treasury, and all the worshippers took turns reciting the benediction and waving the branch. In the United States today—and more so in Israel—a mass of swaying palm branches in the synagogue, and the perfume of esrogs diffused through the air, make this one of the loveliest of Jewish rites. The impression on children is deep.

Like Passover, Sukos runs all week long, but only the first and the last days are full festival observances.

Sh'mini Atzeres: The Eighth Day

At the end of Sukos there is an eighth day, called Atzeres in the Bible, a separate feast without the symbols of hut, palm branch, and fruit.

This day has become one of the merriest in the Jewish calendar. The reading of the Torah comes to an end with the last chapter of Deuteronomy and begins again with Genesis; for this reason the holiday has acquired another name, the Celebration of the Law: *Simkhas Torah*. Outside Israel this fete takes place on the added ninth day.

Nobody who has been in a synagogue during the Celebration of the Law needs to be told what it is like. For one who has never seen it, description will be pale. The manner varies from the exalted frenzy of the Hasidic congregations to the decorous dancing and singing in the elegant Manhattan synagogues. The essence everywhere is the same: excitement, music, joking, joy within the usually solemn precincts of worship. Seven times, chanting processions circle the synagogue with all the Holy Scrolls. Flag-waving children march behind in cheery disorder. Hoary jests sprung year after year draw the same laughter always. The honors of the day, grand prizes of congregation life, go to members distinguished in learning, philanthropy, or hard work for the synagogue. The man who speaks the benediction over the last verses of the Torah is Bridegroom of the Law. He is immediately followed by the Bridegroom of Genesis, saying the blessing over the first chapter of the Bible, "In the beginning . . . " which the sexton chants forthwith. A powerful jubilation irradiates the synagogue. The time comes when the rabbi is himself drawn into the rejoicing and solemnly dances with a Holy Scroll in his arms. My grandfather, patriarchal and reserved all year long, was still performing this dance in his nineties, a few shuffling, tottering steps, his face alight with pleasure as he clasped the Torah in his old arms.

LITURGY

The words and actions that make a rite or festival into a service are often called liturgy, especially in Christian context. The following are some lines from the long liturgy of St. John Chrysostom, the basic rite of the Eastern Orthodox Churches such as the Russian Orthodox and Greek Orthodox. These lines present the reading of the Gospel lesson for the day and certain prayers in litany form that follow. Notice that the reading of the Gospel, which comes toward the beginning of the service, is a solemn procession with candles and the opening of a pair of grand doors. This suggests the great sacred and devotional importance that the Gospels have in the Eastern Orthodox Church. This reading is followed by "the prayer of fervent suppli-cation" and prayers for the departed, if any are to be commemorated.

After these lines would come the offering of the bread and wine, their consecration, and the communion. Notice the recurring emphasis on wisdom and the resurrection of Christ. The stately language of the Orthodox liturgy is apparent here, though to gather its full impact one would have to see the interior of an Orthodox church, with its rich colors, icons, robes, incense, and royal doors in and out of which participants process, and to hear the soaring music that accompanies the liturgy. This rite is powerfully an orchestration of symbols.

The Orthodox Liturgy

The Lesson being ended the Priest saith:
    Peace be with thee who readest.
    Reader: And with thy spirit.
    Deacon: Widsom.
    Reader: Alleluia.

The Alleluia

And the Choir sings the verses appointed for the Alleluia.
*The Deacon lays down the censer in its place, and going to the
Priest he bows his head to him, and then, holding his stole with the tips of
his fingers and pointing to the book of the Gospel, he saith:*
    Pray, Father, bless him that preacheth the gospel of the holy
Apostle and Evangelist N.
The Priest, signing him with the sign of the cross, saith:
    May God, through the prayers of the most renowned holy and
glorious Apostle and Evangelist N., grant thee to preach the word
with much power, unto the fulfilling the gospel of his well-beloved
Son our Lord Jesus Christ.
And he gives the book to the Deacon.
    Deacon: Amen.
*And first bowing to it he takes up the book and, coming out of the
holy doors preceded by tapers, goes to stand in the customary place. The
Priest standing still by the holy table turns towards the west and saith
aloud:*
    Wisdom, be steadfast, let us hear the holy Gospel.
    Then: Peace be with you all.
    Choir: And with thy spirit.
    Deacon: The Lesson of the holy Gospel according to N.
    Choir: Glory be to thee, O Lord, glory to thee.
    Priest: Let us give heed.

The Gospel Lesson

The Deacon then reads the Gospel.
    At that time . . .
Which being finished, the Priest saith:
    Peace be with thee that preachest the Gospel.

From *The Orthodox Liturgy* (London: The Society for Promoting Christian
Knowledge, 1939, 1960), pp. 46–51. Reprinted by permission of The Society for
Promoting Christian Knowledge.

The Common Prayers

Choir: Glory be to thee, O Lord, glory to thee.

The Deacon then coming to the holy doors delivers the book to the Priest and the doors are again shut. Then standing in the customary place the Deacon begins thus:

The Litany of Fervent Supplication

Let us all say with all our soul, and with all our mind let us say:

Choir: Lord, have mercy upon us.

Almighty Lord, the God of our fathers, we pray unto thee, do thou hear and have mercy upon us.

Choir: Lord, have mercy upon us.

Have mercy upon us, O God, after the multitude of thy mercies, we pray unto thee, do thou hear and have mercy upon us.

Choir: Lord, have mercy upon us. *Thrice, and so thereafter.*

Also we pray for our most blessed Metropolitan N., for our Archbishop (*or* Bishop) N., and for all our brethren in Christ.

(Also we pray for the suffering country of Russia, and for all her people, whether dwelling therein, or now scattered abroad.)

Also we pray for all Christian armies.

Also we pray for our brethren the priests, for the monks, and for all our brethren in Christ.

Also we pray for the blessed, ever-memorable, holy orthodox patriarchs, for all devout kings and right-believing queens, for the founders of this holy house, and for all our orthodox fathers and brethren who are gone before and now rest in this place, or wherever else.

Also we pray for them that bring forth the fruit of good works in this holy and venerable temple, for them that toil and them that sing and for the rest of the people that wait for thy great and bountiful mercy.

The Priest meanwhile saith secretly the Prayer of Fervent Supplication:

O Lord our God, accept this devout supplication of thy servants which pray unto thee; and after the multitude of thy mercies, shed forth thy bounties upon us and upon all thy people which look unto thee for rich mercy:

Aloud:

For thou, O God, art merciful, thou lover of mankind, and we give glory to thee, the Father, the Son, and the Holy Ghost, now and for ever and world without end.

Choir: Amen.

Here, in the churches of the emigration, the Priest adds this Prayer following; the Deacon first saying:

Let us pray to the Lord.

Choir: Lord, have mercy upon us.

Accept, O Lord our God, this heartfelt supplication which we thine unworthy servants make before thee, that thou, forgiving us all our offences, wouldst remember all our enemies which hate and evilly entreat us: reward them not after their works, but turn thou such among them as believe not unto the right faith and true worshipping of thee, and such as yet believe that they may forsake evil and do good. Mercifully deliver thy holy Church from all the evils which beset her, preserve her from all heresy and schism, and stablish her in peace and concord. Preserve our motherland from the power of the ungodly, and from the evil men. Grant unto us all that, being speedily reconciled, we may lead a quiet and peaceable life in all godliness and honesty, and may have brotherly love one towards another in thy Christ. Hear the cry of affliction which thy faithful servants in grief and necessity raise unto thee day and night. Manifest thyself also unto them that have forsaken thee and seek not after thee, that none of them may perish, but all be saved and come unto the knowledge of the truth. That so we all with one mind and one mouth may glorify the majesty of thy most honourable name, of the Father, and of the Son and of the Holy Ghost, now and for ever and world without end.

Choir: Amen.

The Litany of the Departed

If there be any offering made for the dead, then the Deacon or Priest saith this litany following:

Have mercy upon us, O God, after the multitude of thy mercy, we pray unto thee, do thou hear and have mercy upon us.

Choir: Lord, have mercy upon us. *Thrice, and so thereafter.*

Also we pray for the souls of the servants of God now departed, N. and M., that thou wouldest grant them repose and forgive them all their wilful sins and unwitting transgressions.

Make their souls to rest, O Lord our God, where the righteous do rest.

For the mercy of God, the kingdom of heaven, and release of their sins, O Christ our immortal king and our God, we beseech thee.

Choir: Grant this, O Lord.

Deacon: Let us pray to the Lord.

Choir: Lord, have mercy upon us.

The Priest thereupon saith the Prayer following:

O God of the spirits of all flesh, who hast destroyed death and trodden down the devil, and hast given life unto the world: do thou, O Lord, give rest unto the souls of thy departed servants N. and M. in a place of refreshment, light, and peace, from whence pain, sorrow, and sighing flee away: forgive, O blessed Lord, thou lover of mankind, forgive the sins they have committed in thought, word and deed: for there is not a man that liveth and sinneth not: thou only art without sin, thy righteousness is everlasting righteousness, and thy word is truth:

Aloud:

For thou art the resurrection and the life, and the repose of thy departed servants N. and M., O Christ our God, and we give glory to thee, together with thine unbegotten Father, and thy most holy and gracious and life-giving Spirit, now and for ever and world without end.

Choir: Amen.

FAST

A common feature of the symbolic and practical expression of religion, as stylized as the festival and the rite in its time—and usually in a dialectical relationship to them—is the fast, or time of abstinence and emotional release of transcendental grieving and repentance. This is a period such as the Christian Lent, the Jewish Yom Kippur, and the Muslim Ramadan. Though the fast may be a stylized and annually recurring ritual, it is no less deeply felt for that. The following is an account by an American woman, who lived in an Iraqi village for a year with her anthropologist husband, of a *kraya*, or women's meeting during the yearly Muslim fast of Ramadan. During this month devout Muslims neither eat nor drink from dawn to dusk, but they often sleep as much as possible in the daytime and meet at night to break the fast and hear the *Koran* and devotional stories from a mullah, or Muslim teacher. The commemoration in the passage below was of the Shi'ah tradition, which puts great emphasis on the heroic death of Hussein, a relative and successor of the prophet Muhammad who was, in Shi'ah eyes, cruelly killed by false Muslims. It was to that tragedy that these people turned to find a vehicle for their sorrowing emotions.

Guests of the Sheik

Elizabeth Warnock Fernea

Finally, when it seemed that not a single person more could be jammed into the court, the mullah stood up and clapped her hands to quiet the crowd. The two young women who sat near us took their places on each side of her (they were novices, I later found out, in training to be mullahs themselves) and the kraya began.

The mullah sat down and the two young girls stood to lead the congregation in a long, involved song with many responses. Gradually the women began to beat their breasts rhythmically, nodding their heads and beating in time to the pulse of the song, and occasionally joining in the choruses, or supplying spontaneous responses such as "A-hoo-ha!" or a long-drawn-out "Ooooooh!" This phase lasted perhaps ten minutes, the girls sank down into their places, and the mullah arose to deliver a short sermon. She began retelling the story of the killing and betrayal of the martyr Hussein, which is told every night during Ramadan and is the beginning of the important part of the kraya. At first two or three sobs could be heard, then perhaps twenty women had covered their heads with their abayahs and were weeping; in a few minutes the whole crowd was crying and sobbing loudly. When the mullah reached the most tragic parts of the story, she would stop and lead the congregation in a group chant, which started low and increased in volume until it reached the pitch of a full-fledged wail. Then she would stop dead again, and the result would be, by this time, a sincere sobbing and weeping as the women broke down after the tension of the wail.

I sat silently, frozen by the intensity of it all, and hoping that none of the women, and especially the mullah, would notice that I was sitting without beating my breast, without chanting or weeping —in fact without participating at all. I contemplated throwing my abayah over my head, as all the other women had done, so the hawk-eyed mullah would not be able to tell whether I was crying or not, but by this time I thought she was sufficiently carried away by the force of her own words so that she wouldn't have cared. I was right. Real tears were coursing down that hard, shrewd face as she told, for the hundred thousandth time probably, the story of the death of the martyr.

Excerpts from *Guests of the Sheik* by Elizabeth Fernea. Copyright © 1965 by Elizabeth Warnock Fernea. Used by permission of Doubleday & Company, Inc.

Abruptly the weeping stopped, the women were drying their eyes and everyone stood up. I nearly tripped and fell as I tried to rise, for my abayah was caught under me and one leg had fallen asleep in the cramped position in which I had been sitting for the past hour. Sherifa caught my shoulder as I stumbled—fortunately, for the mullah was beginning the third stage of the kraya. Flanked by her two novices, she stood in the center of the court rocking forward with her whole body at each beat, slowly but regularly, until the crowds of women formed concentric circles around her, and they too rocked in unison, singing and beating their breasts. Three older women joined the mullah in the center, throwing aside their chin veils so they might slap their bared chests.

"A-hoo-ha!" sounded the responses.

All her veils flying as she rocked, the mullah struck her book with her right hand to indicate a faster tempo, and the novices clapped and watched to make sure that all were following correctly. I shrank back out as the circles of women began to move counterclockwise in a near-ceremonial dance. A step to the left, accompanied by head-nodding, breast-beating, the clapping of the novices, the slap of the mullah's hard hand against the book, and the responses of "A-hoo-ha!" "*Ya Hussein*," they cried. The mullah increased the tempo again, the cries mounted in volume and intensity, the old women in the center bobbed in time to the beat, there was a loud slap against the Koran, a high long-drawn-out chant from the mullah, and everyone stopped in her tracks. The three old ladies who had bared their chests readjusted their veils, and many of the women stood silently for a moment, their eyes raised, their open hands held upward in an attitude of prayer and supplication. But the mullah was already conferring with her novices. The kraya was over.

The women began to stream out, smiling and chattering, drawing their veils over their faces and bidding each other good night. Sherifa was laughing with one of the novices. Fadhila led me over to our hostess, where we sat down for a final chat and cigarette before departing. It was hard to believe that these decorous and dignified ladies were the same women who, five minutes ago, had thrown themselves into a ritual of sorrow for the martyr. I was quite overcome by the episode and found it difficult to respond easily to the conversational overtures being made by my hostess.

Almost every evening during Ramadan I went to krayas—at the sheik's house, at Laila's house, at Abdulla's and Mohammed's. The tone of each kraya depended on the personality of the mullah, but the basic ritual remained the same: The *latmya* invocation with preliminary chant and breast-beating; the sermon, different for each day of Ramadan, but followed by the telling of Hussein's betrayal (*hadith*); the latmya again, at a faster pace, with the circles of women moving together in strict tempo, the spontaneous cries and wails, the profession of inspired penitence by the few women who join the mullah in the inner circle and finally the *da-a,* or moment of silence and prayer at the end. This final moment is considered to be the climax of the kraya, I was told, for then, in a state of purification, the women may ask great favors from Allah and expect to have them granted. Often these favors are requested conditionally. A woman may pray for a son, and vow that if her prayer is granted, she will hold krayas in her house during Ramadan for a stipulated number of years. Such vows are sacred, and if for some reason the woman cannot fulfill them, she may be released only by a gift to the mosque or to the mullah.

INITIATION

An essential component of the symbolic expression of any religion is initiation, or some formal process of entry into it that tells what is important about the nature of the individual and the divinely ordained cosmos and how the two can be symbolically and experientially brought together. There can be many initiations, however, even within one religion—simple rites for everyone, extremely strenuous passages for professionals, moderately difficult ones within religious sects that are voluntary but in principle open to all desirous of withdrawing to some extent from mass society. Some initiations presuppose a prior inner experience that has led the seeker to the rite, such as that expected by those Christian groups that practice believer's baptism; others expect the rite itself to induce the experience.

Fundamental to almost any initiation, though, are three steps outlined in books such as Arnold van Gennep's *The Rites of Passage* and Victor Turner's *The Ritual Process.* These are first a clear separation of the candidates from ordinary society, then a stage of what is called marginality or liminality when they are in a state of dissociation from ordinary society but extremely accessible to spiritual influx, and finally reaggregation or reincorporation when in a definite way they are rejoined to the religious community in their new status.

The following passage about baptism in a fundamentalist and pentecostal group on the West Indies island of St. Vincent makes the stages and other overtones of initiation vividly clear. Note how the special, separated role of the initiates is made evident by their white robes, note the dissociated spiritual states in the liminality phase, said to be special yet difficult, and note how reincorporation is handled in part through a spiritual mother-child relationship. Death and rebirth language and symbolism, a very important aspect of almost all initiation, is also evident in this passage. Leader, pointer, and mother are all titles of officers in this church.

Spirit-Possession Belief
and Trance Behavior
in Two Fundamentalist Groups
in St. Vincent

Jeannette H. Henney

The decision to accept baptism is the starting point for a series of rituals focusing on the baptismal candidate. In a ceremony known as "bowing," which takes place during the course of a regular meeting, the aspirant is separated from the congregation and introduced as a candidate. The bowing ceremony I witnessed was divided between two meetings. The pointer was absent on the first evening, and the two leaders and the mother who were officiating in his stead were not qualified to conduct all parts of the ritual. Several evenings later, the pointer completed the ceremony. At the first meeting, except for a lengthy comment on baptism by Leader M., the early part of the service followed the usual pattern. Leader M. then extended an invitation to "anyone who wants to give his heart to Christ Jesus" to "come now and bow." A man and a young woman went forward and knelt on the ground before him. The congregation stood and sang while Leader M. exhorted everyone to come to Jesus. A woman arranged the kneeling candidates, placing their hands in the positions they would be required to hold for the duration of each meeting attended before baptism: each held a lighted candle in the right hand, the left hand being held open with the palm up. Both hands were extended, waist high, at right angles to the body. The candidates kept their eyes closed and were instructed to meditate constantly on their sins.

From Jeannette H. Henney, "Spirit-Possession Belief and Trance Behavior in Two Fundamentalist Groups in St. Vincent," in *Trance, Healing, and Hallucination: Three Field Studies in Religious Experience*, ed. Felicitas D. Goodman, Jeannette H. Henney, and Esther Pressel, pp. 50–53. Copyright © 1974 by John Wiley & Sons, Inc. Reprinted by permission of John Wiley & Sons, Inc.

Leader P. addressed some remarks particularly to "those of you who are about to ax Jesus to give you some of that water." Mother A. spoke next. She put the Bible, with her lighted candle held on top of it, on the head of first one and then the other of the candidates, while praying over them. Holding the Bible and candle balanced on the man's head with one hand, she took the woman candidate's candle in her other hand, held it on the woman's head, prayed, marked the sign of the cross over the woman's head with the candle, and finally handed the candle back to her. She put the Bible on the head of each again and rang the bell over them. Taking the candle of each in turn, she then marked a cross with it before them. She helped them to rise from their knees, explaining that she had not yet had everything revealed to her, so she would leave the rest to the elder (Pointer B.). Before leaving them, however, she said, "Not only are you going to sit there with your hands open but you are going to repent every one of your sins. He is going to make of you a better child."

Pointer B. continued the rites at the next meeting. It was held at another church (Questelles; the first part had taken place at Lowmans), but the composition of the congregation was about the same. The man who had bowed was not present, but the pointer said that, even so, it was his duty to introduce the woman candidate to the Christ Jesus. During one of the early hymns, he used a piece of chalk to make a circle on the floor around the center pole. He made four straight lines out from the pole to the circle and within the quadrants thus formed proceeded to draw designs. Mother A. had put a lighted candle on the floor by the pole. He moved it to a place on one of the lines drawn out from the pole. Taking a glass of water and another candle, he dipped the unlighted end of the candle in the water and sprinkled his drawing with it. He then rang the bell in each of the four quadrants.

After the routine part of the service was over, Pointer B. gave a prayer book to Mother A. He directed the candidate to kneel on a pillow before him (this was a more elaborately furnished church than the other). With his hand on the woman's head, he prayed aloud asking the Holy Spirit to abide in her. While the seated congregation sang a hymn, Pointer B. put on the kneeling woman's head a lighted candle and then the Bible with the candle on top of it. He rang the bell beside her. The mother read the questions for a candidate for baptism from the prayer book, and the woman responded. The congregation sang another hymn while the pointer marked a cross on her head with the lighted candle and gave her three sips of water. He marked a cross on her forehead and her palms with chalk.

The pointer announced that he was going to "take a prove."

Mother A. made a cross on the woman's chest with the edge of the Bible and handed it to her. The candidate held it with both hands, the edges pointed toward her, and made the sign of the cross with it. After she opened it, Mother A. carefully noted where her thumbs touched the pages and took the book from her. Mother A. then read the three verses indicated by her thumbs on each page, and the pointer interpreted the message to the congregation.

The bowing ritual required several hours. The pointer, leaders, and Mother A. were frequently in various stages of dissociation, which, though seemingly hampering and retarding their activities considerably, at the same time seemed to augment the excitement and importance of the proceedings.

A period of preparation lasting from several weeks to several months follows for the candidates. The pointer decides when they are ready for the final baptism rite, but it is likely that he is influenced as much by the number of candidates he has been able to gather as he is by their state of preparedness—it is gratifying to be able to point to a goodly number of "children." According to Mother E., "the leader will give them [the candidates] the 51st psalm to read," to learn and be able to repeat back to him, and "they have to learn plenty other things." Mother O. stated that "when they are in the mercy seat, the leader and mothers teach them where to walk and how to speak in the way leading to the Lord—they [candidates] read and learn things from the Bible—and [they, i.e., leader and mothers] teach them the way to baptism." At the meetings, the candidates sit on the front bench, "the bench of repentance," and they "have their hand open, beggin' and askin' God to forgive them for all their sins while they are on the mercy seat."

The night before the baptism ceremony, the candidates remain in the church, praying, listening to words of consolation, and undergoing a shortened version of mourning. After white blindfolds are tied over their eyes, the candidates are laid on the ground— symbolizing death and eventual rebirth in baptism. Mother A. wrote her description of one baptism as follows:

> *Pointer have had the baptism on the 28th August, and it was a very fine one. . . . The baptism was done at Lowmans. On Saturday night, there was a vast amount of members turned out. The bands [blindfolds] for the candidates were thus signed by Pointer. Pointer have had a long lecturing to his seven Candidates (as you know, when he begins he does not want to stop). Passages of scripture had been read and explained. Candidates were thus question from a certain book. Many other heart touching consolations were given by others (Leaders, Mothers and who had thus gained opportunity). During the meeting, Candidates were ordered to kneel, whilst bands were placed on their hands and shoulders and afterwards tied on head*

by Pointer with the aid of myself and other Mothers; after which Pointer prayed. After a short period of singing and demonstrating, the meeting was thus brought to an end. That was about 1:50 a.m. The candidates were thus lain to have a rest with the company of some of the members.

On Sunday morning, members from various parts gathered in the church (though it was raining a lot). A short meeting was held, after which we all journeyed to the river. After reaching the river, the meeting were commenced, Baptism lesson were read and meeting carried on. One or two persons prayed, hymns were sung, then Pointer taking the cross from cross bearer, pushed his way through water. (Before Pointer go in river the water was consecrated.) He prayed, sung a hymn, then beckoned the cross bearer to come to him. The cross bearer was placed in an opposite direction, so that Candidates can be plunged just to the foot of the cross. A hymn was sung then Candidates were beckon to be brought (one by one). Each Candidate were spoken to before being plunged . . . they were taken to and taken from Pointer by two mothers. At intervals, the Candidates as they go in water were taken to a sheltered place where they were undressed by myself and other Mothers. Even too Mother B., Mother R., Pointer and I replaced fresh bands. After which we all marched from there singing back to church. For a short time in church, meeting was held, then lunch were required. After lunch, meeting was called in. Many sweet sermons were unfurled, by leaders, pointers, mothers and other elders who gained opportunity. Then washing and anointing was done (during service) by myself, Mother B., Mother R. and Pointer B. At intervals candidates were put to prayer and then testified.

Dissociation, more violent than usual for Shakers, is reported to be common for baptismal candidates. One mother described them as shaking so uncontrollably that it was necessary to support them lest they fall back into the water. Shakers obviously enjoy the baptismal ceremony. They describe fondly the beauty of the candidates garbed in white and proudly display their processional banners and the cross under which the candidates are plunged. One woman, however, admitted that it was difficult to be a candidate.

PUBLIC SYMBOLS

It is important to realize that there are at least two kinds of symbols. Public symbols focus and reflect the general sense of meaning and identity of a society, and private symbols reflect what is important to an individual. Public symbols, then, are the American flag or the cross on a church, and private symbols are those of a poet or artist. The following passage, from an important book dealing with these topics, discusses the *public image*, or generally accepted picture of the way the universe is. While the public image may not be precisely the same as a public symbol, it is public religious and other symbols that usually validate and articulate the public image, especially in traditional societies. It was, therefore, Christian public symbols that caused medieval maps to project an image of the world centered on Jerusalem. As the author suggests, in the modern world the standard public image of the cosmos and the world is one based on scientific and mathematical symbol systems, although there are important communities or contexts—more than private but less than public in the fullest sense of the word—in which religious symbols shape the meaning orientation, at least, of the cosmic image.

The Image

Kenneth E. Boulding

The image not only makes society, society continually remakes the image. This hen and egg process is perhaps the most important key to the understanding of the dynamics of society. The basic bond of any society, culture, subculture, or organization is a "public image," that is, an image the essential characteristics of which are shared by the individuals participating in the group. It is with the dynamics of the public image that we shall chiefly be concerned in this chapter. We must not suppose, of course, that society has no influence on private, unshared images or that these unshared images have no influence on society. Indeed, every public image begins in the mind of some single individual and only becomes public as it is transmitted and shared. Nevertheless, an enormous part of the activity of each society is concerned with the transmission and protection of its public image; that set of images regarding space, time, relation, evaluation, etc., which is shared by the mass of its people.

A public image almost invariably produces a "transcript"; that is, a record in more or less permanent form which can be handed down from generation to generation. In primitive nonliterate societies the transcript takes the form of verbal rituals, legends, poems, ceremonials, and the like, the transmission of which from

From Kenneth E. Boulding, *The Image* (Ann Arbor, Mich.: University of Michigan, 1956), pp. 64–66. Reprinted by permission of University of Michigan Press.

generation to generation is always one of the principal activities of the group. The invention of writing marks the beginning of the "disassociated transcript"—a transcript which is in some sense independent of the transcriber, a communication independent of the communicator. As we have already noticed, the transcript of society has been in process of rapid development and elaboration in the past few centuries. Beginning with the inventing of printing, and especially with the coming of the camera, the movie, the phonograph, and the tape recorder the elaboration of the transcript has proceeded to the point where an enormous number of aspects of life and experience can be recorded directly. There are still large parts of the image, however, which can only be transcribed in symbolic form. Generations yet unborn may be able to see President Eisenhower in three-D as he appeared to the present-day observer. They will be able to hear the exact cadences of his voice as well as read the words he has written. We are still, however, unable to record touch, taste, or smell. We have no direct means of transcribing sensations, emotions, or feelings except through the crowded channels of symbolic representation.

An effective transcript has a great effect in creating a public image, that is, in ensuring that the images of the various individuals who have access to the transcript are identical or nearly so. As an example of the building-up of a public image through the development of a transcript we might consider the formation of maps. The spatial image can be transcribed very briefly and commodiously in the form of a map. The map itself, however, has a profound effect on our spatial image. When we look at the crudely constructed charts of the South Sea Islanders they mean very little to us because we visualize the sea as a plain blue surface dotted with multicolored dots which we interpret as islands. The South Sea Islanders probably visualize their space in a somewhat different way in terms of the things you have to do to get from one place to another, the stars you have to observe, the directions you have to go, the courses you have to keep. Instead of being a plain blue surface their space is a series of intersecting lines. The Romans had only vague ideas of the shape of their own empire. They knew pretty well, however, how far it was from Rome wherever they happened to be, and their maps indicate this spatial conception. The maps of the Middle Ages show the world centering in Jerusalem. The shapes were unimportant. The theological symbolism was the vital thing. With the coming of surveying, trigonometry, and accurate measurements the map becomes an exact representative of the bird's-eye view. The invention of latitude and longitude reduced the multidirectional space of earlier days to two simple directions, north-south, east-west. The gradual exploration of the globe leads to a closure of geography. This has profound effects upon all parts of the image. Primitive man lives in a world which has a spatial unknown, a dread frontier populated by the heated imagination. For modern man the world is a closed and completely explored surface. This is a radical change in spatial viewpoint. It produced effects in all other spheres of life.

PRIVATE SYMBOLS

The following poem, "Auguries of Innocence," by William Blake (1757–1827) suggests the nature of private symbolism in a powerful spiritual and poetic imagination. The basic message of this poem is the inter-relatedness of all things, especially on the moral level: heedlessness and cruelty on the smallest microcosmic level represent and lead to the fundamental evils of the universe; conversely all that is good, even if as unobtrusive as wandering deer, images fundamental goodness. As the opening quatrain vividly states, the infinite and eternal appear in very small and almost over-looked details—details, that is, from our ordinary perspective. What makes Blake's images striking is that he was not a person of ordinary observation; unlike most of us, he saw *through* not *with* the eye, seeing things in their eternal meaning and from the perspective of the soul. In this sense, many of his symbols of good and evil are private, for they come from him and no one else. Yet, of course, the figures of poets and artists cannot be wholly private, like the colors of one's most secret dreams, for their task is communication; they must conjure up new images that nonetheless can strike a response in others. In this poem Blake has combined private with public symbols. While the orchestration here is fresh and gripping, individual symbols are often common cruelties of which nearly everyone is vaguely aware or are from folk tradition (the hunted hare, the fly killed by a wanton boy). New Testament images are woven through the lines (the lamb, the mocker of the infant's faith), and the incarnation of God in human form in Jesus Christ is subtly but forcefully suggested in the last four lines. Yet so unusual is Blake's angle of vision that even old public symbols become new private symbols—with just enough of the old remaining to make the new meaning stick in the reader's mind.

Auguries of Innocence

William Blake

To see a world in a grain of sand,
*   And a heaven in a wild flower;*
Hold infinity in the palm of your hand,
*   And eternity in an hour.*

A Robin Redbreast in a cage
Puts all heaven in a rage;
A dove-house filled with doves and pigeons
Shudders hell through all its regions.
A dog starved at his master's gate
Predicts the ruin of the state;
A game-cock clipped and armed for fight
Doth the rising sun affright;
A horse misused upon the road
Calls to Heaven for human blood.
Every wolf's and lion's howl
Raises from hell a human soul;
Each outcry of the hunted hare
A fibre from the brain doth tear;
A skylark wounded on the wing
Doth make a cherub cease to sing.
He who shall hurt the little wren
Shall never be beloved by men;
He who the ox to wrath has moved
Shall never be by woman loved;
He who shall train the horse to war
Shall never pass the Polar Bar.
The wanton boy that kills the fly
Shall fell the spider's enmity;
He who torments the chafer's sprite
Weaves a bower in endless night.
The caterpillar on the leaf
Repeats to thee thy mother's grief;
The wild deer wandering here and there
Keep the human soul from care:

From *The Poems, with Specimens of the Prose Writings, of William Blake,* prefatory notice by Joseph Skipsey (London: Walter Scott, 1888), pp. 208–13.

The lamb misused breeds public strife,
And yet forgives the butcher's knife.
Kill not the moth nor butterfly,
For the last judgment draweth nigh;
The beggar's dog and widow's cat,
Feed them and thou shalt grow fat.
Every tear from every eye
Becomes a babe in eternity;
The bleat, the bark, bellow and roar,
Are waves that beat on Heaven's shore.
The bat that flits at close of eve
Has left the brain that won't believe;
The owl that calls upon the night
Speaks the unbeliever's fright.
The gnat that sings his summer's song
Poison gets from Slander's tongue;
The poison of the snake and newt
Is the sweat of Envy's foot;
The poison of the honey-bee
Is the artist's jealousy;
The strongest poison ever known
Came from Caesar's laurel-crown.

Nought can deform the human race
Like to the armourer's iron brace;
The soldier armed with sword and gun
Palsied strikes the summer's sun.
When gold and gems adorn the plough,
To peaceful arts shall Envy bow.
The beggar's rags fluttering in air
Do to rags the heavens tear;
The prince's robes and beggar's rage
Are toadstools on the miser's bags.
One mite wrung from the labourer's hands
Shall buy and sell the miser's lands,
Or, if protected from on high,
Shall that whole nation sell and buy;
The poor man's farthing is worth more
Then all the gold on Afric's shore.
The whore and gambler, by the state
Licensed, build that nation's fate;
The harlot's cry from street to street
Shall weave Old England's winding-sheet;

The winner's shout, the loser's curse,
Shall dance before dead England's hearse.

He who mocks the infant's faith
Shall be mocked in age and death;
He who shall teach the child to doubt
The rotten grave shall ne'er get out;
He who respects the infant's faith
Triumphs over hell and death.
The babe is more than swaddling-bands
Throughout all these human lands;
Tools were made, and born were hands,
Every farmer understands.
The questioner who sits so sly
Shall never know how to reply.
He who replies to words of doubt
Doth put the light of knowledge out;
A puddle, or the cricket's cry,
Is to doubt a fit reply.
The child's toys and the old man's reasons
Are the fruits of the two seasons.
The emmet's inch and eagle's mile
Make lame philosophy to smile.
A truth that's told with bad intent
Beats all the lies you can invent.
He who doubts from what he sees
Will ne'er believe, do what you please;
If the sun and moon should doubt,
They'd immediately go out.

Every night and every morn
Some to misery are born;
Every morn and every night
Some are born to sweet delight;
Some are born to sweet delight,
Some are born to endless night.
Joy and woe are woven fine,
A clothing for the soul divine;
Under every grief and pine
Runs a joy with silken twine.
It is right it should be so;
Man was made for joy and woe;
And, when this we rightly know,
Safely through the world we go.

We are led to believe a lie
When we see *with* not *through* the eye,
Which was born in a night to perish in a night
When the soul slept in beams of light.
God appears and God is light
To those poor souls who dwell in night;
But doth a human form display
To those who dwell in realms of day.

CHAPTER FIVE

TRANSCENDENT
ASSEMBLIES:
SOCIOLOGY OF RELIGION

Religion, as we know it, is never really solitary. Faith reaches upward toward the transcendent that every person wishes to know inwardly, but it also reaches outward into the surrounding community. The greater-than-self experience religion offers is both cosmic and social. In religion, we can lose the burden of lonely individuality both to harmonize with the infinite and to unite with a band of fellow-believers. Indeed, these two dimensions reinforce each other. Even the most estranged hermit, worshipping alone in the heart of the loneliest desert on earth, is still worshipping as a member of religious society. Somewhere he must have learned at least the seeds of the words and concepts through which he now calls on whatever gods are his; these imprints bind him from within to society, however isolated from it is his physical frame. Most of us, of course, exchange words and feelings about religion along with other things almost daily, and although each of us may sort them out in a somewhat different way, we cannot honestly say that very much of what we think is ours alone and not born from these matrices of social interaction. At the same time, society with its structures is usually seen as dependent on the sacred that gives it authority. It is the religion that shows why the particular institutions of the society and its moral norms have divine as well as human sanction. Religion can implicitly threaten dissidents against them with spiritual as well as temporal adversity.

In studying religious groups and the relation of religion to society, there are several things to look for. First, we must remember that no social group of any sort is really static and unchanging. Every human group is in process and is changing, whether slowly or rapidly, from one form and one stage to another. It is important, then, to look for signs of process as well as at the present structure of a group. Changes are particularly likely to be far-reaching and significant during the first two or three generations of a religious movement, as it transits from a fluid but spirit-filled group to an institution with channels for continuing the teaching in a systematic way; it is very important and instructive to look for evidences of this process in new movements.

Second, we must look for the relation of the religion to its surrounding society and its relation to the elites, the holders of power, privilege, and education, in the society. Is it an *established* religion that pervades the culture, or a new *emergent* group rising up over against the prevailing faith and estranged from it in important ways? Is it a *great tradition* religious system with close ties to the elite and the literate cultural stream, or are we looking at popular or folk beliefs? If it is an emergent group, is it *intensive*, seeking a stricter adherence to the accepted religion and scriptures than that attributed to the run-of-the-mill ecclesiastics, or is it *expansive*, striving to bring together ideas from near and far and perhaps seeking mystical experience more than legalistic purity?

Third, we must look for types of leadership and with them for the structures of interpersonal relationship within the religion. Is the leadership authoritarian or open? Does the group essentially center on the charisma of the leader, or is the leader just a functionary within a group who commands loyalty for other reasons? On the matter of interpersonal relations, religious groups can range from total institutions, such as monasteries and communes where virtually every detail of daily life is religiously and institutionally conditioned, to groups whose members have no interpersonal contact except at occasional services.

In this chapter we look at examples of most of these patterns within the sociology of religion and then at religion in two kinds of social settings: as the legitimation of a relatively stable social and political order and in a time of rapid social change. Writers in this chapter include Max Weber and Joachim Wach on religious groups; Wladimir D'Ormesson and Oscar Lewis on established religion; Melford E. Spiro and Jacob Needleman on emergent religions; S. C. Hughson, O. H. C., on monastic life; Peter Worsley and S. Wells Williams on religious leadership; and William Theodore de Bary and George Weller on religion and society.

PROCESS
IN RELIGIOUS GROUPS

The following selection from the writings of the influential sociologist of religion Max Weber (1864–1920) gives insight into the developmental life of religious movements. In the first section, we note that religions begin with the type of person who may broadly be called a prophet and that his appeal depends in large part on a powerful charisma. In the second passage, we see something of what happens next. A community or congregation forms around the prophet and after the founder's departure perpetuates his work as it becomes *routinized,* or organized, with priestly or bureaucratic leadership and regular services.

The Sociology of Religion

Max Weber

The Prophet

What is a prophet, from the perspective of sociology?

We shall forego here any consideration of the general question regarding the "bringer of salvation" (*Heilbringer*) as raised by Breysig. Not every anthropomorphic god is a deified bringer of salvation, whether external or internal salvation. And certainly not every provider of salvation became a god or even a savior, although such phenomena were widespread.

We shall understand "prophet" to mean a purely individual bearer of charisma, who by virtue of his mission proclaims a religious doctrine or divine commandment. No radical distinction will be drawn between a "renewer of religion" who preaches an older revelation, actual or supposititious, and a "founder of religion" who claims to bring completely new deliverances. The two types merge into one another. In any case, the formation of a new religious community need not be the result of doctrinal preaching by prophets, since it may be produced by the activities of non-prophetic reformers. Nor shall we be concerned in this context with the

From Max Weber, *The Sociology of Religion,* translated by Ephraim Fischoff, pp. 46–47, 60–62. Copyright © 1922, 1956 by J. C. B. Mohr (Paul Sieback). English translation (from the fourth edition) copyright © 1963 by Beacon Press. Reprinted by permission of Beacon Press.

question whether the followers of a prophet are more attracted to his person, as in the cases of Zoroaster, Jesus, and Muhammad, or to his doctrine, as in the cases of Buddha and the prophets of Israel.

For our purposes here, the personal call is the decisive element distinguishing the prophet from the priest. The latter lays claim to authority by virtue of his service in a sacred tradition, while the prophet's claim is based on personal revelation and charisma. It is no accident that almost no prophets have emerged from the priestly class. As a rule, the Indian teachers of salvation were not Brahmins, nor were the Israelite prophets priests. Zoroaster's case is exceptional in that there exists a possibility that he may have descended from the hieratic nobility. The priest, in clear contrast, dispenses salvation by virtue of his office. Even in cases in which personal charisma may be involved, it is the hierarchical office that confers legitimate authority upon the priest as a member of a corporate enterprise of salvation.

But the prophet, like the magician, exerts his power simply by virtue of his personal gifts. Unlike the magician, however, the prophet claims definite revelations, and the core of his mission is doctrine or commandment, not magic. Outwardly, at least, the distinction is fluid, for the magician is frequently a knowledgeable expert in divination, and sometimes in this alone. At this stage, revelation functions continuously as oracle or dream interpretation. Without prior consultation with the magician, no innovations in communal relations could be adopted in primitive times. To this day, in certain parts of Australia, it is the dream revelations of magicians that are set before the councils of clan heads for adoption, and it is a mark of secularization that this practice is receding.

On the other hand, it was only under very unusual circumstances that a prophet succeeded in establishing his authority without charismatic authentication, which in practice meant magic. At least the bearers of new doctrine practically always needed such validation. It must not be forgotten for an instant that the entire basis of Jesus' own legitimation, as well as his claim that he and only he knew the Father and that the way to God led through faith in him alone, was the magical charisma he felt within himself. It was doubtless this consciousness of power, more than anything else, that enabled him to traverse the road of the prophets. During the apostolic period of early Christianity and thereafter the figure of the wandering prophet was a constant phenomenon. There was always required of such prophets a proof of their possession of particular gifts of the spirit, of special magical or ecstatic abilities.

The Religious Congregation, Preaching, and Pastoral Care

If his prophecy is successful, the prophet succeeds in winning permanent helpers. These may be apostles (as Bartholomaeus translates the term of the Gathas), disciples (Old Testament and Hindu), comrades (Hindu and Islamic), or followers (Isaiah and the New Testament). In all cases they are personal devotees of the prophet, in contrast to priests and soothsayers who are organized into guilds or official hierarchies. We shall devote additional consideration to this relationship in our analysis of the forms of domination. Moreover, in addition to these permanent helpers, who are active co-workers with the prophet in his mission and who generally also possess some special charismatic qualifications, there is a circle of followers comprising those who support him with lodging, money, and services and who expect to obtain their salvation through his mission. They may, on occasion, group themselves into a congregation for a particular temporary activity or on a continuous basis.

A "community" or "congregation" in the specifically religious sense (for this term is also employed to denote an association of neighboring groups which may have originated for economic or for fiscal or other political purposes) does not arise solely in connection with prophecy in the particular sense used here. Nor does it arise in connection with every type of prophecy. Primarily, a religious community arises in connection with a prophetic movement as a result of routinization (*Veralltäglichung*), i.e., as a result of the process whereby either the prophet himself or his disciples secure the permanence of his preaching and the congregation's distribution of grace, hence insuring the economic existence of the enterprise and those who man it, and thereby monopolizing as well the privileges reserved for those charged with religious functions.

It follows from this primacy of routinization in the formation of religious congregations that congregations may also be formed around mystagogues and priests of nonprophetic religions. For the mystagogue, indeed, the presence of a congregation is a normal phenomenon. The magician, in contrast, exercises his craft independently or, if a member of a guild, serves a particular neighborhood or political group, not a specific religious congregation. The congregations of the mystagogues, like those of the Eleusinian practitioners of mysteries, generally remained associations that were open to the outer world and fluid in form. Whoever was desirous of salvation would enter into a relationship, generally temporary, with the mystagogue and his assistants. The Eleusinian mysteries, for example, always remained a regional community, independent of particular localities.

The situation was quite different in the case of exemplary prophets who unconditionally demonstrated the way of salvation by their personal example, as did, for example, the mendicant monks of Mahavira and the Buddha, who belonged to a narrower exemplary community. Within this narrower community the disciples, who might still have been personally associated with the prophet, would exert particular authority. Outside of the exemplary community, however, there were pious devotees (e.g., the *Upasakas* of India) who did not go the whole way of salvation for themselves, but sought to achieve a relative optimum of salvation by demonstrating their devotion to the exemplary saint. These devotees tended to lack altogether any fixed status in the religious community, as was originally the case with the Buddhist *Upasakas*. Or even might they be organized into some special group with fixed rules and obligations. This regularly happened when priests, priest-like counselors, or mystagogues like the Buddhist *bonzes*, who were entrusted with particular responsibilities, were separated out from the exemplary community. This had not been the case in the earliest stages of Buddhism, but the prevailing Buddhist practice was the free organization of devotees into occasional religious communities, which the majority of mystagogues and exemplary prophets shared with the temple priesthoods of particular deities from the organized pantheon. The economic existence of these congregations was secured by endowments and maintained by sacrificial offerings and other gifts provided by persons with religious needs.

MEANING
IN RELIGIOUS GROUPS

The establishment of routinized religious groups does not mean a lessening of the religious quality of the experience from that of the days of the founder, though it may to some extent mark a change in its nature. The following passage from the sociologist of religion Joachim Wach explores the religious meaning of the fellowship that routinization ideally allows to continue to be felt and shows that this dimension is essential to religion.

The Comparative Study of Religions

Joachim Wach

There are three traditional ways in which religious experience has found expression: in thought, in action, and in fellowship. It would be a great mistake to look upon expression in fellowship as one which may or may not be added to expression through belief and through *cultus*. All three forms are constitutive, yet only in the context of communion can the intellectual and the practical attain their true meaning. Myth and doctrine comprise the articulation in thought of what has been experienced in the confrontation of Ultimate Reality. *Cultus* is the acting out of this confrontation in worship and service. Both give direction and "center" the community formed by those who are united in a particular religious experience, while the community cultivates, shapes, and develops in thought and action the expression of its religious experience.

The religious act will always be *somebody's* religious act. Modern Western man is all too prone to think of the solitary individual first and last, yet the study of primitive religions shows that, individual experiences notwithstanding, religion is generally a group affair. Marett puts it thus: "Primarily and directly, the subject, the owner as it were, of religious experience is the religious society, not the individual," and "the religious society rather than the religious individual must be treated as primarily responsible for the feelings, thought and actions that make up historical religion." A Hasidic rabbi once said that a prayer which is not spoken in the name of all Israel is no prayer at all. In most important religious ceremonies a large number of people participate in order to make them possible. Even the highly individualistic sectarians of Scandinavia believe that

From Joachim Wach, *The Comparative Study of Religions* (New York: Columbia University Press, 1958), pp. 121–24. Notes omitted. Reprinted by permission of Columbia University Press.

conversion can only be experienced in the cult-community of the brethren. There is no denying that on a higher level of civilization a more strongly individualized attitude developed. Not only the outstanding individual (king, priest) but also the average devotee will cultivate his communion with the numen, say his own special prayer, and perform his personal worship. This is eminently the case in the great world religions. The Christian theologian Ferré says that man, being God's creature and child, is "by nature more of a *socius* than of an individual." Throughout the history of religious thought, the action of one man has been indissolubly tied to the thought and action of another. The old phrase *unus Christianus nullus Christianus* ("One Christian is no Christian") is true of all other religions as well. The French scholar Mouroux has stated it well: "In union with his brethren, a person gives himself to God who is the Father of all. The religious relationship which is profoundly individual cannot be individualistic." And he has added that one can seek and find God only on the condition of helping others to seek and find Him jointly. In this respect contemporary attempts to recreate religious fellowship in modern industrial societies and large urban areas are very significant. "The new *community*, built on a religious basis, about a 'charged' symbol, is the important thing."

Numerous minds of many generations help to weave the fabric of myth, and doctrine is often the result of the reflection and deliberation of a long line of religious thinkers. It takes equally long until, through the cooperation of the members of a group over many generations, the ritual which both creates and directs action and interaction has evolved. Frequently a group is considered indispensable for a valid religious act.

In and through the religious act the religious group is constituted. There is no religion which has not evolved a type of religious fellowship. Hocking asked why the *homo religiosus* tries to build a group; he answered it by saying that "the presence of his group is the continued experimental corroboration (and development) both of his truth and of his way of putting it to work." From the point of view of the anthropologist, Malinowski and Radcliffe-Brown have stressed the role and particularly the effect of religion on society. In several other of my works, I have stressed the double relationship which characterizes the religious group, as distinct from other types of grouping. The collective and individual relation of its members to the numen is primary and the relation of the members of the group to each other is secondary. In personal experience the latter relationship comes first but it is ontologically dependent upon the orientation to the numen. In another context we have said that "the nature, intensity, duration, and organization of a religious group depends upon the way in which its members experience God, conceive of, and communicate with Him, and upon the way they experience fellowship, conceive of it, and practice it." We further stressed that "the religious group more than other types of association, presents itself as a microcosm with its own laws, outlook on life, attitude and atmosphere." Except for certain developments in the modern Western world, there has always been a consciousness of the numinous character inherent in the religious communion, in the primitive cult-group, in the *ecclesia*, the *Kahal*, the *ummah*, or the *samgha*. Only where historical developments have led to a degeneration in the life of the fellowship and hence to a weakening of this feeling will the rationalist or the mystic or the spiritualist protest against the actual manifestation or even the idea of a communion and community in religion. The numinous character of the fellowship which might be reflected in myths or formulated in doctrine is not necessarily the result of a venerable age, as some think, but is due to the "power and glory" which the fellowship assumes as a divine foundation. It is important to realize that there is this dimension to the notion of the religious community, because the secularized minds of many modern Westerners cannot understand it except in purely sociological terms.

THE GREAT TRADITION IN ESTABLISHED RELIGION

Established religion is not necessarily religion maintained in a privileged position by the state but indicates a religion overwhelmingly privileged and pervasive in a culture, such as Catholicism in Spain or Islam in Arabia. Such a religion has certain characteristics. It is deeply intertwined with the land's literature and art and also with its folk customs. Holidays, burial customs, ways of initiating newborn infants, and even greetings and sayings reflect it. Its churches or temples are generally conspicuous, and its clergy important figures. Its institutional expression is highly routinized. Its intellectual life is replete with books and well-trained scholars, even though the folk participants may have little access to this side of the tradition. It has, theoretically, strict doctrinal and moral codes but must find ways in practice of adjusting these since it also has responsibility for all members of its community regardless of level of spiritual advancement. Apart from sectarian movements within them that may be emergent religion, the great religions of the world and the major denominations therein function as established religion in most of their respective culture areas.

Within established religion, however, two styles of religious life appear: they may be called, following Robert Redfield, the great and little traditions. The first is the religion of the religious elite—the clergy, scholars, and highly educated laity. The second is that of the ordinary participants for whom, in traditional society, it merges with folk religion. The great tradition is literate, historical-minded, and bureaucratic in its understanding of the religion's institutional life; its people are oriented toward the worldwide and historical perspective, toward systematic doctrine and worship, toward their role as custodians of the tradition, toward facts and figures, and toward a sense of paternal responsibility for but not identity with more ordinary members.

Two selections depicting aspects of Roman Catholicism about the time of the 1950 Holy Year illustrate the meaning of the great and little traditions. The first, by a French Roman Catholic writer, discusses the role of the papacy; the terms in which it is discussed beautifully reveal the quintessentially great tradition way that office was conceptualized at the time—with sense of its administrative supremacy, ancient heritage, and worldwide vision. There is even a certain revealing note in the author's saying that the pilgrims who came to Rome in the Holy Year "confusedly but profoundly" sensed this. To give a contrasting picture of the little tradition from within the same religion, the second passage is an account of Roman Catholic life in a Mexican peasant community; it is based on anthropological field work done at about the same time.

It should be emphasized that neither of these two accounts portrays Roman Catholicism as it is now, whether in Rome or Mexico or anywhere else. Since 1950, immense changes have been wrought by the Second Vatican Council and its aftermath (the Vatican Council referred to in the D'Ormesson passage is the first, of 1870, which defined papal infallibility) and by rapid social change that has transformed peasant life in Latin America and elsewhere. The 1950 Holy Year, a high point in the pontificate of Pope Pius XII, is in fact selected as the year for this comparative study since it was one of the last years when traditional styles of both great and little traditions still persisted in much of the world with a fairly high degree of integrity, making their distinctive characters easily detectable. Both traditions still exist but are now much more fluid.

The Papacy

Wladimir D'Ormesson

More than three million pilgrims of all nationalities and all races made their way to Rome during the Holy Year of 1950; in the Holy Year of 1900 there were only 300,000, and in 1925, 582,000.

Most of these pilgrims—and especially all those who came long distances—in a sense "discovered" the papacy. In a disjointed world, rent by opposing forces, they came to understand better than before what the unity of a spiritual society which has existed for twenty centuries and has brotherly harmony as its earthly principle should mean. The opinions and comments constantly to be heard from the lips of these visitors were striking and unanimous in this respect. As in a flash, they came to realize what is meant by the plenitude of the high office of the papacy. To this I can testify.

That office is in fact complex in its nature. To understand all that it comprises it is perhaps necessary to live for some time in Rome, and little by little to realize all that is contained in the history of that capital of the Christian world and remains so miraculously alive today. Then will it be seen that there are in the papal office, if I may put it so, ten distinct elements. Let us try to define them, and then to show their significance.

1. According to the Catholic faith the pope is the Vicar of Jesus Christ on earth; that is, the 258th successor of St. Peter, the Prince of the Apostles. We have seen in the first part of this small book on what facts, traditions and texts we Catholics base this conviction.

2. The pope is the Bishop of Rome, and it is precisely because he is the Bishop of Rome—that is, the head of the Church of Rome—that he exercises supreme magistracy over the whole Catholic Church. It is to be observed in this connection that the Sacred College which elects the pope is composed of seventy cardinals, and that each of these cardinals is either one of the six titular bishops of the suburbicarian sees of Rome, or one of the priests of the fifty-eight parishes which composed the ancient diocese of Rome, or one of the deacons of those parishes. The pope, then, is still elected by the senior clergy of Rome. It is, I repeat, as head of the Church of Rome that he is pope.

By permission of Hawthorn Books, Inc., from *The Papacy* by W. D'Ormesson, translated by Michael Derrick, pp. 106–12. Hawthorn Books, Inc., copyright © 1959. All rights reserved.

3.   The pope is the head of that immense international society called the Catholic Apostolic and Roman Church, spread—unevenly—through the five continents of the world and including about 472 million members, as well as a highly-organized ecclesiastical hierarchy. He alone has the power to "feed" this flock; to rule and govern this Church.

4.   The pope is the head of the clergy of the Catholic Church, which comprises seventy cardinals, ten resident patriarchs, five titular patriarchs, 307 resident metropolitan archbishops, 42 resident archbishops who are not metropolitans, 1,232 resident bishops, 883 titular archbishops and bishops, 79 prelates and abbots nullius, twelve apostolic administrators, nineteen prelates of Eastern rite, 206 vicars apostolic, 122 prefects apostolic, seven missions *sui juris*, 365,000 priest, one million nuns, and about 270,000 male religious.

5.   The pope is the guardian of the deposit of Catholic faith and of revelation, a deposit which enshrines the sacred books of the Old and New Testaments and a tradition which has been handed down from generation to generation until today.

6.   The pope is the supreme Doctor of the Church. When he speaks *ex cathedra*—that is when in his capacity as Shepherd and Teacher of all Christians he defines a doctrine concerning faith or morals—he is infallible, which means that the definitions of the Sovereign Pontiff are unchangeable. (We shall return to this later, and will examine more closely this supreme attribute of the pontifical power which, having been the object of passionate controversy for centuries, was solemnly defined by the Vatican Council.)

7.   The pope is a sovereign. He reigns over a state that is recognized by all states. It is worth observing that even the Soviet Union recognizes him to be a head of state. We had proof of this in the *démarche* made in 1956 by the *Chargé d'Affaires* of the Soviet Embassy in Italy, to the Apostolic Nuncio in Italy. The Soviet *Chargé d'Affaires* was instructed by his government to communicate to the Holy See—and for this he made use of the services of the Nuncio in Italy as an intermediary—certain documents concerning proposals for disarmament; and it was specified that this *démarche* should be made to the pope as Head of the State of the Vatican City. As I have already indicated, the sovereignty of the pope is illustrated by various facts, among which is the presence of forty-seven foreign diplomatic missions at the Holy See. The pope, by the very nature of his sovereignty, holds a rank apart among the heads of states whether they be monarchs or presidents of republics. He receives their ceremonial visits, and does not return such honours except through a cardinal.

8. Historically, the pope is the heir of the Roman Pontiffs, and this title covers both the old Roman Empire and the Christian era. By a gradual substitution which came about after the time of Constantine, the papacy—we have already seen this briefly—little by little filled the gaps caused by the decline and fall of the Empire. After the darkness of the barbarian invasions, a Christian Rome arose from the ashes of pagan Rome. In a certain sense it was the pope who became the head of this new empire. This historic power is shown in numerous rites and in the splendour of many monuments.

9. The pope—or rather the papacy—is the crucible where spiritual currents from the Hebrew, Asian, Egyptian, Greek, Celtic and German worlds meet and are re-formed. What we call the Roman Church is a fusion of these diverse spiritualities, reduced to their very essence and condensed and clarified by the Latin genius.

10. The pope, then, if I may put it this way, is a keystone. The papacy commands and upholds an enormous structure; one that is and must be the most many-sided that exists. Is it possible to imagine, despite the unity of Catholic faith and discipline, moods and temperaments more different than those of the Church in France, Spain, the United States, Britain, Latin America, Ireland and so on? Nevertheless, all these Churches form but one single Church. They march together, so to speak, keeping in step. They are sheep of the same flock, and the pope is their only shepherd. It is in him that the unity of the Catholic Apostolic and Roman Church is expressed, which is the greatest strength of the Church.

Such are, I believe, the various aspects or traditions of the supreme Magisterium of the Church, and it is impossible to separate them. One cannot grasp the traditional role of the papacy, the reality that is both Roman and universal, without admitting each one of its sources, and their fusion. Anyone who took into account only one of these aspects, traditions or sources would make a grave error. It is this that sometimes makes the supreme Magisterium difficult to grasp for those who are only mindful of its purely evangelical side. On the other hand, when these various elements are brought together, and when it is understood that they are commanded and ordered, then all that the office of the papacy entails, that of a lord and that of a servant, with its abstractions and realities, spiritual heights and temporal commitments, purity and pomp, gentleness and inflexibility, authority and prudence, its "Romanity" and its universality, can be judged.

Confusedly but profoundly the pilgrims who came to Rome

during the Holy Year, and took part in some of the magnificent jubilee celebrations, felt all this. Pilgrims of all languages and races who came to kneel at the tomb of the first Apostle and, after the passage of twenty centuries, before the throne of his successor, gave Rome its highest sense of being the capital of Christendom. When Pius XII appeared he personified the fact of Catholic unity. In this world, torn apart by feverish passions and ideologies, where those who oppose a civilization based on Christian faith use all their strength and tenacity to break such a unity and to undo the bonds which hold it together, the office of the Roman Pontiff assumed a vital significance such as can only be matched by looking far back into history.

On November 26th, 1950, one month before the end of the Holy Year, there took place in St. Peter's basilica a great ceremony, and one which was particularly filled with meaning. The Greek or Byzantine rite was followed when, in the presence of the pope, the Melchite Patriarch celebrated and seventeen archbishops and bishops of the Byzantine rite—among them two Russians, a Ukrainian, a Ruthenian and a Greek—concelebrated with him. This unusual Mass not only illustrated the union of the non-dissident Eastern Churches in the See of Peter. The very fact that it was celebrated according to the Byzantine or Greek rite—which differs only very slightly from the Orthodox Russian rite—showed that the unity of the Christian Church in all that part of the world depends only on the question of the supreme authority. The faith, the holy sacrifice of the Mass, the liturgy, are the same. I pen these words in hope.

We return now to one of the essential attributes of the papacy— the question of papal infallibility, as defined by the Vatican Council. This attribute is so unique that it alone would be enough to characterize the papacy; it is its supreme distinguishing mark. It is therefore useful to examine its meaning and its scope. In this way we shall obtain a better idea of what the papal power really is.

The constitution *Pastor aeternus* by which the powers and prerogatives of the pope were specified and dogmatically defined dates from July 18th, 1870—a few weeks before the end of the temporal power. But in no way was this an improvisation of the Vatican Council. Dogmas are not improvised; they are elaborated. The essential dogma of the Holy Trinity did not receive its definitive expression until the Council of Nicaea in 325; that of the Divinity of the Holy Ghost until the Council of Constantinople in 381; that of the supernatural motherhood of Mary until the Council of Ephesus in 431.

In fact, the constitution *Pastor aeternus* was the settlement of an ancient problem which had given rise to heated controversy throughout the Catholic world, especially in France during the second half of the seventeenth century and the first half of the eighteenth. The question of papal infallibility was indeed one of the elements of Gallicanism, and gave rise to one of the four paragraphs of the famous "Declaration of the Clergy" of 1682, to which Bossuet contributed.

What I have tried to show in this study is essentially the primacy of Peter in action, through the heads of the Church of Rome, the popes, his successors. That primacy had been solemnly proclaimed at the Council of Florence in 1438, while the conciliar theories professed at Basle were threatening the traditional teaching about it. And the decree of the Council of Florence was all the more remarkable for the fact that the two Churches, of the West and of the East, united then for the last time, both took part. "We define", declared the Council, "that the apostolic Holy See and the Roman Pontiff possess the primacy over the whole world; that this same Roman Pontiff is the successor of Peter, Prince of the Apostles; that he is the true Vicar of Christ, head of the whole Church, Father and Teacher of all Christians, and that to him was granted by Jesus Christ, in the person of Peter, the power to feed, rule and govern the universal Church, as is contained in the acts of the ecumenical Councils and in the holy canons."

Such a text was already formulated. However, it did not prevent Gallicanism, Febronianism or Josephism from developing and upholding theses which conspicuously limited the exercise of the papal primacy. The object of the Vatican Council was simply to bring these vagaries to an end and to define the plenitude of the papal power in a manner that would be both clear and final.

That power, it may be said, is the conclusion of a chain of logic. This is how the Vatican Council expresses that chain; it is necessary to read the text carefully, for it is explicit:

> The eternal shepherd and bishop of our souls, in order to confer a perennial character on the saving work of redemption, ordained the building of the Holy Church, in which, as in the abode of the living God, all the faithful should be included by the bond of one same faith and charity. To this end, before he was glorified, he prayed his Father not only for the apostles but also for those who by their word were to believe in him, that they should be one, as the Son himself and the Father are one. Just as he sent out the apostles whom he had chosen from the world, and as he himself had been sent by the Father, so he wished to have shepherds and teachers in his Church even unto the consummation of the world. But in order that the

episcopacy itself should be one and indivisible, and so that, by mutual agreement amongst the priests, the whole multitude of believers should be kept in the unity of faith and communion, he established blessed Peter above the other apostles and thus instituted, in him, the principle and the visible and perpetual foundation of both these unities, on the solidity of which the eternal temple will be raised, and the sublimity of the Church destined for heaven will be made safe in the firmness of this faith.

This is indeed the living chain of which we have spoken. And it is also the unity which descends from heaven and forms itself anew, spiritually, upon the earth. God; Christ; his Church; the apostles and their leader; a perpetual line of successors of the apostles; a perpetual line of successors of the chiefs of these apostles, so that the bishops, the successors of the apostles, may be ever united in the person of the pope, the successor of Peter. Such is the organization of the Church of Christ, as he wished it to be, and valid until the end of the world. The cornerstone of this edifice, then, is the papacy. Without it there is no unity.

THE LITTLE TRADITION
IN ESTABLISHED RELIGION

The following account of religion in a Mexican village is based on field work done from 1943 to 1948. The first passage links it to the preceding, for it is through the hierarchy of parish priest, bishop, and archbishop that the faithful of this village are linked finally to the Pope who, as a function of his worldwide supervision of the Church, bestows authority upon the archbishop and bishop. Nonetheless, it is clear that the same religion looks different from the perspectives of Tepoztlán and Rome. The little tradition is essentially a local and nonliterary experience, borne through family, community, and peer group oral transmission. It is closely linked to the seasonal cycle and to agriculture, and so to festivals and prayers for local concerns. It is conceptually vague and unsystematic, yet deeply rooted in a person's sense of community identity and experience of the miraculous. It is full of particularism—for example, belief that different figures of Christ have different powers—rather than the rational consistency usually much vaunted by the great tradition. Notice, however, that as a person becomes more cultured he or she is expected to be more systematic about religion. Yet all in all, the faith is probably no less, and no more, fervent or spiritually satisfying in Tepoztlán than in Rome, but just somewhat different.

Life in a Mexican Village: Tepoztlán Restudied

Oscar Lewis

The complex organization of the church includes seven levels of ecclesiastic hierarchy. The first and highest in the nation is the archbishop of Mexico. He maintains connections with Tepoztlán through the medium of circulars, pastorals, and general orders. Few if any Tepoztecans have ever seen him. Next is the bishop of Cuernavaca who is in charge of the churches in the state of Morelos. He visits Tepoztlán about once every five years, but has been seen occasionally by Tepoztecans when in Cuernavaca.

On the third level in the hierarchy is the local priest, the main figure in the central church of Tepoztlán, and the highest spiritual authority in the municipio. The fact that he is a native of Tepoztlán has facilitated his work there. Tepoztecans feel more comfortable with this priest than with all of his "foreign" predecessors, and are less inclined to complain and criticize him. His lack of mysticism and religious fervor and his attitude of detachment suits them well. However, being a native son has diminished somewhat the aura of respect which generally surrounds a village priest and has encouraged some Tepoztecans to make direct appeals to him to lower his fees and to settle family conflicts and personal problems. He has also been drawn into some small conflicts, a result of which was his being denounced to the archbishop of Mexico City by a group of Tepoztecans.

In the fourth place are the Monjas Carmelitas, the aforementioned nuns, who, although a recent addition, are to reside permanently in the village. These nuns are all outsiders and are treated with great respect by Tepoztecans. In addition to their other activities, the nuns have assumed the direction of some of the religious associations, particularly the *Juventud de Acción Católica*. They have greatly extended the activities and increased the membership of these associations and by their work have brought about a religious revival in Tepoztlán.

On the fifth level of the hierarchy are various lay functionaries of the church. These are:

From Oscar Lewis, *Life in a Mexican Village: Tepoztlán Restudied* (Urbana, Ill.: The University of Illinois Press, 1951, 1963), pp. 263–67, 272–78. Copyright © 1951, 1963 by the Board of Trustees of The University of Illinois Press and of the author. Notes omitted.

1. The sacristan or sexton hired by the priest as his personal aid and caretaker of the church building. Specifically, the duties of the sacristan are to help the priest dress for ceremonial occasions, to memorize several prayers in Latin in order to assist at Mass, to care for the altar and the sacred vessels, to clean the temple, and to keep a record of the priest's religious program. At the time of this study the sacristan was a young unmarried man of twenty of an acculturated family in the barrio of Santo Domingo. He was paid a wage of from three to five pesos a day and more on certain fiesta days when there is an excess of work.

2. The cantor or church singer is an assistant to the sacristan but is selected by the priest and responsible to him. He is expected to play the organ and sing religious songs in Spanish and Latin. He participates in the singing during Mass and in leading the hymns and *Te Deums*. He is paid one peso for each Mass and fifty centavos for each *Te Deum*.

3. The *rezanderos* are men who make a vocation of religion by memorizing many prayers and hiring themselves out to intone these prayers for others on special occasions. For example, if someone loses a horse or cow and wishes to ask San Pedro to help him find the animal he will pay one or two pesos to a *rezandero* to go to the chapel in the barrio of San Pedro and recite the appropriate prayer.

Although the *rezandero* is not recognized by the church as a functionary he is thought of as such by the populace. Some *rezanderos* play an important role in local religious life and enjoy certain prestige. The more skilled have a large repertory of prayers and deliver them with the impressive skill of a priest. It is interesting to note that the two most important *rezanderos*, both of whom were our informants, were also political leaders; one in the Cristero movement, the other in the opposing leftist group. The latter, incidentally, became the first Protestant in Tepoztlán. At present there are approximately ten *rezanderos* in the village and the majority of these live in the barrio of Santo Domingo.

4. The members and respective officers of the religious associations are a type of lay church functionaries. Many of these associations were founded in colonial times and had a long history of ups and downs. They suffered misfortunes during the struggle for independence and during the Reform and the Revolution but were always reorganized in times of peace. Some of these associations are national and international in character, such as the Asociación Guadalupana, the Apostolado de la Oración, and the Acción Católica; others are essentially local and lack externalities. We shall describe the more important of these organizations.

a.   The Asociación de la Vela Perpetua, the objective of which is to give homage to the *Santísimo Sacramento* by permanently maintaining a lighted candle on the altar. The Asociación consists of thirty-one women who identify themselves by wearing a medal suspended on a white ribbon. Each member dedicates one day a month to keeping vigil at the altar. Membership is limited to the maximum number of days in a month and this society is considered honorific and select. In the days of Díaz only the wives of *caciques* were members. The organization has a president, secretary, and treasurer; apart from its routine religious activity, this society serves no other social function.

b.   Asociación del Apostolado de la Oración celebrates the first Friday of each month. Although men may join, the present membership consists of twenty-five to thirty women. The distinguishing mark is a medal worn on a red ribbon. It is interesting to note that although this organization has different levels of membership to stimulate the mystic devotion of its members, in Tepoztlán the members fulfill only the rituals of the first order without aspiring to the superior orders.

c.   Asociación Guadalupana celebrates the twelfth day of each month in honor of the Virgin of Guadalupe. Membership is made up of thirty women.

d.   The Cofradía de la Virgen del Carmen is a sisterhood of about thirty women who celebrate the sixteenth day of each month. The scapulary of the Virgen del Carmen is used widely in the village because of the numerous virtues attributed to it. It is useful to frighten away devils and other fear-inspiring beings. It also saves lives by deflecting bullets or machetes. If carried at the time of death, it insures the possibility of "dying well" and the certainty that the Virgen del Carmen will soon remove the soul from purgatory. For these reasons approximately three hundred men, women, and children customarily carry this scapulary.

e.   Sagrado Corazón de Jesús celebrates Mass on the first Friday of each month in homage to the Sacred Heart of Jesus. Again membership consists of thirty women. This association is considered most powerful because its members are "the best women in the village." The present president is the priest's sister.

f.   Asociación de la Adoración Nocturna is made up exclusively of men. The forty members are obliged to confess each month and keep vigil all night of the first Saturday of each month, praying and giving praise to the Holy One. On the following Sunday each member takes communion. However, this society scarcely functions because the majority of the members refuse to fulfill the requirement of confession.

g.   Acción Católica de Jóvenes Mexicanos consists of two sections, one for each of the sexes. There are about eighty youths and thirty girls in the organization. The members work to arouse the religious spirit of the people, to organize fiestas to raise funds, and to attract the youth to join. Under the stimulation of the nuns this organization has become extremely active. For the first time, young Tepoztecans have manifested a militant Catholicism of a modern type and have become interested in understanding the religious dogma and in recruiting new members. It is also the only religious association which has a sense of solidarity and imposes mutual obligations upon its members. Members visit each other when ill, celebrate each other's birthdays, and attend weddings and funerals.

h.   Vanguardia is an association for children from seven to fourteen years of age. They are required to attend Mass, to confess, and to take communion every Sunday. Membership varies considerably during the year.

Other associations which function only once or twice a year also exist. Some of these are the Hermandád de las Ánimas which celebrates All Saints' Day on November first, the Sociedád de la Virgen de la Natividad which is in charge of preparations for the fiesta of the patron of the village on September eighth. Before the Revolution there was an Asociación de Caridad called San Vicente de Paul which distributed food and clothing to the poor. The society disappeared during the Revolution and was never reorganized.

The Annual Cycle of Religious Fiestas

The religious fiestas in which Tepoztecans participate are of four types (1) the barrio fiestas in which each barrio celebrates its patron saint; (2) the village-wide fiestas which celebrate the holy days in the central church; (3) the fiestas of other surrounding villages of the municipio; and (4) the fiestas of villages and towns outside the municipio. In all, there are a total of 63 named fiestas in which Tepoztecans participate. Of these, 27 are village-wide fiestas, 12 are barrio fiestas (some barrios celebrate two separate days), 7 are fiestas of surrounding villages within the municipio, and 7 are fiestas of villages outside the municipio.

Of the village-wide fiestas, the most important are the Carnaval, Ash Wednesday, the fiestas of Holy Week, the fiestas for El Tepozteco and María on September 8, the blessing of the *pericón* on September 28, the Days of the Dead, and the Days of the Posadas.

It is difficult to estimate accurately the total number of days during the year devoted to the fiestas. Some of the 63 fiestas last three or four days, and a conservative total estimate would be about 100 days. It would be quite erroneous, however, to conclude that most Tepoztecans spend approximately a third of the year in fiestas. Most fiestas are attended by only a small portion of the population. Certainly less than five per cent of the populace attend the 14 fiestas of the surrounding villages and other towns. And less then ten per cent of the villagers attend the fiestas of barrios other than their own. And there are probably only about a half-dozen village-wide fiestas during the year in which the village as a whole participates. Much time is also consumed in preparations which may begin two to four weeks before the celebration of the fiesta.

Barrio fiestas follow a more or less definite pattern. The religious ceremonial which takes place within the barrio chapel is generally celebrated with three Masses given by the priest. The first Mass is called *preparación;* the second, *función;* and the third, *consumir.* The first two are conducted *sin vinar* (without taking wine), but in the third, the priest takes the sacred wine. In the afternoon the priest conducts the *exposición del Santísimo,* some church music is played and sung, and finally a *rosario* is prayed. If the barrio has insufficient funds, some parts of the ceremonial are dispensed with.

The secular aspects of barrio fiestas overshadow the religious aspects in popularity and attendance. These festivities generally consist of a display of fireworks, both day and night, which have been arranged on a *castillo* or wooden framework. The *castillo,* in the shape of a bull, is most often used. Entertainment may also be supplied by a *jaripeo,* which is a type of rodeo devoted to a display of roping and mounting bulls. Music may be supplied by a band of hired musicians, and some fiestas include groups of religious dancers. Finally, all in the barrio, except the poorest families, prepare a meal of *mole* and other festal dishes and entertain visitors from other barrios or villages. Those who participate in a fiesta, dress in their best clothing, often purchasing new clothing for this annual occasion.

Barrio fiestas and some village-wide fiestas are supported by popular subscriptions which are more in the nature of voluntary taxes. The *mayordomo* of each fiesta collects the money in a ceremony called the *Moxotlaloyan y Cerapah* at the place where the money for candles for the church is paid. A similar payment is made for the *castillo*, either at the same time or, in some cases, in a separate ceremony called the *castillopah*. This ceremony is usually held one day after the fiesta so as to collect the *limosna* a year in advance. The amount paid is generally fifty centavos, or one peso, according to how much had been promised to the *santo* the year before. The people, who had been reminded earlier of the coming payment by the *huehuechique* or *limosnero*, convene at the *mayordomo's* house to leave their money. Upon payment, each receives a portion or two, according to the amount contributed, of *mole verde*, tamales, and a drink called *tepache*. Contributions are carefully recorded and there have been few cases of misuse of these funds.

The calendar of religious fiestas is a typical Catholic calendar which includes moveable and fixed fiesta days. The dates upon which many of the fiestas fall are calculated from the key date, Ash Wednesday.

Religious Practices and Beliefs

Just as the cycle of religious fiestas in Tepoztlán follows Catholic practice, with some local modifications, so does the individual Tepoztecan. Only a few persons, mostly women, in the village fulfill all the ritual and other obligations set by the priest and church. These people are looked upon by the rest as fanatics who are "always dressing the saints." The priest does not consider his flock to be "good Catholics." The older people maintain a respectful passivity toward most church activities, while the adult males and many older youths, although not irreligious, tend to scoff at the nuns, the Acción Católica and other "fanatics." Among these recalcitrants there is much more interest in the barrio fiestas and one or two of the nearby village fiestas than in the regular daily and weekly religious acts which are required of them. On the other hand, the nuns and the religious associations tend to emphasize the latter. The school, too, so far unsuccessfully, discourages attending fiestas because of the disastrous effects upon school attendance. Regular participation in church ritual is associated with becoming "more cultured." Those who go to boarding schools or who have occasion to live in Mexico City for some time learn to attend Mass, to confess, and to take communion more often than is customary in the village.

Prayers for various occasions are memorized by Tepoztecans. The older generation learn them in Náhuatl, the younger in Spanish. The people do not know how to improvise prayers, and when their memory fails they prefer to keep silent, or merely cross themselves, or kiss a scapulary to invoke the protection of the appropriate saint. The obligatory morning prayers are seldom said with regularity. Some of the old people still say a prayer at noon when the bell of the municipal clock strikes; the men remove their hats and give thanks to God because they still have strength to work. When the evening church bell rings, the men are again supposed to take off their hats and the women to kneel to give thanks because the day has passed without mishap. We cannot estimate the number of people who fulfill the latter obligation, but in all the time we were in the village we never observed anyone kneeling in prayer outside the church. But men returning home from the fields lift their hats respectfully whenever they pass a cross, and on the bus from Tepoztlán to Cuernavaca all hats go up in unison each time a church is passed. Some Tepoztecans recite prayers on special occasions, such as planting corn, lighting a charcoal furnace, or pruning a tree.

As indicated earlier, most Tepoztecans do not feel strongly the need to attend Mass every Sunday or even on holy days. On the basis of our own observations and informants' estimates, it appears that, on the average, about two hundred, mostly women, attend church on Sundays. The 6:00 A.M. Mass is preferred; those who attend the 8:00 A.M. Mass risk being called lazy. Mass, like other public gatherings, is a welcome form of diversion. It is one of the opportunities for sweethearts to see one another; young people are said to attend not out of devotion but to flirt. Everyone puts on his best clothes for Mass. The older men wear huaraches, white *calzones*, and shirts; the youths wear trousers and modern shirts, and many wear jackets. The women use *rebozos* to cover their heads. Upon entering the church, the women cross themselves with holy water and take seats up toward the front. The men generally do not cross themselves and remain in the rear. Some of the youths stand at one side of the nave, leaning against the pillars so as to be able to see the girls during the service. The children sit with their mothers and sisters. Five- and ten-centavo pieces are dropped into the plate passed by the sacristan.

After Mass the young men are the first to leave. They remain at the church door, talking, joking, and laughing quietly among themselves, until the girls appear. The older men are the next to leave the church, and then the women. Most of the men go off to drink, while the women go home in little groups of relatives.

Tepoztecans do not rigorously observe Sunday or other holy days as days of rest. During planting and harvesting, everyone works in the fields, and the storekeepers in the center who profit by the week-end tourist trade always work on Sundays and holidays.

Informants say, "It is no sin to work on Sunday when it is done out of necessity." Some of the very old people believe that he who works on Sunday ruins himself economically for the rest of the week.

Tepoztecans do not like to confess; the majority do so only once a year. Not giving much importance to sin, Tepoztecans do not regard confession as necessary. Most men consider confession important only when one is about to die but "with the pangs of death, who's going to remember to confess properly?" Women, particularly married women, are less reluctant to confess, and about fifty women are known to take communion and confess quite often. Through the Acción Católica the number of young people of both sexes who do this has increased. Perhaps the most important deterrent to confession, especially among the older people, is that the priest may exact from the confessor the recitation of certain prayers which most people cannot say accurately. Fearing a scolding from the priest, they prefer to avoid the situation. There is no such difficulty with communion. "We would all take communion more often if we didn't have to confess; that we always avoid."

In general, the Tepoztecan feels obliged to contribute to the church and does so by paying *limosnas*. There is a belief that he who refuses to give alms will find that no one receives his soul in heaven and that therefore he must go to hell. He who always gives alms finds that when he dies and his soul goes to heaven, "the Saint to whom he has given alms comes to receive the soul and intercedes with God to allow him to enter, and so he gets to heaven." Thus, when a Tepoztecan lights a candle to some saint or deposits a coin or two in the box, he considers himself deserving of the protection of that saint.

Tithes, which were obligatory and were collected by the government for the church before the Revolution, no longer exist. The local priest, however, hires a *limosnero* at harvest time to go about the fields, riding on a mule, to collect contributions from the farmers. As a rule, each farmer gives about twelve ears of corn, so that the priest collects a good amount for his stores.

Religious beliefs in Tepoztlán reflect Tepoztecan social character and world view. The profoundly practical nature of Tepoztecans precludes religious fantasy, mysticism, and any preoccupation with metaphysics; they seek from religion concrete solutions to problems of daily life and go about it in as direct a manner as their religion permits. Their religious world, like the world in which they live, is full of hostile forces and punishing figures which must be propitiated to secure good will and protection. The act of propitiation is direct and simple, consisting of giving something or doing something which is known to please a particular saint, such as lighting a candle, giving a few coins, offering flowers, burning incense, reciting a special prayer, or performing a certain dance; these offerings incur an obligation on the part of the recipient to favor the donor.

As in most mestizo communities in Mexico and Central America, Tepoztecan religious beliefs represent a fusion of Catholic and pagan elements. The people's concept of God is vague at best; the one characteristic which is clear to Tepoztecans is that he is a punishing God who acts in ways hostile to men. Most misfortunes are ascribed to him; good fortune rarely.

The Holy Trinity is viewed as consisting of three distinct gods. One is God the Father, who is usually pictured with a long, white beard and a large ball in his hand, "that one is the Lord of the World." The second is "the one who died for us, the one who was crucified." The third is "the Holy Ghost or the Holy Dove," who is frequently depicted with the symbol of a dove to which Tepoztecans give divine attributes.

El Tepozteco occupies a special place in Tepoztecan religion and is unique to this community. The process by which he was deified and confused with Catholic figures was paralleled in localities all through Mexico during the colonial period. He continues to play an important role in Tepoztlán, is constantly evoked, and is one of the few legendary figures in the village. He is described to the children in the following manner:

> *Tepozteco cannot be known; his house is on the hill near El Parque. There he has his* comal, *his* metate, *and everything which he needs in his house, but he himself does not appear. He always lives far off among the clouds. When they don't give him a good celebration on the eighth of September he sends a great wind; when the celebration is a good one then he does nothing, he is content. Tepozteco is a god who is lovable and cruel. He has only one punishment for the village—he takes away the water. He makes* los aires *and they cause illness. He has a mother who is in the church. We say a Mass for his mother. His mother is named* Tonantzin *and also* Natividad.

Legends about El Tepozteco continually spring up. The most recent of these was told in the early days of World War II, after Mexico declared war on the Axis and obligatory military service was established:

> *In those days of worry and confusion, a conscript was walking the streets of Cuernavaca. He was crying because he had been called to the army. Suddenly at the corner he saw a boy, dressed like a peasant. The boy asked the youth why he was crying. "Why shouldn't I cry, for I must be a soldier,*

and they have ordered me to the war to defend the United States, and I must leave my old parents. If it were to fight for my country it would be bad enough but to fight for the gringos. . . ." Then the boy said, "Go in peace. Your tears are not in vain. Neither you nor other young Mexicans will have to go to fight for a foreign government. You will learn to be a soldier, but you will never leave the country. Go to the village of Tepoztlán and take an offering to my mother, the Virgen de la Natividad." Then the boy disappeared mysteriously.

The soldier was very impressed by what had happened. He told his parents and they decided to go to Tepoztlán with an offering. After that they began to tell the people of that village what had happened, and everyone understood that El Tepozteco had spoken again. El Tepozteco kept his word, for none of the conscripts went to fight for the United States.

Tepoztecans do not distinguish clearly between those misfortunes which might be considered punishments of God, or the work of the devil. Tepoztecans believe firmly in the devil, who is generally called *el pingo*, and to whom is attributed many of the evils which befall them. The powers of the devil, however, are relatively few; he cannot cause drought but he can cause harm to a person, making him an idiot or carrying him off bodily. The devil always appears dressed as a Mexican horseman or as "a tall gentleman, dressed in black like respectable people, with a suit of fine cloth." He is almost always met on lonely roads or in the woods during the night. To combat his evil influence, Tepoztecans recite a prayer to some saint, especially to St. Michael and St. Gabriel. When a Tepoztecan brings an offering to St. Michael he considers it necessary to light a candle to the devil as well, even though it be a small candle, so that he will not be angered.

Despite four hundred years of Catholicism, most Tepoztecans do not yet have a clear concept of the Catholic heaven and hell. According to Aztec religion the equivalent of heaven was a pleasant place where dead warriors and women who died in childbirth went to live. The existence of hell as a place for expiating sins committed in life was totally unknown. There was only Mictlán, the region of the dead, where souls continued to live the same life as they had on earth. Tepoztecans have no concept of eternal punishment. Hell is a form of purgatory to which only the greatest sinners are sentenced. Ordinary people do not fear hell, for "the temperate ones, those who believe in God, those who have done some good," go to heaven. The threat of hell is chiefly used to control the conduct of children; adults are not generally concerned with life after death.

Tepoztecans view heaven simply as a place of glory, "that is, a place where one has no necessities." Although hell may be described as "a place where there is a lot of fire and where sinners are burned," Tepoztecans do not actually view hell this way. To them going to hell means being condemned to wander over the earth at night, dragging chains until the period of punishment and suffering is over and the soul is admitted to heaven. Many accounts of such punishment are told in the village. The following is typical:

> A woman who was a witch didn't leave her property well distributed, nor any written directions about it. Her children did not know what belonged to each and wanted to give the younger brother only a small share. He didn't agree to this, and it would have been better if he had, for after that every night at a late hour the children heard chains dragging and the sound of weeping. The sounds stopped at the door of their house and then began again. The brother consulted several people, and they advised him to confess and tell the priest what he had heard. He did this, and the priest told him to wait a day, and he would tell him where he would find his mother. The next day the priest said he could not locate his mother, but that he should go to where they sent the bones from the butcher's. He did so, and at midnight he found his mother tied to a post with a strong chain. When she saw him, she began to cry and told him that if he did not wish to see her in this state, he should accept the small share. The son was convinced and took his portion of the inheritance and after that they never again heard the noise, and the mother ceased to suffer.

All accounts include the dragging of chains by the soul and the scene at the slaughterhouse. The soul is released from suffering by some of the living who make up for the sins of the dead.

The saints are viewed as intermediaries with God, and Tepoztecans devote themselves to cultivating their favor. The saints are endowed with personal qualities, and their images are worshipped directly as divine beings rather than as mere symbols of living saints. This is evident when, in times of drought, the saints of each of the barrios, as well as of some of the villages, are appealed to for rain. All the images are shut up in the parish church and are taken out in procession only in the afternoon when the sun is high, so that the images will feel the heat and notice the people's discomfort and sadness.

The saints with greater punishing powers are most assiduously worshipped. Saint Peter, of the barrio of San Pedro, is one of these. If there are not enough dancers at his feast day, he brings illness and misfortune to those who did not participate. Saint Peter, whose image is accompanied by a lion, is said to use this animal to frighten children into dancing for him and sometimes to appear to a father who has refused to permit his children to dance. It is also believed that if a person does not accept the office of *mayordomo* of the barrio of San Pedro, the lion will be sent to frighten him.

In their view of the saints, Tepoztecans reveal a tendency toward polytheism. This is indicated in the distinct attitudes toward the different images of the same saint. For example, the various local figures of Christ do not all have equal powers and are not all worshipped with equal fervor. The Christ of Ixcatepec is considered "very miraculous" and is called upon when there is great misfortune, such as extreme drought. He is rendered special homage by taking children, dressed in white tunics and wearing a crown of thorns and little thorn crosses on their backs, to the chapel of Ixcatepec to do penance.

INTENSIVE EMERGENT RELIGION

Emergent religion stands out in the sea of society pervaded by established religion. It includes new movements, sectarian withdrawals, cultic syncretism—whatever provides a religious vehicle for people who say, "I'm different from others; I know more, and I want more," and express it by a self-conscious, deliberate choice to follow a path other than the ordinary within or outside the normative religion.

The following passage offers an example from Burma of the *intensive* way of making this choice, the way of one who wants to go deeper into or follow more strictly the dominant faith. The quasi-political overtones of some emergent religion are evidenced by the fact that these sects center around persons who are believed by their followers to be not only *weikza* or wizards but also future kings, meaning that they had accumulated so much good karmic merit and magical power that soon, in this or another incarnation, their power would be manifest in their becoming earthly sovereigns.

Note several common characteristics of emergent religion, especially of the intensive sort. The movements insist on strict following of normative precept and practice of the established religion and then on going beyond it. They center on charismatic persons. They claim to have secret powers and to know secret facts about momentous historical-spiritual future events that are not known outside their circle, though the subject of rumor. The circle has a more intense spiritual life and a more intense relation to invisible spiritual realities (the *nat* spirits) than the ordinary established religion.

Buddhism and Society

Melford E. Spiro

Two Future Kings

Since, unlike those esoteric sects whose primary emphasis is eschatological, messianic sects are rare, and since moreover they are even rarer on the village level, it was by accident that I encountered the existence of two of them in Upper Burma. In the midst of a discussion of the Future King notion in Yeigyi, one of the villagers noted that a putative Future King was living in Mandalay. Neither he nor any of the other men with whom I was engaged in conversation placed any credence in this Future King—none of them (nor any other inhabitant of Yeigyi) was a member of a messianic Buddhist sect, nor did any of them know where he lived. Nevertheless, with the assistance of a young Mandalay monk who did know his address but had never been there himself, I was able to spend a day in what turned out to be the "palace" of this royal pretender, where I interviewed him and some of his devotees. By chance, this particular "palace" had been visited a few years earlier by Mendelson, and although he was unable at that time to interview the king, his description of the establishment and of the ideology of this sect obviates the necessity of repeating what he has already set forth.

The ground floor of the "palace," a building in the center of the city, consists of rooms for secular activities of various kinds—eating, sleeping, study, discussion, and so on. The two upper stories include the chambers of the king; administrative offices; altar rooms for various gods, spirits *(nat)*, *weikza*, Buddhas, and so on; and a throne room with all the regalia, including the throne, associated with the traditional Burmese court. This is the throne of *bou:do sakya* (hereafter anglicised Bodaw Setkya) Future King of Burma.[1] Although he denied, in our interview, that he himself was that person, this man is referred to by his followers as Bodaw Setkya, and it is by that name that I will refer to him.

Although disavowing any claim to be the Future King, Bodaw Setkya admits to being a powerful exorcist *(ahte:lan: hsaya)* and a Master of Buddhist meditation. In short, rather than making any

From pp. 174–80 in *Buddhism and Society* by Melford E. Spiro. Copyright © 1970 by Melford E. Spiro. Reprinted by permission of Harper & Row, Publishers, Inc.

[1]*Bou:* designates a grandfather, and by extension, an old man. *Daw* is a royal honorific. *Sakya* is the Burmese corruption of the Sanskrit, *cakra* (pali, *cakka*), the Wheel or discus, which (as the king said) "circumambulates the globe and destroys all enemies in its way."

admissions that would render him liable to charges of treason, he established instead, and in one sentence, his *bona fides* as a wonderful being: he has power over the supernatural world, and as a master meditator he is a contender for nirvana (claims traditionally associated with the statuses of Buddhahood and emperorship). In general, both Bodaw Setkya and a second king (described below) spoke circumspectly, by means of indirection and allusion, and neither granted me permission to take notes during our interview. Their followers, however, are not as circumspect as their Masters. With respect to nirvana, for example, Bodaw Setkya's followers claim explicitly that (to render the Burmese expression literally) he has "found a way out to a blissful place," a discreet way of saying that he has attained nirvana.

Bodaw Setkya is a short, plump man, flabby and effeminate in appearance, who gives the appearance of great shrewdness. Before attaining his present position he had been, so he claimed, an electrician and a trustee of the pagoda adjacent to the "palace" in which he now resides. Hoping to become a Buddha, he began some years ago to recite the Virtues (*goung:do*) of the Three Jewels, and giving up his electrical work he devoted full time to meditation. Indeed, for a year he meditated while sitting on top of the pillar which is now enshrined in the courtyard of the "palace." As a result of these activities, he is now under the protection of the *deva* whose images are in the various altar rooms. Ten years ago, having "completed" his meditation (another indirect way of saying that he had achieved the aim of his meditation, either Buddhahood or nirvana), he entered the present building, which he has never left. All these years he has continuously observed the Nine Buddhist Precepts; hence his yellow robe—yellow, he pointed out, being the sign of purity. Since in adhering to the Nine Precepts it was necessary to abstain from all sexual behavior, he also abandoned his wife. He is attended instead by a woman who sat in his room with us during the entire interview, whom he identified as his "sister," but whose sensuous appearance did not at all accord with the sibling role he imputed to her.[2]

From his present chambers, the Bodaw conducts his occult medical practice; and it is a lucrative practice indeed, for it permits him, he said, to feed his many poor followers. But his fees are not his only source of wealth; in addition, he has been successful in making gold by means of his alchemic skills. (This was his only

---

[2]It is of interest to compare the miraculous details of his life provided by his followers with the rather pedestrian summary provided by the Bodaw himself.

allusion to the possibility that he might be a *weikza*, although his followers had no reticence in telling Mendelson that he was the incarnation of Bou: min: gaung.) He leaves his chambers only four times a year, on the four important Buddhist festivals, when—carried on a palanquin—he grants an audience to his followers in the throne room.

Royal symbolism—Burmese kings, too, did not touch the ground, and they too were carried on palanquins—was practiced by those few members of the sect who were privileged to enter his chamber during our interview. Prostrating themselves when they entered the room, they bowed themselves out when they left his presence, their backs always away from him, which of course was the stylized manner of approaching and leaving the presence of the Burmese king.

In order to become a follower of Bodaw Setkya it is necessary, he stressed, to adhere to Buddhist discipline in detail. His followers must observe the Five Precepts, practice meditation, cleave always to the truth, practice both love and tolerance, and do homage to the Three Gems. This is why, he explained, so many monks, in addition to recognizing his "greatness," are included among his followers. Indeed, the day before our interview he had fed, so he claimed, five hundred monks in a special dining room set aside in the "palace" for monks. As for lay followers, he estimated their numbers at a hundred thousand! (His steward told Mendelson that their number was five thousand.)

What can we make of all of this? Piecing together the information Mendelson elicited from his followers with what I obtained from the Master himself, and in both cases reading between the lines, it is fair to conclude that this Bodaw Setkya claims to be and/or is viewed by his followers as a master *weikza*, probably the incarnation of Bo Min Gaung, who either already is—or in a future rebirth will become—the Future Buddha and/or Future King. This conclusion, moreover, is supported by a description in a Burmese language newspaper *(Bahosi)* of a *nat* ceremony held in the "palace" in which he is referred to, alternatively, as Dhammazedi Min Gaung and as Bodaw Setkya.[3]

This meeting with Bodaw Setkya took place soon after I began

---

[3]The same article, incidentally, emphasizes that the participants in the ceremony were preponderantly Shan peasants. That Shans, being Buddhists, should be involved in these messianic sects is not surprising, especially when it is noted that even non-Buddhist hill tribes have been infected by the same beliefs. Stern has provided us with a remarkable account of a sect of this type among the Karen, a non-Buddhist Burmese hill people.

my field work and some months before I knew enough about esoteric Buddhism to be able to probe beyond the obvious. (Unfortunately, becoming involved in many other research problems which I then considered of greater importance, I did not find an opportunity to return.) Although my second encounter with a Future King was also confined to a single interview, it took place some months after I had been in Burma, by which time I had acquired sufficient information about esoteric Buddhism to ask intelligent questions. As with Bodaw Setkya, my encounter with the second King—Bo Min Gaung *weikza* himself, as some of his followers referred to him—was almost entirely due to chance.

Close to Mandalay, on the highway leading to the Shan States, is a large spirit shrine holding the images of certain local as well as national spirits *(nat)*. Travelers frequently stop before the shrine to do homage to them. Behind this shrine, and situated on a lower plot of land, is a small but especially lovely pagoda, with a tall brick tower near by. One afternoon I stopped my car by the side of the road in order to explore this religious complex, which I passed every week on my trip from Yeigyi to Mandalay. Walking through the pagoda compound, I noticed a typical resthouse *(zayat)*, which it turned out was the dwelling of a very old, very friendly monk. This man was deeply involved in esoteric Buddhism. The tower, he explained, was a receiving station, which took messages transmitted by distant *weikza*. He invited me inside the resthouse, where I noticed on his bed a large photograph of a handsome man dressed in white. To my query he responded that it was a picture of Bo Min Gaung, the famous *weikza*, in whose behalf he (the monk) had built the pagoda. At the beginning of our conversation he said that Bo Min Gaung had died, or left the world, some years earlier; later he said that Bo Min Gaung was living on Mt. Popa; still later he said that Bo Min Gaung was even now living among men, and that I could find him in Mandalay. When I expressed an interest in meeting this famous *weikza*, who was both dead and alive, and who lived simultaneously both in Mandalay and on Mt. Popa, the monk not only gave me his address but provided me with a letter of recommendation.[4]

The following day, I set off for Bo Min Gaung's residence in Mandalay. I arrived with my assistant at a fairly large house, surrounded on all sides by a high wall. In order to get into the compound, we had to pass through a guardhouse where, despite our

[4]For the importance of Mt. Popa, as a center for esoteric Buddhism, see Mendelson. As F. K. Lehman has pointed out (by personal communication), a true Buddhist monarch controls the country insofar as he controls the *nat* spirits of its constituent territories and/or replaces them with those of his own appointment. That this Bo Min Gaung resides on Popa is, therefore, of the utmost symbolic significance.

letter of recommendation from the old monk, we were detained for quite some time while the guards held a long conference among themselves. Finally, after an exchange with messengers called from the house, we were allowed to pass and were ushered directly into the *weikza's* consulting room. When we entered he was holding a consultation with two women traders who, he later told us, had come for advice concerning their business. On the floor were various offerings the women had brought him.

Sitting on the floor and wearing the pointed hat of a *weikza*, Bo Min Gaung appeared to be an effeminate, middle-aged man— younger than Bodaw Setkya—with very light skin and a soft voice. On the wall behind him were three copies of a curious photograph, showing a normal-sized man sitting in the meditation posture, holding a much smaller man, about one-fourth his size, on his lap. The large man was the putative *weikza* seated before us, and the small one was the man in the photograph owned by the monk who had sent us to this *weikza*, whom he had identified as Bo Min Gaung. To my query, the man seated before us immediately resolved the problem. He, so he claimed, is not Bo Min Gaung; rather, the spirit of Bo Min Gaung is inside of him. In short, he was claiming to be the reincarnation of Bo Min Gaung (which resolved the apparent contradiction in the monk's statements that Bo Min Gaung was both dead and also living in Mandalay. The physical body of Bo Min Gaung was dead, but his spirit survived in this man who—and this was physically exemplified in the picture—is self-consciously aware that he is the reincarnation of the former).

When I asked him directly if he were a Future Buddha or a Future King—he did not conceal the fact that he was a *weikza*—he circumvented the question by saying, "I have only come to advise people on how to live a Buddhist life." I tried again, this time indirectly, by asking whether he knew of Bodaw Setkya or had any relationship with him. To this he said in a flat tone that he had nothing to do with him.

While we talked, he kept pouring hot tea into small cups which, after blowing into the cup, he would give us to drink (thereby imparting some of his power to us—a cherished privilege). Before we left him, he also gave us an *in:*, a cabalistic square which he said would protect us from all harm.[5]

As we were ushered out, our host told us he could see us again

---

[5]Like most magical power, *in:* too can be harnessed for both benevolent and malevolent ends. In itself, its power—essentially amoral—can become manifest in destructive ways. When, a few weeks after this incident, I offered this *in:* to a Western-educated professional woman, she (literally) expressed horror. "You must stay away from *in:* even good ones can do harm! I might take it into my house today, and then someday it might blow up."

in about an hour if we wanted to wait, which we did. Later, after receiving the message that he would see us, we were taken to another room in a different part of the house. When we entered this small and simple room, the man we knew as Bo Min Gaung was seated with a monk and was no longer wearing his *weikza* hat. When we had seen him earlier, he explained, he was Bo Min Gaung (an ellipsis, I assume, for the notion that the spirit of Bo Min Gaung had been inside him); but now Bo Min Gaung had (temporarily) left his body and we could speak to him as Ba Pwa (his proper name), the ordinary mortal, rather than as Ba Pwa the reincarnation of, or one possessed by, the mighty Bo Min Gaung.

In answer to my question, he said that the first time Bo Min Gaung came to him, he appeared in physical form, and they had slept together in the same bed. Since then the ancient *weikza* has possessed him—i.e., his spirit enters into him—every day.[6] (So we now have still another interpretation of the relationship between Ba Pwa and Bo Min Gaung. Alternatively: Ba Pwa *is* Bo Min Gaung, he is the reincarnation of Bo Min Gaung, he is the body in which the spirit of Bo Min Gaung resides, he is the body whom Bo Min Gaung regularly possesses.) When Bo Min Gaung first possessed him, he ordered him to live with love and concentration, and to help people to observe the Buddhist precepts. He taught him all his occult arts in subsequent possessions.

When the interview ended and we began walking down the stairs, we were approached by a follower of Ba Pwa (alias Bo Min Gaung), a philosophy graduate of the University of Mandalay. He was eager to talk about his Master, and we were eager to listen. When we first saw Ba Pwa, he said (as Ba Pwa himself had said), he was possessed by Bo Min Gaung. The latter, he said, had the choice, after becoming a *weikza*, of becoming a Buddha or of entering nirvana. Because of his love for others and his desire to help them, he chose instead to stay in the world. (Here, then, is the Mahayanist *Bodhisattva*, and indeed the young devotee used that term in connection with Ba Pwa.) Bo Min Gaung, he continued, is both an Embryo Buddha and a *weikza*, and like all *weikza* he is immortal. Although his physical body is in the Himalayas—like Popa, the abode of *deva*—his spirit travels. Hence it is that he possesses Ba Pwa.

[6]In the Burmese *nat* religion, shamans (typically females) are possessed by various spirits or *nat* (typically male), whom they marry and with whom (typically in their dreams) they have coitus. Ba Pwa's possession by Bo Min Gaung is reminiscent of this type of *nat* possession, except that in this case the relationship is homosexual rather than heterosexual. This is consistent with my first impression of Ba Pwa as being highly effeminate.

But Ba Pwa is also *weikza*. Many people, including many monks, have become apprenticed to him in order to become *weikza*. Ba Pwa himself was a mill-owner when he was possessed by Bo Min Gaung twenty-three years earlier. Forsaking his mill and all his other property, he had lived ever since on alms and donations from his followers. He was—and still is—married, but after his first possession by Bo Min Gaung, he repudiated conjugal life forever.

Ba Pwa, our informant continued, has followers all over Burma, including university graduates like himself, because they all recognize his power. When I asked about Bodaw Setkya, he not only said he knew of him, but immediately identified him as a competitor to Ba Pwa. Bodaw Setkya, he admitted, is "powerful," but "we will soon see who is the more powerful. Within the year strange things will occur." I asked if these "strange things" referred to the appearance of the Future King. He said he could not divulge such information, but he did say, in answer to my direct question, that neither Bodaw Setkya nor Bo Min Gaung is the Future King, although "Bo Min Gaung has a plan to be followed by the Future King."

This suggested rather strongly that Ba Pwa—he who has followed Bo Min Gaung—is viewed as the Future King. When I put this to him directly, he was reluctant to talk about it. Finally, however, he admitted that it was so. "In a year or two," he said, "Bo Min Gaung—[or did he mean Ba Pwa?]—will show his power, and everyone will worship him." But what about the present government, I asked. Will they oppose him or submit to him? "All of them," he said, "including [Premier] U Nu, will bow down before him and worship him."

EXPANSIVE EMERGENT RELIGION

Expansive emergent spiritual movements, unlike intensive movements that are focused on one aspect of the traditional faith, are concerned with relating ideas old and new, and from near and far, to the current religious situation. Generally their emphasis is on states of consciousness, and a basic assumption is that if the individual is really in harmony with the infinite cosmos, his or her state of consciousness will be blissful. The following account from a highly regarded book about the spiritual movements that characterized the sixties indicates some of the basic assumptions of the expansive perspective, exemplified here as reflected in astrology: the convergence of truth wherever found, whether scientific or subjective; the emphasis on harmony with the universe; the allusion to ancient teachings of wisdom; the complexity of the system and the regard in it for individual differences; and of course, the characteristic emergent opposition to the dominant symbol systems—indicated by the use of a pattern like astrology that is widely regarded as either unscientific or unorthodox.

The New Religions

Jacob Needleman

A More Fundamental World

What is the nature of that more fundamental world which the followers of the new teachings seek to penetrate? Does it actually exist?—not above the clouds or beyond the grave, but here and now in the midst of our own familiar world? If it does exist, what is the nature of its power or its call?

Such questions must be brought if we wish to think about the significance of these teachings and about the impact of the whole "spiritual explosion." Otherwise, we may naïvely turn to the sociologists, the psychologists, the theologians, or even to our poets and belle-lettrists for ways of understanding this phenomenon. And we will then find our judgment tied to forms of thought in which the question of a more fundamental world either does not arise or does not arise as a question.

The teachings we have just described are but part of a phenomenon which in a wider view seems almost apocalyptic. The number of Americans engaged in some sort of spiritual discipline is impressive enough. When we add to that number those who now seek to guide their lives simply by ideas which are associated with these traditions, we cannot avoid the picture of a "spiritual explosion."

For a moment let us take this wider view before attempting to assess the individual and collective significance of the various teachings.

Excerpts from *The New Religions* by Jacob Needleman, pp. 194–99. Copyright © 1970 by Jacob Needleman. Used by permission of Doubleday & Company, Inc.

On the level of ideas, a whole new set of categories has taken root which expresses the search for new ways of relating to other people and to the events of one's life. Where before one heard talk of anxiety, guilt, anal and oral personalities, superego, and so forth, one now hears of "working out one's karma," "past incarnations," "rising signs" and "sun signs." Where dreams were once taken as an index of suppressed desires, they are now scanned for prophetic messages and extrasensory communications. The language of existentialism, with its concepts of "the absurd," "dread" and "radical freedom" is also giving way to the language of astrology, psychism and mysticism. Even Marx and Chairman Mao now have to compete with the I Ching and the Tarot cards. Suddenly, the ideal of pleasure or momentary fulfillment is no longer the sexual orgasm, but the spiritual insight, the "flash" of "cosmic meaning."

I am speaking now not only of the radical or alienated young in or out of the drug scene, but of great millions of people throughout the country. Of course, much of the interest in such things as astrology remains on the level of a fad. And even a more serious study of such ideas is very far from the commitment to a spiritual discipline or teacher. And yet, since the ideas which attract the mind are expressions of our relationship to the world and to ourselves, the new ideas represent the beginnings of a searching which eventually leads many people to the new teachings themselves. Their prevalence is a clear sign of the great shift in the consciousness of the West.

Astrology

The Idea of Influences. Concerning astrology, it is as easy and justifiable to scorn its popular side as it is difficult to deny the sense of its cosmological basis: the idea that all elements in the universe, from atoms to galaxies, are interrelated. Everyone agrees that the sun, moon and planets, and even the stars, exert an influence on the earth. What separates modern science from the ancient systems of astrology is the question of the nature and extent of that influence. In the modern scientific world-view, the idea of levels of reality is meaningless. This is because science has found it pragmatically useful to exclude purpose and intention from its conception of reality. Now, the idea that something is on a higher level than something else only makes sense if the "lower" serves the purposes and intentions of the "higher." The intentions of the higher act, very strictly, as an influence upon the lower. Thus, if there is a higher or more fundamental world than our own, it is because our world serves its purposes.

In this sense our organism, for example, is "higher" than various organs of the body, which in turn are higher than the tissues, and so forth down to the cells and their components. If the idea of intention and purpose is excluded from our conception of the organism—as it is in the scientific view—then it becomes just as true to say that the organism serves the liver as it is true to say that the liver serves the organism. And the very idea of influence dissolves into mere cause and effect which in turn is relative to our conception of time and our subjective opinions about the nature and composition of the entities we are observing. To be influenced by something, however, means to participate in its intention, to serve its purpose.

Pursuing this analogy, the cells in our body would be "astrologers" to the extent that they studied the intentions and purposes of the tissues and organs which their lives served. Self-knowledge, the observation of the forces that influence one's life, is thus the basis of astrology. And from this point of view, mere astronomy, without the study of the purposes served by the mind and the senses, and without the study of the interlocking influences and intentions that make up the organic universe, can lead nowhere. A non-hierarchical and non-psychological study of the universe reveals only patterns, but not meaning.

This is only one aspect of the idea of astrology as it existed in those systems of knowledge which originated in ancient Egypt, Greece, India, Tibet and elsewhere. It was never an isolated science in these cultures, but part of a system of teachings that were integrated by the symbolic forms which we know as myths. These symbolic forms are the language of a purified emotional perception that had as its object the great unitary intentions of the cosmos itself. They thus embrace a knowledge not only of the stars and planets, but of human psychology and physiology, plants and animals, physics and chemistry—all placed within the context of man's divine mission of self-perfection through the service of God. If we have lost the key to these ancient systems and myths, it is not because there are insufficient archeological findings, but because we have lost the means of verifying even the findings we have. That verification begins with the purification of the emotional life and the uncovering of real, not imaginary, intuition. Thus, even the largest aspects of those systems which embraced astrology were tied to existential goals similar to those we have found in the new teachings.

What we are witnessing in this country is therefore a renewal of the interest in astrology, but hardly a renewal of astrology itself. As long as we are quite clear about this, the turning to astrology is significant in its own right. The symbols of astrology, however subjectively they are understood, provide a potentially far richer framework than our contemporary psychology for approaching people and human relationships—richer, that is, in questions and hence in openness. There is the ram, the bull, the scorpion, the archer. There are the planets and the associations they call forth— Jupiter, the symbol of magnificence; Saturn, the principle of resistance and instruction; Uranus, the force of transformation. There are the *houses* of the horoscope in which the pattern of celestial signs is applied to every sphere of an individual's life from the trivial to the momentous. There are the elements of fire, air, water and earth whereby character traits are linked to an idea of various forms of energy in the universe. There are the *aspects* of the solar bodies with their sense of a constantly shifting relationship of forces generating everything from whole destinies to momentary life-events. And there is much, much more.

How pale psychoanalytic concepts seem next to all this, not only in nuance, but in the sense of alienation from the whole of nature and the universe. The general interest in astrology represents, at the very least, a rebellion against the idea of an unalive cosmos which modern science has given us, a cosmos in which man is at best a lonely anomaly. If I think of you as, say, a Scorpio rather than as an "extrovert" or "oral type," I have room in my mind to see you in relationship to the great cosmic forces of destruction and regeneration, symbolized by the sign of the scorpion. I could not thereby say that I understand you any better than if I labeled you an extrovert—obviously not, since I cannot say I understand anything at all about such great forces. But for that very reason, I may be more able to resist passing judgment on you; to do so would be like passing judgment on the universe itself. When taken like this, astrology can open relationships, rather than close them.

In terms of the "spiritual explosion" it is this sense of greater forces at work which makes the interest in astrology significant and which is congruent with the emotion of wonder. One cannot say that present-day astrology is knowledge, much less a spiritual path. But it can be the expression of an intimation that it is contemporary man, rather than the universe, which is blind and purposeless. That is surely why so many followers of the new teachings maintain a fascination with such things as astrology, the Tarot and the I Ching.

The open-minded or skeptical astrologer is, of course, the exception. The intricate mathematical computations that go into the erection of a horoscope and into the reading of what is called "the progressed chart" can lull one into equating arithmetical precision with real knowledge. And the exciting symbolism of astrology can close the mind as easily as it can open it—for exciting labels are still only labels. Moreover, one can come from a session with an ardent astrologer absolutely stuffed with a phantastic sense of one's own cosmic importance. These are no doubt some of the reasons why the Judaeo-Christian tradition, as we know it, has always scorned astrology. But things are different now, and the present interest in astrology can be as much a sign of the incipient spiritual search as was, for example, St. Augustine's turning away from astrology in his day.

MONASTIC LIFE

An important aspect of the sociology of religion is that it frequently produces *total institutions*. In sociology, total institutions are institutions such as communes, armies, monasteries, residential schools, hospitals, and prisons that—for very different reasons, with varying degrees of voluntarism, and in very different ways—manage not only one side of a person's life as does an ordinary club or church but also nearly all of one's visible life as evidenced in such things as clothes, quarters, time of rising, work and purpose, and as far as possible, inner thoughts. This kind of life, dedicated to religious ends, is expressed in the lives of the monks and nuns who have long been major exemplars of several spiritual traditions. Unmarried, living communally without personal possessions and in obedience, and always available for divine work, they represent a high subordination of self to faith. The passage following is by a monk of the Episcopal Church in the Order of the Holy Cross and describes a typical day at its home monastery in West Park, New York. Notice the religious symbols and attitudes that surround everything said or done. The Offices are an ancient series of seven brief services, consisting largely of psalms said or sung throughout the day in most monasteries and convents of the Roman Catholic and Episcopal churches.

An American Cloister

S. C. Hughson, O.H.C.

If we should take this day upon which I happen to be writing we would begin with a scene of rare winter beauty. If you can, without too much violence to your feeling, imagine yourself abroad at so early an hour as 5:30 a.m., you would find the air keen and still. The mercury is hovering a little above zero, and the frost hangs hoar on every limb, and silvers the long line of the farm fences and every forest tree with a million gleaming crystals. Around the eastern half of the horizon sweeps a belt of clear ruddy gold, the earnest of the dawn, shining through the lacework of the trees that fringe the hilltops across the river. Dark shadows still lurk beneath the riverbanks, and amongst the thickets of wild shrubbery; but the alchemy of the coming day is swiftly dissolving them, while the stars, undimmed by the least fleck of mist, are glittering pale against a turquoise sky.

Morning and light are coming in their beauty.

Suddenly along the halls, through the stillness, as the caller passes from door to door, there sounds the salutation with which for immemorial centuries Religious have greeted the dawn, "Let us bless the Lord"; and from within each cell is heard the hearty response, "Thanks be to God"; fitting words indeed to be the first that Religious take upon their lips with each returning day.

Lights glimmer along the passages and stairs, and by 6 the brethren have taken their places in the choir. The morning Offices then proceed, followed by the Masses. . . .

Breakfast is then served, after which the housework is done, cells are cared for, and all with much expedition, as a little later begins the morning meditation, "the daily renewal of the Upper Room on the morning of Pentecost," as our Rule describes it.

Fresh from this blessing of the Holy Spirit, the daily Chapter of the Community is held every morning for the purpose of disposing

From S. C. Hughson, O.H.C., *An American Cloister* (West Park, N.Y.: Holy Cross Press, 1948). Slightly abridged. Reprinted by permission of the publisher.

the day's work, and arranging various programmes of the activities of the Community.

This would give our enquiring guest a still more bewildering glimpse, for here what is to be done for our Lord is canvassed, counsel is sought, brains, experience and knowledge are freely borrowed.

The Office of Terce is then sung; and a half hour later, as the morning silence begins, one would find no languid group on a sunny cloister, but a corps of men, alert and intense, each claiming every minute for the manifold duties that are assigned him.

Everywhere are signs of activity. There are dishes to be washed, sacristy work to be done with reverence and despatch, dinner to be prepared, outdoor work to be superintended, for wherever it is possible, the dwellers in a monastery do all their own work.

Often our guests are able to be of much help in certain of these activities. Indeed, not infrequently the dawn of a vocation to the Religious Life is found in the practical co-operation of a visitor in the ordinary duties of the monastery.

And this has to be done with system in order to leave time for the minimum period of study which the Rule contemplates each day, and—more important than anything else—for the required times of prayer. In a Religious house nothing is so carefully guarded as the devotional life. Often the work has to be retrenched, but prayer never.

Time never hangs heavy on the hands of a busy man, and the morning period is drawing to a close before one realizes it. Each one is still deep in his task when a clear peal sounds from the great bell in the tower above the chapel. This warning signal tells us that we have fifteen minutes in which to bring the work to a close, and repair at noon to the Chapel for Sext and None.

These Offices concluded, dinner follows, and after a short visit to the Chapel, the Community recreation is held in the common-room. This observance is universal in Religious Communities. . . .

Later in the afternoon, there is perhaps a walk. In summer, much work is done in the monastery gardens . . . we raise a large part of the vegetables we use on our table, and thus by the labour of our hands seek to supplement, for our support, the offerings which our friends send for the upkeep of the mother-house of our Order.

By work and thrift we are able to raise not only our vegetables for the summer, but to put up a substantial amount for use during the winter.

Thus the pleasant and at the same time profitable work goes on in the garden, until the Chapel bell again sounds, calling all to Vespers which is followed by the evening meditation.

Supper is then served, and shortly after eight Compline, the last office of the daily round of prayer, is sung. This service, in many respects more than any other, expresses the confiding trust of the soul through the darkness of the night in the good God, and His tender compassion towards His people.

The final words of the Compline Office are: "The divine help remain with us always. Amen." With this appeal to God the "Great Silence" comes down upon the house, a silence not only from open speech, but "a silence of the heart." And now all through the night no word is spoken until across the stillness of the dawn is heard the summons: "Let us bless the Lord."

One by one the lights go out until only the heart of flame that throbs perpetually above the Holy Place where the Blessed Sacrament reposes, or that burns before the statue of the Mother of God, shows here and there a figure kneeling before altar or shrine.

Again the hours that are gone are passed in review; the silent confession of the sins of the day is being made; the last act of adoration to the Most Holy is offered; the last Ave is spoken in love to God's Holy Mother.

Cor ad cor loquitur. At no other time does heart so speak to heart as in this holy silence when the oblation of the day's work is made at the feet of God, and the spirit is once more commended into His Hands. Kneeling in this worshipful place one realizes the deeper meaning of what our Rule tells us of silence:

"As the contemplative gazing up to the glory of his ascended Lord is the type of the perfect Religious, so forgetfulness of all about, and the hushing of all earthly converse and intercourse with others concerning transitory things, is the normal atmosphere of the Religious house. We are really never in such close intimacy as when we are drawn together in blessed stillness before our Lord in the Sacrament of His Love, communing one with another even while absorbed in loving adoration of Him."

And so the day ends. In another hour the last light is out, and God's servants go to their rest signing themselves with the Sign of the Cross, with the prayer on their lips and in their hearts:

O Saviour of the world, who by Thy Cross and Precious Blood hast redeemed us: save us and help us we humbly beseech Thee, O Lord.

AUTHORITARIAN
RELIGIOUS LEADERSHIP

The following passage describes an emergent religious movement in New Guinea that is centered around the teaching and charisma of one individual. Notice the strongly political overtones of this movement. It is an early but representative example of the *cargo cult*. These striking activities sprang up in colonial areas, especially Melanesia, as religious movements affirming native values (here, the inspiration from a traditionally sacred tree, the return of the spirits of the native dead). They predicted even greater benefits from adherence to native leaders than those offered by the white man in his religion and economy. Note that this movement, as long as it lasted, centered on the experience of one person that others, because of his power and their own inner needs, were willing to accept.

The Trumpet Shall Sound

Peter Worsley

The Milne Bay Prophet Movement

In 1893, Mr. R. J. Kennedy, Native Magistrate at Samarai, described in the Annual Report how a young native named Tokerua (correctly Tokeriu) of Gabagabuna village on the north side of Milne Bay had become inspired by a spirit which resided in a traditionally sacred tree.

Seligman, however, states that 'it was not uncommon for living men and women to journey to Hiyoyoa [the other world—P.W.] and return to this world'. According to his account, Tokeriu claimed to have visited Hiyoyoa itself. On his return, he prophesied the coming, in two or three months' time, of a great storm which would submerge the whole coast with a gigantic tidal wave. Existing villages, including Wagawaga and Gabagabuna, would be submerged by this wave which would cause the emergence of a new island in the middle of the bay.

Believers, however, were to be saved. The prophet enjoined

Reprinted by permission of Schocken Books Inc. from *The Trumpet Shall Sound* by Peter Worsley. Copyright © 1968 by Peter Worsley. Notes omitted.

various measures on his followers as the only way to ensure salvation. The White man's goods were banned: tin match-boxes, pocket-knives, and other such possessions were discarded, and the natives were to return to the use of stone implements. The people were also to wear long, narrow leaves in their armlets, as a sign of their 'entire repudiation of the White man'. They were to abandon their houses and retreat inland to seek refuge from the storm. Houses were burnt down and the people moved: the inhabitants of Gabagabuna village, for example, built a new village half a mile inland. It differed from the traditional type of village in that the houses were built in long rows with a long platform running alongside. In the centre was a larger house, the residence of Tokeriu.

Abel, the missionary, discovered the existence of the movement when, one Sunday, he found his morning service attended only by children. Everyone had gone to Tavara, the district where Tokeriu lived, he discovered, so with a colleague he immediately set out for Wagawaga, where there was a mission station with a native 'teacher', Biga. Only Biga and his wife and family greeted the party. Men, women and children had fled inland with their pigs and dogs.

Abel eventually found that the prophet had been told by a spirit that after the storm the south-east wind, the wind of the pleasant harvest season, would blow continually. Then the land would prosper, and yams and taro multiply in the gardens. Besides these traditional attractions, a sail would be sighted on the horizon, heralding the coming of a huge ship with the spirits of the dead on board, and the faithful would then be reunited with their dead kinsmen. Tokeriu would form a government, and have at his disposal a steamer much larger than the government steamer, the *Merrie England*. Since food would be so abundant, all pigs were to be killed and eaten, and food in the gardens consumed.

The people heeded his message. No work was done, and some 300–400 pigs were killed and eaten. This latter action indicates the powerful appeal of the prophet's message, for pigs were not only the major source of animal protein to these people, but also reservoirs of wealth, and invested with the greatest social value.

The people of Wagawaga, who had had experience of similar prophecies years before, asked the missionaries whether these prophecies were true. When Biga and the Whites exposed the stories as lies, they became enraged and prepared to wreak their vengeance on Tokeriu and on Gabagabuna. The mission party, with more peaceable aims, then went with them to Gabagabuna.

They found it practically deserted. Pushing inland, they came across the new village of Gabagabuna. The natives had received prior warning of their coming, for no women or children were to be seen, and the men sat in 'sullen silence' on the long platform, making no reply to the Whites' greetings. All inquiries were fruitless—Tokeriu had gone inland, the people said. Uninvited, the missionaries climbed on to the platform, but attempts to ingratiate themselves failed: 'I had in my wallet a long thin stick of trade tobacco, a delicacy very much prized by these people, and as I was sitting in the doorway of the chief's house I took it out, and threw it to some men who were sitting behind me in the dark. Almost before they had time to pick it up, it was hurled back and struck me on the ear.'

Biga warned them that their lives were in danger every minute. Then, suddenly, Tokeriu arrived. 'He was not the grey-headed wizened man we had expected to see—the kind of old man who, in his dotage, might imagine he had held converse with a spirit in the night. Tokeriu was in the prime of life . . . he was a refined man, for a savage; and the marvel to us was that he could restrain his people, who were not in sympathy with him in the conciliatory course he was taking'.

He was obviously trying to control his strong emotions, and listened in silence to the missionaries, but made no response.

Suddenly, he began to recite his prophecies. The people became more and more excited and hostile, and the visiting Wagawaga men, equally, were only held back with difficulty by the Whites.

Eventually, the Whites' party made for safety: they split up and found their way back to the coast in small groups, reaching their boats just before their pursuers could attack them.

The followers of Tokeriu eventually became disillusioned with him, when the slaughter of their valuable pigs turned out to have been in vain. The people now threatened to kill him; Government intervened, arrested him, and gave him two years' prison sentence in Samarai jail. Gabagabuna received a Christian teacher, and when Abel visited the village Tokeriu offered him a present of a large, new garden, full of crops.

It will be noted that although Tokeriu made his peace with Abel, anti-Europeanism was marked in this movement. Later we will see that anti-European feeling was not necessarily present in the earlier stages of many movements though it quickly became added to most of them. The Tokeriu movement is, therefore, of particular interest since it is one of the earliest Melanesian manifestations in embryonic form of that consciousness of common cultural community, and of difference from other communities, that we call nationalism.

RELIGION
WITH MINIMAL LEADERSHIP

A great deal of religious practice, of course, is quite independent of strong leadership or rigid belief, and yet it is observed anyway. Just as millions of American homes celebrate Christmas according to fairly specific traditions —the tree, talk of Santa Claus, and so forth—so in traditional China was New Year's celebrated with countless customs enforced by no one yet always there. Most of the little tradition kind of observances, in fact, are done without benefit of explicit leadership or prescription. The following passage on New Year's in old China gives colorful examples of religion that is enforced by custom itself, not by any institution or charismatic leader.

The Middle Kingdom
S. Wells Williams

The return of the year is an occasion of unbounded festivity and hilarity, as if the whole population threw off the old year with a shout, and clothed themselves in the new with their change of garments. The evidences of the approach of this chief festival appear some weeks previous. The principal streets are lined with tables, upon which articles of dress, furniture, and fancy are disposed for sale in the most attractive manner. Necessity compels many to dispose of certain of their treasures or superfluous things at this season, and sometimes exceedingly curious bits of bric-a-brac, long laid up in families, can be procured at a cheap rate. It is customary for superiors to give their dependents and employees a present, and for shopmen to send an acknowledgment of favors to their customers; one of the most common gifts among the lower classes is a pair of new shoes. Among the tables spread in the streets are many provided with pencils and red paper of various sizes, on which persons write sentences appropriate to the season in various styles,

From S. Wells Williams, *The Middle Kingdom*, vol. 1 (London: W. H. Allen and Co., 1883), pp. 810–16.

to be pasted upon the doorposts and lintels of dwellings and shops, or suspended from their walls. The shops also put on a most brilliant appearance, arrayed in these papers interspersed among the *kin hwa*, or 'golden flowers,' which are sprigs of artificial leaves and flowers made in the southern cities of brass tinsel and fastened upon wires; the latter are designed for an annual offering in temples, or to place before the household tablet. Small strips of red and gilt paper, some bearing the word *fuh*, or 'happiness,' large and small vermilion candles, gaily painted, and other things used in idolatry, are likewise sold in great quantities, and with the increased throng impart an unusually lively appearance to the streets. Another evident sign of the approaching change is the use of water upon the doors, shutters, and other woodwork of houses and shops, washing chairs, utensils, clothes, etc., as if cleanliness had not a little to do with joy, and a well-washed person and tenement were indispensable to the proper celebration of the festival. Throughout the southern rivers all small craft, tankia-boats, and lighters are beached and turned inside out for a scrubbing.

A still more praiseworthy custom attending this season is that of settling accounts and paying debts; shopkeepers are kept busy waiting upon their customers, and creditors urge their debtors to arrange these important matters. No debt is allowed to overpass new year without a settlement or satisfactory arrangement, if it can be avoided; and those whose liabilities altogether exceed their means are generally at this season obliged to wind up their concerns and give all their available property into the hands of their creditors. The consequences of this general pay-day are a high rate of money, great resort to the pawnbrokers, and a general fall in the price of most kinds of produce and commodities. Many good results flow from the practice, and the conscious sense of the difficulty and expense of resorting to legal proceedings to recover debts induces all to observe and maintain it, so that the dishonest, the unsuccessful, and the wild speculator may be sifted out from amongst the honest traders.

De Guignes mentions one expedient to oblige a man to pay his debts at this season, which is to carry off the door of his shop or house, for then his premises and person will be exposed to the entrance and anger of all hungry and malicious demons prowling around the streets, and happiness no more revisit his abode; to avoid this he is fain to arrange his accounts. It is a common practice among devout persons to settle with the gods, and during a few days before the new year, the temples are unusually thronged by devotees, both male and female, rich and poor. Some persons fast and engage the priests to intercede for them that their sins may be pardoned, while they prostrate themselves before the images amidst the din of gongs, drums, and bells, and thus clear off the old score. On new year's eve the streets are full of people hurrying to and fro to conclude the many matters which press upon them. At Canton, some are busy pasting the five slips upon their lintels, signifying their desire that the five blessings which constitute the sum of all human felicity (namely, longevity, riches, health, love of virtue, and a natural death) may be their favored portion. Such sentences as "May the five blessings visit this door," "May heaven send down happiness," "May rich customers ever enter this door," are placed above them; and the doorposts are adorned with others on plain or gold sprinkled red paper, making the entrance quite picturesque. In the hall are suspended scrolls more or less costly, containing antithetical sentences carefully chosen. A literary man would have, for instance, a distich like the following:

> *May I be so learned as to secrete in my mind three myriads of volumes:*
> *May I know the affairs of the world for six thousand years.*

A shopkeeper adorns his door with those relating to trade:

> *May profits be like the morning sun rising on the clouds.*
> *May wealth increase like the morning tide which brings the rain.*
> *Manage your occupation according to truth and loyalty.*
> *Hold on to benevolence and rectitude in all your trading.*

The influence of these mottoes, and countless others like them which are constantly seen in the streets, shops, and dwellings throughout the land, is inestimable. Generally it is for good, and as a large proportion are in the form of petition or wish, they show the moral feeling of the people.

Boat-people in Kwangtung and Fuhkien provinces are peculiarly liberal of their paper prayers, pasting them on every board and oar in the boat, and suspending them from the stern in scores, making the vessel flutter with gaiety. Farmers stick theirs upon barns, trees, wattles, baskets, and implements, as if nothing was too insignificant to receive a blessing. The house is arranged in the most orderly and cleanly manner, and purified with religious ceremonies and lustrations, firing of crackers, etc., and as the necessary preparations occupy a considerable portion of the night, the streets are not quiet till dawn. In addition to the bustle arising from business and religious observances, which marks this passage of time, the constant explosion of firecrackers, and the clamor of gongs, make it still more noisy. Strings of these crackling fireworks are burned at the doorposts, before the outgoing and incoming of the year, designed to expel and deter evil spirits from the house. The consumption is so great as to cover the streets with the fragments, and farmers come the week after into Canton city and sweep up hundreds of bushels for manure.

The first day of the year is also regarded as the birthday of the entire population, for the practice among the Hebrews of dating the age from the beginning of the year, prevails also in China; so that a child born only a week before new year, is considered as entering its second year on the first day of the first month. This does not, however, entirely supersede the observance of the real anniversary, and parents frequently make a solemnity of their son's birthday. A missionary thus describes the celebration of a son's sixth birthday at Ningpo. "The little fellow was dressed in his best clothes, and his father had brought gilt paper, printed prayers, and a large number of bowls of meats, rice, vegetables, spirits, nuts, etc., as an offering to be spread out before the idols. The ceremonies were performed in the apartment of the *Tao Mu,* or 'Bushel Mother,' who has special charge of infants before and after birth. The old abbot was dressed in a scarlet robe, with a gilt image of a serpent fastened in his hair; one of the monks wore a purple, another a gray robe. A multitude of prayers, seemingly a round of repetitions, were read by the abbot, occasionally chanting a little, when the attendants joined in the chorus, and a deafening clamor of bells, cymbals, and wooden blocks, added force to their cry; genuflexions and prostrations were repeatedly made. One part of the ceremony was to pass a live cock through a barrel, which the assistants performed many times, shouting some strange words at each repetition; this act symbolized the dangers through which the child was to pass in his future life, and the priests had prayed that he might as safely come out of them all, as the cock had passed through the barrel. In conclusion, some of the prayers were burned and a libation poured out, and a grand symphony of bell, gong, drum, and block, closed the scene."[1]

A great diversity of local usages are observed at this period in different parts of the country. In Amoy, the custom of "surrounding the furnace" is generally practised. The members of the family sit

[1]Presbyterian Missionary Chronicle, 1846.

down to a substantial supper on new year's eve, with a pan of charcoal under the table, as a supposed preservative against fires. After the supper is ended, the wooden lamp-stands are brought out and spread upon the pavement with a heap of gold and silver paper, and set on fire after all demons have been warned off by a volley of fire-crackers. The embers are then divided into twelve heaps, and their manner of going out carefully watched as a prognostic of the kind of weather to be expected the ensuing year. Many persons wash their bodies in warm water, made aromatic by the infusion of leaves, as a security against disease; this ceremony, and ornamenting the ancestral shrine, and garnishing the whole house with inscriptions, pictures, flowers, and fruit, in the gayest manner the means of the family will allow, occupy most of the night.

The stillness of the streets and the gay inscriptions on the closed shops on new year's morning present a wonderful contrast to the usual bustle and crowd, resembling the Christian Sabbath. The red papers of the doors are here and there interspersed with the blue ones, announcing that during the past year death has come among the inmates of the house; a silent but expressive intimation to passers that some who saw the last new year have passed away. In certain places, white, yellow, and carnation colored papers are employed, as well as blue, to distinguish the degree of the deceased kindred. Etiquette requires that those who mourn remain at home at this period. By noontide the streets begin to be filled with well-dressed persons, hastening in sedans or afoot to make their calls; those who cannot afford to buy a new suit hire one for this purpose, so that a man hardly knows his own domestics in their finery and robes. The meeting of friends in the streets, both bound on the same errand, is attended with particular demonstrations of respect, each politely struggling who shall be most affectedly humble. On this day parents receive the prostrations of their children, teachers expect the salutations of their pupils, magistrates look for the calls of their inferiors, and ancestors of every generation, and gods of various powers are presented with the offerings of devotees in the family hall or public temple. Much of the visiting is done by cards, on which is stamped an emblematic device representing the three happy wishes —of children, rank, and longevity; a common card suffices for distant acquaintances and customers. It might be a subject of speculation whether the custom of visiting and renewing one's acquaintances on new year's day, so generally practised among the Dutch and in America, was not originally imitated from the Chinese; but as in many other things, so in this, the westerns have improved upon the easterns, in calling upon the ladies. Persons, as they meet, salute each other with *Kung-hí! Kung-hí!* 'I respectfully wish you joy!'—or *Sin-hí! Sin-hí!* 'May the new joy be yours,' either of which, from its use at this season, is quite like the *Happy New Year!* of Englishmen.

Toward evening, the merry sounds proceeding from the closed doors announce that the sacrifice provided for presentation before the shrines of departed parents is cheering the worshippers; while the great numbers who resort to gambling-shops show full well that the routine of ceremony soon becomes tiresome, and a more exciting stimulus is needed. The extent to which play is now carried is almost indescribable. Jugglers, mountebanks, and actors also endeavor to collect a few coppers by amusing the crowds. Generally speaking, however, the three days devoted to this festival pass by without turmoil, and business and work then gradually resume their usual course for another twelvemonth.

RELIGION LEGITIMATING THE SOCIAL ORDER

Religious cosmologies and doctrines are often used to show that one should obey the rulers of society, for they have been approved by God or the Absolute and their laws are part of the makeup of a sacred society that reflects the divine will for earth. The following passages are by the Muslim writer Ziā ud-Din Barni (c. 1285–1357), associated with the Muslim Dehli sultanate that ruled much of India from about 1210 to 1556. In the first passage he shows that the rulers of the Baghdad caliphate, the greatest and archetypal Muslim empire, should be given respect due the prophet Muhammad himself because they are related to him by blood. In the second he takes up a theme often presented by defenders of a social order as ordained by God: the division of labor in society is a part of God's plan and does not negate the fact that in principle all are equal before God—even though to advance people out of their station would be to go against God's plan and could do no good. In the third passage, however, Barni indicates that rulers themselves should follow the order willed by God or they will be equally worthy of scorn and divine punishment.

Sources of Indian Tradition

William Theodore de Bary

Social Precedence

The essentially religious color of the medieval Muslim ideal social order is brought out in the following passage, which purports to be an order by the Caliph Ma'Mūn establishing social precedence. The passage is from the Rulings on Temporal Governments, *by Ziā ud-dīn Barnī.* [From Barni, Fatāwa-yi-Jahāndārī, folios 128a–129b passim]

It is commanded that the inhabitants of the capital, Baghdad, and the entire population of the Muslim world should hold in the greatest honor and respect all men of the Hāshimite family who are related to the Prophet by ties of blood, especially the 'Abbāsids to whose line the caliphate of the Muslim community has been confirmed, and, in particular the saiyids whose descent from and relationship to the Prophet is certain. In all circumstances they should strive to reverence and honor them and not allow them to be insulted and humiliated. They should consider the rendering of honor and respect to them to be among their religious duties and a way of doing homage to the Prophet himself. People should consider the causing of any harm or injury to them as equal to infidelity and unbelief.

In accordance with God's commands, a share of the fifth of the spoils of war which accrues to the public treasury, after having been converted to cash, should be delivered to them at their homes for their maintenance. They are to have precedence in seating over all my [the Caliph Ma'mūn's] helpers, supporters, courtiers, and high officers and dignitaries of the realm. In other assemblies and meetings, religious scholars, shaikhs, wazirs, maliks [princes], and the well-known and distinguished people of Baghdad are to sit below them. All classes of the Baghdad population are to pay them due regard and to deem the salvation of Muslims of all classes attainable through paying the relations of the Prophet honor and respect.

As regards the Sunni religious scholars and the Sufis of Baghdad, it is commanded that they should be respected in the capital; to do them honor is to be considered a part of piety. It

From Wm. Theodore de Bary, ed., Sources of Indian Tradition (New York: Columbia University Press, 1964), pp. 505–509. Copyright © 1958 Columbia University Press. Reprinted by permission of Columbia University Press.

should be thought that the mandates of the True Faith are adorned by their words and deeds and the elevation of the banners of Islam is a result of honor paid to them.

[And Ma'mūn ordered that] in accordance with the instructions of the Chief Qādī and with the records kept by the Shaikh ul-Islām, they should cause religious scholars and Sufis to be given what would be sufficient and salutary for them, and enable them to live in the best of circumstances and to avoid that neediness which makes both knowledge and the learned contemptible.

For the warriors and champions of the Faith, he commanded sufficient salaries, allowances, and assistance to be given them in cash from the public treasury of the Muslims, in accordance with the instructions of the muster master at Baghdad and the ranks and grades named and fixed by the muster master's department. Respect and honor are to be paid to holy warriors both in the caliph's palace and in all Baghdad, for they are the protectors of the territory of Islam and of its inhabitants. They fight in the way of God and overthrow the enemies of God and of His Prophet.

Divine Origin
of the "Division of Labor"

Ideally a man's status in the godly society is related to his innate virtues or vices for which God as Creator is responsible. A man's occupation denotes his moral degree in God's sight. The superior social rank of the learned and the literary, implied in the first reading, should be noted. [From Barnī, Fatāwa-yi-Jahāndārī, folios 216b–217b]

All men in creation are equal and in outward form and appearance are also equal. Every distinction of goodness and wickedness which has appeared among mankind has so appeared as a result of their qualities and of their commission of acts. Virtue and vice have been shared out from all eternity and were made the associate of their spirits. The manifestation of human deeds and acts is a created thing. Whenever God obliges good actions and wicked actions, and good and evil, He gives warning of it so that those good and bad deeds, that good and that evil, may be openly manifested, and when, in the very first generation of Adam, the sons of Adam appeared and multiplied, and the world began to be populated, and in their social intercourse the need for everything befell mankind, the Eternal Craftsman imparted to mens' minds the crafts essential to their social intercourse. So in one he implanted writing and penmanship, to another horsemanship, to one the craft of weaving, to another farriery, and to yet another carpentry. All these crafts, honorable and base, from penmanship and horsemanship to cupping and tanning, were implanted in their minds and breasts by virtue of those virtues and vices which, in the very depths of their natures, have become the companions of their spirits. To the hearts of the possessors of the virtues, by reason of their innate virtue, have fallen the noble crafts, and in those under the dominion of vice, by reason of their innate vice, have been implanted the ignoble occupations. Those thus inspired have chosen those very crafts which have been grafted upon their minds and have practiced them, and from them have come those crafts and skills and occupations with which they were inspired; for them the bringing of those crafts into existence was made feasible.

These crafts, noble and ignoble, have become the hidden companions of the sons of the first sons of Adam. In accordance with their quickness of intelligence and perspicacity, their descendants have added to the crafts of their ancestors some fine and desirable features, so that every art, craft, and profession, of whose products mankind has need, has reached perfection.

As virtues were implanted in those who have chosen the nobler occupations, from them alone come forth goodness, kindness, generosity, valor, good deeds, good works, truthfulness, keeping of promises, avoidance of slander, loyalty, purity of vision, justice, equity, recognition of one's duty, gratitude for favors received, and fear of God. These people are said to be noble, freeborn, virtuous, religious, of high lineage, and of pure birth. They alone are worthy of offices and posts in the realm and under the government of the ruler who, in his high position as the supreme governor, is singled out as the leader and the chief of mankind. Thus the government of the ruler and his activities are given strength and put in an orderly condition.

But whenever vices have been inserted into the minds of those who chose the baser arts and the mean occupations, only immodesty, falsehood, miserliness, perfidy, sins, wrongs, lies, evil-speaking, ingratitude, stupidity, injustice, oppression, blindness to one's duty, cant, impudence, bloodthirstiness, rascality, conceit and godlessness appear. They are called lowborn, bazaar people, base, mean, worthless, "plebeian," shameless, and of impure birth. Every act which is mingled with meanness and founded on ignominy comes very well from them. The promotion of the low and the lowborn brings no advantage in this world, for it is impudent to act against the wisdom of creation.

**Rulers to Preserve
the Social Order Willed by God**

[From Barni, Fatāwa-yi-Jahāndāri, folios 58a–58b, 130a]

It is a [religious] duty and necessary for kings whose principal aims are the protection of religion and stability in affairs of government to follow the practices of God Most High in their bestowal of place. Whomsoever God has chosen and honored with excellence, greatness, and ability, in proportion to his merit so should he be singled out and honored by kings. . . . He whom God has created with vile qualities and made contemptible in his sin, rascality, and ignorance, who as a sport of the Devil has been brought into existence as a slave of this world and a helpless victim of his lower self, should be treated and lived with according to the way he was created, so that the wisdom of the creation of the Creator may illumine the hearts of all. But if the ruler, out of a natural inclination or base desire, self-will, or lack of wisdom honors such a scoundrel, then the ruler holds God in contempt and treats Him with scorn. For the ruler has honored, in opposition to the wisdom of creation, one whom God has dishonored and treats him as one distinguished and honorable, making him happy out of the bounty of his power and greatness. Such a ruler is not worthy of the caliphate and deputyship of God. To use the name of king for him becomes a crime for he has made the incomparable bounty of God into an instrument of sin. Opposition to the wisdom of creation hurts him in this world and finally he will be punished in the next world.

RELIGION IN SOCIETY
IN TIMES
OF RAPID CHANGE

When the structures of society are rapidly changing, as has happened so much in the twentieth century as vast sectors of the world have experienced nationalism, revolution, and modernization, religion is likely to be lost if it does not respond in some way true to both its own tradition and the new conditions. People in such times are immensely concerned with political and economic reform, for age-old injustices are challenged by the idea that anything can be turned on its head. Yet, the very pace of change makes many people eager for symbolic ties with the stable spiritual traditions of the past. The following passage is about the modern Hindu spiritual leader in India Vinoba Bhave, who has combined these two sides. A disciple of Mohandas K. Gandhi, the advocate of nonviolence who more than anyone else won Indian independence, Vinoba concerns himself with the practical social change issue of land reform, yet works through the personality of a traditional saint. As the following account of his methods makes clear, Vinoba is able to effect social change precisely because he has the aura of a traditional mahatma, a great soul or holy man. This passage depicts a positive response by religion to times of rapid change.

Vinoba Bhave:
India's Walking Messiah

George Weller

At three o'clock every morning, in some dark village of India, the slumber of the poor is broken by a series of strange noises. Twelve handclaps, dry and commanding, echo through the labyrinth of mud houses where men and animals sleep. A little bell tinkles. Then twenty pairs of sandals move out, slip-slapping among the houses. A kerosene lantern winks by. Presently, when the shuffling sandals are gone, there drift back the notes of a hymn of peace, sung in marching rhythm. Vinoba Bhave, India's walking messiah, and his disciples have taken to the road again.

Vinoba is fifty-seven. A duodenal ulcer is gnawing at his stomach, and dysentery plagues his daily journey of fifteen to twenty miles. Somewhere among the thousands of villages awaiting him is one where he will lie down forever. When he does, the Communist Party will be relieved of its most formidable unarmed antagonist in Asia, perhaps in the world; for Vinoba has undertaken single-handed a program of redistributing India's land. Already Indian landowners have given him nearly 50,000 acres, often in single acres or fractions, though his only weapons are moral suasion and his own prestige as a mahatma, a "great soul."

From George Weller, "Vinoba Bhave: India's Walking Messiah," *The Yale Review*, vol. XLII, no. 2 (December 1952), 236–39. Copyright Yale University.

Vinoba does not badger the landowners, as the Communists do, before a mob of land-hungry peasants steered by a claque of party members. When he arrives at a village he calls the landowners together quietly, under a tree or by a brook, and they are surprised and mollified at being invited to express their views to him privately. He listens closely, lying at full length like a withered Caesar, a brown skinny shoulder exposed, supporting himself on one elbow. "We are sorry, but we cannot help you," the landowners mutter, between pious fear and indignant martyrdom. "We simply cannot spare any land." "I have three sons and only twenty acres. Do you expect me to cut off my sons to help out some stranger?" Experience has taught Vinoba how to handle this objection. Patting the farmer on the shoulder, he says quietly, "Consider me as your fourth son. Father, I am asking you for my own share, no more." The idea of having a mahatma in the family is almost irresistible, even to a hardboiled farmer. Then Vinoba speaks confidentially of his belief that rich and poor are brothers, quoting Sanskrit wisdom on the uses of property and proverbs on the virtue of giving.

The quiet meeting with the landowners lasts usually an hour or so, and ends in a gentlemanly deadlock. The landowners politely stall off a decision. Nobody wants to break the common front by giving anything. "All right," says Vinoba. "So be it. Tomorrow I shall be gone and you will all keep your land. But I warn you: trouble is ahead." A long, painful silence follows, Vinoba lying on his back with his eyes closed, the owners trying to read each other's faces. "We have so little now," mourns one. Vinoba snaps upright: "You have little, but others have less." His nurse brings him his collapsible spinning wheel in its case like a trombone, and he sets it up and begins spinning. The owners shuffle away.

But they are still not free of Vinoba. Indians are proud. Can a mahatma be permitted to walk on to the next village and avow the fact—which will arrive there hours before him—that the rich here are both impious and mean? There is another, more local danger. In the public meeting an hour hence, when Vinoba apears before the whole village, not just the landowners, some little two-acre man, mesmerized by Vinoba or simply mischievous, may rise and give away a sixth of his puny holdings. Then how will the great ones look? Anyone who holds village office by virtue of landed eminence will seem indifferent to his local good name. It is necessary to give Vinoba something—a token, say.

By the time the public meeting opens the landowners have put their heads together behind a tree and scraped together a few acres. Hoping Vinoba will stay at a safe distance, they send him a message that they will "help him," without mentioning any figures. Sometimes they resort to floral flattery to get him on the road sooner. "Have I come for garlands?" demands Vinoba. "I have a garden if I want a bouquet. Tell me how much land you will give." He walks nervously around in a circle of squatting farmers, with their wives and children. He denounces nobody. Does any small farmer want to set an example to the rich? One or two hands are timidly elevated.

The substantial landowners now see themselves outflanked. When they break down, their answer is usually the one I heard given to Vinoba in the United Provinces. "We cannot actually spare you an inch of land. But because you are a mahatma, we cannot let you leave us empty-handed."

Yet Vinoba somehow leaves the farmers with a sense of having solved their own troubles, respectably and independently. The rich, because they have given "voluntarily," are ennobled and dignified. The poor have a divided gratitude—to the departed Vinoba, to the remaining rich, and to God, whom Vinoba summons to witness and sanctify the gift.

Being a practical saint, Vinoba is not satisfied with the almighty registrar of deeds. He also ties up giver and getter with a regular lawful deed, signed and humanly witnessed. Knowing the poor man's temptation to make an easy rupee, Vinoba nails down the new owner with a clause forbidding transfer for ten years. He has even squeezed the state into a little giving. The farmers are exempt from the three percent transfer tax. And if the land has been waste and the farmer clears and plants it within two years, he pays no taxes.

"When you awaken tomorrow I shall be gone. But in reality I shall still be with you," he tells his villages. He is, too. He leaves helpers behind with the villagers, in joint committee, to see that the land is fairly handed out, with preference for the landless and the untouchables. He keeps his rear guard alert. "People know loopholes in any law better than the lawmakers themselves," he warns them. Gandhi, who never was fooled by Vinoba's self-depreciation, once said: "He has an army of disciples and workers who would rise to any sacrifice at his bidding." To lock the stitches after Vinoba has passed is no pretty task, because on one pilgrimage in northern India he averaged 285 acres a day, and on another in Hyderabad he averaged 200 acres a day.

Vinoba's method has this drawback: it hits the man with middle-sized holdings but not the large absentee owner. Among 563 donors in Madhya Pradesh, 541 gave less than 25 acres and only thirteen over a hundred. Vinoba has not worked out any sure way of getting at the remote rich. The best he can do is to sour the lesser landowners against them, and thereby increase the tension on their local overseers. Some day he may enter the cities, which he calls a "jungle of brutes," and hunt down the big owners.

However, only the rich-and-obscure dare go underground in the cities when Vinoba approaches; the rich-and-prominent must line up humbly to be plundered by the apostle. At Delhi, the President of India, Dr. Rajendra Prasad, entered shoeless the grass shack erected by the government for Vinoba beside the memorial altar where Gandhi was cremated, and invited Vinoba to help himself to his estates in Bihar.

"People want a revolutionary program," he tells India, "and think that a revolution cannot be wrought without bloodshed. I cannot accept their contention. They are not revolutionists at all. They are status-quo-ists. Their object is not a revolution, but to cause an exchange of places between the present happy and unhappy ones. A revolution must signify universal happiness without exception. While the Western mind is trained to think in terms of the greatest good of the greatest number, the Indian mind from childhood is taught to think in terms of the good of all."

CHAPTER SIX

UNEARTHLY PATTERNS
IN THE MIND:
THE CONCEPTUAL LIFE
OF RELIGION

The expression of religion in practices and groups is oriented to transcendence; as we have seen, rituals and spiritual groups predicate meanings. It is important to realize that religion always has forms of outward expression. It is not merely that religion *thinks* about meanings; it reveals this concern in rites, groups, and institutions that have no ostensible point if the transcendent is not real. Religion is not only inward beliefs or pieties but also something that can be seen in the art, actions, and social configurations of a society.

Religion, however, does have a side that dwells in the mind in the form of ideas, beliefs, processes of thought, and attitudes. Some people, in fact, think of religion as a matter of beliefs about God, life after death, and morals, and that first people held such beliefs, then devised rites and groups in order to express and perpetuate them. Actually, the question of which came first, religious beliefs or practices and sociology, may be as unanswerable as the similar question about the chicken and the egg. The important fact is that the two go together and are both essential to what religion is, in distinction from simple philosophy on one hand and magic or social clubs on the other. In religion these two sides are mutually reinforcing, like the two sides of a coin. What we think is reflected in what we do and the human relationships we form; and, conversely, what we do, together with the emotional feelings directly engendered by what we do, is reflected in what we think. We need, and the religious process can help supply, ideas to go with experience and concepts to answer the questions about the world and society in which we participate.

These are ideas that express the more-than-earthly meanings of human life, as do rites and transcendent assemblies. As thought, they are the inner counterparts to the outer forms of expression. Like the outer, they bear several messages at once. There are messages in what religious conceptual statements say, in how they say it, and in who says it and when—just as, for example, there is a message not only in what a religious group explicitly does but also in whether it is established or emergent in relation to its social milieu.

That is not all, however. Religious teachings, and claims to truth in religious statements, certainly need to be taken seriously in their own terms. In order to evaluate them, we need to understand what they are saying and what methods they are using for determining truth or value in religion.

In this chapter, religious conceptual language—ideas, styles of teaching, and methods for determining truth—are examined. We begin with a passage by a distinguished philosopher and theologian who expounds the close relationship between religious statement and action —a theme already alluded to in a different sense that points to some very deep things about religious language. We then look at the great importance of verbal communication in religion—the role of the word in religion's process of inner transformation. Then we compare three contrasting lights in which religious conceptual systems can be put: traditional beliefs, liberal theology, and intentionally conservative theology. Afterwards, we compare three broadly contrasting religious conceptual systems oriented toward (1) nature, (2) salvation, and (3) mystical unity. Finally, we consider reason, experience, and existential choice, three ways of determining truth in religion.

RELIGIOUS STATEMENT
AS ACTION-ORIENTED

The following passage by the religious philosopher Nicolas Berdyaev (1874–1948) provides a thought-provoking introduction to the consideration of language and truth in religion. Berdyaev talks of *Logos*, word or principle, and we are reminded that in religion language can be a way of knowing. To know something to be true is to be able to say something about it; even to know something to be beyond words—which much of religious reality is said to be—is to express its transcendence in words. Even more important, Berdyaev believes that truth, especially in the religious sense, is not dead fact, which can enslave, but is absolutely linked to meaning and is that which liberates the person to be creative and free. In looking at various sorts of religious truth or claims to truth, we should keep these lines in mind—all statements that are genuinely claimed to be religious truth are intended to be not only mere factual propositions but also truths that are important because they liberate one to be creative and free as does all absolute truth.

The Meaning of the Creative Act

Nicolas Berdyaev

Obedience to necessity (of nature or of categories) is understood as intellectual honesty and conscientiousness. Men believe that the criteria of truth are intellectual and that truth is accepted positively by the intellect, that knowledge of truth is honest and conscientious obedience. They doubt everything else but believe firmly in this. If truth lies in this, that the world is necessity and not freedom, that there is no meaning in the world, then it is dishonest and conscienceless to turn away from this truth and invent non-existent freedom and meaning, to recognize as truth whatever you will. And all the efforts of our spirit along the line of least resistance, the line of the given world, all the passive obedience of the spirit, speak for the assumption that there is neither freedom nor meaning in the world, that that towards which the spirit strives is non-existent. The *pathos* of obedience to necessity, to the world as it is, is transformed into the *pathos* of truth. The passive philosophy of necessity may be a sad and hopeless, but yet a true, philosophy, not thought out according to our desire. This customary opinion, proclaimed with a false *pathos* of nobility, puts more acutely the question whether the knowledge of truth is passivity, obedience of the intellect, or activity, the creativeness of the spirit? Is not the "truth" of the passive intellect with its purely intellectual conscience only a spectre, the self-hypnosis of a spirit oppressed and divided within itself? The obedience to "truth" of the passive intellect is slavery and palsy, not honesty and conscientiousness. The "truth" of a passive intellect simply does not exist—it is merely an intellectual expression of

From Nicolas Berdyaev, *The Meaning of the Creative Act*, translated by Donald A. Lowrie (New York: Collier Books, 1962), pp. 42–44.

spiritual depression and dependence. Truth is revealed only by the creative activity of the spirit; outside this, truth is incomprehensible and unattainable. The absolute reply of the Gospel: "I am the Truth" has also absolute philosophical and gnosseological meaning. The Absolute Man is Truth. Truth is not that which is, that which is forced upon us as a given condition, as necessity. Truth is not the duplication, the repetition of being in the knower. *Truth is comprehension and liberation of being, it presupposes the creative act of the knower within being; Truth is meaning and may not deny meaning. To deny meaning in the world means to deny truth, to recognize nothing but darkness. Truth makes us free. To deny freedom is to deny truth.* There cannot be truth in the idea that the world is merely a meaningless necessity, for the exclusive power of necessity is the power of darkness in which there is neither truth nor any way to liberation. Either truth does not exist at all, and then we should cease all philosophic assertions, or truth is a creative light giving meaning and liberation to being. Truth is light and one cannot acknowledge truth and deny all the light in the world. Truth is the enlightenment of darkness and hence there cannot be truth about the meaningless and utter darkness of being. Truth presupposes the Sun, the Logos; and He who was the Sun and Logos of the world could say: "I am the Truth." The passive, intellectual, abstract "truth" must be sacrificed and by this sacrifice must be purchased victory over a slavish oppression of the spirit. The passive slavery to this "truth" is a great hindrance in the way of knowing the genuine truth. Dostoevski has a moving word about how, if truth were on one side and Christ on the other, it would be better to refuse truth and to go with Christ, that is to sacrifice the dead truth of a passive intellect for the sake of the living truth of the integral spirit. And to-day all philosophy must pass through the heroic act of denying the "truth." Then philosophy will become a creative act of knowing, i.e. active knowledge. What is, what is given and forced upon the intellect, this is not at all the truth; neither is it obligatory, for it may be that it is given and forced upon us only because of the slavish oppression of the spirit and will disappear like a mirage with the spirit's liberation. Knowledge of the truth means the provision of a reasoned meaning for being, its bright liberation from the dark power of necessity. Truth itself resists the world as it is, as it is given, otherwise truth would not be value, meaning; otherwise the Logos would not be living in it. Lowering truth to those scientific concepts which were a result of adaptation to necessity is a fall of the spirit, its renunciation of creative activity. Therefore creative philosophy cannot be scientific philosophy. There is a gnosis which goes beyond science and is independent of it. But creative gnostic philosophy is not a sentimental philosophy either, not a philosophy of the feeling, of the heart. A philosophy of feeling is also passive, obedient and not creatively active. Philosophy is not dreaming but action.

THE IMPORTANCE OF VERBAL COMMUNICATION

The use of words with thoughts behind them is an essential part of religious experience and its interpretation. Words can take many forms and play many roles: books, sermons, dialogues, chants, philosophical reflection, prayer, the chatter of organizing groups. Zen Buddhism is sometimes considered a religion that negates the importance of the word. It is true that its absolute cannot be put into words, but only experienced and demonstrated, and that its central form of practice is meditation intended to stop rather than agitate the thinking mind in order to get to the One Mind beneath it.

Nonetheless, words do have an important role in Zen; even if used only to show the inappropriateness of words to enlightenment, they can themselves lead one to the point of grasping this. Thus, examples from Zen are chosen to illustrate the essential role of words in religion. The first selection is a translation of a book containing traditional dialogues on koans between a Zen master and his disciple. Koans in Zen are seemingly nonsense expressions upon which the disciple concentrates his thoughts; in the following selection, the riddle is "What is the sound of the one hand?" When the disciple goes to the master for training, he is asked about the koan on which he has been working. What the master is looking for is not an intellectual answer but a *demonstration*, perhaps nonverbal and undoubtedly not very rational, that the student has assimilated the koan and the view of reality that underlies it on every level of his being. (In this case, the intellectual meaning is probably that the one hand is the One Mind—the Buddha-mind or absolute essence and being of the universe beyond all words—that is coexistent with the universe and fills all, which is both before birth and after death. The point is not to *say* this but to thrust oneself forward, alive with the realization of it.)

Another form of verbal religious communication is the sermon, and it is also used in Zen. The koan passage is followed by a passage from a sermon on the topic of the one Buddha-mind. The sermon is by Bankei (1622–93), a famous Japanese Zen master who stressed the presence of the "unborn mind" everywhere as the true essence of all things. The first passage, then, shows the demonstration of a truth that the second puts into more rational words.

The Koan on the Sound of the One Hand

In clapping both hands a sound is heard; what is the sound of the one hand?

Answer. The pupil faces his master, takes a correct posture, and without a word, thrusts one hand forward.

Discourse

Master. If you've heard the sound of the one hand, prove it.

Answer. Without a word, the pupil thrusts one hand forward.

Master. It's said that if one hears the sound of the one hand, one becomes a Buddha [i.e., becomes enlightened]. Well then, how will you do it?

Answer. Without a word, the pupil thrusts one hand forward.

Master. After you've become ashes, how will you hear it?

Answer. Without a word, the pupil thrusts one hand forward.

Master. What if the one hand is cut by the Suimo Sword?

Answer. "It can't be."

Or:

"If it can, let me see you do it." So saying, the pupil extends his hand forward.

Or:

Without a word, the pupil thrusts one hand forward.

Master. Why can't it cut the one hand?

Answer. "Because the one hand pervades the universe."

Master. Then show me something that contains the universe.

Answer. Without a word, the pupil thrusts one hand forward.

Master. The before-birth-one-hand, what is it like?

"The Koan on the Sound of the One Hand" from *The Sound of the One Hand: 281 Zen Koans With Answers*, translated, with a commentary, by Yoel Hoffmann. Translation and commentary copyright © 1975 by Yoel Hoffmann. Published by Basic Books, Inc., and Bantam Books Inc. Reprinted by permission of the publishers.

Answer. Without a word, the pupil thrusts one hand forward.

Master. The Mt.-Fuji-summit-one-hand, what is it like?

Answer. The pupil, shading his eyes with one hand, takes the pose of looking down from the summit of Mt. Fuji and says, "What a splendid view!" naming several places to be seen from Mt. Fuji—or others would name places visible from where they happen to be.

Master. Attach a quote to the-Mt.-Fuji-summit-one-hand.

Answer.

Floating clouds connected the sea and the mountain,
And white flat plains spread into the states of Sei and Jo.

Master. Did you hear the sound of the one hand from the back or from the front?

Answer. Extending one hand, the pupil repeatedly says, "Whether it's from the front or from the back, you can hear it as you please."

Or:

"From the back it's caw! caw! [the sound of a crow]. From the front it's chirp, chirp [the sound of a sparrow]."

Master. Now that you've heard the sound of the one hand, what are you going to do?

Answer. "I'll pull weeds, scrub the floor, and if you're tired, give you a massage."

Master. If it's that convenient a thing, let me hear it too!

Answer. Without a word, the pupil slaps his master's face.

Master. The one hand—how far will it reach?

Answer. The pupil places his hand on the floor and says, "This is how far it goes."

Master. The before-the-fifteenth-day-one-hand, the after-the-fifteenth-day-one-hand, the fifteenth-day-one-hand, what's it like?

Answer. The pupil extends his right hand and says, "This is the before-the-fifteenth-day-one-hand." Extending his left hand he says, "This is the after-the-fifteenth-day-one-hand." Bringing his hands together he says, "This is the fifteenth-day-one-hand."

Master. The sublime-sound-of-the-one-hand, what is it like?

Answer. The pupil immediately imitates the sound he happens to hear when sitting in front of his master. That is, if it happens to be raining outside, he imitates the sound of rain, "Pitter-patter"; if at that moment a bird happens to call, he says, "Caw! Caw!" imitating the bird's call.

Master. The soundless-voice-of-the-one-hand, what is it like?

Answer. Without a word, the pupil abruptly stands up, then sits down again, bowing in front of his master.

Master. The true-[mental]-sphere-of-the-one-hand, what's it like?

Answer. "I take it to be as fleeting as a dream or phantom, or as something like an illusory flower. That's how I think of it."

Master. The source-of-the-one-hand, what is it?

Answer. "On the plain there is not the slightest breeze that stirs the smallest grain of sand."

*All communication with places north of the White Wolf River is
disconnected,
And south to the Red Phoenix City, autumn nights have grown so long.*

Or:

"It is from the place where there is not even one rabbit's hair that I have struck the sound of the one hand."

*The wind blows and clears the sky of all floating clouds,
And the moon rises above those green hills like a piece of round white jade.*

Or:

*Arriving at the river, the territories of the state of Go seem to come to an
end,
Yet on the other bank, the mountains of the state of Etsu look so far away.*

Zen: Poems, Prayers, Sermons, Anecdotes, Interviews

Lucien Stryk
and Takashi Ikemoto

The mind begotten by and given to each of us by our parents is none other than the Buddha-mind, birthless and immaculate, sufficient to manage all that life throws up to us. A proof: suppose at this very instant, while you face me listening, a crow caws and a sparrow twitters somewhere behind you. Without any intention on your part of distinguishing between these sounds, you hear each distinctly. In

Excerpt from *Zen: Poems, Prayers, Sermons, Anecdotes, Interviews* by Lucien Stryk and Takashi Ikemoto, pp. 79–80. Copyright © 1963, 1965 by Lucien Stryk and Takashi Ikemoto. Used by permission of Doubleday & Company, Inc.

so doing you are hearing with the birthless mind, which is yours for all eternity.

Well, we are to be in this mind from now on, and our sect will be known as the Buddha-mind sect. To consider, once again, my example of a moment ago, if any of you feel you heard the crow and the sparrow intentionally, you are deluding yourselves, for you are listening to me, not to what goes on behind you. In spite of this there are moments when you hear such sounds distinctly, when you hear with the Buddha-mind of non-birth. This nobody here can deny. All of you are living Buddhas, because the birthless mind which you possess is the beginning and the basis of all.

Now, if the Buddha-mind is birthless, it is necessarily immortal, for how can what has never been born perish? You've all encountered the phrase "birthless and imperishable" in the sutras, but until now you've not had the slightest proof of its truth. Indeed I suppose like most people you've memorized this phrase while being ignorant of birthlessness.

When I was twenty-five I realized that non-birth is all-sufficient to life, and since then, for forty years, I've been proving it to people just like you. I was the first to preach this greatest truth of life. I ask you, have any of you priests heard anyone else teach this truth before me? Of course not.

TRADITIONAL
BELIEF SYSTEMS

To illustrate different approaches to religious statement, the following three passages are all taken from texts and theologians of the Church of England, the Christian church established in a country that contains both Protestant and Catholic elements. First there is the Catechism, or instruction in question and answer form regarding Christian faith and life, that is supposed to be learned before one is confirmed into full participation in church life. *The Book of Common Prayer* in which it is found is the standard book of services and other rites and teachings in the Church of England; the official version dates from 1662 and is based on versions over a century older.

The following selection represents traditional teaching in an established religion. It is taken seriously; yet it is fair to say that these words in their archaic language also suggest social continuity and the atmosphere of old English churches and support the *meaning* and *authority* of tradition as such. Note the underlying assumption of a stable society in which there are those in authority and those who are higher than others; a feel for religion intertwined with social order is a characteristic part of traditional belief systems. Note also the inclusion of much older Christian or biblical texts, such as the Nicene Creed, the Ten Commandments, and the Lord's Prayer.

The Book of Common Prayer of the Church of England

A Catechism

That is to say, an instruction to be learned of every person before he be brought to be confirmed by the bishop

Question. What is your Name?

Answer. N. or M.

Question. Who gave you this Name?

Answer. My Godfathers and Godmothers in my Baptism; wherein I was made a member of Christ, the child of God, and an inheritor of the kingdom of heaven.

Question. What did your Godfathers and Godmothers then for you?

Answer. They did promise and vow three things in my name. First, that I should renounce the devil and all his works, the pomps and vanity of this wicked world, and all the sinful lusts of the flesh. Secondly, that I should believe all the articles of the Christian faith. And thirdly, that I should keep God's holy will and commandments, and walk in the same all the days of my life.

Question. Dost thou not think that thou art bound to believe, and to do, as they have promised for thee?

Answer. Yes verily: and by God's help so I will. And I heartily thank our heavenly Father, that he hath called me to this state of salvation, through Jesus Christ our Saviour. And I pray unto God to give me his grace, that I may continue in the same unto my life's end.

From *The Book of Common Prayer of the Church of England. The Book of Common Prayer 1662* of the Church of England is Crown Copyright in England and extracts used herein are with permission.

Catechist.   Rehearse the Articles of the Belief.

Answer.   I believe in God the Father Almighty, Maker of heaven and earth:

And in Jesus Christ his only Son our Lord, Who was conceived by the Holy Ghost, Born of the Virgin Mary, Suffered under Pontius Pilate, Was crucified, dead and buried: He descended into hell; The third day he rose again from the dead; He ascended into heaven, And sitteth at the right hand of God the Father Almighty; From thence he shall come to judge the quick and the dead.

I believe in the Holy Ghost; The holy Catholick Church; The Communion of Saints; The Forgiveness of sins; The Resurrection of the body, And the life everlasting. Amen.

Question.   What dost thou chiefly learn in these Articles of thy Belief?

Answer.   First, I learn to believe in God the Father, who hath made me, and all the world.

Secondly, in God the Son, who hath redeemed me, and all mankind.

Thirdly, in God the Holy Ghost, who sanctifieth me, and all the elect people of God.

Question.   You said that your Godfathers and Godmothers did promise for you, that you should keep God's Commandments. Tell me how many there be?

Answer.   Ten.

Question.   Which be they?

Answer.   The same which God spake in the twentieth chapter of Exodus, saying, I am the Lord thy God, who brought thee out of the land of Egypt, out of the house of bondage.

    I.   Thou shalt have none other gods but me.

    II.   Thou shalt not make to thyself any graven image, nor the likeness of any thing that is in heaven above, or in the earth beneath, or in the water under the earth. Thou shalt not bow down to them, nor worship them. For I the Lord thy God am a jealous God, and visit the sins of the fathers upon the children unto the third and fourth generation of them that hate me, and shew mercy unto thousands in them that love me and keep my commandments.

    III.   Thou shalt not take the Name of the Lord thy God in

vain: for the Lord will not hold him guiltless, that taketh his Name in vain.

IV.   Remember that thou keep holy the Sabbath day. Six days shalt thou labour, and do all that thou hast to do; but the seventh day is the Sabbath of the Lord thy God. In it thou shalt do no manner of work, thou, and thy son, and thy daughter, thy man-servant, and thy maid-servant, thy cattle, and the stranger that is within thy gates. For in six days the Lord made heaven and earth, the sea, and all that in them is, and rested the seventh day: wherefore the Lord blessed the seventh day, and hallowed it.

V.   Honour thy father and thy mother; that thy days may be long in the land which the Lord thy God giveth thee.

VI.   Thou shalt do no murder.

VII.   Thou shalt not commit adultery.

VIII.   Thou shalt not steal.

IX.   Thou shalt not bear false witness against thy neighbour.

X.   Thou shalt not covet thy neighbour's house, thou shalt not covet thy neighbour's wife, nor his servant, nor his maid, nor his ox, nor his ass, nor any thing that is his.

Question. What dost thou chiefly learn by these Commandments?

Answer.   I learn two things: my duty towards God, and my duty towards my Neighbour.

Question.   What is thy duty towards God?

Answer.   My duty towards God is to believe in him, to fear him, and to love him, with all my heart, with all my mind, with all my soul, and with all my strength; to worship him, to give him thanks, to put my whole trust in him, to call upon him, to honour his holy Name and his Word, and to serve him truly all the days of my life.

Question.   What is thy duty towards thy Neighbour?

Answer.   My duty towards my Neighbour is to love him as myself, and to do to all men as I would they should do unto me: To love, honour, and succour my father and mother: To honour and obey the Queen, and all that are put in authority under her: To submit myself to all my governors, teachers, spiritual pastors and masters: To order myself lowly and reverently to all my betters: To hurt nobody by word nor deed: To be true and just in all my dealing: To bear no malice nor hatred in my heart: To keep my hands from picking and stealing, and my tongue from evil-speaking, lying, and slandering: To keep my body in temperance, soberness, and chastity: Not to covet nor desire other men's goods; but to learn and labour truly to get mine own living, and to do my duty in that state of life, unto which it shall please God to call me.

Catechist.   My good child, know this, that thou art not able to do these things of thyself, nor to walk in the commandments of God, and to serve him, without his special grace; which thou must learn at all times to call for by diligent prayer. Let me hear therefore if thou canst say the Lord's Prayer.

Answer.   Our Father which art in heaven, Hallowed be thy Name, Thy kingdom come, Thy will be done, in earth as it is in heaven. Give us this day our daily bread; And forgive us our trespasses, As we forgive them that trespass against us; And lead us not into temptation, But deliver us from evil. Amen.

Question.   What desirest thou of God in this Prayer?

Answer.   I desire my Lord God our heavenly Father, who is the giver of all goodness, to send his grace unto me, and to all people, that we may worship him, serve him, and obey him, as we ought to do. And I pray unto God, that he will send us all things that be needful both for our souls and bodies; and that he will be merciful unto us, and forgive us our sins; and that it will please him to save and defend us in all dangers ghostly and bodily; and that he will keep us from all sin and wickedness, and from our ghostly enemy, and from everlasting death. And this I trust he will do of his mercy and goodness, through our Lord Jesus Christ. And therefore I say, Amen, So be it.

Question.   How many Sacraments hath Christ ordained in his Church?

Answer.   Two only, as generally necessary to salvation; that is to say, Baptism, and the Supper of the Lord.

Question.   What meanest thou by this word *Sacrament?*

Answer.   I mean an outward and visible sign of an inward and spiritual grace given unto us, ordained by Christ himself, as a means whereby we receive the same, and a pledge to assure us thereof.

Question.   How many parts are there in a Sacrament?

Answer.   Two: the outward visible sign, and the inward spiritual grace.

Question.   What is the outward visible sign or form in Baptism?

Answer.   Water: wherein the person is baptized, *In the Name of the Father, and of the Son, and of the Holy Ghost.*

Question.   What is the inward and spiritual grace?

Answer. A death unto sin, and a new birth unto righteousness: for being by nature born in sin, and the children of wrath, we are hereby made the children of grace.

Question. What is required of persons to be baptized?

Answer. Repentance, whereby they forsake sin: and faith, whereby they stedfastly believe the promises of God, made to them in that Sacrament.

Question. Why then are infants baptized, when be reason of their tender age they cannot perform them?

Answer. Because they promise them both by their sureties: which promise, when they come to age, themselves are bound to perform.

Question. Why was the Sacrament of the Lord's Supper ordained?

Answer. For the continual remembrance of the sacrifice of the death of Christ, and of the benefits which we receive thereby.

Question. What is the outward part or sign of the Lord's Supper?

Answer. Bread and Wine, which the Lord hath commanded to be received.

Question. What is the inward part, or thing signified?

Answer. The Body and Blood of Christ, which are verily and indeed taken and received by the faithful in the Lord's Supper.

Question. What are the benefits whereof we are partakers thereby?

Answer. The strengthening and refreshing of our souls by the Body and Blood of Christ, as our bodies are by the Bread and Wine.

Question. What is required of them who come to the Lord's Supper?

Answer. To examine themselves, whether they repent them truly of their former sins, stedfastly purposing to lead a new life; have a lively faith in God's mercy through Christ, with a thankful remembrance of his death; and be in charity with all men.

The Curate of every Parish shall diligently upon Sundays and Holy-days, after the second Lesson at Evening Prayer, openly in the Church instruct and examine so many Children of his Parish sent unto him, as he shall think convenient, in some part of this Catechism.

And all Fathers, Mothers, Masters, and Dames, shall cause their Children,

Servants, and Prentices, (which have not learned their Catechism,) to come to the Church at the time appointed, and obediently to hear and be ordered by the Curate, until such time as they have learned all that is here appointed for them to learn.

So soon as Children are come to a competent age, and can say, in their mother tongue, the Creed, the Lord's Prayer, and the Ten Commandments; and also can answer to the other questions of this short Catechism; they shall be brought to the Bishop: And every one shall have a Godfather, or a Godmother, as a witness of their Confirmation.

And whensoever the Bishop shall give knowledge for Children to be brought unto him for their Confirmation, the Curate of every Parish shall either bring or send in writing, with his hand subscribed thereunto, the names of all such persons within his Parish, as he shall think fit to be presented to the Bishop to be confirmed. And, if the Bishop approve of them, he shall confirm them in manner following.

LIBERAL THEOLOGY

The following passage is by a contemporary, and controversial, bishop of the Church of England. This passage, from a book for a popular audience, is an example of one theological response to a tradition like that of the last selection. That style of response, commonly called liberal, basically asserts that all religious language, whether ancient or modern, comes out of a culture and shares the culture's particular world view. In order for the real meaning of religion to live in other cultures, its concepts must be continually translated into language and concepts that are living in the other culture and that harmonize with its world view and experience of life. Thus, Christianity should be translated out of the language of two thousand years ago, which Robinson says modern people cannot *really* believe, and into terms compatible with the world of modern science and the modern social order in which we live. These, in Robinson's terms, make God the reality found in the depths of existence, rather than a being up in heaven, and make Christ a manifestation of God for us as humans, rather than a fantastic being with a peculiar biology. The old-fashioned heaven and virgin birth merely get in the way today; we should, Robinson believes, look at the *meaning* behind them.

But That I Can't Believe

John A. T. Robinson

> *You can blame it on to Adam,*
> *You can blame it on to Eve,*
> *You can blame it on the apple,*
> *But that I can't believe.*
>   Sydney Carter, *Friday Morning*

But that I can't believe! It's a typical reaction to much of Christian doctrine to-day. And time and again I catch myself saying: 'In the sense in which you think you're being asked to believe it, nor can I.'

People suppose that being a Christian means swallowing a whole string of statements, of which the following might be samples:

> *There's a Being called God in heaven who made the world, as a potter makes a pot.*
>
> *He created Adam and Eve as the first man and the first woman to live on this planet.*
>
> *They sinned, and we've all been suffering the consequences ever since.*
>
> *But to save the situation God sent his Son down from heaven to earth.*
>
> *Jesus hadn't got a human father, but God took the man's part.*
>
> *As a God-man Jesus could have done anything he wanted to, and sometimes did.*
>
> *When he died, his body vanished into thin air and was reconstituted as one that could pass through closed doors.*
>
> *Jesus then went back up to heaven, where we shall go when we die—unless, of course, we are bad, when we shall go to hell.*
>
> *At the end of the world Christ will be seen returning on the clouds to wind things up.*

That's a caricature, but I suspect it's a pretty fair picture of what many people *think* the Church *expects* them to believe.

Certainly when I am asked, 'Do you believe in the Virgin Birth or the Resurrection or the Divinity of Christ?', I am aware that the answer 'Yes' will be taken by the questioner to mean that I accept

From John A. T. Robinson, *But That I Can't Believe* (London: Collins Fontana Books, 1967), pp. 11–14. Reprinted by permission of William Collins, Sons & Co., Ltd.

that sort of picture more or less literally. The answer 'No' will be taken to mean that I'm not a Christian (and therefore ought to resign).

And there are people of very different kinds who see it like this and want to keep it that way.

There are many conservative and middle-of-the-road churchmen who regard one as diluting the Faith or confusing the simple if one can't return a straight 'Yes.'

Equally, there are powerful vested interests on the other side— humanists who would like Christianity kept as traditional and incredible as possible and regard one as dishonestly slithering out of it if one suggests one simply is not interested in defending the target they know how to knock down.

So one gets caught both ways. But the only thing to do is to pick oneself up again and refuse to be presented with this false 'either-or.'

For the answer I want to give is that I believe profoundly in what these doctrines are concerned to say but that the traditional ways of stating them so often put the crunch at quite the wrong place. One's faith is made to turn on questions to which the answer should well be 'Don't know' or even 'No.' Let me illustrate.

A century ago . . . both traditional Christians and non-Christians were agreed that the truth of Genesis depended on whether Adam and Eve were actual historical characters. One can well understand how those who denied this were thought to be betraying the Faith and selling the pass.

But we can now see that this was really the wrong question. People could give quite different answers to this—and in fact the great majority have now given a negative answer—and still be Christians. For Christianity commits one to a certain interpretation of human nature—which is given classic expression in the Genesis story. It does not commit one to any particular anthropological or biological theory.

In the same way, Christianity stands for a certain commitment to Christ as 'God for us.' It does not bind us to a particular view of where his genes came from or of what happened to the molecules of his corpse.

As I hope to make clear, I accept as strongly as anyone what the New Testament writers are seeking to affirm by the Virgin Birth or the Resurrection. But I refuse to have this faith made dependent for me or for anyone else on answers to questions which the New Testament doesn't set out to answer, on which there can never be certainty, and on which Christians should be free to differ.

Let me make it absolutely clear that I am *not* saying that a modern Christian *cannot* take these and other miracles literally as physical phenomena. He may well be convinced by the evidence that something quite unusual physically took place.

I myself find the evidence for the empty tomb (which is much stronger documentarily than that for the virgin birth) very compelling. I find it difficult to get away from the fact that the tomb was found empty. But I believe strongly that a Christian can be *free* to say that the bones of Jesus lie around somewhere in Palestine. For the conviction of Christ's living power—which is what belief in *the Resurrection* means—does not *turn* on any theory of what happened to the body.

The same applies to what statements of the Christian faith one takes purely factually as history and what as affirming some spiritual conviction or theological truth.

Consider, for instance, the central clauses of the Apostles' Creed:

a. He was conceived by the Holy Ghost, born of the Virgin Mary,

b. He suffered under Pontius Pilate, was crucified, dead and buried,

c. He descended into hell,

d. On the third day he rose again from the dead,

e. He ascended into heaven,

f. And sitteth on the right hand of God the Father almighty;

g. From thence he shall come to judge the quick and the dead.

Of these, *b* is a series of straight historical statements. Others, like *f*, are clearly symbolic expressions of faith. Most are a mixture of both.

On the face of it, all the sentences sound alike and appear to speak of happenings. But they are certainly not all literal events.

In the past men have not worried very much to ask what *kind* of truth they are asserting.

But to-day we are acutely conscious of the difference. We cannot lump everything together and simply say, 'Do you believe this?', without asking a lot of questions. This makes the situation a good deal more complicated. But the same is true of any period of transition—in science or anything else.

Much sifting and counter-questioning is necessary. And the immediate result is bound to appear negative and confusing. For one has to clear the ground so often in order to get down to the real issues.

INTENTIONALLY
CONSERVATIVE THEOLOGY

Another form of contemporary religious thought is intentionally conservative theology. Its proponents endeavor to support the full meaning of the tradition within which they find themselves, feeling that its explicit language and concepts are as valid now as ever. It should be distinguished from writing that is strictly traditionalist in the sense of being done from within a tradition when that tradition is culturally dominant and virtually unquestioned. In very few cases can one write religiously in that manner today. Rather, modern religious conservatism represents a deliberate choice made in full awareness of other options. Often it is not so much support of an established religion as it is asserting doctrines in a way that goes counter to the prevailing culture. (In present-day America, though, it seems that both liberal and conservative perspectives find strong cultural support.)

The following passage, by a Church of England theologian, is a moderately conservative response to the kind of liberal theology exemplified by Bishop Robinson. (The book *Honest to God* referred to in the passage is another book by Robinson.) Austin Farrar, also writing for a popular audience, is concerned to show—in opposition to Robinson's kind of liberalism—that the traditional meaning of God's transcendence is viable and that simply calling God reality or the universe makes no sense and is a way of not believing in God. Farrar's final point in this selection is the classic one: it is really traditional theology that offers the highest and fullest honor, respect, and trust toward God and toward humanity made in his image.

Reflective Faith

Austin Farrar

We are told repeatedly that religious faith might still be the force it always has been among mankind, if it could only shed an overload of 'transcendence'. It has become plain, however, that the anti-transcendence men are in some disagreement among themselves. At a casual glance, you might take the difference for a matter of

From Austin Farrar, *Reflective Faith* (Grand Rapids, Mich.: William B. Eerdmans Publishing Co., 1974), pp. 171–75. Reprinted by permission of The Society for Promoting Christian Knowledge, London.

degree—some of our radical theologians will swallow a bit more transcendence than others, much as one diner will take more mustard with his beef than another.

Well, but is 'transcendence' really the sort of thing you can have more or less of? It is time we considered what 'transcendence' means; so let's do a bit of verbal definition.

I propose to you one main distinction. 'Transcendence' is used in theology—in *theology*, mind you—in two senses which are utterly different. According to sense one, 'God transcends' means 'God is something over and above other things'. To assert God's transcendence in this sense is just a pompous and unnecessary way of saying that you believe in God; and, equally, to deny his transcendence is to renounce belief in him. According to sense two, 'God transcends' means 'God outsoars us'. To cry up his transcendence is to give a one-sided emphasis to your account of the relation between God and his creatures; to cry down transcendence is to throw the emphasis in the other direction. Sense one does not admit of degrees, for either you assert God, or you don't. Sense two admits of degrees, for you can give a more or less one-sided account of the relation of things to God. Take the two senses, and beat them up together, and you will have a high old philosophical muddle.

I will now take the two senses one by one, and in more detail. In sense one, to say that God transcends things or persons is just to say that he is himself, and that he isn't any of those things or persons, whether taken one by one, or taken all together. To make the point clear, I will adopt what many people would regard as a very un-transcendent view of the divine being: a view I by no means hold—but never mind; for the sake of argument, let's suppose it. Let's suppose that the things in this world of ours constitute the whole field of God's activity and the whole sphere of his being. Let's allow him no other action but what issues in things being the way they are and doing the things they do. Let him find his whole employment, so to speak, in making nature natural—which will of course include making man human. Then his field of action is our field—the field we share with all created things. None the less—and this is the point I wish to make—his living in that field, or focusing of that field, is his living or his focusing; it is none of ours. To take the obvious comparison: you and I may both enjoy the same piece of music, and can (if you like to think so) enjoy it in exactly the same way. The field and form of our awareness are identical; yet mine is inalienably mine, and yours yours: the experience finds a different actual existence in you and in me. So too with God and any of his creatures. His living of our world must be his, and not ours, even if it is our world and no other that he focuses. For otherwise, is it not obvious that talk about God can add nothing to a story about the world and its constituents? If you mean by 'God' just things being things and men being men, then why not be content to talk about men and about things? What is added to the picture by talking about God at all? What can the name of God still serve for but a piece of slang, an appreciative noise? During our Bach Festival I see scribbled on Oxford walls 'Bach is God'. But we know perfectly well that it means no more than 'Bach is tops'. Bach fans are talking about Bach, not about God. If we really wanted to say that the Bach-person is one with the God-person, we should have to presume a God-person existent in his own right, whose fusion with the Bach-person was seriously, though mysteriously, asserted. In order to flow together with the Bach-person, God would have first to transcend—to be over and above—the Bach-person as such; and, presumably, over and above all other persons and creatures as well.

To sum up: in sense one of 'transcendence', to say that God transcends natural beings is just to say he is himself, however much he overlaps them; while to deny that God transcends is to confess that his name stands for nothing real, but only for an emotional gilding on the cosmic ginger-bread. So 'God is transcendent' comes to the same thing as 'God is'. 'Transcendent' is a platitudinous addition, which may just as well be dropped off.

So much for sense one. Or no—wait a bit—there's an objection I think I must consider before proceeding to sense two, for it isn't a mere debating-point, it has much practical importance. The objection is this: Granted that, to be anything real, God must transcend you and me and every particular creature, he still need not transcend the universe as a whole. Or as some would prefer to say, natural reality as such. Why can't the assertions we make about God be assertions about the substance of reality or about the character and tendency of the universe as a whole?

I say the objection is important, because people who wish to compromise between believing in God and not believing in him can time and again be found seeking refuge in the suggestion it embodies. Perhaps there is no such being (they think) as the traditional—or, as they may like to say, the mythical—God-figure; but why should not that figure be a poetical peg on which to hang statements about Reality, or about the Universe as a whole? Well, I'll tell you why not—because there's no such thing as Reality, there are just all the things that are real; the question is, whether God is one of those, or not. And as for the Universe as a whole—the Universe isn't a whole; the question is, whether there is a God to give it the wholeness it lacks by projecting it in the single focus of his mind. I do not think we need spend time in exploding Reality with a big R—not at the present phase of philosophical development. 'Good old Auntie Reality!' burst out an undergraduate reviewer of *Honest to God*, a book for which in general he had considerable respect; but Reality—that was a drop too much for the young man, and I myself feel disinclined to be solemn over such a moth-eaten Aunt Sally at Philosophers' Fair. What does need to be said, and said again, is that there's no such being as the Universe. The universe isn't *an* organism or *a* system or *a* process: it's an unimaginable free-for-all of innumerable bits of organism, system, process; or, if you'll allow me an antiquated piece of slang, it's not a thing, it's just one damned thing after another. If natural science has told us anything, natural science has told us that much. The universe is one only in the sense that its multifarious constituents condition one another, positively or negatively, in the great web of space-time relations. We can make statements about the universe, as we can make statements about the contents of the British Museum. We can make general or statistical statements about the way things go; we can make diagrammatic statements about the patterns into which they fall. We cannot make statements about a common substance or ground of things, nor about a general purpose or trend in things, for there's nothing to constitute the common substance and there's nothing to have the purpose or to do the trending. There's only one way to pin God-type statements on the universe, and that is to pin the universe to a real God: a God who has unity and entity in himself; who (to use our present language) transcends the universe, and so is in a position to draw its multiplicities into the focus of a unity they themselves lack.

To have done, then, with the objection we raised: Reality or 'the Universe' does not provide a half-way house between belief and disbelief in theology. We must either assert or else deny that God transcends every creature—not only this creature or that creature, but all creatures collectively. If he doesn't transcend in this first sense, the sense we have so far considered—then the issues connected with transcendence in the second sense simply don't arise. For a God who is no more than the world cannot stand in any relation to the world, about which we could inquire *how* transcendent that relation is. So, to get on with the story, we will assume sense one transcendence, i.e. we will assume belief in God, and try to ask *how far* he transcends, or outsoars, his creatures.

Surely, though, as a question asked in sober philosophy, our new question is absurd. How high does the divine stature tower above ours? How much more masterly is his grip on the universe of things than ours? How much? One can only answer, as much as one can stretch to think, and then some! For us to cut God down to size, or to keep his monarchy within our paper-constitutions, is surely a ridiculous enterprise.

What, then, are people really talking about, when they are inflating or deflating the divine transcendence? They are talking bugbears. They say: 'If we let God be God, he will crowd us out of the picture. If he is the Creator, then we are mere wax in his hands. If he is the fixer of values, we are the slaves of his decisions. If he is a general providence, we are not to provide for ourselves. If he is infinitely above our nature, we can approach him only by denying what we are, and turning our backs on life.' Those are a few of the bugbears; one could easily lengthen the list. Bugbears are the children of distrust; distrust, in this case, of whom? Either of God or, presumably, of mankind. We should be distrusting God, if we thought him not big enough to stand out of his own light or to bestow on his creatures the degree of independence which would make their existence most worth having. We should be distrusting mankind, if we thought them incapable of contemplating God's greatness, without sinking under the weight into repression and infantility. As to distrust of God, that is not, perhaps, very rational; but distrust of mankind in this connection can find all too much historical justification. Has not theology served to keep a multitude in tutelage, to excuse laziness, and to cloak despair? The corruptions of religion must be taken along with the corruptions of all things human. But unless we will despair of man, why should we specially despair of his religion?

RELIGION GROUNDED IN NATURE

The next three passages reflect three different, though not entirely inconsistent, points of orientation for religious meaning: nature, salvation, and mystical monism. The first, by a distinguished Chilean diplomat and writer, begins with an account of the famous Khajuraho temples of Hindu India, noted for their statues of divine figures in erotic relationships. The writer shows that these reflect an experience of religion as a sublime manifestation of the creative union of heaven and earth, absolute and phenomenal reality, and male and female. They indicate that the sexual act—the most ecstatic, biologically and spiritually creative, and mystical human act, with its self-forgetting in the timeless moment of joy—can be regarded as the supreme sacrament of union of humanity with the divine. The Khajuraho temples lead to a discussion of the ritual sexual act, maithuna, in Tantric Hinduism. It is an example of religion grounded in nature, which at the same time is an act of the transcendence of nature that may be called salvation—and so builds a bridge between religion grounded in nature and religion of salvation, showing they flow one into the other.

The Serpent of Paradise

Miguel Serrano

From the cave of Amarnath in Kashmir, I decided to continue my pilgrimage to Banaras as the Swami of Ashahabal had advised. But before going there I decided to visit the temples at Khajuraho. These temples are famous all over the world for their erotic sculpture, and are considered one of the highest expressions of the medieval renaissance in India.

Prior to that time Indian art had reached its highest point during the Gupta period of the fifth century. There is nothing quite like the art of that epoch. The sculptors were able to express the mystery of primary forces; they were almost like gods. The stone heads of the Buddhas reflect an infinite pity and a serene acceptance of pain: they express the extraordinary attitude of one who has entered Nirvana at one end of a cord, while remaining voluntarily tied to the earth at the other. The sculpture at Khajuraho, by contrast, seems to have an almost decadent refinement. The carved bodies seem to have been formed by a wind blowing from some other universe, from an almost devilish paradise; their naturalness seems to have been achieved by a forbidden magic. There is nothing like them anywhere else in the world. These figures are not naturalistic, but they are almost painfully attractive.

The earliest temples of India were almost devoid of sculpture, and in primitive Buddhism the image, called Murti, was prohibited. But by the time of the Gupta period it had returned with great forcefulness. This image is Maya, or the Universe, and it is a symbolic expression of the thought of God. The anonymous sculptors

From *The Serpent of Paradise* by Miguel Serrano. Copyright © 1963, 1972, by Miguel Serrano. Reprinted by permission of Brandt & Brandt.

who created these carvings intuitively seemed to understand this thought, and during this golden period many statues of this kind were carved all over India. In the western part they may be found at Ellora and at Elephanta, in the south at Belur and Halebid, and along the eastern shore at Bhubaneshwar, Puri, and Konarak. Who these sculptors were, no one knows, but they really seem to have known the secret of creation. They knew that the Mother, Shakti, one day awoke and looked at herself in a mirror, and then in a second and then in a third until the world was created.

Whereas Shakti, the Mother, is the ultimate model of all the statues, the model of the temples themselves is Mount Kailas. All the temples of south and central India attempt to reproduce the shape of the mountain. The temple also has the shape of the body of a man, and the circular disc at the top of the dome is the halo or coronary *chakra* over the head. Moreover, the form of the temple is always the same. On the outer walls there are always hundreds of images reflecting war, life, death, love, procreation—in a word, Maya, or Illusion. But inside, in the most secret shrines, Siva meditates as a lingam. As has already been explained, the lingam symbolizes ecstatic concentration; it is the erect dorsal spine, along which the fire of the Serpent rises towards Samadhi. The interior Self or god remains unchanged in a profound dream, unaffected by what goes on externally, by its own creation which is reflected in the images on the outer walls of the temple.

Foreigners who visit Khajuraho usually cannot understand it. It is naturally difficult for a Western Christian to appreciate a religious temple decorated wholly by erotic figures. Frequently these visitors are scandalized; they depart full of righteous indignation and write angry articles condemning Indian morality. In the past the Mohammedans were also offended, and with gunfire and hammers they destroyed many of the temples.

Khajuraho was built in a beautiful place, in the midst of forests surrounded by low hills, with a river passing through the center. Yet all of the palaces that were built there have now disappeared, as have some eighty temples. Only seven have survived. Much of the sculpture of the destroyed temples was scattered in a great radius around the area, and many villagers have struck their plows against a dark stone which turned out to be a beautiful statue of Siva and his wife Parvati, affectionately loving each other. These villagers often took these statues to their huts, cleaned them up a little and, after anointing them with red sandalwood paste, made them into household gods.

In the most splendid days of Khajuraho the temples were

attended by devadasis, or sacred dancers, who were in fact prostitutes, or courtesans of the gods. These devadasis were imported from all over India, and were selected for the beauty of their faces and figures. Most of them came from Rajasthan. They were then carefully trained in the art of divine love, and they were initiated into the cult, so they could help in the supreme ecstasy and perfection of the Brahmacharis, or chaste disciples. Possibly they also served as models for the anonymous artists who carved the faces and bodies of Parvati.

When I arrived at Khajuraho I spent a whole day walking about the temples and looking at the statuary. All the postures of carnal love are reproduced here. Everywhere the female is fervent in love; she is wholly enveloped in the supreme passion, engaged in giving herself away. She searches for her lover, taking his head into her hands, enveloping him with her thighs, and bending and swinging her body. On her face is an expression of complete ecstasy, for she is engaged in making him wise and in perfecting him, while her body and her soul are totally lost in the act of giving, or perhaps in the nameless pleasure. Other women help the central couple; these are the servants or contributing forces. The male lover incorporates them in the circle of his enjoyment, and with both hands he caresses them while at the same time he takes possession of his divine consort. But strangely enough, the faces of the servants who are helping the couple, and who support the female so that she may maintain her acrobatic posture, are inscrutable and serene as though they were taking part in a rite or masque. Although they are caressed, and even at times caress themselves, their faces reflect nothing but service and devotion. Moreover, the face of the male lover expresses no desire, but total absence. He is shown as though he were dreaming, with only one part of him remaining to sustain his lover, giving her protection and infinite tenderness. He appreciates her sacrifice and the pain she endures for his cause; he appreciates the technique which she has perfected in order to liberate him. She has wholly descended to the human level, to the level of flesh, for service and for maternity. Thus she is the creation or the world. He meanwhile is beyond her, he is beyond everything at the other end of the cord; and he loves her with an infinite tenderness since he loves her as himself. The male lover is at once ubiquitous and surrounded; he is immobile and abandoned; he holds his lover between his arms and penetrates her. He incorporates her within himself, but at the same time he always keeps her without.

The terrifying mystery expressed in these images seems to reflect the intuitive consciousness or Collective Unconscious of the whole people. Nevertheless, India has already forgotten their meaning. These statues are now a cause of shame to many modern Indians. Yet they are her greatest glory. For sex was sacred; like everything in India, it was symbolic.

The whole world may be conceived of at Khajuraho, except that here the final stages are emphasized. When Krishna said, "I am the desire, the lust which procreates," this statement represented the first creation. The Father coupling with his Daughter who as his Wife produced a Son, the world. This union was sexual, but the sex of the world, considered as illusion, is the furthest reflection of the original act. It is the last of the series of mirrors. The statues at Khajuraho, which are representations in stone of Tantric thought, represent the attempt to return to the union of the Self and the Ego. It does not use sex to procreate, but to destroy creation and to dissolve Maya. It is a forbidden, sterile love; it is magical. It is love without love.

On the temples of Khajuraho there are no statues of children, for the product of the love portrayed here is not a son of the flesh, but the son of death. The product of this love is a lotus flower; it is an ark which allows man to pass over the terrifying waters of death.

At its height, Khajuraho was a sophisticated and almost super-civilized city. As a result, the kind of love that is portrayed on the walls of its temples is likely to have been essentially aristocratic and selective, like a religious initiation for a minority. Such stratification, however, means little in India, for status is temporary and fluctuating. Thus hedonism in India has not quite the same dangers it has for others, for at any moment it can be cast off at will, like a stone thrown into a pond.

The men who practiced the secret love at Khajuraho had to be well versed in various arts: they had to know how to decorate the bodies of their lovers, they had to know all about jewels and food, and they had to be experts in their appreciation of femininity. The women, in turn, were trained from adolescence in the mystical art of love. Their training was quite different from that of a geisha, however, for their art was essentially religious. The woman was not taught to satisfy man physically, but to touch his intimate centers, or *chakras*, and to impel him towards the Self. Thus the woman taught man to abandon her physically and to incorporate her spiritually within himself, so that he married not a woman but his own soul.

Although this religious art had an ancient heritage, coming from an unknown past, in Khajuraho it reappeared as a reaction against the devotional or *bhakti* tendency which had invaded India. It was in fact Tantrism with its accompanying Kaula and Kapalika cults. Kaula is the same as Shakti, the Serpent, and her opposite is Akula, or Siva. The union of these two produced Inkaula, or the Hermaphrodite. The rite which produced this result was called Kolamarga. Kapalika was a much more secret cult than Kaula. It probably involved human sacrifice and also the eating of the flesh and blood of the victim. Those who followed this cult lived secretly with their initiated women, who were called yoginis. The most ancient temple at Khajuraho is dedicated to sixty-four of these yoginis, and is called Chausath-Yogini. The members of the Kapalika cult went about covered with ashes and with their heads shaven, except for a piece of hair which hung down at the back of their necks. They also wore jewels in their ears and around their necks, and they carried a skull in one hand and a staff in the other. The Kapalikas believed that the center of the individual, or of the Self, was located in the *yoni*, or sex, of a woman. By meditating on it, they believed they could attain liberation. They simply considered that all men were Siva and all women Parvati. This cult is considered to be very ancient.

The compiler of these Tantric practices in the seventh and eighth centuries was a king called Indrabhatti, who in his work describes his initiation through an act called Maithuna in Sanskrit. His daughter, the beautiful Laksminkara Devi, was said to be one of the most advanced and enthusiastic members of this aristocratic cult of magic sexual love.

It is always important to remember that this rite was essentially a forbidden love, *contra natura*, for in it everything is contrary to the apparent purpose of creation. It has nothing to do with the procreation of the race. Yet Krishna himself, the blue god—that Pan of India or Christ of Atlantis—gave precedence to the act: he loved a married woman and he danced with her in a jungle within a circle surrounded by *gopis* or servants who were the shepherdesses of Gokul. The secret wedding that took place in the gardens of Vrindavana was the same as the Tantric Maithuna.

Such magic love has to be antisocial and illegitimate; moreover, it is sterile since it is only internally procreative.

Marriage as an institution was not considered advisable for either yogis or yoginis, unless they were used to living a double life.

This mystery is expressed in a sublime way on the walls of the temples of Khajuraho, especially in the expression of the figures who love each other in a way that is at once frenzied and static.

The Tantric hero is forbidden to practice love passionately or compulsively. This is a rule permitted only to the woman, since she is the active participant and because she represents the feminine aspect of the universe and the creative side of Siva himself. She is Shakti or Kundalini. Shakti is in fact the creator of the world, or it is at least through her that God creates the world. Shakti is both the Demiurge and Maya, or Illusion, since Illusion is the multiplicity of forms. God creates the world because of love, or rather out of his love for his Shakti or his active catalyst. Love is always an illusion or a dream; and so God does not really participate in creation. Instead, he remains untouched and immobile. This concept is represented again and again in the images of Khajuraho.

This metaphysical concept of woman playing the active role while man plays the passive is not usually found in the imperfect human world. Nevertheless, in the Tantras the woman is reincorporated into divine life. The Tantras see Shakti, or the Mother, in everything; they consider her to be the pillar of both the macrocosm and the microcosm. Thus liberation can only be achieved through contact with woman in this world, by means of a sexual pilgrimage.

In Tantric yoga, women first have to be recognized externally and then accepted as the only possible means of attaining unity. Marriage with woman is the first step, but it must always be a symbolical marriage.

In all of this it must not be forgotten that what is important is the symbolic meaning or metaphor. Although written language and sculptured images may appear to be heavily overladen with sex, they are so only in appearance. On its highest plane, when it is practiced among the more sophisticated members of the cult, the Tantric ceremony is only a symbolic act, for Maithuna occurs only within the body of the man.

The human body is considered to contain two essential elements: Siva, or the static principle, and Shakti, the dynamic principle. Siva, who is masculine, resides in the empty space which is found between the brain and the skull, and which is called Sunya. Shakti, which is feminine, is the Serpent, Kundalini, which is coiled around the base of the Tree in the Muladhara Chakra. The right side of the body is considered to be masculine and it contains Pingala, or the sun; the left is feminine and holds Ida, or the moon.

What Maithuna really represents is a union of opposites within the same body. The union of Siva and Shakti links Ida and Pingala, and Kundalini with Atman. There are several weddings in one, and opposites are progressively united. By the union of these opposites, totality is achieved and the Hermaphrodite is produced. And on top of the Tree of Life the source of eternal life and eternal youth is found. There the mind and vision become one, and particular organs lose their identity. This is the achievement of Sunya, or Emptiness; it is the Brother of Silence or the Nirvana of the Buddhists. According to the Tantric cult of Mahayana Buddhism, this Emptiness is Compassion, and for that reason the Boddhisattva Avalokitesvara entered Nirvana only at one extreme of the cord, and he always remained bound to the world by the other. This union of opposites, perhaps, has the form and sound of the syllable OM. When extremes are united each fulfills the desires of the other.

This wedding with oneself is a marriage with the Serpent. Once the rites are fulfilled the body grows wings, and the soul is covered with a tunic which allows us to go on living after death. It allows us to enter the state of continued consciousness even after the physical body ceases to exist. The wedding is also a resurrection.

In India Tantrism has led to excesses, and to orgies and aberrations. Such a development was probably inevitable in this dangerous and complicated symbolism; nevertheless, the Tantrism of the Left Hand asserts that the road to liberation excludes nothing. It claims that self-denial and asceticism are absurd, since the Supreme Emptiness achieved in Sunya produces the same results, only more satisfactorily. Yet the Tantric method is the most difficult of all, for it demands continual vigilance over all parts of existence. It is the science of Siva, the Serpent.

SALVATIONIST RELIGION

Salvation in religion can be thought of as fundamentally linked to the image of rebirth. It is an experience, symbolically or psychologically or both, of dying, returning to the womb, and being reborn as a new person. The past is wiped away; the regenerate person is able to start again with the knowledge and divine power to do right what he or she did wrong before. Usually—and this makes rebirth fully salvationist—the new status is not for this life only but is perpetuated on the other side of death in an eternal life of bliss. Sometimes, in fact, the rebirth experience is not so much a definite initiation as it is a new status, the actual realization of which projected to the moment of physical death. In one's religious life now, one is preparing for that moment.

Characteristically, though, salvationist religion puts emphasis on some rite of initiation heavily laden with the symbolism of death and rebirth, like

Christian baptism. As an example, we return to the experience of the salvationist religion of Isis of the hero of Apuleius's *The Golden Ass*. Now we see him ecstatically transformed through the rite of Isaic initiation itself; he passes through the liminal experience of approaching the confines of death and beholding the sun at midnight; he comes out a new person immortal in the goddess.

The Golden Ass

Apuleius

The old man took me by the hand and led me towards the spacious temple; and after he had duly performed the rituals of opening the doors and of making the morning-sacrifice, he produced from the secret recesses of the shrine certain books written in unknown characters. The meaning of these characters were concealed, at times by the concentrated expression of hieroglyphically painted animals, at times by wreathed and twisted letters with tails that twirled like wheels or spiralled together like vine-tendrils—so that it was altogether impossible for any peeping profane to comprehend. From these books the high priest interpreted to me the matters necessary for my mystic preparation.

That done, I set about purchasing, partly at my own cost and partly with the aid of friends, all the required commodities. This I did on a larger scale than I had been bidden; and then, at the time that the priest had appointed as most suitable, I was led to the Baths, surrounded by a crowd of devotees. There, after I had taken the usual bath, Mithras himself washed and sprinkled me with pure water, invoking first the pardon of the gods.

Then he led me back once more into the temple and sat me down at the very feet of the Goddess. Two parts of the day had now gone; and after giving me some secret charges (too holy to be uttered) he bade me aloud to fast for the next ten days, eating no flesh and drinking no wine. This fast I reverently observed; and then at last the day arrived when I was to pledge myself to heaven. The sun swung down and drew the evening on; and lo, hosts of people came eagerly from every direction, each man honouring me with

From Jack Lindsay, translator, *The Golden Ass by Apuleius*. Bloomington and London: Indiana University Press, 1932, 1967, pp. 248–51. Reprinted by permission of the publisher.

various gifts according to the ancient rite. Then, after the uninitiated had withdrawn to a distance and I had donned a new linen gown, the priest grasped my hand and conducted me into the Holy of Holies.

Perhaps, curious reader, you are keen to know what was said and done. I would tell you if it were permitted to tell. But both the ears that heard such things and the tongue that told them would reap a heavy penalty for such rashness. However, I shall not keep you any longer on the cross of your anxiety, distracted as you doubtless are with religious yearning. Hear therefore and believe what I say to be truth.

I approached the confines of death. I trod the threshold of Prosperine; and borne through the elements I returned. At midnight I saw the Sun shining in all his glory. I approached the gods below and the gods above, and I stood beside them, and I worshipped them. Behold, I have told my experience, and yet what you hear can mean nothing to you. I shall therefore keep to the facts which can be declared to the profane without offence.

Morning arrived; and after the due solemnities I came forth sanctified with twelve stoles, an habiliment of deep religious import, but which the bonds of my obligation do not keep me from mentioning, as I was seen by many bystanders. For, by order of the priest, I climbed a wooden pulpit which stood in the middle of the temple before the image of the Goddess. I wore a vestment of linen embroidered with a flower-pattern; a costly cope hung down from my shoulders to my ankles; and from whatever angle you inspected me you saw interesting new animal-shapes among the decorations— here Indian serpents, there Hyperborean griffins (which the Antipodes incubate like birds). This latter garment was what the priests commonly call an Olympic Stole. In my right hand I held a lighted torch; and a comely chaplet was wound round my head, from which the palm-tree leaves jetted like rays of the sun.

Thus decorated like the sun and draped like a statue (the curtains being whisked away) I was suddenly revealed to the gaze of the multitude. After this I celebrated the festal day of initiation (as if it were a birthday) with a sumptuous feasting and merry converse; and the third day was taken up with similar ceremonies, with a ritual-breakfast and the consummation of my priesthood.

Lingering about the temple for several more days, I was granted the delight of viewing the Holy Face: a benefit that no grateful services can ever repay—till at length, after humbly thanking the Goddess (not as she deserved but as I was able), I received her admonition to depart home; and I reluctantly made my preparations. But I could hardly bear to break the ties of intense affection that bound me to the place. Prostrating myself before the Goddess and watering her feet with my tears, I addressed her, gulping back the sobs that disturbed my articulation:

'Most holy and everlasting Redeemer of the human race, you munificently cherish our lives and bestow the consoling smiles of a Mother upon our tribulations. There is no day or night, not so much as the minutest fraction of time, that is not stuffed with the eternity of your mercy. You protect men on land and sea. You chase the storms of life and stretch out the hand of succour to the dejected. You can untwine the hopelessly tangled threads of the Fates. You can mitigate the tempests of Fortune and check the stars in the courses of their malice. The gods of heaven worship you. The gods of hell bow before you. You rotate the globe. You light the sun. You govern space. You trample hell. The stars move to your orders, the sea-sons return, the gods rejoice, the elements combine. At your nod the breezes blow, clouds collect, seeds sprout, blossoms increase. The birds that fly in the air, the beasts that roam on the hills, the serpents that hide in the earth, the monsters than swim in the ocean, tremble before your majesty.

'O my spirit is not able to give you sufficient praises, nor have I the means to make acceptable sacrifice. My voice has no power to utter what I think of you. Not a thousand mouths with a thousand tongues, not an eternal flow of unwearied declaration, could utter it.

'Howbeit, poor as I am, I shall do all that a truly religious man may do. I shall conjure up your divine countenance within my breast, and there in the secret depths I shall keep divinity for ever guarded.'

I thus offered my prayer to the supreme Goddess. Then I embraced the priest Mithras (my father in Her); and clinging upon his neck and kissing him oft, I begged his forgiveness that I could not recompense him adequately for the benefits he had heaped upon me. After expressing my sense of obligation at full length, I left him and prepared to revisit my ancestral home from which I had been so long absent.

So, a few days later (as the Goddess admonished), after hastily packing my luggage I went on shipboard and set sail for Rome. Safely and swiftly carried by a favouring breeze, we soon reached the port of Augustus. There I disembarked; and travelling by post-chariot I arrived at the Holy City on the evening of the day before the Ides of December. Nothing now mattered to me so much as to supplicate daily the supreme godhead of Queen Isis (who is propitiated in this city with the deepest veneration as Campensis: a name derived from the site of her temple). In short, I became an unslackening worshipper, a newcomer to this church of hers, but indigenous to her religion.

MYSTICAL MONISM

The passage following is from the Hindu Katha Upanishad (c. 500 B.C.). It represents the important vein of religious literature that emphasizes that God, here called Brahman or the Self-Existent, is the only real being—all else, even other gods like Brahma (the Creator) and Agni, is but a manifestation of him. This approach is certainly linked to religion grounded in nature and to salvationism, for it stems in part from experience of nature as the One in many forms and itself grounded in mind and in part from inner salvation-like experiences in which the individual transcends the many to realize the One. Yet monism (Hindu philosophers prefer the term *nondualism*) is perhaps more closely related to the way of the philosopher or the mystic than to salvationist religions.

The Upanishads: Breath of the Eternal

The Self-Existent made the senses turn outward. Accordingly, man looks toward what is without, and sees not what is within. Rare is he who, longing for immortality, shuts his eyes to what is without and beholds the Self.

Fools follow the desires of the flesh and fall into the snare of all-encompassing death; but the wise, knowing the Self as eternal, seek not the things that pass away.

He through whom man sees, tastes, smells, hears, feels, and enjoys, is the omniscient Lord.

From Swami Prabhavananda and Frederick Manchester, translators, *The Upanishads: Breath of the Eternal* (New York: Mentor Books, n.d.), pp. 20–23. © 1948 by The Vedanta Society of Southern California. Reprinted by permission of Vedanta Press.

He, verily, is the immortal Self. Knowing him, one knows all things.

He through whom man experiences the sleeping or waking states is the all-pervading Self. Knowing him, one grieves no more.

He who knows that the individual soul, enjoyer of the fruits of action, is the Self—ever present within, lord of time, past and future—casts out all fear. For this Self is the immortal Self.

He who sees the First-Born—born of the mind of Brahma, born before the creation of waters—and sees him inhabiting the lotus of the heart, living among physical elements, sees Brahman indeed. For this First-Born is the immortal Self.[1]

That being who is the power of all powers, and is born as such, who embodies himself in the elements and in them exists, and who has entered the lotus of the heart, is the immortal Self.

Agni, the all-seeing, who lies hidden in fire sticks, like a child well guarded in the womb, who is worshiped day by day by awakened souls, and by those who offer oblations in sacrificial fire—he is the immortal Self.[2]

That in which the sun rises and in which it sets, that which is the source of all the powers of nature and of the senses, that which nothing can transcend—that is the immortal Self.

What is within us is also without. What is without is also within. He who sees difference between what is within and what is without goes evermore from death to death.

By the purified mind alone is the indivisible Brahman to be attained. Brahman alone is—nothing else is. He who sees the manifold universe, and not the one reality, goes evermore from death to death.

That being, of the size of a thumb, dwells deep within the heart.[3] He is the lord of time, past and future. Having attained him, one fears no more. He, verily, is the immortal Self.

That being, of the size of a thumb, is like a flame without smoke. He is the lord of time, past and future, the same today and tomorrow. He, verily, is the immortal Self.

As rain, fallen on a hill, streams down its side, so runs he after many births who sees manifoldness in the Self.

[1]Brahman, the absolute, impersonal existence, when associated with the power called Maya—the power to evolve as the empirical universe—is known as Hiranyagarbha, the First-Born.

[2]The reference is to the Vedic sacrifice. Agni, whose name means fire, is said to be all-seeing, the fire symbolizing Brahman, the Revealer; the two fire sticks, which being rubbed together produce the fire, represent the heart and the mind of man.

[3]The sages ascribe a definite, minute size to the Self in order to assist the disciple in meditation.

As pure water poured into pure water remains pure, so does the Self remain pure, O Nachiketa, uniting with Brahman.

To the Birthless, the light of whose consciousness forever shines, belongs the city of eleven gates.[4] He who meditates on the ruler of that city knows no more sorrow. He attains liberation, and for him there can no longer be birth or death. For the ruler of that city is the immortal Self.

The immortal Self is the sun shining in the sky, he is the breeze blowing in space, he is the fire burning on the altar, he is the guest dwelling in the house; he is in all men, he is in the gods, he is in the ether, he is wherever there is truth; he is the fish that is born in water, he is the plant that grows in the soil, he is the river that gushes from the mountain—he, the changeless reality, the illimitable!

He, the adorable one, seated in the heart, is the power that gives breath. Unto him all the senses do homage.

What can remain when the dweller in this body leaves the outgrown shell, since he is, verily, the immortal Self?

Man does not live by breath alone, but by him in whom is the power of breath.

And now, O Nachiketa, will I tell thee of the unseen, the eternal Brahman, and of what befalls the Self after death.

Of those ignorant of the Self, some enter into beings possessed of wombs, others enter into plants—according to their deeds and the growth of their intelligence.

That which is awake in us even while we sleep, shaping in dream the objects of our desire—that indeed is pure, that is Brahman, and that verily is called the Immortal. All the worlds have their being in that, and no one can transcend it. That is the Self.

As fire, though one, takes the shape of every object which it consumes, so the Self, though one, takes the shape of every object in which it dwells.

As air, though one, takes the shape of every object which it enters, so the Self, though one, takes the shape of every object in which it dwells.

As the sun, revealer of all objects to the seer, is not harmed by the sinful eye, nor by the impurities of the objects it gazes on, so the one Self, dwelling in all, is not touched by the evils of the world. For he transcends all.

He is one, the lord and innermost Self of all; of one form, he makes of himself many forms. To him who sees the Self revealed in his own heart belongs eternal bliss—to none else, to none else!

Intelligence of the intelligent, eternal among the transient, he,

---

[4]The Birthless is the Self; the city of eleven gates is the body with its apertures —eyes, ears, etc.

though one, makes possible the desires of many. To him who sees the Self revealed in his own heart belongs eternal peace—to none else, to none else!

REASON AS THE WAY TO RELIGIOUS TRUTH

Reason and experience have been advanced as means of ascertaining religious truth. Two Jewish writers exemplify these ways, and provide a contrast within the same tradition, in this and the following passage. Moses Mendelssohn (1729–86) reflects a Jewish response to the Age of Reason. The fundamental assumption of reason is that real truth, including the truth about God, can be known through a calm, objective, unemotional following of a logical process. It is also assumed that the universe itself is rational, that God is rational and works in ways compatible with and understandable by the processes of reason. The human mind, as a part of this universe, is capable of real knowledge upon which valid premises for reason can be based and of thinking God's thoughts after him in working from them to valid conclusions about the maker of the universe. This approach, and the attitude toward such aspects of religion as revelation, ethics, and history characteristic of it, is evident in this passage. Notice that Mendelssohn defends Judaism precisely as a religion highly compatible with the rational approach; Christian rationalists, of course, have done the same for that faith.

Jerusalem and Other Jewish Writings

Moses Mendelssohn

It is true that I recognize no eternal verities except those which can not only be comprehended by the human intellect but also be demonstrated and verified by man's reason. It is, however, a misconception of Judaism if Mr. Mörschel thinks I cannot take this position without deviating from the religion of my fathers. On the

Reprinted by permission of Schocken Books Inc. from *Jerusalem and Other Jewish Writings* by Moses Mendelssohn, translated by Alfred Jospe. Copyright © 1969 by Schocken Books Inc.

contrary, I consider this view an essential aspect of the Jewish religion and believe that this teaching represents one of the characteristic differences between Judaism and Christianity. To sum it up in one sentence: I believe Judaism knows nothing of a *revealed religion* in the sense in which Christians define this term. The Israelites possess a *divine legislation*—laws, commandments, statutes, rules of conduct, instruction in God's will and in what they are to do to attain temporal and eternal salvation. Moses, in a miraculous and supernatural way, revealed to them these laws and commandments, but not dogmas, propositions concerning salvation, or self-evident principles of reason. These the Lord reveals to us as well as to all other men at all times through nature and events but never through the spoken or written word.

I am afraid many readers will once again find my views shocking and hard to accept. People have usually paid little attention to this distinction. Supernatural *legislation* has been mistaken for a supernatural *revelation* of religion; and people have spoken of Judaism as if it were merely an earlier revelation of those religious doctrines and tenets which are necessary for man's salvation. Therefore, I shall have to explain my views in some detail in order to avoid further misunderstandings. Let me go back to first principles so that my reader and I can set out and proceed together from the same starting point.

Those principles which are independent of time and remain forever unchanged are called *eternal truths*. They are either *necessary*, and as such, unchangeable, or *contingent*; that is, either their permanence is grounded in their *essence* (they are what they are because logically they cannot be anything else and are not conceivable in any other way), or it is based on their reality (they are universally true because they occurred and became real in this and in no other way, and they could not have achieved reality in any other or better way than they did). In other words necessary as well as contingent truths have a common source—truth. The former originate in reason, the latter in the will of God. The statements of necessary truths are true because God conceives of them this way and not otherwise; the statements of contingent truths are true because God, who in His wisdom has given them, considers them to be good this way and not otherwise. Examples of the first kind are the principles of pure mathematics and logic; examples of the second are the general principles of physics and psychology—the laws of nature according to which this universe, matter as well as spirit, is governed. Necessary truths cannot be changed even by God himself. Even He, notwithstanding His omnipotence, cannot suspend the rules of His unchangeable reason. Contingent truths, however, are subject to the will of God; they are unchangeable only insofar as they are in accord with His holy will and intentions. He can suspend them, permit exceptions [miracles], or introduce different laws in their stead as often as such changes may be useful.

Besides these eternal truths there also exist temporal, historical truths—events which occurred once and may never occur again, or principles which, by the processes of cause and effect, become accepted as truth at a certain point in time and space. They can be considered true only in relationship to this particular point in time and space. All historical truths fall into this category—events which took place long ago and of which we were told by others but which we ourselves can no longer observe.

These categories of truth differ not only in their essential nature but also with regard to the method by which they can be taught, that is, in the way in which men can convince themselves and others of their truth. Necessary truths are based upon reason, i.e., upon the unchangeable logical relationship and essential coherence of concepts, according to which they either presuppose or exclude each other. All mathematical and logical proofs are of this kind. They show whether it is possible or impossible to establish a logical relationship between certain concepts. If we wish to teach these truths to others, we must not appeal to their faith but address ourselves to their reason. We need not quote authorities or refer to the credibility of men who hold the same views but must analyze the components of these concepts and demonstrate their logical connection step by step until our student will understand how they are interrelated. Our function in this educative process, as Socrates put it so well, is merely a kind of midwifery. We cannot put anything into the other's mind that is not already there; we can, however, assist him in his effort to bring to light what was hidden and make him perceive and comprehend what he has so far failed to see.

The apperception of the truths in the second category, however, requires not only reason but also *observation*. If we want to know what laws the Creator has prescribed for His creation or according to what general rules nature changes, we must experience, observe, and analyze individual facts and events. Our first step must be to gather all pertinent data by using the evidence of our senses; the next step must then be to use our reason in order to determine what the different cases may have in common. To be sure, we shall have to accept some conclusions on faith, based on the experience and views of others. Our life span simply is not long enough to allow us to experience everything for ourselves. Hence, in many cases we rely on the findings of reputable scholars, on the assumption that their experiments and observations are correct. But we should rely on them only insofar as we ourselves know or are convinced that the objects of their investigation still exist, that their experiments and observations can be repeated, and that their results can be examined by us or others who have the opportunity or capacity to do so.

Yet if the results of these investigations are of great importance for our own or someone else's happiness, we will rarely be satisfied to rely on the statements even of credible witnesses who tell us of their experiments and observations. In such cases, we will seek an opportunity to repeat the experiments ourselves and let the evidence of our own observations convince us. The Siamese, for instance, may be prepared to trust the reports of the Europeans that in their part of the world water hardens and can carry heavy burdens at certain times. They may accept this finding on faith and perhaps even announce it as a fact in their textbooks of physics, on the premise that is always possible to verify this observation by experiment. Should they, however, find themselves in a situation in which their lives are endangered and in which they might have to entrust themselves or their families to this hardened element, they would hardly feel adequately reassured by a mere report which they have received from someone else. They would want to convince themselves of its truth by their own experiments, tests, and observations.

Historical truths—the passages, so to speak, which occur only once in the book of nature—must, however, be explained by themselves or they will remain incomprehensible. They can have been perceived only by the senses of those who were present at the time and place they occurred in nature. Everyone else must accept them on the authority and testimony of others. Moreover, people who live at a subsequent time must rely unconditionally on the credibility of this testimony, for it testifies to something which no longer exists. The object itself as well as the opportunity for direct observation to which they could appeal can no longer be found in nature, and the senses can no longer convince themselves of the facticity of the object or the truth of the event. Hence, the reputation and credibility of the narrator are the sole evidence in historical matters. Without [the] testimony [of eyewitnesses] we cannot be convinced of any historical truth. Without authority the truth of history vanishes along with the event itself.

Whenever God intends man to understand a certain truth, His

wisdom provides man with the means most suited to this purpose. If it is a necessary truth, God provides man with whatever degree of reason he requires for its understanding. If a natural law is to be disclosed to man, God's wisdom will provide him with the necessary capacity for observation; and if a historical truth is to be preserved for posterity, God's wisdom authenticates its historicity by establishing the narrator's credibility beyond any doubt.

It seems to me that only with regard to historical truths did God, in His supreme wisdom, have to instruct mankind either by human means—through the spoken or written word—or through extraordinary events and miracles, if they were required to confirm the authority and credibility of the event. But the eternal truths that are necessary for man's salvation and happiness are taught by God in a manner that is more fitting for His dignity: not through sounds or letters—intelligible only here or there, to one or the other individual —but through creation itself in all its inter-relatedness, which is legible and intelligible to all men. Nor does He confirm these truths by miracles which would merely fortify our belief in the credibility of certain historical events. Instead, He awakens our mind, which He himself has created, and gives it an opportunity to observe the inter-relatedness of things as well as its own workings and to convince itself of those truths which destiny enables man to understand in this life on earth.

Consequently, I do not believe that human reason is incapable of perceiving those eternal truths which are indispensable to man's happiness or that God, therefore, had to reveal these truths in a supernatural way. Those who cling to this notion subtract from God's omnipotence the very thing they think they are adding to it. They assume He was good enough to disclose to men those truths on which their happiness depends, but that He was neither omnipotent nor good enough to grant them the capacity to discover these truths for themselves. Moreover, those who take this position consider the necessity for a supernatural revelation more universal than revelation itself does. If mankind, without revelation, cannot be but corrupt and miserable, why should by far the larger part of mankind have been compelled to live without benefit of true revelation from the beginning? Why should the two Indies have to wait until it should please the Europeans to send them missionaries with a message of comfort without which, according to this opinion, the Indians can live neither virtuously nor happily? Moreover, it is a message which they can neither fully comprehend nor properly utilize because of their limited circumstances and state of knowledge.

EXPERIENCE AS THE WAY
TO RELIGIOUS TRUTH

Many have criticized reason as a means to religious truth. The grounds are twofold: reason is deceptive because people unconsciously tend to select their assumptions for subjective reasons and, thus, use reason to justify what they want to believe on other grounds; and reason, even if it does provide factual truth, does not provide meaning and so is spiritually empty (on this compare Berdyaev's point). This has led them to affirm that it is really experience—conversion, mystical, or just that of living in a religious tradition—that provides religious truth bearing meaning and power.

The following passage is by a modern Jewish writer fully cognizant of the modern crisis of belief and of ways of finding meaning in existence. He argues for the experience of living in a religious tradition as a source of meaning. That is, in this case, the Jewish tradition shaped by Aggadah (the traditional collection of proverbs and legends of distinguished rabbis) and Halakah (the Law of Moses). Reason itself does not save us from the meaninglessness that makes the universe irrational for us; living in a tradition that gives one experience of warmth and exemplars of purposiveness does. Whether or not this guarantees ultimate truth, it offers experienced truth, which is as far as we humans can actually go.

The Religious Imagination

Richard L. Rubenstein

Perhaps the most difficult burden contemporary man has had to bear has been the loss of the conviction that his existence is ultimately meaningful. Of all the gifts the Aggadah bestowed upon the rabbinic Jew, it is likely that none was as precious as the gift of meaning.

.   .   .

Meaning and purpose had yet to disappear in the world of the Aggadah. The illusion is unassailed save by one pathetic dissident, Elisha ben Abuya. Incidentally, it is possible to view much of the literature of primitive Christianity as a specialized form of a new Aggadah. This is particularly true of those parts of the New

From *The Religious Imagination,* copyright © 1968 by Richard L. Rubenstein. Reprinted by permission of The Bobbs-Merrill Company, Inc. Notes omitted.

Testament which are based upon the conviction that Jesus' ministry is in fulfillment of prophecy.

The Aggadah and the Halakah served related but distinct functions. The Halakah served to define and govern objective behavior in rabbinic Judaism. It gave the rabbinic Jew a very extensive idea of what was expected of him in every significant domain of human behavior. It specified the manifest norms and styles of conduct which enabled the rabbinic community to survive effectively in a multiplicity of religious, historical, and cultural settings. The Aggadah served a no less important need. It helped the community to structure a meaningful psychic world. Without it, Jews might long ago have disintegrated morally and psychologically.

The Aggadah had the power to reach the learned and the ignorant alike. Abstract philosophic ideas would make little impression on most men. The Aggadah used concrete images of legendary figures faced with the same personal conflicts as those experienced by many of the members of the community. Its images had the power to move men and women who were incapable of acting on the basis of abstract concepts. The psychic world of the Jew was largely expressed in the imagery of the Aggadah. A Jew who publicly exhibited disdain for religious tradition could, for example, be identified with Jeroboam ben Nabat. The identification classified his dissidence. It also served as an assurance of future retribution. The moral universe of rabbinic Judaism thus maintained its integrity. The quest for an ordered existence was not abruptly disturbed by behavioral or creedal dissent. Even sin and rebellion had their place in the rabbinic order of things. This limited their capacity to spread. A concrete sense of identification with sinners such as Manasseh or Jeroboam could do more as an instrument of internalized social control than a thousand words of abstract discussion concerning the nature of evil. The principle that a picture is worth a thousand words is also applicable to the mental pictures of legend and myth.

As there were models of sin whose misfortunes served as a warning, there were also models of righteousness to be emulated. The virtue of hospitality was taught through the hyperbolic tale of Abraham sitting in his tent which opened in all four directions so that the patriarch might speedily greet the wayfarer. Peace was not abstractly praised. The image of Aaron and his disciples as pursuers of peace gave substance to the ideal. Through the Aggadah, the Bible became a corpus of ego-ideals to be imitated and negative character-types whose example was to be rejected.

These images were largely realistic. They took cognizance of the human situation in depth. There was assurance in the knowledge that even Moses had transgressed. An overscrupulous or an unduly harsh conscience is not likely to develop when temptation is understood as the problem of everyman. When the Aggadah portrayed Moses as blemished, every Jew was assured that his own failings were not private and isolated peculiarities. His feelings did not separate him psychologically from his peers. No man was free of sin. Neither was any Jew regarded as entirely free of the obligation to do his best in keeping the commandments.

As I have stated, the legends also acted as a safety-valve. Offenses could be committed in fantasy which would have been totally unacceptable in reality. Such tales served as a form of emotional catharsis. Legends of wrongdoing offered the Jew a number of potential identifications. By identifying with the righteous, he assured himself that religious fidelity would not ultimately be in vain. By identifying with the sinner, he was able to give expression to his own conscious and unconscious temptations, if only in fantasy. Imaginary enactment of an illicit act permitted a certain discharge of emotion without harmful social consequence. Such identifications were probably often unconscious. They were no less effective on that account. The same mechanism is at work in the contemporary world of fantasy, the arts, the novel, and the motion picture. The archaic fantasy world of rabbinic legend was more effective emotionally because of the sacred environment of synagogue and school in which it was given expression.

In spite of the manifold miseries inflicted upon the Jewish community throughout its history, it was fortunate not to have had to live beyond meaning. There were burdens enough without the supreme burden of meaningless indignity.

.   .   .

Most men simply cannot live in an ultimately meaningless and irrational universe. The threat of disaster does not reside in the painful affect alone. It resides very largely in the extent to which such a threat upsets the individual's sense of coherence and structure. Rational, purposeful pain is infinitely more bearable than irrational misfortune. Mankind has an extraordinary capacity for self-sacrifice to the point of death where sacrifice is meaningful and ultimately contributes to the individual's wider goals. Sometimes rational pain is sought when it has a meaningful place in the structured cosmos of the individual. Only when pain or disaster loses all meaning does it become ultimately threatening. The gratuity of events rather than their feeling-tone constitutes the worst threat against which men must steel themselves.

Rabbinic Judaism was incapable of rescuing Jews from intensely painful experiences for almost two thousand years. It was, however, able to reduce their pain by assimilating it to a way of life which was both meaningful and durable. This was one of the most precious and lasting therapeutic gifts of the Aggadah to the Jewish community.

EXISTENTIAL CHOICE

There is a third possible approach to the quest for religious truth, existential choice. It is best identified with the Danish philosopher and theologian Soren Kierkegaard (1813–55) and the modern existentialist school. The basic argument is this. The arguments for and against religious truth are equally balanced, and there is no way to make a choice between them solely on the grounds of reason or experience. A person can only make a choice from out of his or her own freedom—a choice that is basically a decision of what he or she subjectively wants to be. Truth is not something objective, to be approached by reason, but is subjective and is known only in the moment of commitment; religious truth is not true unless it is known by faith, that is, by free choice and decision. When an individual makes this choice, however, he or she also has to accept its consequences in his or her life, a life that may be pleasant but meaningless if faith is opted against or difficult and even wracked by objective uncertainty but rich with inner meaning if faith is opted for. In the following passage, Kierkegaard, in his "Concluding Unscientific Postscript," explores these issues.

Concluding Unscientific Postscript

Soren Kierkegaard

When one man investigates objectively the problem of immortality, and another embraces an uncertainty with the passion of the infinite: where is there most truth, and who has the greater certainty? The one has entered upon a never-ending approximation, for the certainty of immortality lies precisely in the subjectivity of the

From Robert Bretall, *A Kierkegaard Anthology* (copyright 1946, © 1974 by Princeton University Press), pp. 212–15. Reprinted by permission of Princeton University Press.

individual; the other is immortal, and fights for his immortality by struggling with the uncertainty. Let us consider Socrates. Nowadays everyone dabbles in a few proofs; some have several such proofs, others fewer. But Socrates! He puts the question objectively in a problematic manner: *if* there is an immortality. Must he therefore be accounted a doubter in comparison with one of our modern thinkers with the three proofs? By no means. On this "if" he risks his entire life, he has the courage to meet death, and he has with the passion of the infinite so determined the pattern of his life that it must be found acceptable—*if* there is an immortality. Can any better proof be given for the immortality of the soul? But those who have the three proofs do not at all determine their lives in conformity therewith; if there is an immortality, it must feel disgust over their manner of life: can any better refutation be given of the three proofs? The "bit" of uncertainty that Socrates had helped him, because he himself contributed the passion of the infinite; the three proofs that the others have do not profit them at all, because they are and remain dead to spirit and enthusiasm, and their three proofs, in lieu of proving anything else, prove just this. A young girl may enjoy all the sweetness of love on the basis of what is merely a weak hope; but she is beloved, because she rests everything on this weak hope; but many a wedded matron more than once subjected to the strongest expressions of love has in so far indeed had proofs, but strangely enough has not enjoyed *quod erat demonstrandum*. The Socratic ignorance, which Socrates held fast with the entire passion of his inwardness, was thus an expression for the principle that the eternal truth is related to an existing individual, and that this truth must therefore be a paradox for him as long as he exists; and yet it is possible that there was more truth in the Socratic ignorance as it was in him, than in the entire objective truth of the System, which flirts with what the times demand and accommodates itself to *Privatdocents*.

The objective accent falls on WHAT is said, the subjective accent on HOW it is said. This distinction holds even in the aesthetic realm, and receives definite expression in the principle that what is in itself true may in the mouth of such and such a person become untrue. In these times this distinction is particularly worthy of notice for, if we wish to express in a single sentence the difference between ancient times and our own, we should doubtless have to say: "In ancient times only an individual here and there knew the truth; now all know it, but the inwardness of its appropriation stands in an inverse relationship to the extent of its dissemination. Aesthetically the contradiction that truth becomes untruth in this or that person's mouth is best construed comically. In the ethico-religious sphere, the accent is again on the "how." But this is not to be understood as referring to demeanor, expression, delivery, or the like; rather it refers to the relationship sustained by the existing individual, in his own existence, to the content of his utterance. Objectively the interest is focused merely on the thought-content, subjectively on the inwardness. At its maximum this inward "how" is the passion of the infinite, and the passion of the infinite is the truth. But the passion of the infinite is precisely subjectivity, and thus subjectivity becomes the truth. Objectively there is no infinite decision, and hence it is objectively in order to annul the difference between good and evil, together with the principle of contradiction, and therewith also the infinite difference between the true and the false. Only in subjectivity is there decision, to seek objectivity is to be in error. It is the passion of the infinite that is the decisive factor and not its content, for its content is precisely itself. In this manner subjectivity and the subjective "how" constitute the truth.

But the "how" which is thus subjectively accentuated, precisely because the subject is an existing individual, is also subject to a dialectic with respect to time. In the passionate moment of decision, where the road swings away from objective knowledge, it seems as if the infinite decision were thereby realized. But in the same moment the existing individual finds himself in the temporal order, and the subjective "how" is transformed into a striving, a striving which receives indeed its impulse and a repeated renewal from the decisive passion of the infinite, but is nevertheless a striving.

When subjectivity is the truth, the conceptual determination of the truth must include an expression for the antithesis to objectivity, a memento of the fork in the road where the way swings off; this expression will also indicate the tension of the subjective inwardness. Here is such a definition of truth: *An objective uncertainty held fast in an appropriation-process of the most passionate inwardness is the truth*, the highest truth attainable for an *existing individual*. At the point where the way swings off (and where this is cannot be specified objectively, since it is a matter of subjectivity), there objective knowledge is placed in abeyance. Thus the subject merely has, objectively, the uncertainty; but it is this which precisely increases the tension of that infinite passion which constitutes his inwardness. The truth is precisely the venture which chooses an objective uncertainty with the passion of the infinite. I contemplate nature in the hope of finding God, and I see omnipotence and wisdom; but I also see much else that disturbs my mind and excites anxiety. The sum of all this is an objective uncertainty. But it is for this very reason that the inwardness becomes as intense as it is, for it embraces this objective uncertainty with the entire passion of the infinite. In the case of a mathematical proposition the objectivity is given, but for this reason the truth of such a proposition is also an indifferent truth.

But the above definition of truth is an equivalent expression for faith. Without risk there is no faith. Faith is precisely the contradiction between the infinite passion of the individual's inwardness and the objective uncertainty. If I am capable of grasping God objectively, I do not believe, but precisely because I cannot do this I must believe. If I wish to preserve myself in faith I must constantly be intent upon holding fast the objective uncertainty, so that in the objective uncertainty I am out "upon the seventy thousand fathoms of water," and yet believe.

In the principle that subjectivity, inwardness, is the truth, there is comprehended the Socratic wisdom, whose everlasting merit it was to have become aware of the essential significance of existence, of the fact that the knower is an existing individual. For this reason Socrates was in the truth by virtue of his ignorance, in the highest sense in which this was possible within paganism. To attain to an understanding of this, to comprehend that the misfortune of speculative philosophy is again and again to have forgotten that the knower is an existing individual, is in our objective age difficult enough. "But to have made an advance upon Socrates, without even having understood what he understood, is at any rate not Socratic." Compare the "Moral" of the *Fragments*.

Let us now start from this point and, as was attempted in the *Fragments*, seek a determination of thought which will really carry us further. I have nothing here to do with the question of whether this proposed thought-determination is true or not, since I am merely experimenting; but it must at any rate be clearly manifest that the Socratic thought is understood within the new proposal, so that at least I do not come out behind Socrates.

When subjectivity, inwardness, is the truth, the truth objectively defined becomes a paradox; and the fact that the truth is objectively a paradox shows in its turn that subjectivity is the truth.

CHAPTER SEVEN

FUTURES BAZAAR: OPTIONS AND ISSUES IN RELIGION TODAY AND TOMORROW

Where is religion going? Whatever the religion of the future is, we can be certain it will not be identical in all respects to any religion of today. We may hold that the essence of religion, or of any particular religion, is unchanging. If the history of religion teaches us anything, however, it is that its forms and attitudes are capable of almost infinite variation and are in a continual process of change.

This is understandable, for religion expresses what the self experiences in the presence of the infinite. While the infinite may always be the same, the side of the equation represented by the human self changes from generation to generation, at least in terms of what we understand an ideal self to be like.

Therefore, matters such as the relative roles of men and women, the power of biological science to alter human life, and rapidly changing political systems that unavoidably modify what it feels like to be human cannot help but interact deeply with religion. If through medical science we can prevent deaths that once seemed the "will of God" and if the age of patriarchal fathers and absolute monarchs who once gave meaning to calling God father or king is now giving place to other kinds of family and political life, then the experience of being a human self, in terms of our implicit concept of what a self can do, how long it can survive, how it can relate to other people and to society, will also change. There is no way the experience of religion can fail to be conditioned by such changes. If we change but leave religion unchanged, then religion inevitably becomes an experience whose main function is to give us access to a past different from the present. This can be a rich and valid experience—for a present without a past, the lot of too many in times of rapid change, can be painfully one-dimensional—but it is only one side of what religion can be and eventually will lock the religion in the past. If we change religion with the times, we face many pitfalls—we may, for example, cut ourselves off too hastily from the past and in so doing undermine the authority and security of religion in the eyes of many. We also, however, give religion a chance to deal with the real issues of the day and even offer some options for the future that do not demand the one thing that seems really impossible in human life, turning back the clock.

An aspect of religion today, especially in America, that cannot be separated from thinking about its future is its far-reaching pluralism. The great diversity of religion in America, while not unknown in the past, is different from the pattern of most earlier cultures with a single, established religion and only a limited range of devotional variations and sects within it. Now we are in a situation in which any religion is both a present minority and also an option offering one possible future. In our religious world, we are in touch with countless pasts from East and West as we shop for a believable and livable future. What meets that criterion, of course, will be a religion that deals convincingly with the changes and issues that condition what it really feels like to be a self.

In this chapter we look at some of today's religious options and at some of the issues shaping experience of the self today with which religion is trying to contend. Then we examine some points of view on what the religious future will be like, and finally we reflect on the persistence of religion in human life

---

RELIGION AND SOCIETY

One of the great issues religion always faces is its relation to the surrounding society and political establishment. When these change in a revolutionary manner, the problem is intensified. Yet religion always seems to have a role; whether supportive or negative, united or divided, it responds in a way that says as much about the society as about the religion. The following selection is an example of one important modern relationship between religion and society. It is an account of the Russian Orthodox Church, the form of religion that is culturally pervasive and numerically dominant in the Soviet

Union. Earlier in this book there was an excerpt from the Orthodox liturgy. Now we can observe the immense importance for Orthodox people of simply celebrating the liturgy in officially atheist Russia. Here we see an example of a religion that is virtually unchanged internally, though existing in highly changed circumstances. In it access to the past and to a sense of transcendent glory in a present that many certainly experience as one-dimensional is the one reward it can bestow. *Samizdat* in the Soviet Union are illegal writings passed around among intellectuals in manuscript form.

Discretion and Valour:
Religious Conditions in Russia
and Eastern Europe

Trevor Beeson

No precise figures are available for the number of Orthodox Christians who now attend church, if they can reach one that is open, but informed observers usually estimate figures ranging between 25 and 30 million. Three specialists in 'scientific atheism' from Kiev published the results of sociological research into religious practice in 1970 which indicated that 15–20% of the entire population were believers. The distribution of believers varied considerably. In Byelorussia, for example, the proportions were 16% in the towns and 39% in the villages. In the Central Russian region of Orel the proportions in the villages ranged from 23% to 33%. The kind of religious life experienced and expressed by some of these Christians has been described by a member of the Russian Orthodox Church, and the rest of this chapter is largely based on his experiences.

An Anglican visitor to Russia once asked Patriarch Alexii for a definition of the Russian Orthodox Church. The answer—A Church which celebrates the divine liturgy—disappointed him. No doubt he understood the remark to mean, 'A Church which only celebrates the divine liturgy.' Had he emphasized *celebrates* and even more, *divine*, he would have come closer to an understanding of the Patriarch's (and the Russian Church's) attitude. For the new and enforced concentration on worship has once more revealed to Russian

From Trevor Beeson, *Discretion and Valour: Religious Conditions in Russia and Eastern Europe* (London: Collins Fontana Books, 1974), pp. 77–83. © The British Council of Churches, 1974. Reprinted by permission of William Collins, Sons & Co., Ltd.

Christians that Liturgy can act as Jacob's Ladder, can be a meeting place between heaven and earth, an area of life in which man communes with God.

Hence their willing acceptance of elaborate and (by Western standards) excessively lengthy services—services throughout which, often in crowded and under-ventilated churches, young and old alike will stand (and stand attentively and devoutly) for several hours on end. Abbreviation of the services is barely tolerated. On the contrary, as Metropolitan Nikodim has remarked, 'faithfulness to our ways of worship—in this lies our salvation.' For it is in the traditional forms that the Church's teaching is most adequately expressed and (as the Old Believers once argued also) to tamper with any aspect of tradition could mean tampering with the faith itself. In any case, however well motivated a reform might be, the simple Christians of Russia would immediately suspect it as a secular attempt to infiltrate and undermine church life. The memory of the 'Living Church' experiments lingers on and prevents even the calendar from being reformed.

So the old ways are cherished and retained. The argument that the new circumstances demand new forms of worship meets with little or no response. And yet the new circumstances have given the old forms a new significance and a new vitality. There can be few countries in Europe where such fervour—uninhibited, yet unhysterical—may be observed and shared.

This is not to say that the services are intellectually understood. The average Russian has neither the theological nor the linguistic training to understand Byzantine formulae in Slavonic translation (and Slavonic remains the principal liturgical language to this day). But the latter is not the whole. And the image (*obraz*) of God is powerfully communicated by a synthesis of poetry, painting, drama and music which has served throughout the centuries as the medium through which Russians were converted and taught their faith.

It is a synthesis that makes its impact also on outsiders. For Soviet society and its institutions can offer no comparable calm and beauty—nor can they provide so easy and so unalloyed a contact with the Russian past (something that attracts a certain category of visitor).

The Church has its twelve major feasts, as well as Easter, and a calendar replete with saints' days and red letter days. Some of these are celebrated nationally, others are patronal feasts with local application. Local feasts may affect a given rural area (and, complain the State authorities, disrupt production there for several days). Others may provide the focal point for distant pilgrimage. The summer festivals of St Iov at Pochaev or of St Sergii at Zagorsk, for example, will attract thousands (in the case of Zagorsk, hundreds of thousands) of pilgrims from all parts of the USSR.

Nor are pilgrimages limited to particular feasts or seasons. At the relics of St Sergii, humble daily services are conducted—largely by the pilgrims—throughout the year, from dawn to dusk. Elsewhere, relics may not even be exposed for veneration and still attract the pilgrims. Thus the Caves Monastery in Kiev is closed and the relics of the monastery's saints are exposed for scientific comment and ridicule. Yet there are pilgrims still, who make the rounds and cross themselves and venerate the relics surreptitiously. Holy springs, no less than icons, are held to mediate divine grace. The Russian Christian is often vividly aware that the material world was not merely the setting for the Incarnation: it has organically participated in it.

Sacraments, *materia sacra* and sacramental actions thus occupy an all-important place in the devotional life. Despite all impediments baptism is sought even by families whose overt links with the Church are tenuous; at the other end of the life-span, the Church's participation in funeral rites (if only, sometimes, to the extent of blessing a handful of the earth intended for the grave) is widely appreciated. The impressive quality of modern crosses in Soviet cemeteries, not to mention the occasional *lampadki,* are evidence of more than a residual faith. The same may be said of the commemorative foods that are shared by relatives at the graveside (and left also for passers-by to share). From baptism to burial, the sacramental system offers comfort and support.

At the same time, the awe which it generates has its negative aspect. Communion is a comparatively rare (albeit therefore extremely important) event in the life of most believers. Four times a year is still considered a desirable norm. Georgi Fedotov wrote of Russian people in the Middle Ages, who 'loved the Church with all the beauty and richness of her ritual and all the spiritual comfort they found in it,' and in which 'so many sacred things—icons, crosses, relics, holy water, blessed bread—surrounded them and nourished them that they did not miss the sacrament which had once been the core of liturgical life but had gradually become practically inaccessible or irrelevant to them.' These strictures, only lightly modified, might still be addressed to their descendants.

Since the four penitential seasons are considered particularly appropriate for communion, and since confession is considered a necessary preliminary to it, there is excessive pressure on confessors at such times. Private confession has given way in many parishes to a mixture of public preparation, common expression of penitence and a brief moment of individual absolution, a moment at which the penitent may speak privately of particular sins that burden him. Those who feel the need for more sophisticated spiritual direction may still occasionally establish a relationship with some *starets*, though he may be far to seek.

The Lenten periods and the period of preparation for communion (*govenie*) are periods of abstinence, as are Wednesdays and Fridays of each week. Many of the faithful—the less sophisticated in particular—will keep the fasts with some rigour, fasts that require abstinence from all foods of animal origin (including eggs and dairy products), as well as from frivolity. Their faith thus has an everyday dimension; it is rooted and expressed in Lenten frugality or, at the appropriate time, in festal foods and joy.

Much less frequently does it have an intellectual dimension or expression. Partly this is because aids to thought, rather than devotion, are rarely available. Texts are difficult to obtain, whether scriptural, liturgical, devotional or apologetic—though a limited production of church *samizdat* is undertaken. At the same time, the rarity of texts increases the receptivity of readers to an extraordinary degree. The occasional, fragmentary typescript has greater impact than the idle rows of religious paperbacks on many a Western Christian's shelves.

Something similar could be said of sermons. Sermons are preached at most services. Their subject matter is based on the day's readings or commemorations: most are unambitious and largely devotional in tone, but whatever their limitations they are listened to with intense seriousness and gratitude.

Contacts between clergy and laity tend to be cordial, though irregular. There is certainly not the regular or extensive visiting of parishioners that British clergy might wish to practise. At the same time, pastoral visits are not out of the question, especially at times of need. Furthermore, some of the clergy will themselves be visited. In the larger cities some, circumspectly, convene discussion groups or take part in them. A zealous clergyman is highly prized. As one parishioner wrote to her priest:

> *Your stature, pastor, is known to God; and we can only observe with wonder how He trusts you and grants you souls that are torn by prayer out of the clutches of death and hell. God can say to you, Go; and you go. And according to the fullness of your obedience there is no barrier on earth that can impede your approach to the unique lost soul that God has found for you. And when you have found it, pastor, you serve it in all its lowliness as you would serve Christ himself.*

According to provincial standards, a pastor's stature is particularly enhanced, not only by his zeal, but also by his devout appearance, his *blagoobrazie*. A bearded, long-haired and—most important— booted cleric conforms to simple people's expectations and to some distant (nineteenth-century-cumiconic) prototype. But a venerable beard is not enough by itself. A cleric's lassitude can lead to low attendance, low parish revenue, poverty-line emoluments for the clergy and, consequently, further lassitude or else withdrawal from the situation. The influx of youthful and dedicated clergy into the parishes from the theological schools is urgently needed. Recent increases in the student intake at these schools will help to ensure such an influx in the years to come—contrary to the expectations of the last decade.

These parishes are unevenly distributed through the USSR. A variety of factors determine this unevenness: the character of the local State Plenipotentiary for Religious Affairs or of his counterpart, the bishop; the nature of the local parish and (not necessarily in harmony with the latter) the Parish Council; the history of the region —particularly the date of its incorporation into the USSR and its war-time situation (1941–1944).

The social stratification of the parish or of the Church at large is more difficult to establish. At least it may be said that the less privileged and the elderly are better placed to manifest their adherence to the faith. But membership of the Church is far from being confined to overt churchgoers. Even among the latter, young people and members of the intelligentsia are no longer difficult to find. Furthermore, Orthodoxy—not necessarily in its 'established' form—attracts even the unattached intelligentsia to a remarkable degree. And such an interest appears to be on the increase.

Part of the attraction has been mentioned: access to a peculiar register of life, access also to the Russian past. For here, indeed, is an alternative Russia, a Russia seeking the sanctification of life, a 'Holy Russia' in some sense. But it is not thereby an anti-Soviet enclave. Inevitably, its adherents regret, resent and suffer from some of the Soviet State's attitudes and actions. At the same time, they evince a Russian (and also Soviet) patriotism, which is genuine—however misguided or inadequate any nationalism may be.

In general, the Orthodox as citizens of the USSR do not seek isolation, but rather integration into the social fabric of the State, the sort of integration which is implied in the 1966 decree of the Supreme Court of the RSFSR, which rendered illegal 'the refusal to accept citizens at work or into an educational establishment; their dismissal from work or exclusion from any educational establishment, any material restriction on the rights of citizens in respect of their religious adherence.' At the same time, as *church members* they would undoubtedly welcome more of the independence allegedly accorded to the Church by Lenin's decree of January 1918.

Meanwhile, the Church as an institution is silent vis à vis Soviet society. But this does not compromise or finally frustrate its witness. Its condition resembles that of the Rublev icon of Christ, found in the autumn of 1918 under a pile of firewood, ready for destruction. Four-fifths of its paintwork is vanished. Yet the steadfast features of a humble Saviour remain. His gaze ignores the barren wood around, renders it insignificant and, simultaneously, provides it with new dignity.

EASTERN MYSTICISM IN AMERICA

The appeal of the East has been a part of American life for a long time, and that appeal has intensified since World War II. For some, Eastern emphasis on meditation, inner mystical experience, closeness to nature, and apparent lack of dogmatism have contrasted favorably with Western religion. One of the most influential forms of Eastern religion in the West has been Zen. We have already looked at some Zen material from Japan; the following passage is an account of life at an American Zen Center. It is at Tassajara Hot Springs, a beautiful wooded site deep in the mountains behind Carmel, California. Notice the influence of Hesse's *Siddhartha*, from which we have had a selection, in this circle of American young people interested in the spiritual experience of the East. (The zendo is the hall where Zen meditation is practiced.)

Turning On

Rasa Gustaitis

After the chaos of the last few weeks, I welcome the Zen way now. My first work assignment is as dishwasher and a more delightful site for the chore I have never seen. Adjoining the zendo, on a platform that is covered with a roof but open on the sides, a sink and some

Reprinted with permission of Macmillan Publishing Co., Inc., from *Turning On* by Rasa Gustaitis. Copyright © 1969 by Rasa Gustaitis.

tables have been piled high with cooking pots and dishes used by guests. (The guests eat solid American fare and to the Zen students, the aroma from the kitchen is often tantalizing.) Beyond the platform's edge is the creek. On its other side the mountainside begins with its maples, oaks and sycamores. So, in washing dishes, you have the sound of the creek, of birds and wind in the trees and see sunlight on water and greenery.

A bearded fellow, John Steiner, is already elbow-deep in a caldron when I arrive. Barclay Daggett, a retired engineer, is sweeping the floor. Jim, a fellow who wandered in yesterday and doesn't quite seem to know what he's into yet, is wiping plates. Since they are all here for only a few days, their heads are not shaved as are those of most Tassajara students.

Barclay has toured the turn-on circuit. He has been to Esalen, to another center, called Bridge Mountain, to assorted gurus, and ashrams.

"I've had three ecstatic experiences in my life," he tells me. "One was a shot of morphine, in a hospital before major surgery. The second was in a womb tank, the third was a little satori on the seventh day of a seven-day sesshin in Honolulu." (A sesshin is a period of intensive Zen meditation. The word means mind-gathering.)

"A womb tank? What's that?"

"That was in the Sensory Limitation Research Laboratory of the Veterans Administration hospital at Oklahoma City," he says. "You float in body temperature water in a small tank. The room is dark, air-conditioned, and soundproofed. You have a face mask on and you float with a snorkel in fetal position. There's a mike in the snorkel and you're told, 'You're going on a trip. Please report all you encounter.' I was in it for eight hours and for five hours and fifty minutes I was completely quiet. Toward the end, my mind relaxed completely, but was still perfectly alert."

"How were your three ecstasies different?"

"They were all similar," he says. "They had in common that you don't care. You just don't care. Everything is perfect. There's nothing to want."

There's something faintly sad in the way that sounds to me. Barclay is a ruddy, healthy looking man in late middle-age. I wonder whether his search is building into anything. He says he plans to stay in Tassajara and be a monk.

A dark-haired girl named Patty joins us. She's a married woman, here for two weeks as a student, but she talks like a thirteen-year-old. "If only I could get Mortie to go on my Zen trip with me," she says. "I've been trying to get him to smoke pot. That might get him to see it a little. I feel it's my duty as his wife to smoke pot with him, even though I'm not supposed to. He just doesn't get it. You know what he says? He says, 'This nonattachment sounds pretty selfish to me.' Can you believe it? He's a physicist. When I give him a koan, like, 'Where does the sound go after it leaves the body?' he says, 'It gets converted into light and heat.' Do you think I can ever? Maybe if he smokes pot. Right now I wish the Roshi would come back."

"How come?" I ask.

"It's just different when he's here," she says.

"Yes it is," agrees John, who hasn't been talking much. He is washing the pots with meticulous attention, practicing Zen. I know he was here last summer, for two months of intense Zen training, and would like to talk with him, but now is not the right time.

"I'm going into tangaryo tomorrow," Patty says. "You'll have to do it too, Jim, if you're staying longer than today."

"What's tangaryo?" Jim asks.

"You don't know? Everyone has to go through it if they're here longer than overnight. You sit by yourself for a long time—at least half a day. If you're here for two weeks or more, you have to sit three days—from four in the morning until ten at night. I'm here for just two weeks so I don't know how long I'll have to do it," says Patty.

Dick Baker told me that the purpose of tangaryo is "to see if you can overcome mental and physical restlessness" and compared it to the practice, among Tibetan monks, of drawing a circle around oneself and sitting in it for a year. "It changes your concept of time and space," he said. Students who come to Tassajara just for a trip and are not serious about Zen generally are put off by tangaryo, so it's a way to weed out the dilettantes. In my case an exception will be made. Because I want to observe student life at Tassajara as thoroughly as possible in a short time, I will not sit in tangaryo.

When the last big spoon has been put away, the tables wiped and the floor mopped, it is almost time for lunch which consists of a barley broth with green squash, potato salad with peels and bread with jam. Afterward there are more dishes.

In midafternoon, John, Jim, Patty and I go down the creek for a swim in a natural pool that spring water has carved in the rock. John strips, dives in and swims around, just as the girl did this morning at the baths. But the water is ice-cold and again I hesitate. Afterward we stretch out in the sun and John tells me how he got into Zen.

He was a graduate student in city planning at Berkeley last spring, he says, when he became ill with mononucleosis and, confined to bed, too weak to read, was forced to reflect on his life.

He found that it had been extraordinarily mental for most of his then twenty-three years. He had been active in a lot of social causes at Harvard and Berkeley, had spent a year in Guatemala on a Peace Corps-type project, but everything seemed to be in the same dimension as his studies. Now he craved something else, though he didn't know what. While recovering, he read Hesse's *Siddhartha* and the term 'inner sanctuary" seemed to be it.

So he began to go the Zen center in San Francisco, dropped out of graduate school—at least for a while—and, in the summer, came to Tassajara for two months. Originally, he thought that this time off would be valuable because it would make him a better city planner. But now it became important in its own right. He took an apartment across the street from the Zen Center, attended zazen daily and spent most of his weekends at Tassajara. He no longer knows exactly where he's going, but is certain that, for him, this is the right path.

John is intelligent and intellectual. In that sense, he is typical of the serious students I meet during my stay at Zen Mountain. Later in the afternoon, I get to talking with Taylor Binkley, a dropout from his last year at the Massachusetts Institute of Technology, whom I find watering the bamboo and the flowers beside the bathhouse.

Taylor, like a lot of people here, came to Zen by the psychedelic drug route. He attended the summer training session, when the schedule was much more vigorous than now, allowing only six hours of sleep and half an hour of personal time every day. At the end of a month, during zazen, he says, he experienced satori. "All the classic problems—greed, anger, pride—flew apart and I rose up into beautiful reds and oranges and came down green and blue." After that, at the baths, he felt his body turn into currents of color and saw ladybugs translucent in the sun against bamboo trees.

Then he left, he went to Berkeley and got into the drug scene again. "I had a marvelous month, one of the happiest in my life, but it wasn't enough. I had the satori but I didn't have the vessel to put in it. So now I'm back building the vessel."

Taylor now looks back on his psychedelic period as wasteful. "It's sort of nonsensical to throw your life away on something that doesn't understand that life is what's happening," he says. "A life should be carefully carved so that it lives up to its own inherent beauty."

His father, he tells me, is a biochemistry professor. "He says you can't save the world by staring at your navel. You can't of course. That's not it. So I just wrote him—biochemistry is your quest. To me this has more meaning."

Like John, Taylor does not know precisely where he is going now, but has no doubts about being on the right course. "Most people here have no plans because they don't know where they'll be when they'll leave," another student tells me later. But most will not stay forever at the monastery. They will take their training back with them when they return to life on the other side of the mountains.

At zazen this same day—after a supper of rice, tomato and lettuce salad, burdock roots and carrots—my legs don't bother me as much. Now there is the sound of crickets together with the quiet rushing of the creek. I go to sleep, around ten o'clock, feeling that, somehow, things are right with the world.

But the following morning dream fragments again crash around in my head and the pain in my legs is so bad that I feel sick to my stomach. What use is this sort of torture, I wonder angrily. It deadens the faculties. Surely in Japan, where people sit cross-legged all the time, they don't go through this. How can I find unity with the universe if I can't get past what's happening to my legs?

When I meet Dick Baker later in the morning, I ask him about that. "I can't get beyond the pain," I tell him.

"Why go beyond it?" he replies. "The pain only exists as long as you compare yourself with someone who has no pain."

"But some people can sit cross-legged easily, others can't. I never could."

"It took me two years to get my knees to the ground," Dick says. "You discover you're much stronger than you realize, that you have physical and psychic second winds."

So now I feel challenged. I continue to sit cross-legged. That evening, beyond a certain point, the pain gets no worse and I can actually concentrate on my breathing. "When you are completely absorbed in your breathing, there is no self," the Roshi has said. The grain of the plywood before me begins to flow and, watching my breath and hearing the sound of the brook and the crickets, I become one with the flowing wood, the sounds, and the sap of the trees rising all around in the valley and the mountains. It is only a moment. The next morning, I wake with a sense of gladness just before the bell. But at zazen, the struggle begins all over again and my mind will not be still.

This is no easy road. But I sense that in this very simple and very difficult life, there exists in distilled form all that is happening so chaotically at Esalen and on the acid scene. Here it lives in the single sunflower glowing in an earthenware pot outside the zendo, in the ritual of every meal, the attention that brings beauty and meaning to the smallest moment. "Actually," the Roshi said in one lecture, "Buddhism is nothing but living your own life, little by little."

One person who seems to know what that means is Phillip

Wilson, who beats the big fish drum or rings a gong during the sutra singing after zazen. He is an advanced student and has spent about a year in Japanese monasteries. I've noticed that when he's talking with someone his face is somehow translucent and the expression is of a steady amusement and surprise. But it is a kind, not at all critical expression. One afternoon, I have a chance to talk with him.

Ten years ago, he tells me, he got a B.A. degree in medieval history from Stanford, and thought of teaching. "But I looked over the whole system, the way everything was being done, and I decided I couldn't do it that way. So I just cut myself loose and let myself wander until something happened to put me in the direction that was right. I went to graduate school for a while at Stanford and San Francisco State in anthropology and education, and then I went to Europe for a while and looked there, and then to the Art Institute and looked there. I had gardening jobs and teaching jobs. But it just wasn't right."

"What was missing?"

He laughs. "*Something* was missing. I had knocked out of existence, I had no respect at that time for what people were doing or for what I felt myself inclined to do. And I think that's a very bad condition for anyone to be in, a very sick one."

"Did you try psychedelic drugs?"

"Yeah, only again I didn't like the way people were doing it. I thought they weren't really going to the source, although I couldn't say what the source was. There's some kind of humanistic renaissance that's supposed to come about but there's no one with the strength. They get around people who have bad vibes or who aren't going their way and they get wiped out. You look at them on television and you love them. You see how beautiful and sensitive and *weak* they are. They can't make their garden anywhere, only on their own ground.

"So I asked myself, what would be the ideal condition? And it was to work with whatever you have wherever you are and to be at peace with whatever people you are with and still follow your own way. That's why I was happy when I found Suzuki, because though he's a little guy and very weak-appearing, he's dynamite. He's like a thief and a mother. He's not held by superficial conditions of existence but he'll work with them and use them and transform them into a spiritual life. Now to do this without drugs and to do it with your everyday life to me is kind of a miracle."

About seven years ago, Phillip went to a lecture by Suzuki Roshi. "I had been loking at Russian ikons and I saw that he was a live one—in his stance, his movements. The look in his eyes was like out of eternity. He was very quiet and no one could understand his language, his images didn't follow a train of thought I was used to. At that time, I could tell how someone's mind was by the obvious— how they dressed, combed their hair, picked up an object and put it down, by a certain quality of feeling. But he had an unusual condition in his mind and when I tried to follow it, it would become invisible. So I said, all right, I accept the challenge.

"So I went to the Zen Center every day for a year, and I thought, how can he do it? I was going batty trying to get up at 5:45 every morning, while he was getting up at 5:45 and then working all day and doing meditation every evening and staying up till ten or eleven with conferences. After one year I got so I could do my morning zazen, a decent amount of work during the day and my evening zazen, and then I'd go out and have a beer or play around but he was still working and still more committed to life."

Phillip is a powerfully built man and, in the beginning, had trouble sitting cross-legged. "One day the sensei told me to put one leg over the other. I did that and after that when I did zazen I would sweat. My whole body would be a blanket of pain. But I kept it up and eventually my whole body became more limber."

"Is the pain important?"

"It's important to the student." He laughs. "If you look at the position you'll see it doesn't demand anything harsh from you. You're sitting, learning to be quiet, alert, keep your back straight, breathe from your stomach, hold your head high; and you're realizing that it takes courage just to sit, to eat, that it takes courage just to live and do the ordinary thing. People have forgotten this and they need it.

"I was a very bad student," he continues. "Instead of being receptive, I was full of my own ideas. But to appreciate nature and things you have to become very quiet so that it can come into you. If you can be quiet and alert with some kind of helpfulness—the quieter you become, the more translucent you are. Things around you begin to do their natural pattern and accept you in that way. You become a kind of reflection of what they're doing, but at the same time you remain yourself.

"Now I listen to people differently. I see that they're expressing their nature or their confusion with it, or their understanding of it, or they're trying to complete themselves. I like people I used to avoid —like greedy, grasping businessmen or politicians, they show an unusual vitality. I see how they're struggling with their life. I don't feel separate now from anyone."

Zen Buddhism has no doctrine or creed. It is a mind-body

discipline, a path toward the awakening to a truth that cannot be taught, explained or conceptualized. It is not accessible through the intellect, through obedience to rules or imitation of a master. The intellect, rules and master can steer a student in the right direction, but ultimately this truth must be experienced by everyone in his own way. It can best be spoken of in paradoxes and contradictions.

Zen stories tend to be illogical, irreverent and often seem non-sensical. Though they are not symbolic, they always point to something beyond themselves. They are always vivid, never abstract.

For example, some monks asked one of the ancient masters to speak to them about Buddhism. The master told them to first work in the fields. They did so and then gathered to hear him. He stood up before them and simply spread his arms.

Or, a monk asked his master, "What is the doctrine that goes beyond the Buddhas and Fathers?" The master held up his staff and answered, "I call this a staff. What would you call it?"

Zen teachers, in these stories, had no orthodox procedures. They were brusque and abrupt, replied to students' serious, thoughtful questions with laughter or slaps or by pulling their noses. The students, in turn, upon experiencing satori, proved they were enlightened by behavior that would be held irreverent in most religions. The masters were invariably pleased. As a result, Zen always remained in touch with simple, daily reality.

NEO-EVANGELICALISM IN AMERICA

Another important facet of American religion suggesting another option for the future is the revival of the interpretation of Christianity called evangelicalism. Evangelicalism has been strong in America for a long time. It is not a particular denomination but a religious style that dominates some and cuts through many. It emphasizes a definite personal decision to accept Jesus Christ as savior and to accept the supreme authority of the Bible. It has a particular flavor and manner of worship that is traceable to the great revivals on the frontier in the last century and that emphasizes fervent preaching, a warm social life, lively and moving hymns in the gospel tradition, and the giving of individual testimony. The resurgence of this tradition, so deeply rooted in the American past, in the 1970s has several causes, one of which was no doubt reaction against the social change and Eastern vogues of the sixties. The evangelical revival began around 1970 with the Jesus movement among young people. The following passage describes some of its institutions at that time.

One Way: The Jesus Movement and Its Meaning

Robert S. Ellwood, Jr.

Time and Religion

A touchstone of meaning in any religion is its handling of man's experience of living in time. In the series of endless moments of which time is composed, things happen one after the other and few of them seem really fulfilling. We are frustrated because the present is always vanishing, good things remembered from the past seem locked in that past, and the future promises hopes that seem always still around the corner. We seek in religion ultimate transformation of self and world to a state where all that is good in all these moments comes together.

Different religions deal with the frustrations of time in different ways and hold out different models for transcendence of its limitations. As we have seen, evangelicalism in general endeavors to collapse the historical (and personal) stream into the immediacy of its alternative world, the world of the New Testament. We have seen that this is almost a mystical experience, but one not attained, like classical mysticism, by techniques of meditation.

Within evangelicalism several models or archetypes for evangelical transcendence of time through assimilation of the alternative world occur: movement in the miraculous New Testament world as contemporary, ecstatic loss of those rational "thinking" aspects of the mind which hold us in the time stream, vision of the present world as permeated with purposes continuous with those of the New Testament, and stress on the imminent end of the present age. In this chapter we shall look at some Jesus movement services

From Robert S. Ellwood, Jr., *One Way: The Jesus Movement and its Meaning* (Englewood Cliffs, N. J.: Prentice-Hall, Inc., 1973), pp. 72–78. Reprinted by permission of the publisher.

with a view to seeing what archetypal model they hold up against the problem of time. In each case, an image of an archetypal *person* which, it is implied, the believer wants to be like, emerges. It may be the childlike believer to whom marvellous things happen and who is greater even than parents, or the woman beloved of the Lord, or the responsible patriarchal father, or the penitent at the end of his rope who accepts all accusations against him.

Calvary Chapel

Probably the best known of all the Jesus people churches is Calvary Chapel in Orange County, California. For some reason it is usually said to be in Costa Mesa, but it is actually on the Santa Ana side of the street which separates the two suburban cities. Calvary Chapel was founded as an independent church by the Reverend Charles Smith in the mid-sixties. In 1969, at the time the present sanctuary was built, a group of a dozen young people met in it for Bible study. By 1971 hundreds if not thousands were attending meetings every night of the week. Most meetings have to be held in a large circus tent on a vacant lot a block from the church.

I attended a service on a Wednesday night, an evening devoted to the instruction of "new Christians." The fleets of folding chairs covering the asphalt floor of the tent were perhaps half filled, indicating an attendance, according to my estimate, of just under a thousand. While this is impressive, it must be remembered that Calvary Chapel draws attendance from an area with a total population of several million. On Saturday nights a "Jesus rock" concert with the evening service fills the tent.

Most of those in attendance were young people of high school and college age, dressed in the diverse costumes of their kind: patched levis, print maxis, and ample hair. Underneath, all looked like well-fed, well-scrubbed suburban youth. Nearly all had a Bible of some sort. I did not see a single non-Caucasian. Here and there was a suited, clean-shaven middle-aged man, or a bewigged and benignly smiling matron—probably curious and approving parents, or church folk supporting this good work by their presence, or visiting ministers seeking to learn the secret of Calvary Chapel's success.

The tent, lighted by an overhead rigging of electric lights and cords, was heated by great oil drums red hot from noisy compressed gas fires. While not exactly nineteenth century, this rather delightful air of improvisation about the tent gave it all the camp meeting's spirit of breaking with the institutionalism of the parish church.

When the long-discussed plans to replace the tent with a new and larger sanctuary materialize, Calvary may well find the change counterproductive for evangelism.

The service started a few minutes before the set time of 7:30. A bearded young man in white jeans and a striped sweater like a French sailor's entered to sit on a high stool on the stage. That platform held a wealth of sound equipment and musical instruments, but no religious symbols, not even a cross or open Bible. The young man began strumming a guitar and singing a song about Jesus. The crowd clapped enthusiastically along with him. Between songs he let fall a scattering of comments and messages. He sang a song about the King's Highway and said that a "highway thing" was on his mind.

He reported that recently when he was driving on the freeway, he had started speeding and had prayed to the Lord there would be no patrolman around. Then the Lord told him that this was wrong; he should "obey every ordinance of man" whether or not an officer was in sight. Then he made a wrong turn and lost twenty minutes, just the amount of time he had gained by speeding, indicating that "what a man sows that shall he reap."

This virtually karma-like experience of the immediacy of Scripture truth and God's retributive action was augmented by a story illustrating the immediacy of miracle, for Jesus people, even in the midst of this modern world. The story was second-hand, but impressive nonetheless. Two "brothers" were hitchhiking on the highway. Although they had stood by the road for several hours, "just praising the Lord," they had not gotten a ride. Recalling a Christian who had told them about a vision she had had of an angel, they decided to pray. Kneeling beside the road and placing their hands on the pavement, they prayed for an angel. They sensed the prayer was heard and that an angel stood on the highway just where they had placed their hands. A big truck then came barrelling down the highway. It roared through where the angel was standing; the Christians winced at the thought of it being crushed. But suddenly the driver put on the brakes, backed up, and gave the pair a lift. As they got into the cab he was scratching his head in bewilderment; he said he never stopped to pick up hitchhikers and had no idea why he did this time. The two said that the same technique worked to get them an early ride the next time they hit the road.

So the service opened with songs and discourses of this type as the oildrums flared and glowed. The atmosphere was casual; while most of the audience was quite attentive, people were always coming and going. A girl in a long red dress like that of a pioneer belle came out with a guitar. She sang several lovely songs of her own composition, mostly in the words of Scripture with haunting folksy melodies in the Joan Baez manner. She said that none of the songs were easy to write, for each came out of a tribulation she had been through. In the end, though, the Scripture had provided an answer; what is given in adversity like this really goes deep in the heart. She also told the story of seeing a blind girl on her college campus with a companion feeling flowers. The sightless one said she wanted to touch the "dull" flowers, those blooms which were soft and appealing to the fingers. Somehow this reminded our speaker of the Scriptural verse, "Now we see through a glass, darkly; but then face to face."

The next singer-speaker was a smiling young blond fellow with the look of a beach boy. He told us his own version of the story of the three pigs, which the Lord wanted him to relate that evening, even though he had prepared something else. Each of the three pigs told the mother pig what he planned to do in life. The first wanted to go to a mountain shack with his girl friend and a store of food and drink. The second planned to go to the city and "make a killing." The third had just "taken Jesus into his heart" and had not presumed to make any plans, saying he would pray and wait upon the Lord's guidance, intending in the meantime to stay around home. This greatly disconcerted the mother pig, for she confided that she and the father pig had only been staying together for the sake of the children, and it was not really considerate of the youngest son not to "give her her freedom" by conveniently leaving home like the others. But the youngest pig told his mother sternly that her divorce intentions were wrong, and that he would stay to pray that she and his father might also soon find the Lord Jesus. At this point the narrator stopped to confess that the story "had no ending." There was gentle laughter, but I had a feeling something about the story was probably uncomfortably familiar to many of the listeners.

The same speaker also mentioned a current tragedy. In another California town, a psychologist had shot his wife, children, cats, and himself. He reminded the audience that the night before, on TV, the room of the murdered fourteen-year-old daughter had been shown. She was a Christian; in the room the cameras picked up a cross and a poster saying "Jesus has a lot to give." We offered deep prayers for all involved in this matter.

The transition to the sermon was made by singing a series of low, soft chant-like hymn verses. There were no formal announcements, and no collection was taken. But the young assistant minister in white jeans who gave the main message started with a plug for Chuck Smith's prophecy class on Thursday night. He then went into a rather unexpected talk about his dealings in Hollywood on behalf of a record called "Love Song" being put out by the church. He indicated that, even though he knew nothing of that crass and cynical world, his trust in God gave him freedom and confidence there, opening doors both for the record and for witnessing. "Where the Spirit of God is, there is perfect liberty." God is your Father, your Dad, he said; if you goof, he'll forgive you, and you're not responsible to anyone else, not to your parents, to the government, to business, or to Satan. The Christian is free of debilitating entanglements and so has the joy of true liberty. As an example of God's influence in Hollywood, he told of a record promoter who wanted to distribute several thousand copies of the record to disc jockeys together with a copy for each of a recently issued edition of the Bible with pictures of the Christian life at Calvary Chapel interspersed throughout the text. The assistant minister leapt at this opportunity to sow the seed of the Word as well as promote the record—also of course an evangelistic vessel. Needless to say, there were numerous expressions of wonder and interjections of "Praise the Lord" amid the narration of these movements of grace.

He then started the sermon proper, which was about the Transfiguration and revealed something of the deeper things of Christian spirituality. The listeners were soon caught up in the glory of the Christian's closeness to Christ, who is in turn close to God. Alluding to 1 Corinthians 2:16, "We have the mind of Christ," the preacher repeated several times, "You can have the mind of the Son of God." He spoke of God's wisdom, given liberally to all who ask. He told us that as Christians we go boldly near the throne of God; we are with God forever. "The Christian's lows are still higher than anyone else's highs."

Afterwards, the service ended fairly swiftly. The Lord's Prayer was sung in unison. Then, after prayer, everyone was asked to bow his head and those who now made a decision for Christ were asked to raise their hands. Fifteen did so. They were asked to meet with the assistant pastor for just four or five minutes for instruction and to receive a free Bible. Anyone else who wanted a free Bible was requested to go to a different part of the room. An "Afterglow Service" was announced for those who wished to stay. It included quiet praise and speaking in tongues.

Several little clues helped establish the tone of the service. Leaders and congregants alike made such frequent use of expressions like "Praise the Lord" and "God bless you" that it seemed almost ritual. In prayer many would point one finger upward, or raise both hands.

Mansion Messiah

The atmosphere of the meeting continued and intensified at a commune affiliated with Calvary Chapel called Mansion Messiah. It is located in a big old house on a mostly commercial street in Costa Mesa between a gas station and a firewood lot. Calvary Chapel has three other communes, including Philadelphia House on the beach.

Mansion Messiah has had as many as 40 members, and will house 30 comfortably. At the time I visited it in early 1972, however, only twelve people were living there. I was told that the reason for the decline was that most stay there for only six months or so after conversion, and that many had grown strong enough in the Word to leave on their own to do the Lord's work elsewhere. Some in the commune are new Christians who had been through drugs and the counter culture, though the "deacon" and a friend who showed me around had been previously in an Assemblies of God Bible college in Texas. They had felt they were just receiving and not giving in that situation. Hearing about the Jesus movement on the Coast, they had ventured west and had been in Mansion Messiah for about a month.

Men live on the first floor and women on the second, except for the "elder," who is married and lives on the second with his wife and three children. The furniture was old but comfortable, and there was little of the grubby atmosphere often present in some youth communes. The beds were made and the floors were spotless; everything was shipshape. Few books were in evidence except Bibles, but they were scattered everywhere, along with volumes on prophecy. I was presented with an autobiographical book by a Dutchman who smuggled Bibles behind the Iron Curtain. All except two or three of the members of Mansion Messiah have outside work, generally at such jobs as driving cars for used car lots. All income is pooled, and much of the food and equipment is donated by church friends.

The backyard of the house was taken up largely by a volleyball court. The garage held a fine assortment of gardening and carpentry tools, most of them gifts. In back of the garage, facing the alley and the gas station, was a curious row of compartments. Like six or eight doghouses set side by side, each compartment was a cell about four feet high and three feet wide. Each was just large enough for a kneeling person, and had a door which locked from the inside. Each was completely bare except for carpeting on the floor. Light and air were admitted only by a few very narrow slits in the door. These are prayer rooms, where members of the commune can retire for devotions. It is a practical idea for a religious community whose members have no privacy since several of them share each bedroom. Yet I was reminded of the tiny cave-cells of ancient Buddhist monks I have seen in Japan and central Asia.

The group kindly asked me to take supper with them. Two things impressed me as I talked with them: the unceasing smiles and the unceasing talk of prophecy. This group shared a strong expectation that these are the last days. The mood was reinforced by the few books around, which seemed to run to commentaries on the Book of Revelation and applications of Bible prophecies to the present day. They generally assumed that virtually all prophecy of what would occur before the Day of the Lord had been fulfilled, and that every curse of the present day, from the atomic bomb to the walking catfish plague in Florida, was connected with the impending "tribulations." Some of the smiling dinner table group said, "I'll give the world five years." Others said, "I don't think we'll see 1975." Like all Jesus people, they were always smiling, yet oddly reticent folk. They failed to reveal much about themselves except what can be put in standardized evangelical language: sin, conversion, assurance, challenge. The rough edges of personality and individuality had been cut and trimmed to the mold for the sake of the greater bounty which oneness with a common archetype yields. We talked about the value of the study of prophecy. Even though some things in religion might be even more important, we concluded, mulling over prophecy can keep the reader watchful, not mentally conformed to this passing world, but close to the Word.

The baptisms in the ocean held by Calvary Chapel have become virtually a symbol of the Jesus movement in the national press. Pictures of attractive girls in bikinis arising out of the baptismal waters radiant with joy make splendid magazine photographs. As many as a thousand have been baptized at one of these events, held every month or two. However there is no systematic preparation or follow-up for candidates who experience the ocean baptism. Calvary Chapel has little use for formal requirements, lists, or certificates. Many attending the mass baptism with friends decide on the spur of the moment to enter the waters. Undoubtedly some then start attending the nightly classes in the tent, and others are never seen again. It all depends, so far as Calvary Chapel is concerned, not on the machinery of church bureaucracy, but on the fast or slow, but always humanly inexplicable, workings of grace.

THE WOMEN'S MOVEMENT
AND RELIGION

Perhaps no contemporary development is likely to have a profounder impact on the religion of the future than the changing relationship between the sexes and changing attitudes on the part of women toward the meaning of their sexual identity. This is because most traditional religions have a deep association in their language and images with past patterns of male supremacy that are no longer acceptable to many women. The following article discusses this issue within a Christian context and particularly emphasizes that the patriarchal traditions associated with Christianity are not necessarily the only interpretation of it. Rather, the movement for the liberation of women is part of a movement for the liberation of many classes of people, a movement the biblical tradition strongly supports.

Human Liberation Waits

Anne McGrew Bennett

If there is any one word which could be used to describe the hopes of almost every person today it is the word "liberation." Liberation from whatever limits self-fulfillment. Liberation from the barriers that prevent the exercise of freedom. Liberation, that is, from economic, social, political, racial, and sexist exploitation and oppression. Liberation movements deal with, and challenge, the very foundations of present-day personal and social life. However, "liberation" has become a slogan and the details of the vision are often vague and blurred.

We approach this subject, human liberation, as women claiming full personhood for all women. This is difficult, for we are not representative of all women. Women are young, old, rich, poor, black, white, well, ill—women are of every nation, every ethnic group, every religious and social group. No woman's experience encompasses the experiences of all women. And yet, as we reflect on

From Anne McGrew Bennett, "Human Liberation Waits," in Clare Benedicks Fischer, Betsy Brenneman, and Anne McGrew Bennett, eds., *Woman in a Strange Land* (Philadelphia, Pa.: Fortress Press, 1975), pp. 110–18. Reprinted by permission of Fortress Press.

the vision of human liberation and on the barriers that bind and limit woman, each of us must try to "feel" what it means to woman seeking to be person today, not just in our own personal life, but as every-woman.

It is commonplace to say that we live in a society that is both racist and sexist. But to speak in condemnation of such a society personally and in official church statements is not enough. The movement for human liberation must deal with the causes of racism and sexism: thought patterns, beliefs, and commitments which are dominant in society and which, therfore, mold and shape not only the individual life of each person but our entire culture.

As we think about the Western world and try to understand why women here have been denied full personhood, we are faced with the fact that for thousands of years woman's life has been molded by the Judeo-Christian tradition. And, because of the power and dominance of the European and North American nations, people in all parts of the world are deeply influenced by the Judeo-Christian traditions even if they are not Jews or Christians. The Scriptures are of central importance because they have been, and are, regarded as revealing the very nature and purposes of God and, therefore, of humankind. In searching for the roots of discrimination against women we find that women who appear in the vast sweep of biblical stories and in their interpretations have an inferior status in the relational structure of men and women. The Old Testament story is about men, fathers and sons: Adam, Cain, Abel, Noah, Abraham, Isaac, Jacob, Joseph, Moses, the kings, the prophets. Sometimes a wife or daughter or sister is mentioned but usually in terms of a derivative relationship with a man. In the New Testament the emphasis is also on men who are related in some way to God's revelation in Jesus of Nazareth: the shepherds, the wise men from the East, the twelve apostles, Paul and the leaders of the early church. Almost all of the women who are mentioned are identified by their relationship to men: the Virgin Mother, mothers, sisters, wives, widows, prostitutes, daughters.

The real issue facing women who are struggling to be "free to be human" is the dominance of men over women. This leads inevitably to women's "inferiority" and men's "superiority." The dominance of men over women has had a long, long history. In our own culture the pervasiveness of this dominance is so total that like the air about us we have difficulty "seeing" it. Our language refers to humankind as "he, him, his" and omits woman who is half of humankind. Our customs in marriage and family rites keep men and women unequal; men are honored as the "head," woman's identity is subservient. Our laws, political institutions, and economic systems discriminate in favor of men. Our written histories, secular and religious, are almost entirely about the great men of history and their activities, especially their wars and theological controversies. Woman's history is hidden history.

It is important as we reflect on human liberation to keep in mind that the "inferiority" of women in our culture is an inferiority of rights and of power which is embodied in customs, laws, and theories. Women, in our country, have been trying since before the founding of our Republic to be recognized as full citizens "with all the rights and duties thereto." The Constitution and bylaws of the United States did not so recognize women. The amendments after the Civil War which gave the black male suffrage rights and equal protection under the law did not include black or white women. Even though women finally got the vote in 1920, women are still struggling to get the Equal Rights Amendment passed. The E.R.A. is subject, of course, to approval by the men who control all of the legislative, judicial, and executive bodies of government and the communications media.

Our churches and religious institutions are also male-led and male-dominated even though the majority of the members are women. Women in the Christian church have long been trying to be recognized as full human beings, "made in the image of God," and to be given an opportunity to minister in whatever capacity they feel called. What is there about our Judeo-Christian heritage which supports the dominance of men over women?

The most important element in understanding a culture is its idea of divinity. The Bible came out of a patriarchal society. God is "He." *Yahweh* is the God of Abraham, Isaac, and Jacob who knew him as *El-Shaddai,* a male God (Exod. 6:2–3). Israel also drew from her own experience a number of names for God to express her faith: Father, Brother, Kinsman, King, Judge, Shepherd—all male names. The legal codes of Israel treat woman primarily as chattel. In the New Testament Paul is quoted as considering women subordinate to their husbands (1 Cor. 14:34–35; 1 Tim. 2:11–15). Scholars question the authenticity of these passages but they are widely used to deny woman's equality. 1 Timothy 2:13–14 makes woman responsible for sin in the world.

The extreme male-centeredness of biblical writers, especially editors, is shown in the hundreds of incidents throughout the Hebrew Bible in which feminine words have been changed to masculine in order to express reverence for the holy. All Hebrew words are either masculine or feminine gender. Feminine words referring to sacred objects or having to do with worship have been changed to masculine; for example, the golden dishes on the altar, the bread, curtains, rings, doorposts, and candlesticks. Even the milk cows that brought back the Ark are referred to as masculine six times! One research scholar comments, "We may formulate the folowing principle: whenever someone or something attained an unusual or elevated status, whether temporary or permanent, the Scribes used masculine pronominal suffixes with reference to feminine words."[1]

If the above statements are all, or the essence, of what biblical religion means, then women are in a very bad situation. We have little hope of claiming whole personhood as long as the male-dominated Judeo-Christian traditions mold our understanding of God/Creation/Man/Woman.

Fortunately, there is another approach to the Bible. The Bible and biblical tradition can be reread, keeping in mind the patriarchal bias of the writers and redactors and interpreters, in an effort to understand our biblical faith without sexist blinders.

We can reflect, for example, on the meaning of personhood for men and women in the ancient story of the creation of humankind: "So God created man in his own image; in the image of God he created him; male and female he created them . . ." (Gen. 1:27). This verse has been interpreted quite differently for men than for women. There is no question in the minds of men who follow the Judeo-Christian faith but that men are created in God's image with all the dignity and power and "superiority" that that means. As for women, it has been widely taught and believed that because they are not male they are an inferior creation.

But reread the story. Begin with the previous verse: "Then God said, 'Let us make man in our image, after our likeness. . . .' " Notice that in this passage the writer does not have God say "Let us make man in my image," but "in our image." The Hebrew word for God in these passages is not *Yahweh* or *El* which are masculine singular nouns used to refer to God. The Hebrew word is *Elohim*. It is a plural word which is used in the Bible to refer to the God of Israel and to other gods, both male and female.[2] Scholars, most of

[1]Mayer G. Slonim, "The Substitution of the Masculine for the Feminine Pronominal Suffixes to Express Reverence," *Jewish Quarterly Review* 29 (1938–39): 397–403.

[2]Alan Richardson, ed., *A Theological Word Book of the Bible* (New York: Macmillan Co., 1951), pp. 94–99; *The Interpreter's Dictionary of the Bible* (New York and Nashville: Abingdon Press, 1962), 2:407–17.

them male of course, have a great deal of trouble with the word *Elohim*. Some of them try to ignore the plural and dismiss it as the plural of majesty. However, Dean Cuthbert A. Simpson, who is the exegete in *The Interpreter's Bible* for the elucidation of these particular passages in the creation story in which *Elohim* is used, writes: "The creation of man is invested with a special solemnity. . . . What seems to be significant is the idea that for the creation of man it was fitting, if not necessary, that there should be something like co-operation on the part of the whole company of heaven."[3]

Another problem for us in this passage, as we think about women, is the use of the word "man": "God created man." The Hebrew word translated "man" in this passage is a generic term, not a male term. It should be translated "persons," "humankind," or some other generic term, not "man" which may mean "male" and always carries a male image.

We all know how language limits and determines thought. How much difference there would be in our understanding of personhood if in the creation story the word *Elohim* were used throughout for the word "God" and the referrent masculine pronouns, and if the generic term "persons" were used instead of "man"! "Elohim said, 'Let us create persons in our image, after our likeness' . . . So Elohim created persons in Elohim's own image . . . male and female Elohim created them."

The ancient creation story, in profound symbolism, describes God as inclusive being, and all persons as made in God's image. The story is universal in scope. There are no inferior persons. Woman is protrayed the same as man, "made in the image of God." Both are persons, sex is secondary. Familiar translations blur the meaning.

The second chapter of Genesis contains another creation myth which is formative in our understanding of "woman's place." According to the usual interpretation of this story woman was made after man to be a helper for him. It is best not to be too literal in interpreting myths. However, the word translated as "helpmeet" or "helper" is the Hebrew word used of divine, or superior, help. The word never refers to inferior help in the Bible.

Probably the story (myth) most often quoted over the thousands of years to justify keeping woman inferior to man is the story of the Fall. Eve (whose name, by the way, means "Life" or "Mother of all living") and Adam are still in the Garden of Eden. They have eaten

[3]*The Interpreter's Bible* (New York and Nashville: Abingdon Press, 1952), 1:482–83.

of the forbidden fruit and God says to Eve, according to modern translators of this story: "I will greatly multiply your pain in childbearing; in pain you shall bring forth children, yet your desire shall be for your husband, and he shall rule over you" (Gen. 3:16). Modern scholars' comments on this passage are most interesting—and very different from the common interpretation! Dean Simpson writes:

> Most significant is the fact that [the writer] far in advance of his time sees that this domination of woman by man is an evil thing. The implication is that the relationship between husband and wife was intended by God to be a mutual and complementary relationship of love and respect, not a relationship in which one dominated the other.[4]

Dr. Phyllis Trible, an Old Testament scholar, writes: "This statement is not license for male supremacy, but rather it is condemnation of that very pattern."[5]

A literal translation of the ancient Greek version of this passage found in the Septuagint reads quite differently from our translations: "Unto the woman [God] said, a snare hath increased thy sorrow and thy sighing; Thou art turning away [from God] to thy husband, and he will rule over thee."[6] In this translation it is very clear that woman is being warned against depending on her husband rather than on God.

Surely biblical scholars know that the translation in our Bible implies a false interpretation. This is obvious from their commentaries, but few people have access to these corrective interpretations. Many an article and sermon have extolled "woman's place" as "helper" to her husband, not to mention statements blaming woman for bringing sin into the world and justifying treatment of women as inferior persons and second-class citizens. Half the human race—men—grow up with an exalted ego because God and humankind are always referred to by their identification, by the use of masculine nouns and pronouns, while woman is referred to as man's "helpmeet." What violence these interpretations have done, and continue to do, to both women and men! How do we go about overcoming this destructive pattern of life?

[4]Ibid., p. 510.

[5]"Depatriarchalizing in Biblical Interpretation," *Journal of the American Academy of Religion*, March 1973, p. 41.

[6]Katherine C. Bushnell, *God's Word to Women* (Oakland, Calif.: The Author, 1923), sec. 114–45.

First, women must insist on rereading and reinterpreting the old myths in the Bible. Our faith is passed on from generation to generation through myths and symbols. When a particular culture has distorted the meaning of the myths and symbols which mold our lives, then those myths and symbols must be reinterpreted so that they no longer perpetuate discrimination and oppression.

Women must also insist that women be accorded their rightful place in history. It is the past on which a person depends to build a self-identity. Historians recognize the fateful importance of the way the past is interpreted. The British historian J. H. Plumb emphasizes the fact that history is not the past. He points out that the past is a created ideology in order to control and motivate societies, individuals, and classes.

If an easily identifiable group is portrayed as never having made any general contributions to society—that is, if their contributions are always thought of as within one very limited sphere (with women this would be giving birth and nurturing the family)—then that group of persons are thought of as "other" and the dominant group in the culture continues to hold them in an inferior, usually servant role. Oppressed groups often come to accept the second-class, subservient, not-quite-human role because they know little or nothing about their past which would lead them to have any other opinion. Any change in their societal role may be resisted by them. A traumatic experience for many women today is the emphasis on zero-growth population. Women have been conditioned for millennia to find their identity and self-regard in motherhood. Now there is almost unanimous agreement in developed and developing countries that the two-child family must very soon become the worldwide norm or the human race will breed itself into extinction. The woman's movement for liberation with its emphasis on full personhood for women comes at a time when church and society must provide alternatives for women that are meaningful and socially rewarded in place of a life that has been child-centered, subservient, "other."

Minority groups and women must research their past and insist that it be remembered and celebrated, or they will continue to be considered an inferior "other," not to be counted as full members of the commnity. Also, when one is able to recognize that the group to which one belongs has been involved in significant human events, one feels a part of human experience beyond oneself. One has a sense of participation in the human community and in the making of history. One has a sense of self-esteem. Men have a sense of participation and belonging, whether in the reading of history or in the rituals of celebration. Women do not because, with the exception of the Virgin Mary in Christian liturgies, only men are named in the celebrations of praise and thanksgiving.

Why aren't women named for celebration along with Abraham, Isaac, Jacob, Moses, the prophets, the apostles, Peter and Paul and the great men of history? Why not Sarah, as well as Abraham? Even the name of the Jews, Israelites, comes not from Abraham but from Sarah. Her name has the same root as that of Israel. Why not Miriam as well as Moses? According to the legends of the Jews it was Miriam who taught the wandering Hebrews to dig for water, to till the ground, to cultivate the tree. Why not celebrate Priscilla and Phoebe as well as Paul? Why are women—ancient and modern—excluded from history and from liturgical celebrations?

Many social as well as personal tragedies have their roots in the division of humankind into "superior" and "inferior" beings. Over and over during the long centuries Western nations, Christian people, have glorified war and sanctioned torture. Could it be that the separation of "masculine" from "feminine" qualities leading to the emphasis on aggression, physical force, military power, pride of place, and domination has led to the failure of Christians to stop the killing of the neighbor? Could it be that the ecological crisis—the wanton destruction and pollution of land, sea, air, plants and animals—is related to a drive to dominate without the corresponding drive to nurture? Could it be that when religious sanction is given for man to hold woman, whom he loves and who loves him, in an inferior, submissive place, there are no limits to rationalizing violence toward, and exploitation of, others?

Women's liberation cannot be separated from the struggles of oppressed races because at least half of every oppressed race are women. All women and all oppressed groups share a common victimization; and there will be liberation either for all of them or for none. Human liberation is for everyone—men as well as women. It seeks to overcome the division of humankind into superior and inferior peoples which means the redressing of the imbalance of rights and of power. It seeks the end of the alienation within the individual person of feminine and masculine attributes because each attribute must be nurtured in both the female and male if a person is to be a whole person. It seeks a theology which in symbol and language will help people understand the wholeness of God and the oneness of humankind. The Spirit is moving. Human liberation waits. Tomorrow depends upon us today.

SPACE EXPLORATION
AND RELIGION

In future history textbooks (if books are still written and published), the twentieth century will probably be chiefly remembered for the beginnings of travel in space. In the future, humankind will undoubtedly be traveling and living in space and on other worlds in ways and under conditions we can scarcely imagine, but they will no doubt recall, just as we recall Columbus and the date 1492, that it was in the twentieth century it all began.

How will this life in space affect religion? We can only speculate at this point. That it will deeply affect religion seems beyond question; religion has hardly gone untouched by comparable past changes in technology, living conditions, and human vistas—though it should be remembered that, at least on the short perspective, the religious changes impelled by technical advances have as often been conservative as they have been radical. The long-range effect of space exploration is likely to be a slow but far-reaching deepening of feeling for our ultimate environment and destiny that engenders a sense of the open-endedness of all things and the power and wonder of being itself. At least, that is the realization one gets from reading this beautiful essay by a distinguished writer of science fiction on the meaning of space exploration.

Across the Sea of Stars

Arthur C. Clarke

At some time or other, and not necessarily in moments of depression or illness, most men have known that sudden spasm of unreality which makes them ask, "What am I doing here?" Poets and mystics all down the ages have been acutely aware of this feeling, and have often expressed the belief that we are strangers in a world which is not really ours.

This vague and disturbing premonition is perfectly accurate. We don't belong here, and we're on our way to somewhere else.

The journey began a billion years ago, when one of our

From "Across the Sea of Stars" in *Report on Planet Three and Other Speculations* (1972) by Arthur C. Clarke. Copyright © 1958 by Arthur C. Clarke. Reprinted by permission of Harper & Row, Publishers, Inc.

forgotten ancestors crawled up out of the sea and so started life's invasion of the land. That great adventure was nature's most spectacular triumph, but it was achieved at a heavy price in biological hardship—a price which every one of us continues to pay to this day.

We are so accustomed to our terrestrial existence that it is very hard for us to realize the problems that had to be overcome before life emerged from the sea. The shallow, sun-drenched water of the primitive oceans was an almost ideal environment for living creatures. It buffered them from extremes of temperature and provided them with both food and oxygen. Above all, it sustained them, so that they were untouched by the crippling, crushing influence of gravity. With such advantages, it seems incredible that life ever invaded so hostile an environment as the land.

Hostile? Yes, though that is an adjective few people would apply to it. Certainly I would not have done so before I took up skin diving and discovered—as have so many thousands of men in the past few years—that only when cruising underwater, sightseeing among the myriad strange and lovely creatures of the sea, did I feel completely happy and beyond the cares and worries of everyday life.

No one who has experienced this sensation can ever forget it, or can resist succumbing to its lure once more when the chance arises. Indeed, there are some creatures—the whales and porpoises, for example—who have heeded this call so completely that they have abandoned the land which their remote ancestors conquered long ago.

But we cannot turn back the clock of evolution. The sea is far behind us; though its memories have never ceased to stir our minds, and the chemical echo of its waters still flows in our veins, we can never return to our ancient home. We creatures of the land are exiles —displaced organisms on the way from one element to another. We are still in the transit camp, waiting for our visas to come through. Yet there is no need for us to regret our lost home, for we are on the way to one of infinitely greater promise and possibility. We are on our way to space; and there, surprisingly enough, we may regain much that we lost when we left the sea.

The conquest of the land was achieved by blind biological forces; that of space will be the deliberate product of will and intelligence. But otherwise the parallels are striking; each event—the one ages ago, the other a few decades ahead of us—represents a break with the past, and a massive thrust forward into a new realm of opportunity, of experience, and of promise.

Even before the launching of the Earth satellites, no competent expert had any doubts that the conquest of space would be technically feasible within another generation, or that the new science of astronautics was now standing roughly where that of aeronautics was at the close of the last century. The first men to land on the Moon have already been born; today we are much nearer in time to the moment when a man-carrying spaceship descends upon the lunar plains than we are to that day at Kitty Hawk when the Wright brothers gave us the freedom of the sky.

So let us blithely take for granted the greatest technical achievement in human history (one which, by the way, has already cost far more than the project which made the atom bomb) and consider some of its consequences to mankind. Even over short periods they may be impressive; over intervals long enough to produce evolutionary changes they may be staggering.

The most important of these changes will be the result of living in gravitational fields lower than Earth's. On Mars, for example, a 180-pound man would weigh about 70 pounds; on the Moon, less than 30. And on a space station or artificial satellite he would weigh nothing at all. He would have gone full circuit, having gained—and indeed surpassed—the freedom of movement his remote ancestors enjoyed in the weightless ocean.

To see what that may imply, consider what the never-relenting force of gravity does to our bodies here on the surface of the Earth. We spend our entire lives fighting it—and in the end, often enough, it kills us. Remember the energy that has to be exerted pumping the blood around and around the endless circuit of veins and arteries. It is true that some of the heart's work is done against frictional resistance—but how much longer we might live if the weight of the blood, and of our whole bodies, was abolished!

There is certainly a close connection between weight and the expectation of life, and this is a fact which may be of vast importance before many more decades have passed. The political and social consequences which may follow if it turns out that men can live substantially longer on Mars or the Moon may be revolutionary. Even taking the most conservative viewpoint, the study of living organisms under varying gravitational fields will be a potent new tool of biological and medical science.

Of course, it may be argued that reduced or zero gravity will produce undesirable side effects, but the rapidly growing science of space medicine—not to mention the experience of all the creatures in the sea—suggests that such effects will be temporary and not serious. Perhaps our balance organs and some of our muscles might atrophy after many generations in a weightless environment, but what would that matter since they would no longer be needed? It would be a fair exchange for fallen arches, pendulous paunches, and the other defects and diseases of gravity.

But mere extension of the life span, and even improved health and efficiency, are not important in themselves. We all know people who have done more in forty years than others have done in eighty. What is really significant is richness and diversity of experience, and the use to which that is put by men and the societies they constitute. It is here that the conquest of space will produce an advance in complexity of stimulus even greater than that which occurred when life moved from water to land.

In the sea, every creature exists at the center of a little universe which is seldom more than a hundred feet in radius, and is usually much smaller. This is the limit set by underwater visibility, and though some information comes from greater distances by sound vibrations, the world of the fish is a very tiny place.

That of a land animal is thousands of times larger. It can see out to the horizon, miles away. And at night it can look up to the stars, those piercing points of light whose incredible explanation was discovered by man himself more recently than the time of Shakespeare.

In space, there will be no horizon this side of infinity. There will be suns and planets without end, no two the same, many of them teeming with strange life forms and perhaps stranger civilizations. The sea which beats against the coasts of Earth, which seems so endless and so eternal, is as the drop of water on the slide of a microscope compared with the shoreless sea of space. And our pause here, between one ocean and the next, may be only a moment in the history of the Universe.

When one contemplates this awe-inspiring fact, one sees how glib, superficial, and indeed downright childish are the conceptions of those science-fiction writers who merely transfer their cultures and societies to other planets. Whatever civilizations we may build on distant worlds will differ from ours more widely than mid-twentieth century America differs from Renaissance Italy or, for that matter, from the Egypt of the Pharaohs. And the differences, as we have seen, will not merely be cultural; in the long run they will be organic as well. In a few thousand years of forced evolution, many of our descendants will be sundered from us by psychological and biological gulfs far greater than those between the Eskimo and the African pygmy.

The frozen wilderness of Greenland and the steaming forests of the Congo represent the two extremes of the climatic range that man has been able to master without the use of advanced technology. There are much stranger environments among the stars, and one day we shall pit ourselves against them, employing the tools of future science to change atmospheres, temperatures, and perhaps even orbits. Not many worlds can exist upon which an unprotected man could survive, but the men who challenge space will not be unprotected. They will remold other planets as we today bulldoze forests and divert rivers. Yet, in changing worlds, they will also change themselves.

What will be the thoughts of a man who lives on one of the inner moons of Saturn, where the Sun is a fierce but heatless point of light and the great golden orange of the giant planet dominates the sky, passing swiftly through its phases from new to full while it floats within the circle of its incomparable rings? It is hard for us to imagine his outlook on life, his hopes and fears—yet he may be nearer to us than we are to the men who signed the Declaration of Independence.

Go further afield to the world of other suns (yes, one day, we shall reach them, though that may not be for ages yet), and picture a planet where the word "night" is meaningless, for with the setting of one sun there rises another—and perhaps a third or fourth—of totally different hue. Try to visualize what must surely be the weirdest sky of all—that of a planet near the center of one of those close-packed star clusters that glow like distant swarms of fireflies in the fields of our telescopes. How strange to stand beneath a sky that is a solid shield of stars, so that there is no darkness between them through which one may look out into the Universe beyond. . . .

Such worlds exist, and one day men will live upon them. But why, it may reasonably be asked, should we worry about such remote and alien places when there is enough work to keep us busy here on Earth for centuries?

Let us face the facts; we do not have centuries ahead of us. We have aeons, barring accidents and the consequences of our own folly. A hundred million years will be but a small fraction of the future history of Earth. This is about the length of time that the dinosaurs reigned as masters of this planet. If we last a tenth as long as the great reptiles which we sometimes speak of disparagingly as one of nature's failures, we will have time enough to make our mark on countless worlds and suns.

Yet one final question remains. If we have never felt wholly at home here on Earth, which has mothered us for so many ages, what hope is there that we shall find greater happiness or satisfaction on the strange worlds of foreign suns?

The answer lies in the distinction between the race and the individual. For a man "home" is the place of his birth and childhood —whether that be Siberian steppe, coral island, Alpine valley, Brooklyn tenement, Martian desert, lunar crater, or mile-long interstellar ark. But for Man, home can never be a single country, a single world, a single Solar System, a single star cluster. While the race endures in recognizably human form, it can have no one abiding place short of the Universe itself.

This divine discontent is part of our destiny. It is one more, and perhaps the greatest, of the gifts we inherited from the sea that rolls so restlessly around the world.

It will be driving our descendants on toward myriad unimaginable goals when the sea is stilled forever, and Earth itself a fading legend lost among the stars.

THE MEDICAL REVOLUTION
AND RELIGION

An issue of widespread current discussion is religious and ethical response to the profound questions of values raised by decisions that have to be made in the practice of medicine—and by reflection on the even greater questions that will come with advances in biological science. Today, issues old and new— birth control, abortion, euthanasia, organ transplants, and the allocation of such devices as artificial kidneys— force decisions of life and death. These decisions ultimately reveal not only values but also images of what it means to be a human self. Tomorrow, issues centering around the artificial creation of human life—or the morality of mass euthanasia in the face of worldwide famine resulting from ecological disaster—may be among the problems requiring difficult but urgent choices. The following passage is given as an example of current discussion in medical ethics; it presents one point of view on the matter of euthanasia, or deliberate termination of human life in a medical setting.

Morals and Medicine

Joseph Fletcher

A Time to Plant,
a Time to Pluck

To draw our thinking together, we ought to repeat that there are
three schools of thought favoring euthanasia. First, there are those
who favor voluntary euthanasia, a personalistic ethical position.
Second, there are those who favor involuntary euthanasia for
monstrosities at birth and mental defectives, a partly personalistic
and partly eugenic position.[1] Third, there are those who favor
involuntary euthanasia for all who are a burden upon the
community, a purely eugenic position. It should be perfectly obvious
that we do not have to endorse the third school of thought just
because we favor either the first or the second, or both. Our
discussion has covered only the first one—voluntary medical
euthanasia—as a means of ending a human life enmeshed in
incurable and fatal physical suffering. The principles of right based
upon selfhood and moral being favor it.

Defense of voluntary medical euthanasia, it should be made
plain, does not depend upon the superficial system of values in
which physical evil (pain) is regarded as worse than moral evil (sin)
or intellectual evil (error). On the contrary, unless we are careful to
see that pain is the least of evils, then our values would tie us back
into that old attitude of taking the material or physical aspects of
reality so seriously that we put nature or things as they are *out there*
in a determinant place, subordinating the ethical and spiritual values
of freedom and knowledge and upholding, in effect, a kind of
naturalism. C. S. Lewis has described it by saying that, "Of all evils,
pain only is sterilized or disinfected evil."[2] Pain cannot create moral
evil, such as a disintegration or demoralization of personality would
be, unless it is submitted to in brute fashion as opponents of
euthanasia insist we should do.

We repeat, the issue is not one of life or death. The issue is
which kind of death, an agonized or peaceful one. Shall we meet
death in personal integrity or in personal disintegration? Should

From Joseph Fletcher, *Morals and Medicine* (Copyright 1954 by Princeton
University Press), pp. 207–10. Reprinted by permission of Princeton University Press.

[1]It has always been a quite common practice of midwives and, in modern times,
doctors, simply to fail to respirate monstrous babies at birth.

[2]*The Problem of Pain*, London, 1943, p. 104.

there be a moral or a demoralized end to mortal life? Surely, as we have seen in earlier chapters, we are not as persons of moral stature to be ruled by ruthless and unreasoning physiology, but rather by reason and self-control. Those who face the issues of euthanasia with a religious faith will not, if they think twice, submit to the materialistic and animistic doctrine that God's will is revealed by what nature does, and that life, qua life, is absolutely sacred and untouchable. All of us can agree with Reinhold Niebuhr that "the ending of our life would not threaten us if we had not falsely made ourselves the center of life's meaning."[3] One of the pathetic immaturities we all recognize around us is stated bluntly by Sigmund Freud in his *Reflections on War and Death*: "In the subconscious every one of us is convinced of his immortality." Our frantic hold upon life can only cease to be a snare and delusion when we objectify it in some religious doctrine of salvation, or, alternatively, agree with Sidney Hook that "the romantic pessimism which mourns man's finitude is a vain lament that we are not gods."[4] At least, the principles of personal morality warn us not to make physical phenomena, unmitigated by human freedom, the center of life's meaning. There is an impressive wisdom in the words of Dr. Logan Clendenning: "Death itself is not unpleasant. I have seen a good many people die. To a few death comes as a friend, as a relief from pain, from intolerable loneliness or loss, or from disappointment. To even fewer it comes as a horror. To most it hardly comes at all, so gradual is its approach, so long have the senses been benumbed, so little do they realize what is taking place. As I think it over, death seems to me one of the few evidences in nature of the operation of a creative intelligence exhibiting qualities which I recognize as mind stuff. To have blundered onto the form of energy called life showed a sort of malignant power. After having blundered on life, to have conceived of death was a real stroke of genius."[5]

As Ecclesiastes the Preacher kept saying in first one way and then another, "The living know that they shall die" and there is "a time to be born and a time to die, a time to plant and a time to pluck up that which is planted."[6] And in the New Covenant we read that "all flesh is as grass" and "the grass withereth, and the flower thereof falleth away." Nevertheless, "who is he that will harm you, if ye be followers of that which is good?"[7]

[3]*Human Destiny*, New York, 1943, II, 293.
[4]Quoted by Corliss Lamont, *The Illusion of Immortality*, New York, 1950, p. 191.
[5]*The Human Body*, New York, 1941, 3rd ed., pp. 442–443.
[6]Eccl. 9:5 and 3:2.
[7]I Pet. 1:24 and 3:13.

Medicine contributes too much to the moral stature of men to persist indefinitely in denying the ultimate claims of its own supreme virtue and ethical inspiration, mercy. With Maeterlinck, we may be sure that "there will come a day when Science will protest its errors and will shorten our sufferings."[8]

WORLD HUNGER

It's a strange world of spiritual and ethical deprivations that we live in—for some, a surfeit of affluence threatens sensitivity; for many more, very marginal economic existence and the threat of real starvation kills joy and meaning even before it kills life itself. Moreover, the two threats are linked, and between them they threaten the future of all people on this tiny and teeming globe. The issues clustering around this situation, in itself an affront to any religious concept of moral order and a challenge to any image of what it means to be human, cannot be escaped by religion. The following passages are from a sensitive book by an evangelical Christian and deal with world hunger as moral and spiritual crisis. The first part is from the preface and introduces the issue; the second, from later in the book, is an imagined reply by a Hindu to a question, which is commonly asked by well-meaning but insensitive Westerners, about the problem of hunger in India. It can be taken to exemplify the kind of intercultural understanding that must occur before the necessary solutions can be found to a global problem.

What Do You Say to a Hungry World?

W. Stanley Mooneyham

Television commentator John Chancellor said not long ago at the conclusion of an NBC White Paper on the world food problem, "If the world is not fed, it will be a different and more dangerous world."

Daily headlines chronicle the deteriorating situation:

From W. Stanley Mooneyham, *What Do You Say to a Hungry World?* (Waco, Texas: Word, Inc., 1975), pp. 11–14, 226–27. Reprinted by permission of the publisher.

[8]Quoted by Jacoby, p. 206. [G. W. Jacoby, *Physician, Pastor and Patient*, New York, 1936.]

National Observer, March 30, 1974: "The Next Crisis: Universal Famine."

New York Times, August 21, 1974: "Expert Says World has 27 Days' Food."

Honolulu Advertiser, October 24, 1974: "On The Road to Famine."

Times of India, October 8, 1974: "FAO Chief Warns of Big Human Disaster."

Ethiopian Herald, October 2, 1974: "Drought, Famine Will Overtake the World."

Los Angeles Times, October 9, 1974: "One Billion Face Not Deprivation but Death."

The doomsayers are not wild-eyed, hair-shirted prophets. They are responsible, respected scientists. The principal architect of the "green revolution" and president emeritus of the Rockefeller Foundation, Dr. J. George Harrar, soberly admits: "I'm scared. We could have a lot of starvation by 1980. It is unrealistic to think that this could not happen."

Newsweek quotes a worried U.N. official: "The food problem today is probably the most serious one in the world's history. It now quite literally threatens the survival of hundreds of millions of human beings around the world."

An assessment of the world food situation by the U.S. State Department, a sober bureaucracy not given to exaggerated statements, concludes: "it is doubtful whether such a critical food situation has ever been so worldwide."

But the food crisis does not stand in isolation from the rest of the world's problems. If we were dealing with just an agricultural shortfall, the solution would be relatively simple. But add changing climatic conditions and you complicate the problem. Link it with an uncontrolled world population—as you certainly must—and you further intensify the dilemma.

Now compound it by introducing ecological factors plus deficiency of medical services, inadequate educational programs, discriminatory distribution systems, global economic inequity and repressive political regimes—add these and you've got an apocalyptic situation.

Which is right where we are.

And some of my friends would suggest—even insist—that I stop right there. Their reasoning is something like this: Since the situation seems obviously beyond solution, and since the apocalyptic nature of our times indicates that the return of Jesus Christ is near, and since the wrongs of this world can be made right only by the establishment of his kingdom, there is no need to do anything about the human crisis, so let's concentrate on "eternal" things.

I suggest—rather, insist—this is a cop-out and differs from the "lifeboat ethic" espoused by some secularists only in approach. (It is called an ethic, but to me it sounds like callous elitism.) It goes something like this: The function of a lifeboat is to saves lives in case of a disaster. Each country is like a lifeboat and some of them have their support systems taxed almost to capacity. When the boat is full, the fortunate ones on board are faced with the terrible task of pushing away the others, who are doomed to drown.

The end result of both views is the same—millions of human beings are consigned to die. Of course, the Christian might do something which the secularist wouldn't. He would likely put a tract in each outstretched hand.

I reject both approaches. The first because I am a humanitarian; the second because I am a Christian.

I have accepted my dual citizenship—earthly and heavenly. The earthly was not negated when I took on the heavenly. Rather, for me, the second enhanced the first. The nearer I come to the true person of Jesus Christ, the closer I feel to suffering humanity. Or is it vice versa? I haven't got that part sorted out yet. I only know that one day I saw people as whole persons, not just disembodied souls, and my view of man was perceptibly heightened.

Believing that God is for man (does that make God a humanitarian, too?), I know I must care about man in his hungry suffering and oppressed physical condition as well as his alienated and lost spiritual state. That makes it impossible for me to limit my concern to man's spiritual needs while ignoring his other problems.

At the same time, my Christian conscience will not permit me to accept as a viable alternative the "full lifeboat" theory. I am not a Pollyanna about the situation. I know the hard choices which face us all. I just happen to believe that if those in the lifeboat adopt a policy which cynically denies a place to those who are unfortunate enough to be born too late, it will no longer be a lifeboat but a floating insane asylum in which I would not feel very much at home.

I refuse to opt out without a struggle.

Even though one man is not required to do everything, I firmly believe each of us is responsible to do what he can. I know I cannot feed the whole world, heal every sick child, liberate every oppressed person. I accept this as my human limitation even though it frustrates me. But I know I can help some people as I tackle the problems common to all. I know others can do the same, and I am optimistic that if enough of us act responsibly and decisively we can make a difference, and the difference might be just enough to turn the tide.

This book is one man's attempt to grapple with some of the problems. If this effort has any unique contribution to make on a subject about which a great deal is being written, it will be its moral and ethical approach to the use and misuse of resources, to our view of persons, and to the problems of food production, distribution and consumption.

Most authors whom I have read generally agree that the basic issues of hunger are moral and ethical. But many of them seem to have no apparent belief in absolute values, so they avoid or ignore answers which suggest moral and ethical absolutes. While they brilliantly diagnose and analyze the crisis, their prescriptions are, for the most part, sociological placebos which cannot reach the root of the problem—man's alienation from God and his resulting alienation from his fellow man and his environment.

.   .   .

Why don't you kill all those so-called "sacred" cows that litter up your streets?

Why don't you kill all the dogs and cats that litter your homes? I have heard how much you spend on food for your animals. Why don't you kill them? Does that seem like a rash statement? It does? Then you know how I feel when you tell me to kill an animal that is part of my cultural and religious tradition. I can hardly believe how totally insensitive you are. I guess I need to tell you why the cow is important.

It is a source of milk for our children. Milk isn't plentiful but these cows give some. We plaster the dung on the walls of our houses and when it dries, we burn it for fuel. Wood is scarce and processed fuels are completely out of the question.

We also make the dung into a paste and use it as an antiseptic, cleansing agent in the courtyards of our homes. That might seem strange to you, but it works and we cannot afford commercial sprays and disinfectants. As fertilizer for our crops, this saves us another expense which we can't afford.

You know, of course, we believe the souls of our ancestors live in some of these animals. That is our traditional belief. If you think that is strange, perhaps I could tell you how strange I feel some of your so-called religious beliefs are. But that is another subject.

Please, I ask you, don't come in and suggest we kill all our cows. If you want to learn to be truly sensitive, ask the bigger question: Why the cows? I'll try to explain and then we'll talk about it. But listen to us, hear us, empathize with us. You upset us so greatly by shouting from an ocean away about matters so unfamiliar to you.

---

(1) HOW MUCH IS RELIGION CHANGING?

Few would deny that religion has changed in the past and is changing now, but one can get arguments about the rate of change. Some say that just as the pace of change in material dimensions of life is speeding up, so must be changes in the social and spiritual dimensions. Others deny that religion works that way. They argue that the great changes in spiritual culture heralded by the mass media and some social scientists are much overblown, that in times of rapid change people are likely to want to keep religion stable, and that since this change has to do with human nature rather than human contrivance it cannot happen at more than a slow, evolutionary pace. A proponent of the latter point of view is the distinguished sociologist of religion Andrew Greeley. The following passage is from his book on what religion will be like in the year 2000; his answer, as the passage makes evident, is that it will not be too much different from what it was in 1969.

Religion in the Year 2000

Andrew M. Greeley

I have the sneaking suspicion that this rather small volume will make me more enemies than anything I have ever written, for I am sure many readers will find this an infuriating book. Virtually all the expectations for the future of religion held by many devout Americans—both devout religionists and devout agnostics—are judged by this book to be highly improbable. Yet the social scientist finds himself thinking that most revolutionary expectations are highly improbable.

From *Religion in the Year 2000* by Andrew M. Greeley. Copyright 1969, Sheed & Ward, Inc. Reprinted by permission.

It is extremely instructive to compare that genera of science fiction which deals with mechanical wonders to that much more fascinating genera which may be called social science fiction. The famous TV program *Star Trek* is a model example of the latter, for despite all the wonderful gimmicks that the *Star Trek* Enterprise and its crew are equipped with, both they and the "aliens" they encounter in their journey through the quadrants face the same very human behavioral problems that we face today and our ancestors faced before us. Human society does improve, man does become somewhat more skillful in his relationships, but not very much, and progress is relatively slow. Therefore, to project into the next thirty to fifty years a religious situation that is not greatly different from the present one is the only course open to someone who believes that moral and social growth in the human race can only accelerate somewhat over its past rate. The acceleration may even be very impressive compared to the past, and yet the behavior patterns, the social structures, the human relationships of the beginning of the twenty-first century are not likely to be too different from those of the middle of the twentieth century. Therefore, much that is expected to happen to religion will not happen.

1. Religion will not lose its adherents. In the United States this means that membership, church attendance, and doctrinal orthodoxy will persist at the levels reported in the 1952–1965 surveys. In countries such as England where organizational participation and church attendance levels are much lower, this means minimally that levels are likely to fall no lower than they are, and even as Professor Martin suggests, they may begin to rise slightly.

2. Nor is religion likely to lose its "influence." It will still provide at least a substantial component of the ultimate interpretive scheme or meaning system with the overwhelming majority of the population. It will still have indirect impact on society through the religiously influenced ethical decisions of its members, and it will also have direct influence over society both because it provides part of the underpinning for general social consensus and because in certain critical situations the direct confrontation between religion and social problems contributes to the amelioration of these problems.

3. The sacred is not being replaced by the secular. Scientific rationalism will not generate a new faith. It will not provide satisfactory alternatives to those modes of coping with problems of interpretability currently popular with the overwhelming majority of the population. The transcendent may no longer be coterminous with

all human activity, but the "really real" will still persist where the core problems of interpretability are faced. On the contrary, in fact, the popularity of the current revolt against scientific rationalism suggests that new and deviant forms of the sacred will emerge.

4.   Full-time parochial clergy may diminish in relative proportion to part-time specialized or limited-term clergy, but the full-time clergy working with the local congregations will continue to be the majority of religious functionaries.

5.   Simple, dignified, Low-Church Apollonian ritual will not replace all other forms of liturgy. Rather, on the contrary, Dionysian and ecstatic ritual may be at least as common as the Low-Church liturgy of the underground.

6.   Religious institutions will no more wither away than will the Marxist state. On the contrary, they will become more elaborate and more sophisticated and more dependent on academic experts than they are at the present time.

7.   Neither will denominations cease to be characteristic of the Western religious scene. Whatever ecumenism is likely to exist at the end of the present century and the beginning of the next century will, in all probability, continue to be denominational ecumenism.

8.   Doctrinal orthodoxy has not breathed its last, and there probably lurks in divinity schools even now some *fin de siècle* Karl Barth ready to rise up and bear prophetic witness for orthodox traditions.

9.   The local congregations will not perish. They may become smaller and more diversified, but the tendency for man to worship in the community where he lives with his wife and family and where he sleeps at night will not be eliminated—not, at least, as long as there are suburbs.

10.   The crusade for social and secular relevance will not either sweep away the passivity of the religious masses or drive the masses out of the churches. Neither will the this-worldly religious concerns currently so popular eliminate the otherworldly residue which survives even in American religion. On the contrary, it is possible, perhaps toward the end of the present century, that the otherworldly and the monastic will undergo a notable resurgence in American religion. The monastic element within deviant social movements such as the hippies might even lead us to expect that this resurgence could occur much sooner.

Yet when one asserts that religion at the end of this century and the beginning of the next century will not be so very different in many important respects from what religion is now, one is not necessarily taking a conservative position unless it is decreed that anyone who denies the predictions of the self-defined liberals is *ipso facto* a conservative. There will be a number of very dramatic changes in North Atlantic and American religion in the next three to five decades. But these trends toward change receive somewhat less publicity than those revolutions that, according to this book, will not occur. This does not diminish the importance of those changes that will occur.

1.   There will be a tremendous increase in the dialogue between religion and the social sciences, with both religion and the social sciences learning something in the process.

2.   Social science will realize that religion plays a pervasively important role in human behavior, and no group of social scientists gathering together in the year 2000 to prepare a symposium on the year 2050 will assume that man's ultimate interpretive schemes are not worth considering.

3.   Religion, and theology in particular, will be increasingly concerned about the interpretability of man and the human condition; those signals of transcendence that Peter Berger so ably describes point the way, it seems to me, to a much more intensive investigation of the meaning of man's life and death and new life by religion, with the aid of the categories of thought and the insight of the behavioral sciences.

4.   There will be much more emphasis in religion on personality development being equivalent to religious development, and on the central role of sexuality in this developmental process. Religion will not be equated with psychiatry; indeed, on the contrary, the tendency to make this equation will decline. But the role of man's ultimate interpretive scheme in guiding and defining his personal and sexual development will be much more thoroughly explored and much more comprehensively taught than it is at present.

5.   For both theological and organizational reasons, religion will be much more concerned about small, intimate, fellowship congregations and will use the insights of social psychology to facilitate the religious and personal development of the members of the intimate friendship religious groups.

6.   The next thirty years will see a consolidation of democratic and tolerant organizational theories and practices in most American religious denominations. Religion will be much better able to cope at the end of the century than it is at the present time with internal diversity.

7.   There will also be considerably more sympathetic understanding of the wisdom of alternative religious traditions (both Christian and non-Christian) and also of those who profess these alternative traditions. Religion, therefore, will be able to tolerate not only more internal diversity but also more external diversity, and indeed we can begin to profit from these two kinds of diversities, or at least to realize that we can profit from them.

8.   There will be a further strengthening, both in theory and in practice, of the responsibility of the individual as the ultimate religious and ethical agent in the context of the circumstances in which he finds himself and of his personal relationships with those around him. The individual agent will not be seen as a lonely protestant, other-directed man making decisions entirely by himself, however; he will be seen, rather, as a responsible agent within an historical and existential community.

9.   There will be substantially more emphasis in religion on the nonrational than there is today—both the ecstatic and Dionysian nonrational and also the reflective and the contemplative and mystical nonrational. One suspects that there will also be a further decline of puritanism, as part of which one may even begin to see the verification of Marshall McLuhan's prediction that sexuality will be much "cooler" (that is to say, better integrated with the rest of life) than it is at present.

10.   It will be much clearer at the end of the century than it is at the present time that the clergyman's role function as "God's man" in contemporary society implies a considerable development of his skills as an expressive and affectionate leader—a man who generates authentic personal warmth, trust, and reassurance.

If all of these projections of change are pondered carefully, it would seem that they do represent very important religious developments—developments which will make religion at the end of the twentieth century something very, very different from what it was at the beginning of the twentieth century. It may even seem, in fact, that they are more meaningful, more exciting, and more "revolutionary" than the popular and almost mystical predictions of a religionless, secular, and institutionless Christianity. Whether or not they are more exciting is open to debate, but what I think is not open to debate, at least on the basis of present sociological theorizing and data collecting, is that the second list of ten projections are reasonably likely to occur, and the first set of ten are most unlikely to occur.

Will this religion of the future have more or less influence than the religion of the present? Will it have more or less members? Will it have more or less impact on the world of ideas? Will it be more this-worldly or more otherworldly? To a considerable extent, the answers to these questions depend on how one defines one's terms. But to hazard some guesses, religion will have about the same proportion of members as it has at present. It will surely not have less influence on society than it does now, and it may even have more impact on the world of ideas, since the NORC data cited earlier suggest that a greater number of young intellectuals are more religious than were their predecessors.[1] It probably will be simultaneously more this-worldly and more otherworldly, as we finally begin to understand that the sacred and the secular and the this-worldly and the otherworldly are not necessarily contradictions, and that indeed they have coexisted down through the whole history of religion, particularly through the history of American religion.

What we are predicting, then, is that in the next thirty to fifty—even a hundred—years we will not witness the rapid, or even the gradual evolution, but rather the slow evolution of religion. Of course it is possible that the whole process of human history has been so shaken in the last half century that the projection of trends in the future, on the basis of the past and the present, is no longer valid. It may be that one can no longer assert that just as religion has evolved into the present, so it will continue to evolve into the future, perhaps at an accelerated rate. Furthermore, even though religion has outlived all those who prophesied its doom in the past, it may be that the human condition has changed so much that this time the prophets of doom are correct.

But the assertion that gradual evolution is being replaced by revolutionary doom must be made on the basis of poetic insight or metaphysical abstraction, or, quite possibly, revelation. Nothing in the data or the theories of behavioral science enables the sociologist to cope adequately with propositions made on the basis of data from poetry, metaphysics, or access to the plans of the Deity. All he can reply to such arguments is to observe that we will just have to wait and see—and if there happened to be a bookmaker present, he could add that the prophetic revolutionary might put his money where his mouth is.

---

[1] As we noted before, this may simply be the result of the appearance of large numbers of Roman Catholics on the American scene for the first time.

Alvin Toffler, in his widely discussed book *Future Shock,* takes the point of view that values and life styles and so, by implication, the visible manifestations of religion are changing at a fast and ever-accelerating rate. Indeed, Toffler believes that the basic crisis today is dealing with a rate of change that is more than we are psychologically prepared to handle. Inseparable from the pace of change is the glut of options in both products and life styles. This means that even what appears to be conservative, in religion or life style, may not really be that—it may just be another life style that someone, like Lifton's protean man, is consuming for the sake of its old-fashioned flavor. In five or ten years, at the most, he or she may be into something else. The unavoidable observation, Toffler says, is that values and life styles, like products, are plural and changing in an unprecedented way, and *this* is the insight that must be the key to any interpretation of where we are and where we are going in contemporary culture.

Future Shock

Alvin Toffler

Quite a different alternative lies in the communal family. As transience increases the loneliness and alienation in society, we can anticipate increasing experimentation with various forms of group marriage. The banding together of several adults and children into a single "family" provides a kind of insurance against isolation. Even if one or two members of the household leave, the remaining members have one another. Communes are springing up modeled after those described by psychologist B. F. Skinner in *Walden Two* and by novelist Robert Rimmer in *The Harrad Experiment* and *Proposition 31.* In the latter work, Rimmer seriously proposes the legalization of a "corporate family" in which from three to six adults

From *Future Shock,* by Alvin Toffler. Copyright © 1970 by Alvin Toffler. Reprinted by permission of Random House, Inc.

adopt a single name, live and raise children in common, and legally incorporate to obtain certain economic and tax advantages.

According to some observers, there are already hundreds of open or covert communes dotting the American map. Not all, by any means, are composed of young people or hippies. Some are organized around specific goals—like the group, quietly financed by three East Coast colleges—which has taken as its function the task of counseling college freshmen, helping to orient them to campus life. The goals may be social, religious, political, even recreational. Thus we shall before long begin to see communal families of surfers dotting the beaches of California and Southern France, if they don't already. We shall see the emergence of communes based on political doctrines and religious faiths. In Denmark, a bill to legalize group marriage has already been introduced in the Folketing (Parliament). While passage is not imminent, the act of introduction is itself a significant symbol of change.

In Chicago, 250 adults and children already live together in "family-style monasticism" under the auspices of a new, fast-growing religious organization, the Ecumenical Institute. Members share the same quarters, cook and eat together, worship and tend children in common, and pool their incomes. At least 60,000 people have taken "EI" courses and similar communes have begun to spring up in Atlanta, Boston, Los Angeles and other cities. "A brand-new world is emerging," says Professor Joseph W. Mathews, leader of the Ecumenical Institute, "but people are still operating in terms of the old one. We seek to re-educate people and give them the tools to build a new social context."

.   .   .

Seldom has a single nation evinced greater confusion over its sexual values. Yet the same might be said for other kinds of values as well. America is tortured by uncertainty with respect to money, property, law and order, race, religion, God, family and self. Nor is the United States alone in suffering from a kind of value vertigo. All the techno-societies are caught up in the same massive upheaval. This collapse of the values of the past has hardly gone unnoticed. Every priest, politician and parent is reduced to head-shaking anxiety by it. Yet most discussions of value change are barren for they miss two essential points. The first of these is acceleration.

Value turnover is now faster than ever before in history. While in the past a man growing up in a society could expect that its public value system would remain largely unchanged in his lifetime, no such assumption is warranted today, except perhaps in the most isolated of pre-technological communities.

This implies temporariness in the structure of both public and personal value systems, and it suggests that *whatever* the content of values that arise to replace those of the industrial age, they will be shorter-lived, more ephemeral than the values of the past. There is no evidence whatsoever that the value systems of the techno-societies are likely to return to a "steady state" condition. For the foreseeable future, we must anticipate still more rapid value change.

Within this context, however, a second powerful trend is unfolding. For the fragmentation of societies brings with it a diversification of values. We are witnessing the crack-up of consensus.

Most previous societies have operated with a broad central core of commonly shared values. This core is now contracting, and there is little reason to anticipate the formation of a new broad consensus within the decades ahead. The pressures are outward toward diversity, not inward toward unity.

This accounts for the fantastically discordant propaganda that assails the mind in the techno-societies. Home, school, corporation, church, peer group, mass media—and myriad subcults—all advertise varying sets of values. The result for many is an "anything goes" attitude—which is, itself, still another value position. We are, declares *Newsweek* magazine, "a society that has lost its consensus . . . a society that cannot agree on standards of conduct, language and manners, on what can be seen and heard."

This picture of a cracked consensus is confirmed by the findings of Walter Gruen, social science research coordinator at Rhode Island Hospital, who has conducted a series of statistical studies of what he terms "the American core culture." Rather than the monolithic system of beliefs attributed to the middle class by earlier investigators, Gruen found—to his own surprise—that "diversity in beliefs was more striking than the statistically supported uniformities. It is," he concluded, "perhaps already misleading to talk of an 'American' culture complex."

Gruen suggests that particularly among the affluent, educated group, consensus is giving way to what he calls "pockets" of values. We can expect that, as the number and variety of subcults continues to expand, these pockets will proliferate, too.

Faced with colliding value systems, confronted with a blinding array of new consumer goods, services, educational, occupational and recreational options, the people of the future are driven to make choices in a new way. They begin to "consume" life styles the way people of an earlier, less choice-choked time consumed ordinary products.

THE PERSEVERANCE
OF RELIGION

Another condition of the modern situation, and certainly of the future, is the new closeness of all of humanity and, thus, of all religions. This proximity of the world's faiths may actually be a positive factor for the perseverance of religion because it reminds us of the universality and necessity of the quest for the spiritual meaning of human life. Those are thoughts advanced by the famous historian Arnold Toynbee.

An Historian's Approach
to Religion

Arnold Toynbee

The Task of Disengaging the Essence
from the Non-essentials
in Mankind's Religious Heritage

In the second half of the twentieth century of the Christian Era a Westernizing World has been overtaken by two historical events which, together, make it now an obviously urgent task for us to try to disengage the essence in Mankind's religious heritage from non-essential accretions.

On the one hand the West's disillusionment with the idols which it took to worshipping in the Late Modern Age of its history has now brought the West back, once more, face to face with its ancestral Christianity. The West cannot avoid this re-encounter, and cannot have the experience without finding itself compelled to reconsider how it stands towards its discarded religious heritage. At the same time 'the annihilation of distance' through the achievements of a Late Modern Western technology has brought all the living higher religions, all over the World, into a much closer contact with one another than before. This closer contact is making the relations between them more intimate. In A.D. 1956 a stage could

From Arnold Toynbee, *An Historian's Approach to Religion* (London and New York: Oxford University Press, 1956), pp. 263–65. Reprinted by permission of the Oxford University Press, Oxford.

BL
25
2 23
R

334

2,1,285

CAMROSE LUTHERAN COLLEGE
LIBRARY

already be foreseen at which the hereditary adherents of each living religion would have become well enough acquainted with the other living religions to be able to look at their own ancestral religion in the light of its contemporaries; and, in this light, they would have an opportunity of seeing it with new eyes. Within Western Christendom itself, this was already happening as between the different, and once rival and hostile, Western Christian sects. Protestantism and Catholicism were learning from one another; and individual Western Christians, who had been brought up in one or other of the Western Christian churches, were deliberately choosing their church for themselves in after life. This change in the relations between Protestantism and Catholicism, and this new possibility of making an individual choice between the two, were portents of what might be going to happen as between Christianity, Judaism, Islam, Zoroastrianism, Hinduism, and Buddhism. It looked, in fact, as if the living higher religions of the World would now, once again, have to face the same intense comparative scrutiny that they and their forerunners had formerly faced in those *soi-disant* oecumenical empires that had been foretastes of a literally world-wide society.

Thus, in our society in our time, the task of winnowing the chaff away from the grain in Mankind's religious heritage is being forced upon us by a conjunction of social and spiritual circumstances; but these circumstances are not unique, and the task is not an extraordinary one. It is a perennial task, with which the adherents of every higher religion are confronted all the time. 'The Reformation' is not just a particular past event in the Early Modern chapter of the history of the Western branch of Christianity. It is a perpetual challenge which is being presented at every moment to all higher religions alike, and which none of them can ignore for one moment without betraying its trust.

In the life of all the higher religions, the task of winnowing is a perennial one because their historic harvest is not pure grain. In the heritage of each of the higher religions we are aware of the presence of two kinds of ingredients. There are essential counsels and truths, and there are non-essential practices and propositions.

The essential counsels and truths are valid at all times and places, as far as we can see through the dark glass of Mankind's experience up to date. When we peer into the records of Man's religion as it was before any of the higher religions made their epiphany, we find the light of these counsels and truths already shining there, however dimly. And, if we could imagine to ourselves a future world in which every one of the living higher religions had become extinct, but in which the human race was still surviving, it would be difficult to imagine human life going on without still having these same essential counsels and truths to light its path and guide its steps, as in the past. In fact, the counsels and truths enshrined in the higher religions would appear to have still longer lives than the higher religions themselves. They would seem, indeed, to be coeval with Mankind, in the sense of being intimations of a spiritual presence accompanying us on our pilgrimage as a pillar of cloud by day and a pillar of fire by night—an accompaniment without which Humanity would not be human.

These guesses carry us beyond the narrow limits of our historical knowledge; and this knowledge also does not tell us how the spiritual light reaches, or is reached by, us. Yet, whether it comes to us by discovery or by intuition or by revelation, and whether it is abiding or transitory, it is a matter of indisputable historical fact that it shines in all the higher religions, and it is also clear that this light in them has been the cause of their historic success. The higher religions have had a longer hold on a greater number of minds and hearts than any other institutions known to us up to date; and this hold has been due to the light that they have thrown, for Man, upon his relation to a spiritual presence in the mysterious Universe in which Man finds himself. In this presence, Man is confronted by something spiritually greater than himself which, in contrast to Human Nature and to all other phenomena, is Absolute Reality. And this Absolute Reality of which Man is aware is also an Absolute Good for which he is athirst. Man finds himself needing, not only to be aware of It, but to be in touch with It and in harmony with It. That is the only condition on which he can feel himself at home in the world in which he finds himself in existence.